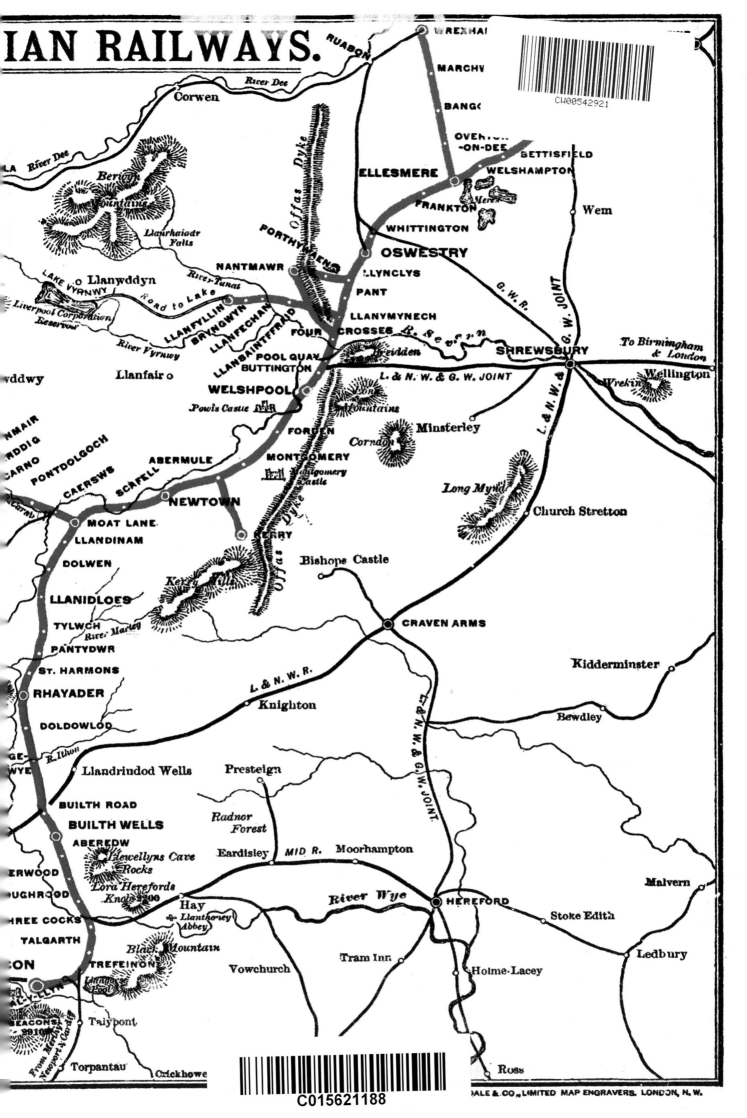

# THE
# CAMBRIAN RAILWAYS

## A NEW HISTORY

*This history of the Cambrian, from the date*
*of its first inception, should be forced, again and again,*
*on the attention of Parliament, as well as rehearsed in the ears*
*of credulous subscribers who are considered by speculating*
*solicitors, engineers and contractors as their lawful prey.*

*Railway Times*, 3 December 1870

# THE
# CAMBRIAN RAILWAYS

## A NEW HISTORY

PETER JOHNSON

An imprint of
Ian Allan Publishing

First published 2013

ISBN 978 0 86093 644 2

All rights reserved. No part of this book may be reproduced or transmitted in any form or by any means, electronic or mechanical, including photocopying, recording or by any information storage and retrieval system, without permission from the Publisher in writing.

© Peter Johnson 2013

Published by Oxford Publishing Co

an imprint of Ian Allan Publishing Ltd, Hersham, Surrey, KT12 4RG

Printed in England

Distributed in the United States of America and Canada by BookMasters Distribution Services

Visit the Ian Allan Publishing website at
*www.ianallanpublishing.com*

**Copyright**
Illegal copying and selling of publications deprives authors, publishers and booksellers of income, without which there would be no investment in new publications. Unauthorised versions of publications are also likely to be inferior in quality and contain incorrect information. You can help by reporting copyright infringements and acts of piracy to the Publisher or the UK Copyright Service.

**Picture credits**
Every effort has been made to correctly identify picture credits. All uncreditied pictures are from the author's collection. Should any errors have occurred, this is entirely unintentional.

FRONT COVER: A classic Cambrian Railways scene, as 1895-built Sharp, Stewart 4-4-0 No 82 climbs Talerddig with a passenger train. No 82 was to be destroyed in the collision at Abermule in 1921. *J. M. Tomlinson/John Alsop collection*

FRONT ENDPAPER: A map showing the extent of the Cambrian network, c1895. *Cambrian Railways*

REAR ENDPAPER: A copy of the gradient profiles given to the Board of Trade in 1889 showing the locations of accidents involving mixed trains. *National Archives*

HALF TITLE PAGE: A smart Edwardian group and their dog pose with Cambrian Railways' carriage No 20, which has brought them from Manchester to Aberystwyth.

TITLE PAGE: A train hauled by Sharp, Stewart 2-4-0 No 54, built in 1865, crosses the original bridge at Barmouth, c1899. *T. F. Budden/John Alsop collection*

# Contents

# Introduction

The Cambrian Railways was absorbed into the Great Western Railway in 1922, following the 1921 Railways Act. Formed by amalgamation in 1864, it had the largest route mileage of any Welsh railway.

It served a large part of Wales to the west of Shrewsbury, from the market town of Whitchurch and industrial Oswestry, which straddled the Welsh-English borders in the east, to Cardigan Bay resorts ranging from Aberystwyth to Pwllheli in the west, via the market towns of Welshpool, Newtown and Machynlleth. To the south it served a sparsely populated and mountainous area to reach Brecon and South Wales; the largest communities were Llanidloes and Builth Wells. Wrexham, Porthywaen, Llanfyllin, Kerry and Dolgellau were served by branches.

Before the railways, regional transport had been largely dependent on turnpike roads, with an incursion by the Montgomeryshire Canal that reached Newtown in 1817. In 1859 Shrewsbury's Lion Hotel advertised three coach services into Wales. The 'well-appointed' four-horse coach named *Greyhound* ran to Aberystwyth, calling at Welshpool, Newtown and Llanidloes, three days a week, taking 9 hours. The *Royal Mail* ran daily, serving Welshpool, Newtown, Machynlleth, Aberdovey and Towyn before reaching Aberystwyth, taking 10 hours. The *Alliance* served Welshpool and Newtown daily except on Sundays.

In July 1852 the promoters of the Shrewsbury & Aberystwyth Railway had claimed that 'in the whole of central Wales, for 110 miles from north to south, and 70 from east to west, there is not one single railway'. This sweeping statement was not quite true, but it was true that there were no standard-gauge lines in the hinterland.

The Cambrian's constituents were the Llanidloes & Newtown Railway, the Oswestry & Newtown Railway, the Oswestry, Ellesmere & Whitchurch Railway, and the Newtown & Machynlleth Railway. They were soon joined by the Aberystwyth & Welsh Coast Railway, bringing Aberystwyth, Aberdovey, Dolgellau, Barmouth, Portmadoc and Pwllheli into the network. The Mid Wales Railway, which extended the Newtown & Llanidloes Railway to a junction with the Brecon & Merthyr Railway at Talyllyn, was worked 'in perpetuity' from 1888 and absorbed in 1904. At its eastern extremity, the nominally independent Wrexham & Ellesmere Railway was operated from 1895, and to the north-west a short extension to the coast line at Pwllheli was completed in 1906. The independent Van Railway, which made a junction at Caersws, was operated from 1896.

The Cambrian had not altogether successful relationships with four light railways, the Welshpool & Llanfair, Vale of Rheidol, Mawddwy and Tanat Valley, two of which it came to own; the first two were narrow gauge. Traffic was exchanged with them and the London & North Western, Great Western, Manchester & Milford, the Potteries, Shrewsbury & North Wales (later the Shropshire & Montgomeryshire Light), Midland, and Brecon & Merthyr railways. The Corris, Talyllyn, Festiniog, Croesor and Gorseddau narrow-gauge lines were also sources of traffic.

Engineering features that ensured the Cambrian Railways stood above many other standard-gauge lines included three summits of more than 600 feet, at Talyllyn (610 feet), Talerddig (693 feet) and Pantydwr (947 feet). The steepest gradients were at Talerddig, 1 in 52, on the main line, and Kerry, 1 in 43. Talerddig also had the deepest cutting. The coast line was notable for its estuarial crossings of four rivers, the Dyfi, Mawddach, Dwyryd and Glaslyn.

The Cambrian's core routes were developed during an era of railway mania, when contractors and investors were clamouring to build railways to every conceivable location, allowing their thirst for profits to overcome any practical consideration for the likely traffic. The participation of contractor Thomas Savin and numerous battles in Parliament and the courts saddled the company with considerable debts, which hampered its development, and its ability to pay interest on its borrowing and dividends to its shareholders, through most of its existence.

Physical features brought their own problems: landslips in Talerddig cutting, unstable ground on the sea cliffs at Friog, and low embankments along the Dovey estuary and the sea coast. The entire system was, in any event, difficult to work, being mostly single track, and the Cambrian soon established a reputation for poor timekeeping. That said, 124 of the railway's 241 miles are still in regular use as part of the national network, and a large swathe of rural Wales would be seriously deprived without it.

The promoters of the coast railway expected the railway to benefit from tourism, a dream that was only partially fulfilled, for the Cambrian never attracted the numbers that the LNWR enticed to the North Wales coast resorts. The line from the Dovey to Pwllheli did, however, become an attraction in its own right and remains to be enjoyed and appreciated. The sea is rarely out of sight and travellers enjoy a splendid variety of seaside and mountain views, not to mention the castles at Harlech and Criccieth, but it was 1916, and wartime, before observation carriages were provided. Now it is tourism that provides much of the summer traffic on those parts of the Cambrian that remain in use, and which sustains seasonal traffic on its narrow-gauge light railways and a short section of the main line.

Never an affluent railway, the Cambrian had its own charm. It was rarely innovative and barely overcame its financial burdens. Its story is worth revisiting.

## Acknowledgements and Sources

Nearly 30 years ago I started as an author of railway books, compiling a photographic album on the Cambrian Railways that was published in 1984. In the interim I have written books about railways that were clients of the Cambrian, particularly the Festiniog Railway and the Shropshire & Montgomeryshire Light Railway. The book about the narrow-gauge railways that came to be owned by the Great Western Railway included the Welshpool & Llanfair Light Railway, which the Cambrian operated, and the Vale of Rheidol Light Railway, which it acquired in 1913. The time has come, therefore, to tackle the railway that linked them together.

In 1922 C. P. Gasquoine, editor of the Oswestry-based *Border Counties Advertiser*, published *The Story of the Cambrian – a biography of a railway*, a rose-tinted memorial to the Cambrian as it lost its independence. He had the company's support and access to its records. The few minor errors that he made show that some of those who who followed him writing about the Cambrian also used him as a source of information.

This book has been mostly compiled from the records of the Cambrian and its constituents held at the National Archives, Kew. The Cambrian series at RAIL92 was particularly useful, containing the officers' reports as well as board and committee minutes. The Board of Trade inspection and accident reports are also at Kew. The Acts of Parliament, 55 obtained by the Cambrian and its constituents and more than 40 of peripheral relevance, were viewed at the University of Leicester and the National Archives' libraries.

A convenient scrapbook of newspaper cuttings from the 1860s is contained in National Archives RAIL92/132. Additionally, *The Times* and the *Manchester Guardian* were viewed on-line, as were the newspapers contained in the British Library's British Newspaper Archive and British Newspapers 1800-1900 projects. Papers not yet available digitally were viewed at Gwynedd Archives, Dolgellau, and at the British Library Newspaper Library, Colindale. The *Railway Times* was seen at the National Archives and the University of Leicester library. The latter also provided copies of *The Railway Magazine*, *Railway Engineer* and the *Locomotive*.

Dates cited here were taken from contemporary records, some of them being at a variance to those published elsewhere, although I notice that I am not the first to make that claim in respect of the Cambrian. In view of the complications of the early years, opening dates are tabulated in Appendix 2.

Except for the Aberystwyth & Welsh Coast Railway 1860 plan viewed at Gwynedd Archives in Dolgellau, the deposited plans were examined at the Parliamentary Archives. Copies of the notices were obtained from the *London Gazette*.

The decision to use only contemporary material to illustrate this book has necessarily restricted the choice. However, there was still more material available than the space to accommodate it. No great cache of previously unpublished photographs was revealed to me so I am afraid that some of them may be familiar to those already acquainted with the subject. In a book about the Cambrian Railways, however, there cannot be too many photographs of Barmouth bridge, or of Aberdovey.

I am indebted to John Alsop, Sara Eade and Ted Talbot for making material from their collections available. Unacknowledged illustrations are from my own collection. Many thanks, too, to Patricia Ward and Adrian Gray, who took the time to read the manuscript and make some useful observations. Responsibility for any errors, of course, remains with me.

The award of a Railway & Canal Historical Society research grant towards the expenses incurred in researching this book was much appreciated.

*Peter Johnson*
Leicester, April 2013

## Parliamentary procedures

With a large number of Acts of Parliament to be discussed it will save space and repetition to comment on the procedure for obtaining an Act and on the authorised capital.

Private bills were deposited in the House of Lords by the end of December each year. Notices advising the intention to deposit a Bill and outlining its purpose were therefore published in local newspapers and the *London Gazette* a few weeks before. Bills were examined for compliance with standing orders and, if there were objections to a scheme, either in principle or detail, passed through opposed private Bill committees in both houses of Parliament. There, objectors had an opportunity of cross-examining the promoters, their engineer and their supporters. They were rarely debated. Successful Bills took up to seven months to be processed and gain the Royal Assent.

The authorised share capital was expected to be sufficient to pay for the line's construction and its preliminary expenses. Shares, usually of £10, were paid for in instalments, called to match construction expenditure. Before the practice was stopped, would-be investors would commit to a subscription contract, agreeing to subscribe when a Bill was enacted, avoiding the need to make payment in advance.

To pay for stations, locomotives and rolling stock, borrowing of one-third of the share capital was permitted once all the share capital had been subscribed and half of it paid up. Therefore, any reference to authorised share capital must be accompanied by an assumption of borrowing of one-third of the capital additionally. The borrowing was secured by the issue of debentures with a guaranteed interest rate, usually 5%, that took priority over the payment of dividends.

If the promoters were unable to raise the ordinary capital from among their friends and acquaintances they would issue a prospectus, which might also be published in one or more newspapers. Failure here could see them turning to bankers, financiers and other sources of funds.

In the event of expenditure exceeding both the original capital and borrowing, authority would be sought for further borrowing that would be secured by the issue of fixed-rate preference shares. In the payment of interest and dividends these ranked after debentures and before the ordinary shares; in common with the debentures, they had no voting rights.

Short-term borrowing, often from the contractor, would be secured by the issue of Lloyds bonds, a form of IOU. They were sealed by the borrower and stamp duty was paid on them as a percentage of the debt.

With the deposit of a Bill the promoters were required to lodge 8% of the ordinary capital in Chancery to provide compensation for anyone affected if the Bill failed. If the Bill succeeded the deposit could be released on application when half of the capital had been subscribed and spent. A Bill that had popular support would be able to use the deposits paid for shares by subscribers for this purpose, otherwise the promoters would have to look elsewhere for it.

It was usual for three years to be allowed to exercise compulsory purchase powers and five years to complete the works.

## Miscellanea

Crown copyright is reserved for illustrations sourced from the National Archives, the Parliamentary Archives and the Ordnance Survey.

## Welsh place names

During the period covered by this book many Welsh place names were anglicised. The archaic forms are mostly used here. The use of Aberystwith for Aberystwyth was ended as early as 1867 in Bradshaw, although perpetuated until 1892 by the Railway Clearing House; only the Welsh form is used here. For clarification, the other places concerned are:

Aberdovey = Aberdyfi
Barmouth = Y Bermo/Abermaw
Carnarvon = Caernarfon
Dolgelly/Dolgelley = Dolgellau
Dovey = Dyfi
Festiniog = Ffestiniog
Kilkewydd = Cilcewydd
Portmadoc = Porthmadog
Towyn = Tywyn

## Counties

Cardiganshire – part of Dyfed
Carnarvonshire – part of Gwynedd
Merionethshire – part of Gwynedd
Montgomeryshire – part of Powys

## Abbreviations

| AWCR | Aberystwyth & Welsh Coast Railway |
| CR | Carnarvonshire Railway |
| GWR | Great Western Railway |
| LNR | Llanidloes & Newtown Railway |
| LNWR | London & North Western Railway |
| MMR | Manchester & Milford Railway |
| MSLR | Manchester, Sheffield & Lincolnshire Railway |
| MWR | Mid Wales Railway |
| NMR | Newtown & Machynlleth Railway |

Although Aberdovey residents succeeded in getting the coast railway routed away from the front it maintained a dominant presence on the wharf for more than 100 years. Amongst the Cambrian's own wagons in this view is a Cannock Old Coppice Colliery, Cheslyn Hay, coal wagon.
*D. George*

| NOR | Newtown & Oswestry Railway |
| OEWR | Oswestry, Ellesmere & Whitchurch Railway |
| ONR | Oswestry & Newtown Railway |
| PSNWR | Potteries, Shrewsbury & North Wales Railway |
| REC | Railway Executive Committee |
| SAR | Shrewsbury & Aberystwyth Railway |
| SMLR | Shropshire & Montgomeryshire Light Railway |
| TVLR | Tanat Valley Light Railway |
| VRLR | Vale of Rheidol Light Railway |
| WER | Wrexham & Ellesmere Railway |
| WLLR | Welshpool & Llanfair Light Railway |
| WMCQR | Wrexham, Mold & Connah's Quay Railway |

## Currency, weight and distance

£1 = 240d (pence) = 20s (shillings); 1s = 12d; 1 guinea = £1 1s
1 ton = 20 hundredweight (cwt)
1 mile = 8 furlongs = 80 chains = 1,760 yards = 1.60 kilometres;
1 yard = 3 feet = 0.91 metres; 1 chain = 22 yards

## The value of money

Equivalent value of £1 in 2012

| 1850 | £83.40 |
| 1860 | £73.30 |
| 1870 | £74.60 |
| 1880 | £77.60 |
| 1890 | £85.80 |
| 1900 | £84.40 |
| 1910 | £79.60 |
| 1915 | £62.50 |
| 1920 | £31.30 |

Retail price index data courtesy of *www.measuringworth.com*

# 1
# Laying the foundations
# 1852-1860

'…this meeting cordially adopts the project of a railway from Llanidloes to Newtown.' With these words, recorded after a public meeting held at the Queen's Head Inn in Llanidloes on 30 October 1852, the active development of what became the Cambrian Railways was started.

The initiative followed the announcement in July of the Shrewsbury & Aberystwyth Railway (SAR), to be routed via the Rea Valley near Shrewsbury, Newtown and Llanidloes. Shortly afterwards the Shrewsbury & Chester Railway proposed the Montgomeryshire Railway to connect Oswestry to Newtown. When the second scheme came under the control of the Great Western Railway the first allied itself to the London & North Western Railway. Its route was re-surveyed, diverting from the Rea Valley and Llanidloes to serve Criggion, Welshpool and Machynlleth and adding a branch from Criggion to Oswestry. Failing to have Llanidloes reinstated, George Hammond Whalley MP decided to promote his own railway.

There were good practical reasons for not routing the line via Llanidloes, the 'zigzag line from Llangurig … through wild narrow mountain ravines that cannot become populous' being one of them, according to the *Shrewsbury Chronicle*. The lower summit at Talerddig on the alternative route was another.

An ongoing hindrance to railway development in the area, substantially the Welsh county of Montgomeryshire, was disagreements over whether it could sustain one railway or two and, if only one, whether it should be southwards from Oswestry through Welshpool and Newtown to Llanidloes with the possibility of going

onwards to the port at Milford Haven, or whether it should be westwards from Shrewsbury through Welshpool, Newtown and Llanidloes or Machynlleth to reach Aberystwyth and the coast. If there were to be two railways the question was, 'Who would control the overlapping section in the middle, which was likely to generate most traffic, in the short term if not in the long term?' Railway politics came into play, too, with the Great Western Railway supporting the north-south option and the LNWR preferring the other.

The SAR was particularly well-connected, its board of management including the banker George Glyn Carr and the Liverpool & Manchester Railway's Henry Booth as well as the principal landowners. Its engineer was Joseph Locke and its secretary Edward Watkin. Originally routed via Welshpool, Newtown, Llanidloes, Carno, Machynlleth and Aberdovey, its purpose was to connect central Wales with the manufacturing counties of England and to provide a short route between them and Ireland, via Wexford. Coal from the Shropshire coalfield was expected to be a staple of westbound traffic while manufactured goods and livestock would be carried eastwards.

The Montgomeryshire Railway did not attract the big names, although it did have, on its board of management, David Pugh MP, a wealthy tea merchant of Llanerchydol, Welshpool, who was to become a Cambrian Railways director. The engineers were Henry Robertson and Thomas Penson Junior; the former was to play a part in the development of railways in the vale of Llangollen and in the GWR, while the latter's father had given David Davies his first contract, the Severn Bridge foundations at Llandinam, in 1846. Twenty-eight miles

George Hammond Whalley MP

long, the railway was intended to serve the needs of central Wales and the 'rich and populous vales' of Montgomeryshire by making connections to the North Wales coalfield, Chester, Birkenhead and Liverpool and the manufacturing districts of Lancashire and Yorkshire.

There had been earlier proposals, Shrewsbury-Newtown in 1844 and Crewe-Newtown, Crewe-Aberystwyth and South Wales-Oswestry in 1845, which failed to obtain powers. Writing to the *Shrewsbury Chronicle* in April 1853, a correspondent had suggested that if a large company like the LNWR would not take the initiative and push the development forward, a union of railways should be developed, each the responsibility of the area through which it ran, working towards the common goal of opening up Montgomeryshire to the four compass points.

The LNWR had produced plans for a line from Shrewsbury to 'New Town' and a branch to Oswestry in 1851; the engineers were Locke and Robert Stephenson.

Whalley had chaired the Llanidloes meeting. No record was kept of how many attended or who they were. During the year Whalley, of Plas Madoc, Ruabon, had been busy, being appointed Sheriff of Carnarvon, Deputy Lieutenant of Denbighshire and commissioned as a captain in the Denbighshire Yeomanry Cavalry. At the year's general election he had failed to be elected MP for Montgomery but succeeded at a by-election in Peterborough in December. Born in Gloucester in 1813, he was distantly related to Oliver Cromwell. In 1845 he had been on the provisional committees of the Direct Western Railway, the Tring & Reigate Railway and the Direct Birmingham, Oxford, Reading & Brighton Railway. A barrister and colliery owner in Ruabon, his interest in Llanidloes was that of a landowner; he leased the Clochfaen estate, 1,600 acres, in Llangurig.

There was no delay. A notice dated 2 November was published in the *London Gazette* on 23 November. The railway proposed was 12 miles long and 29 miles from the nearest railhead at Oswestry, the termini being small market towns. Llanidloes had a population of 4,604 at the 1851 census, Newtown 3,784. Founded in the 13th century, Newtown sits on the Severn, 10 miles inside Wales. Growth came with the development of textile and flannel industries in the 18th and 19th centuries. The significance of its adoption as the eastern terminus lay in it being the terminus of the Shropshire Union Canal and on the SAR's route. Also on the Severn but 276 feet above Newtown, Llanidloes was founded in the 9th century, receiving a market charter in 1289. Silver and lead were mined in the locality, while flannel was also made in the town.

A committee was appointed to promote the railway and to solicit interest from would-be investors. Meetings were held in Newtown, Aberystwyth and Rhayader. Sixteen provisional directors, including the Mayor of Llanidloes, were appointed on 11 November. Rice Hopkins was appointed engineer and charged with the task of taking the project forward. Born in 1807, he had assisted his father in the construction of the Plymouth & Dartmoor Railway and was engineer of the West Somerset Mineral Railway.

The company's Bill received the royal assent on 4 August 1853. The subscribers, Whalley, William Lefeaux, John Lefeaux, Edmund Cleaton, Thomas Edmund Marsh and others, were united into a company incorporated by the Act. They, together with eight others, were nominated as the first directors with a requirement to hold a minimum of 25 £10 shares. The capital was £60,000.

An account of the Parliamentary process was given at the first general meeting on 13 September. Hopkins had done his job well. Of six proposals for railways in the area dealt with during the session, only the Llanidloes & Newtown Railway (LNR) had received its Act. The Welsh Union Railway's plans had not complied with standing

orders and the Shrewsbury & Aberystwyth and North & South Wales railways had failed to serve their notices correctly. The directors had decided to establish 'friendly relations' with the other schemes, the LNWR's Shrewsbury & Newtown Railway and the Montgomeryshire Railway (Oswestry-Newtown), so that a junction could be made at Newtown with whichever was successful.

Objections had been made by the LNWR, the Montgomeryshire turnpike trustees and the Misses Hamer. The nature of the latters' objection was never specified, but on 27 January the directors 'considered it due to their shareholders to express their determination to protect the company from vexatious or excessive demand and especially to protect against any compromise on the payment of costs as proposed…' After protracted negotiations the ladies withdrew their opposition in return for some minor works already allowed for; they also recouped, from the LNR, £150 expenditure incurred by them in testing the LNR plans before the standing order committee.

An agreement for the LNWR to have joint use of the Newtown-Caersws section, 5 miles, and to pay for half of its construction came to naught when the LNWR's own Bill was rejected in the Commons. Minor modifications to bridges and alignments of roads saw the turnpike's objection withdrawn.

The Montgomeryshire Railway Bill had been approved in the Commons at the expense of the LNWR Bill, but the latter's objection to the former in the Lords won out and that Bill had been lost as well. The LNR directors had no objection to the development of adjacent routes, telling the shareholders that a policy for extending their own line to Shrewsbury, Aberystwyth and Milford Haven should be adopted.

Gathering before the shareholders' meeting, the directors had already instructed Hopkins to complete the necessary surveys, plans and sections preparatory to letting the contract and to issue notices to affected landowners. Despite this apparent haste, a month later Whalley explained why he had countermanded Hopkins's instructions, and the secretary why he had not issued the notices.

The company's intention to extend the railway to Llangurig was published on 8 November 1853. Whalley had taken this action at his own initiative and expense, agreeing to pay for the survey, plans and book of reference. Hopkins had made the survey. The proposal fell when the LNWR and GWR withdrew their schemes for lines to Oswestry and Shrewsbury.

Another Montgomeryshire railway proposal made a brief appearance towards the end of 1853, with the deposit of a Bill for the Montgomeryshire & Rea Valley Railway, intended to connect the LNR to Shrewsbury and Oswestry, via Welshpool; the plan shows a junction near Forden. Nothing came of it.

Meeting on 2 February 1854, the LNR directors considered the situation of a Mr Parry. He had been working for Hopkins as a surveyor and valuer but had not been paid despite Hopkins having been paid £250 on account in January. Anxious for Parry to continue with his survey, the directors paid him £50.

Hopkins was paid another £250 on 28 February, when Parry's plans had been produced. Hopkins was instructed to report on the survey and to lay out the line on the basis that he would only be paid out-of-pocket expenses until construction was started. No reference had been made to the appointment of a contractor, but the accounts for the half year to 30 June included a payment of £11 3s 6d under the heading of 'Mr Thompson (contractor)'. The payment had been authorised on 2 February with the remark 'in discharge of … Mr Thompson's [claim]'. Another claim discharged on the same date was that of a Mr Richardson, £28 1s 6d, for his services as an engineer.

By this date the LNWR and the GWR had withdrawn their proposals for railways in Montgomeryshire. Even without these links and depending on the Shropshire Union Canal, shareholders were told, there was no excuse for delaying construction. However, if the residents of the area to be served by the connecting lines did not promote a line the LNR shareholders should be prepared to take it on themselves. Powers would be needed for a short extension to the canal at Newtown.

Hopkins had set out the line but had not passed the plans and specifications to the valuer, so no land had been acquired, the shareholders were informed on 1 September.

It was necessary to keep in with influential landowners. Anne Warburton Owen had inherited the Glansevern estate, 4,482 acres, approximately 1% of Montgomeryshire, on her husband's death in 1837. To obtain her co-operation, on 18 October the directors pledged not to adopt any other line in the county without her approval. A large LNR shareholder, Mrs Owen makes several appearances in this story.

The directors' ambition for the LNR to form part of a Manchester-Milford Haven route would have been fulfilled at one fell swoop had the Direct Manchester & Milford Haven Junction Railway come to pass. Connecting to the LNR at either end, its Bill was deposited in November. The Newtown & Oswestry Railway Bill was deposited at the same time, seeking authority for a route 'commencing near the new parish church in the parish of Newtown … by a junction with the Oswestry branch of the Shrewsbury & Chester Railway …', about 19 miles.

This had been started on Whalley's initiative, when he had asked the London solicitor S. F. Noyes to assist in forming a company and obtaining an Act on 31 October. The haste with which they acted was to have a detrimental effect on their railway for some years. Noyes undertook to find a 'responsible contractor' who would construct and equip the line for a fixed price, taking half of the capital. For taking such a large proportion of the capital the directors and engineer would have to be acceptable to the contractor, Noyes explained.

An inaugural meeting was held in Montgomery on 15 November. Without having the benefit of any survey, the figure of £250,000 was plucked out of the air as the estimated capital; half was to be raised locally, three-eighths by the contractors in shares, and one-eighth in debentures. Noyes introduced 'his friends' Messrs McCormick and Thornton as the contractors on 23 November; the *Railway Times* was to refer to this partnership as Thornton, McCormick and Furness.

When the Bill was deposited, Benjamin Piercy had produced the plans and signed the estimate for £250,000. He was a Montgomeryshire man who had started his career with Charles Mickleborough, estate agent and surveyor, in Montgomery. In 1851 he had worked on plans for the Shrewsbury & Chester Railway Bill before going into independent practice. He was acting engineer to G. W. Hemans on the Vale of Clwyd Railway in 1855 and was to be the engineer of all the Cambrian Railways' constituents.

An unsigned pamphlet dated December 1854 said that the estimated cost for a single track on a double-track formation was £300,000. Traffic would be foreign wool for Newtown, the Welsh flannel centre, and cattle, sheep, timber, bark, flannel, slate and lead ore for export. Local traffic would be lime and coal with direct links to the former at Llanymynech and Porthywaen and to the latter in Denbighshire and Shropshire. Without a railway, agricultural profits were at least 20% less than they could be. With it, the price of steam coal would be reduced sufficiently for the flannel manufacturers to compete with their Yorkshire rivals.

When the contractors signed subscription contracts on 30 December 1854 Noyes gave them an undertaking that not only indemnified them against expenses connected with the Bill but cancelled their liability if they had not made agreements with the provisional directors by 13 January 1855, when the deposit was due. The undertaking was made without the promoters' approval. When

they found out it 'created considerable sensation'. Giving the contractors the right to veto the engineer rendered 'the directors useless and the subscribers their creatures'.

At a meeting of both parties' solicitors on 9 January 1855 Thornton maintained his position concerning the veto, resisting an offer to modify it to a pledge that the engineer should be 'a known man'. He seemed to be concerned that the company would appoint someone with whom he had disagreed in the past. The solicitors thought they had a verbal agreement on this point so the provisional directors signed a contract based on it on 11 January, the occasion of their first formal meeting under the identity of the Newtown & Oswestry Railway (NOR). Local dignitaries were appointed directors, including Sir Watkin Williams Wynn Bt MP (1820-85, 6th Baronet, MP for Denbighshire 1841-85), William Ormesby Gore MP, David Pugh MP and Arthur James Johnes.

The deposit, £18,750, was due to be lodged the next day, but share deposits of £13,040, including £6,250 from the contractors, were insufficient to meet it. Some shareholders had agreed to loan £3,605, leaving a deficiency of £2,105. Edward Williams then offered to loan another £2,000 providing four of the directors and the solicitor guaranteed it. The deposit would be lodged 'with the understanding that the Bill is to be withdrawn unless further shares are taken hereafter to an extent to justify the directors in proceeding.' Here was a project that was struggling even before it had found its deposit, although Williams's loan was to be redeemed by 12 October.

An attempt was made to drum up more support in March 1855 by publishing an eight-page pamphlet signed by Johnes, a judge sitting in north-west Wales and Aberystwyth. Entitled 'A plain statement of the claims of the Oswestry, Welshpool & Newtown Railway Company in a letter to the inhabitants of Montgomeryshire, of Aberystwyth and other districts interested in the proposed railway', it explained that most railways were promoted by commercial interests that did not attract local support. This was different, being promoted by local interests.

The community should treat the railway's appeal for support in the same way that it would appeals for churches, schools and hospitals because, like them, it existed for the public good. Johnes anticipated the payment of dividends, but even if there were none there would be diversified collateral benefits for all classes. Everyone should subscribe in proportion to their means and to the benefits they would receive.

Peter William Barlow (1809-85) was appointed the NOR's engineer on 27 April 1855; Piercy was his resident. They agreed to subscribe £10,000 capital and were to be paid £375 per mile. Barlow was the brother of William Henry Barlow, a Midland Railway employee who became consulting engineer for the MR's London Extension and designed St Pancras station. The contractors had already rejected a previous appointment, but Noyes intimated that they had accepted this one. However, Thornton refused to subscribe for his share of the additional £20,000 capital supposedly consequential upon it.

LNR progress was slow and it appeared difficult to keep both the directors and shareholders motivated. The former had been offered 1 guinea to attend meetings, usually at the Queen's Head in Llanidloes. The general meeting called for 1 March 1855 had to be postponed for want of a quorum; when only the secretary attended the resumed meeting the next day, it was not re-called.

Although the LNR was affected by the NOR's proposals, the directors did not mention it until 26 April 1855, when the solicitor was to secure facilities for making a through route between Oswestry and Llanidloes and to protect the ambition of a route via Montgomeryshire from Manchester to Milford Haven.

On 23 June Leonard Charles Wyon was asked to furnish a design for an NOR company seal that incorporated the arms of Shropshire and Montgomeryshire. Like his father before him, Wyon was renowned as an engraver of dies for coinage, medallions and postage stamps. The seal cost 10 or 12 guineas plus £5 5s for a lockable box to keep it in.

Incorporating the company as the Oswestry & Newtown Railway (ONR), the Bill was enacted as the Oswestry, Welchpool [sic] & Newtown Railway Act on 26 June. The subscribers were Wynn, Gore, Pugh and John Naylor. They, together with Herbert Watkin Williams Wynn (1822-62, second son of the 5th baronet, brother of the 6th baronet, MP for Montgomeryshire 1850-62), Johnes and six others were the first directors. The owner of Powis Castle had the right to appoint a director and the capital was £250,000.

Level crossings on 12 highways or turnpikes required stations or lodges. Any crossing of the navigable River Severn had to be approved by the Admiralty, and the crossing of the Shropshire Union Canal or its tramways by the Shropshire Union Railways & Canal Company. To ensure that Newtown would not be isolated from Shrewsbury, the LNR secured a clause preventing the ONR from opposing any line from, or near, Welshpool to Shrewsbury, unless it was promoting its own line, for seven years.

The ONR's first shareholders' meeting was held on 21 July, when the nominated directors were re-elected. They intended to proceed with construction with as little delay as possible, a declaration that proved to be somewhat optimistic.

Reviewing extension prospects on 23 August, the LNR directors explained that not only would there be no competition for Manchester-South Wales traffic via Oswestry, but the Shrewsbury connection would also feed traffic to and from the Midlands and London. Extension beyond Llanidloes had been hindered by engineering difficulties; a route through Radnorshire to the Vale of Towy Railway at Llandovery might be preferable to one through Cardiganshire.

They took a pragmatic view about competition. The line from Llandovery to Craven Arms, promoted as part of a route for traffic between Shrewsbury and Milford Haven, might take traffic from Llanidloes, but they saw it as a feeder. They felt the same about the proposal to extend the Knighton line to Llandovery. As these schemes would follow a similar route between Builth and Llandovery to that required by a Llanidloes-Llandovery route, the success of either or both of them would reduce the distance of the Llanidloes line by about 20 miles.

Even the railway proposed from Newtown to Machynlleth and Aberystwyth, which would share 5 miles of the LNR's route, did not concern them. The east-west route would provide traffic for their north-south line.

The LNR could make no progress, however, until the remaining £15,000 of shares had been subscribed. Landowners who would benefit from the railway should support it, either by taking shares or by making their land available at moderate rental instead of sale. They thought that the company would be better off if the railway was built for cash rather than being financed by a contractor. Would that these insightful words had been heeded by others in this story.

Hopkins reported on arrangements he had made with the 21 LNR landowners on 19 September 1855. Nearly all had 'met the company in a liberal spirit,' he said, and land valued at £3,000, nearly half, would be taken in shares. The Misses Hamer, despite previous agreements, had still not come to terms, preferring the railway to be routed away from their property. £26,000 of shares had been subscribed, which, with the land shares, left only £1,000 to be subscribed before the company could exercise its borrowing powers. A further £10,000 was still required, therefore, for the company to be capable of funding the construction estimate of £60,000.

The question the LNR directors had to answer, Hopkins told them, was whether they wanted to start construction and rely on the shortfall being subscribed as work proceeded or would they delay construction until all of the shares had been taken? He thought they would be better by having more time for construction and, if they started immediately, fencing, earthworks and bridges could be let in small lots to 'satisfactory contractors' and completed in 18 months for about £22,000. Track-laying, which would cost about the same, could be carried out as funds became available.

In his report to the LNR shareholders, Hopkins explained that of his own volition he and Parry had examined the route between Llanidloes and Newbridge, near Builth, and concluded that Parry's proposal for a line via St Harmons to Rhayader would be best. The steepest gradient would be 1 in 100 that way.

The LNR directors decided that arrangements should be made for cutting the first sod on 3 October 1855. Mrs Owen should perform the ceremony and Hopkins was to arrange access to the field where the Llanidloes terminus was to be made; its owner was to be invited to the event. Hopkins was also to advertise for contractors, specifying that the work should start at Llanidloes and proceed at the rate of £50 per week. Progress was to be slow until the ONR was started, then co-ordinated in order that they could be completed together.

Mrs Owen disrupted the LNR plans by announcing the ceremony's postponement in the *Shrewsbury Chronicle* on 28 September 1855, notifying the directors on 2 October that she would be available on 8 October instead. Whalley performed the ceremony himself, the event incurring expenses of £43 5s 6d. Apparently it rained.

The angry LNR directors devoted some effort to a post-mortem of the failed ceremony. Correspondence, carefully recorded in the minutes and copied to the protagonists, continued until December. It transpired that the advertisement had been placed by Mrs Owen's solicitor's clerk, acting on her instructions, the solicitor was away, and it was drafted by Johnes, an ONR director who would be her nominee to the LNR board.

For her part, Mrs Owen blamed inexperience in the requirements of inaugurating a railway. Whalley had asked her to perform the ceremony on the evening of 20 September and she had asked for time to consider her response, to obtain the attendance and support of influential persons to give credence to the event, and to obtain more information about the company's financial status, as she had been asked to nominate a director.

Receiving the *Shrewsbury Chronicle* the next day she had been surprised to read of her involvement in an announcement that had clearly gone to press before she had been asked. Seeking to extricate herself from the ceremony, she arranged the advertisement, accepting that she should have merely announced her non-attendance rather than postponing the event. It seems rather odd that she had, she said, insufficient time to communicate with the company in Llanidloes yet could arrange for the advertisement to be published in Shrewsbury.

The directors took offence, the solicitor took offence and Hopkins took offence, all at some length. Mrs Owen and Whalley carefully skirted around each other, taking care not to cause offence. Eventually, they all tired of it and the correspondence fizzled out.

The LNR directors had considered the tenders submitted by seven contractors on 2 October, accepting the lowest, less than the estimate, from a local man, David Davies of Gwernerin, Llandinam. Born to a farming family in 1818, the start of his contracting career has already been mentioned. The LNR was his first railway. He had done worked valued at £103 10s by 8 November. The directors resolved to obtain powers of deviation and to extend the line to the canal at Newtown.

Meanwhile a group of ONR shareholders took exception to the company's administration and on 11 September petitioned for an extraordinary meeting. They wished to consider the appointment of its secretary, where that personage should reside, the location of the company's office, the location of directors' and shareholders' meetings, and the location for the first sod ceremony. Most of the directors' meeting had been held in London. William H. Prinsep, who had been the GWR's secretary, had been appointed secretary on a salary of £300 on 17 August. On 14 September the appointment was deferred until the outcome of the meeting was known.

The meeting was set for 5 October. Two days before, the directors decided that the capital represented by the supplicants was insufficient for the meeting to be valid. As there was insufficient time to postpone it they agreed to let it go ahead, however. It seems that the principal complaint was that Prinsep's previous position with the GWR would make him liable to favour that company over the LNWR. On 12 October the directors agreed to adopt the shareholders' proposal to postpone the appointment for two months and to find a candidate who could not be accused of favouring either of the larger companies.

The directors also adopted proposals that the company's offices should be in Welshpool and that the meetings should be held there. The first sod ceremony should be held in Montgomeryshire.

The nature of a traffic agreement with the LNWR over the use of the ONR from Buttington to Newtown was considered on 9 November. The Earl of Powis had suggested that the company should try and obtain a minimum of 4½% on half of the cost of that portion of the line in exchange for giving the LNWR free access to it.

The LNR's application for further powers was published on 12 November. It required three deviations, the canal extension, four level crossings, extensions of time for compulsory purchase and construction, operating agreements with the ONR, and authority to use a joint station at Newtown. ONR objections led to the canal extension being withdrawn.

Two days later the notice for the Shrewsbury & Welshpool Direct Junction Railway (SWR) was published. Intended to connect with the ONR at Buttington, the directors supported it as a feeder to the LNR. After considering a request from Barlow submitted on 2 October, the ONR directors had agreed that he and other officers could act for the SWR, 'so far as is consistent with their engagements with this company.'

Since the ONR Act had received the royal assent, Barlow and Piercy had fallen out over the allocation of fees. On 12 January 1856 the solicitors were requested to see them 'with the object of bringing about a harmonious co-operation between them.'

The contractors had expressed disquiet about the lack of progress in a letter dated 9 January 1856. They had been told that they would start on 1 March 1856, yet the plans were not ready and were unlikely to be for some time. Even when they were completed it would take a while to finalise details of the contract and for them to prepare to start work. At the least, the delay meant that they would have to buy in bricks rather than digging clay for them on site. The directors sent the letter on to Barlow and asked him to explain the delay to the contractors. Evidently

David Davies

they thought it was Barlow's fault, blaming him for the disputes with Piercy.

The ONR committee appointed to deal with the recruitment of an unbiased secretary submitted its report on 12 January 1856. There were numerous applications – 106, reported *The Times* – and six names were submitted with a recommendation in support of a Richard Stephens. He had been secretary of the Liverpool & Southport Railway, losing his position in an amalgamation. The committee ended its report with the observation that none of the candidates had submitted better testimonials or were better qualified than Prinsep.

Stephens was in post by 4 February 1856, having moved from Southport. By 8 February he had taken up temporary accommodation in the solicitor's office, but sought approval to obtain offices for himself and the engineers. He recommended engaging a bookkeeper and an office messenger who should sleep on the premises. He wanted approval to employ temporary assistance to prepare and issue 19,000 share certificates and wanted to obtain plans and estimates for rolling stock. By 15 March a house had been rented for £25 per annum. A bookkeeper and office keeper/messenger had also been appointed, but Stephens was going to have to deal with the share certificates as best he could.

Back in January there had been a rapid change in strategy concerning the LNR's river bridge at Morfodion, near Llanidloes. Hopkins was instructed to obtain tenders for the supply of timber and ironwork on 23 January, but the next day he was told to arrange for a temporary bridge to be built at a cost not exceeding £40. He was to obtain 'about' 2 miles of 65lb per yard wrought-iron rail and the 'necessary chairs, wedges and nails' at the lowest market price. Davies's offer to supply sleepers at 3s 9d each was refused in anticipation of being able to obtain them at 2s 6d, Hopkins's estimated price.

When Hopkins reported to the shareholders in February, agreements had been made for more than three-quarters of the land required. One-eighth would be paid in cash, the remainder either being paid for in shares or in rental at 4% per annum on valuation. Three miles of route were under construction and Davies would soon be ready to move on. While he had consulted with the Vale of Towy Railway over a route from Llanidloes via Rhayader 'towards' Llandovery, he cautioned against committing to expense or guarantees for branches or extensions. 'You have now a main line which is sure to pay well if not encumbered as many railway companies now are.'

On 29 February Davies offered to purchase 1-1½ miles of iron rail for use during construction providing the company would buy them from him at cost price when the contract was completed. If the company exercised its right, he would abate his haulage rate by a halfpenny per cubic yard per quarter-mile. The offer was accepted.

An acceleration of work was approved on 18 April. Hopkins was to arrange with Davies to proceed towards Penstrowed, close to Newtown, at the rate of £500 per month until further notice. When the shareholders' met on 16 August the line to Penstrowed was expected to be opened 'early next summer' and the entire line completed shortly afterwards. The deviation Act had received the Royal Assent on 5 June, when the Shrewsbury & Welshpool Railway Bill had also been enacted.

On 11 June Hopkins was authorised to act as the joint engineer of the Llanidloes-Llandovery line. Whalley was also authorised to attend meetings promoting it, being awarded 10 shares on account of his expenses on 15 August. In September the shareholders approved the allocation of £300 in shares as a guarantee towards half of the expenses incurred in promoting the line in the event of its failure, the Vale of Towy Railway also guaranteeing £300.

On the ONR, Barlow had been told to arrange the contracts and the solicitor to produce the draft contract and notices to landowners on 26 April. The works were to be completed 'at an early day'.

Notwithstanding the instruction given to Barlow, the dispute between him and Piercy had not been resolved. Each of them had put his case on 8 April, a committee deciding that Piercy was 'not chargeable with improper or unprofessional conduct'. Barlow made it clear that he would not work with Piercy, leading the committee to resolve, on 29 May, 'that as the progress of the works is suspended from the course adopted by Mr Barlow it is necessary to appoint another gentleman to perform the duties of engineer in chief.' Barlow was sent a copy of the resolution and requested to deliver all plans, sections, drawings and other documents in his possession and to say what he was owed.

The ONR's draft contract was ready on 13 June but the solicitor informed the board that before the notices to enter could be served the capital should be fully subscribed and a justice's certificate obtained to that effect; 6,249 £10 shares remained unsubscribed. Two calls for payment had been made, the second of them deferred.

The conduct of the ONR's affairs took Stephens to the Lords committee dealing with the Shrewsbury & Welshpool Railway Bill to give evidence during June. At the 23 June meeting for ONR shareholders to assent to the company's inclusion in the Bill, a group of Oswestry shareholders had tried to obtain a pledge that their line would be built and a guarantee that construction would be started at that town. The directors declared the motion failed because the capital represented by the shareholders voting in favour of the SWR clause had not met the required three-fifths majority by £329.

In Parliament the Oswestry shareholders complained about the shortage of time between the meeting and the committee, obtaining access to the ONR's records and postponing Stephens's appearance at the committee. Questioned about the lack of a minute referring to the deferral of the second call, he explained to the directors on 12 July that the committee chairman 'expressed surprise … considered it a very loose way of doing business', but found the explanation satisfactory.

Apparently unsolicited applications for the post of engineer had been received from Piercy and William Billinton by 12 July. On the 23rd the name of a Mr Woods, who 'has been employed on several lines in the north of England' and was willing to work with Piercy, was submitted. The directors interviewed both of them on 29 July and resolved to appoint Piercy, who had the support of shareholders, on 2 August. He would be paid £275 per mile and would work with a consulting engineer to be appointed separately.

Counsel's opinion was obtained on Barlow's claim. A claim £1,100 submitted by Piercy on 19 June was also the subject of scrutiny. The directors had advanced £700 but asked Sir William Cubitt to arbitrate on the account. They had already found it worthwhile to submit legal bills to arbitration, saving £140.

The ONR's finance committee reported on 2 August. £1,106 10s of deposits, including £1,000 from McCormick the contractor, remained unpaid. Some directors and others had agreed to take extra shares to ensure that the Bill would be passed, expecting that the extra shares would be passed to new subscribers at a later date, and £2,385 deposits on them were unpaid; only one holding was paid up. Arrears on shares taken by the contractors and others expected to take them in lieu of

payment totalled £16,984 6s 1d, on the extra shares £4,630, and on subscribers' shares £1,023 8d. The last included £100 due from Whalley.

The unpaid extra shares had caused the Lords committee to disenfranchise the entire holdings of those concerned. The ruling also meant that any transfers involving these holdings were invalid. The only resolution was for the deposits and arrears to be paid. No action seems to have been taken, however, and the matter was left in abeyance.

Royal assent was given to the Shrewsbury & Welshpool Railway Act on 29 July. The subscribers included Thornton and McCormick, the ONR's contractors, who had provided the deposit. Among the nominated directors were five who served on the ONR board. The authorised railway comprised the main line from a junction with the ONR at a point 3 furlongs to the south-west of Cefn farmhouse in Buttington to a junction with the Shrewsbury & Hereford Railway at Shrewsbury, and a branch line to Minsterley. With £150,000 capital, the main line could not be opened before the branch line.

The ONR directors told the shareholders that they had been unable to obtain powers to make traffic agreements with the SWR on 23 August 1856. The engineers' dispute and Piercy's appointment were the reason for not starting construction.

During the year the ONR had made several attempts to obtain its contractors' assent to Piercy's appointment as engineer. On 13 September Stephens was instructed to go to London to ascertain their views on the appointment of Joseph Cubitt, John Fowler or G. W. Hemans as chief engineer. Having obtained their opinion, Stephens was to visit those engineers in London to see if any of them were prepared to take on the ONR with Piercy as their resident.

Stephens reported on 26 September. He had met Thornton, who was willing to work with Cubitt but not with Piercy. Saying that Thornton 'expressed very liberal views as to settling with Piercy', Stephens had told him that the directors and the shareholders would not accept Piercy's removal without just cause, asking him to reconsider but not pressing him for an immediate answer.

Meeting at Cubitt's office the next day, Stephens secured the engineer's participation in the ONR with Piercy as his resident, providing he (Cubitt) had complete charge of engineering matters and that Piercy was responsible to him. Discussion with Thornton followed before Stephens suggested introducing Piercy. 'On Mr Piercy entering, Mr Thornton shook hands with him, and expressed himself pleased to see him.' Stephens should have had a career in diplomacy.

Cubitt agreed to Piercy continuing to work on the Vale of Clwyd Railway but was insistent that he should not seek further work. Cubitt put his conditions in writing on 23 September, asking for payment of £245 per mile inclusive of his expenses and Piercy's wages, payable at the rate of one-tenth quarterly with a further payment if the works took longer than 2½ years.

Accepting Cubitt's conditions, the ONR proposed paying Piercy £100 per mile for services already rendered and, 'in consideration of the peculiar circumstances in which he had been placed', a bonus of £1,500, which would be set against the deposit and first call of his 500 shares. Cubitt was appointed on 3 October and instructed to 'make arrangements for the completion of the contract at an early day', the second time this instruction had been issued.

Barlow's claim was refused on 1 November, after the receipt of counsel's opinion. Not only was he told that the ONR rejected his claim, but also that as he was still liable for the 500 shares he had subscribed, he could not be released from the obligation and must pay the deposit and calls on them. On 6 January 1857 the claim was submitted to Sir William Cubitt for adjudication.

The end of 1856 had been characterised by LNR disputes. In September seven shareholders living in the Rhayader area refused to pay their calls until arrears due from others, £6,159, had been paid. Advice on their powers having been obtained, the directors, meeting on 5 December, did not think that it was in the company's interest to sue for payment or to forfeit the shares, resolving to prepare a list of the defaulting shareholders and make it available to any shareholder who wished to see it. In 1857 a shareholders' committee recommended that the directors pursue the arrears.

At the same time Whalley had been in dispute with his vice-chairman, Lefeaux, over £10,000 shares subscribed by the latter. Lefeaux had agreed to take one-sixth of the capital when the company was first promoted, subject to the issue being fully subscribed, paying a deposit of £1,000. When subscriptions remained static at £30,000 in February 1854, Whalley had agreed to be responsible for them to allow construction to start. On 25 April Lefeaux accepted a proposal to reduce the holding by half, to apply the £1,000 payment to the reduced quantity and to pay the arrears by instalments.

On 23 November 1856 Davies had written proposing conditions for him to take a further £1,000 in LNR shares. With Hopkins absent, the directors instructed him to report to the secretary. Hopkins's non-appearance without notice might have been related to his demise the following year.

The first meeting of the provisional directors of the Newtown & Machynlleth Railway (NMR), held at the Wynnstay Arms Hotel in Machynlleth on 27 December 1856, had followed public meetings in Machynlleth, Dolgelley, Aberystwyth, Towyn and Aberdovey the previous week. The notice of intention to deposit a Bill had been published on 21 November.

At the meetings Piercy, introduced as the engineer of the 23-mile line, had explained that it would commence at a junction with the LNR at Caersws and traverse the vales of Carno, Twymyn and Dovey to reach Machynlleth; his undertaking not to take on further work given to the ONR and Cubitt in September had not lasted very long. Among the provisional directors was Charles Thomas Thruston, whose property had been mentioned in the Corris, Machynlleth & River Dovey Railway or Tramroad Act of 1852; a naval officer, he compiled the NMR prospectus.

Prior to Stephens's appointment it seems that the ONR's record-keeping had been poor. He submitted an eight-page report on the state of the ONR's accounts on 3 February 1857; in essence the books were physically too small to contain adequate detail. Drawing attention to the shareholders' right to inspect and copy the books contained in the Companies' Clauses Consolidation Act of 1845, his request for permission to obtain new books and to transfer the information from the old was approved without demur. It is to be wondered that the auditors had made no comments. Other records had been held at the Welshpool office and with solicitors in Montgomery and Oswestry. He had obtained those from Montgomery but it took two attempts to obtain the rest.

On 18 February Cubitt had informed the ONR directors that he had re-examined the line but had not been able to prepare the plans and sections in time for the meeting. 'A few more days will suffice.' The ONR shareholders were unhappy at the lack of progress reported when they met on 21 February, insisting on adjourning the meeting until 28 March while the directors finalised arrangements with the contractors; if they could not do so then another contractor should be appointed. Thornton, who was present, said that he had had detailed plans only since Christmas and it had taken six weeks to produce the estimates; he would be in a position to make a decision in a few days.

By the time Hopkins had reported to the LNR shareholders' meeting on 17 February the earthworks between Llanidloes and Llandinam were ready for track-laying, and fencing between

Llandinam and Caersws was in progress. He still expected the line to be completed to Penstrowed during the summer and thought a temporary station there would attract traffic from the canal at Newtown. He warned that although the works between Penstrowed and Newtown would be the most expensive on the line, traffic would be 'inconsiderable' until the ONR was opened because it would still have to be carted between the canal and Newtown.

It would be necessary to read between the lines to realise that the completed works referred to by Hopkins did not include the bridges. On 3 April, when the completion target had been moved to October, the directors instructed him to arrange for the erection of the river bridges at Morfodion and Llandinam and the road bridges between Llanidloes and Penstrowed. He was also to order iron rail on the basis that the maker would take payment in shares. The purchase of 1,200 tons of rail and fittings from the Ebbw Vale Company was approved on 19 May.

Provided that joint sleepers cost no more than 3s 9d and ordinary sleepers about 3 shillings, Davies's offer to supply larch sleepers at 1s 6d per cubic foot and to take at least £1,000 shares in payment was also accepted.

Looking forward to the LNR's partial completion, Davies had made a greater offer, to lease and operate it. As rent he would pay 4% on the gross expenditure for three months after opening to Penstrowed, and 5% after opening to Newtown. Two years after any of the connecting lines to Oswestry, Shrewsbury or Llandovery had been opened he would pay 6%, increasing at 1% annually until 10% was reached. The proposed agreement was read to shareholders on 13 June.

Submitting the lease for counsel's opinion, however, the directors discovered that they required fresh powers to complete it. Completion of the works on schedule would only occur if the arrears on calls were paid, shareholders were informed on 22 August, when Hopkins reported that 2 miles of rail had been laid and 9 miles of fencing was nearly complete. The columns of the Llandinam river bridge would be ready for erection within a few weeks and the Morfodion and Penstrowed river bridges would be completed within two months. The road bridges were being built.

Hopkins was responsible for identifying the LNR's first motive power. On 30 October 1856 the directors instructed him to 'purchase the second-hand engine mentioned … at the price of about £350.' A month later he made arrangements with Davies for its transport. 'Mr Sharpe' issued his bill for £350 on 23 December 1857; the locomotive was Sharp, Roberts 2-2-2 *Dove*, built in 1839. Lefeaux hired an engineer to work it.

Running alongside the dispute with the ONR contractors over Piercy's participation was a disagreement over the amount they proposed to charge for the contract – £284,200 – which was not only in excess of the authorised capital but also left nothing for the purchase of land and construction of stations. Estimates of around £200,000 obtained from others, including Piercy, Barlow and Cubitt, indicated that the price was higher than it should have been, but the contractors refused to move on it.

Asked to adjudicate, by 28 March 1857 Sir William Cubitt had valued the contract at £276,200. Adding £70,000 for land, £20,000 for stations, £40,000 for rolling stock and £50,000 for expenses already incurred brought the ONR's projected expenditure to £456,000. Cubitt also set the terms for paying by shares instead of cash, creating a liability for another £49,000, bringing the total to £505,000, £172,000 in excess of the company's powers. The contractors' refusal to accept the award left the directors thinking that their priority was to fulfil their own financial aspirations without regard for the company's interests.

Stephens visited Joseph Cubitt, who expressed surprise at the amount, adding that he thought the original, January 1855, agreement

Cutting the first sod of the Oswestry & Newtown Railway at Welshpool on 4 August 1857.

with the contractors to be 'full of informalities' and recommended taking advice on it.

The ONR shareholders' committee produced a 36-page report on the company's position by 10 July 1857, attributing much of the responsibility to the directors, for not being firm enough with the contractors or with Barlow. Some officials had been acting independently and without authority. Noyes, the solicitor, always took the contractors' side, for example, and the undertaking that he had given them in January 1855 had 'injuriously fettered' the board. Some directors had also acted independently of their colleagues. An executive committee appointed on 3 October 1856 to deal with matters requiring 'prompt attention' between board meetings had put control of the company in the hands of a small group resident near Welshpool; it had acted beyond its remit, only one of 11 meetings had been called in an emergency, and there was no need for it at the present time.

Calls on ONR shares were £57,872 10s in arrears out of £93,755 due. The Welshpool solicitor had been paid a gratuity of £250 for 'special services'; his Bill of £2,168 4s 1d had been reduced by £524 4s 8d at arbitration, so the gratuity appeared to compensate him for half of his 'loss'. The committee was critical of office and travel expenses incurred by Stephens and his staff. Up to incorporation, £16,201 19s 7d had been spent. Since then engineering had generated costs of £16,148 0s 5d. Barlow had claimed £4,250 and Cubitt would be charging £7,350 when Piercy had been willing to do the work for £8,250.

The committee recommended that dealings with Thornton and McCormick be abandoned; any claim made by them should be defended, a new contractor should be appointed, earthworks should be made for a single line to reduce costs, arrears of deposits and calls should be enforced, Noyes should be dismissed, Stephens's position should include that of bookkeeper, and that the directors should review their own position vis à vis their expenses. Nearly £25,000 had

been spent and no land had been purchased, sod turned or brick laid. Stringent economy was called for.

A new ONR contractor, John Rankin Davidson, had been identified by 27 June 1857, and directors met him and Cubitt on 3 and 7 July. McCormick and Thornton had not been discharged and there was disagreement among the directors about the approach to be adopted.

For £206,400 Davidson would build a single-track formation with structures suitable for a double track. He would work with William Oughterson from Carlisle, who had been resident engineer on the Glasgow, Paisley & Greenock Railway. The works excluded station buildings, signalling and cottages at level crossings.

By 1 August the arrears were being pursued and the directors were not claiming their fees. The auditors approved of Stephens's new books, with every entry supported by vouchers and receipts only recorded as they occurred, not in anticipation. The directors had not wanted to transfer the bookkeeper's duties to Stephens but nevertheless had resolved to dismiss the bookkeeper, subsequently extending his notice to three months.

Before a crowd of more than 10,000, Lady Wynn cut the ONR's first sod in the field next to Welshpool's bowling green on 4 August, more than a year since the ONR Act had received the royal assent; contractually, the works had started the day before. Some 400 sat down for lunch in a marquee on the bowling green.

On 7 August Cubitt proposed starting at Oswestry and constructing the line as far as the river bridge at Llanymynech (for £48,000) or Welshpool (£112,000). He also recommended that should the directors decide on the first option they should also take advantage of the state of the river to start on the bridge abutments at Buttington and Pool Quay.

Cubitt issued his first certificate, for £1,200, by 24 October. Davidson was paid £960 in cash. By the end of the year £2,480 had been spent on 'works' and £6,473 12s 4d on land and compensation.

Without opposition, the Newtown & Machynlleth Railway Bill had been enacted on 27 July. The subscribers were Earl Vane, Wynn, Robert David Jones, Thruston, John Foulkes and Laurence Ruck. The last five were named as the first directors, and Vane was to be elected a director at the first shareholders' meeting on 22 August. £150,000 capital was authorised.

Soon afterwards a prospectus was issued. Except for the Chester & Holyhead Railway in the north and the GWR route along the Bristol Channel, Wales was 'absolutely destitute of railways'. Recent acts for lines from Oswestry and Shrewsbury to Welshpool, Newtown and Llanidloes constituted the first step towards filling 'this crying want'. The time was now right to continue these lines to Machynlleth, leaving one short link to complete the route to Aberystwyth and the Irish Sea. Starting from near Caersws, the 23-mile line would follow the turnpike road through Carno and Llanbrynmair.

Intermediate stations would get traffic from lead mines in the Pennant valley. Located at the head of the Dovey estuary, Machynlleth also controlled roads from Dolgelley, Aberdovey and Aberystwyth. The town was known for flannel manufacture. To its north were slate quarries that exported their production by sea; the first stage of its journey, by road, was burdened by heavy charges. With the NMR they would be able to add the inland counties to their markets and reduce costs. A railway to carry slate from Corris to Machynlleth had already been authorised; adapting it for passenger and other traffic would bring Dolgelley and Barmouth closer to Machynlleth.

No gradient exceeded 1 in 60 and only one short tunnel, 176 yards long, was required. The tunnel was at Talerddig, where the line crossed from the Carno to the Dovey; in construction it became a cutting.

Terms for the release of Thornton and McCormick from their ONR agreement were accepted on 21 November. The company would reimburse them the £6,250 they had advanced for the deposit, release them from their share commitments and pay them £500 for the plans and surveys they had made. The shares were transferred to Davidson.

Having dealt with Thornton and McCormick, the ONR uncovered a problem with the bills submitted by Abraham Howell, the Welshpool solicitor, who appeared to be overcharging. A committee reported with a list of ten contentious items on 9 January 1858. The first item was £594 3s 10d for acting as secretary for the eight-month period before Stephens had been appointed. Not only was this £232 17s 2d more than it had cost to run the ONR's own office, including rental, for the same period, but Howell had also discouraged the ONR from setting up its own establishment until the contract had been settled because 'there was not much to do'. Howell also acted for the other Montgomeryshire companies, and by implication had been responsible for the poor bookkeeping.

After a 'protracted illness', Hopkins had died on 18 December 1857; he was 50 years old. Tributes to him were recorded in the LNR minutes on 31 December and in the shareholders' report on 3 February 1858. On 30 December his widow had sent her son, Evan Henry Hopkins, to meet the directors with an offer to determine the state of the railway's construction, particularly with regard to establishing the value of any outstanding debt to Hopkins's estate. She suggested that as the railway was nearly completed to her husband's design, the contract should be continued, and she should be paid for the outstanding work. Hopkins Jnr was then aged 20 and in training as an engineer; he subsequently became a respected clergyman. The directors were prepared to employ him as a consulting engineer in the short term but would prefer to employ someone with experience of contract works in the locality.

The LNR's steam locomotive was out of order when the directors met on 23 January 1858. A Mr Howell, 'engine maker' of Hawarden – coincidentally, it seems, in Llanidloes – accepted the task of reporting on its condition and the repairs required. His estimate of £165 10s gives an indication of the loco's poor condition, but whether it was supplied like that or had been damaged by misuse after delivery can only be surmised. Howell gave the company four months' credit on £100 of the bill; payment of the balance of £57 10s 4d was to be authorised on 1 October.

Evan Hopkins had submitted a report to the shareholders on 3 February. Rail was laid from Llanidloes to Maesmawr, about 8 miles, and several miles had been ballasted. For economy, ballast was to be transported by locomotive rather by horses. The Morfodion river bridge was ready for track-laying. The wrought-iron girders for the Llandinam river bridge were on site and should be erected within a month; the bridge was being supported on oak piles. The Roefach road bridge was approaching completion, but others had not been started. Before the line could be opened the usual railway accoutrements, station buildings, engine and carriage sheds, level crossing gates, mile, gradient, lamp and signal posts, weighbridges and turntables, were required.

The acquisition of a tank engine was recommended for working the traffic. The 'present locomotive' needed its pistons and valves refitting and made steam-tight. When the track to Llanidloes was complete it should be taken there and repaired by W. Thomas, 'who has every convenience in his fitting shop for that purpose'.

Davies had timber in stock for the bridges and could complete the line in six to eight months given sufficient funding; access to more land was required though. While time had undoubtedly been lost due to Rice Hopkins's illness and death, the optimism of the previous year had clearly been misplaced.

Evan Hopkins was appointed engineer on 6 February, undertaking to raise the capital required to enable the railway to be completed to Newtown in accordance with his father's contract.

Notwithstanding this obligation, which was not fulfilled, the LNR was struggling to raise the capital it needed, but the minutes are not explicit on the matter. The solicitors accepted shares in lieu of expenses or were allowed to offset their expenses against calls due on shares. Several bills were paid with notes of hand, promissory notes, and in February and March 1858 several directors gave the company notes for amounts ranging from £30 5s to £600 – £1,063 12s in total. Payments of £600 plus £9 5s interest for sleepers and £696 17s 3d to the Uskside Engineering Company for bridge girders were approved on 29 April 1858. The last time Davies was paid for any work was in April. The minutes recorded payments totalling £8,255 15s since construction had started.

Continuing objections from Mr Herbert, the Misses Hamer and Palmer, whose properties were affected by the route between Penstrowed and Newtown, and the need to contain costs, forced a review of the alignment there during February. The land required was to be valued so the directors knew how much money should be paid into court if the company took possession without agreement.

The LNR directors' optimism over the issue of the debenture stock built up and was dashed down within a few weeks. On 28 May they discussed and accepted an offer of £5,000 to be advanced by 'clients of Messrs Williams & Rathbone', presumably brokers. Whalley and Lefeaux, as chairman and vice-chairman, had to provide personal security for the interest and repayments of principal. The company awarded them 750 shares as security against the liability there were incurring, subject to them being returned when the debt was redeemed. Having secured funding, as they thought, the directors

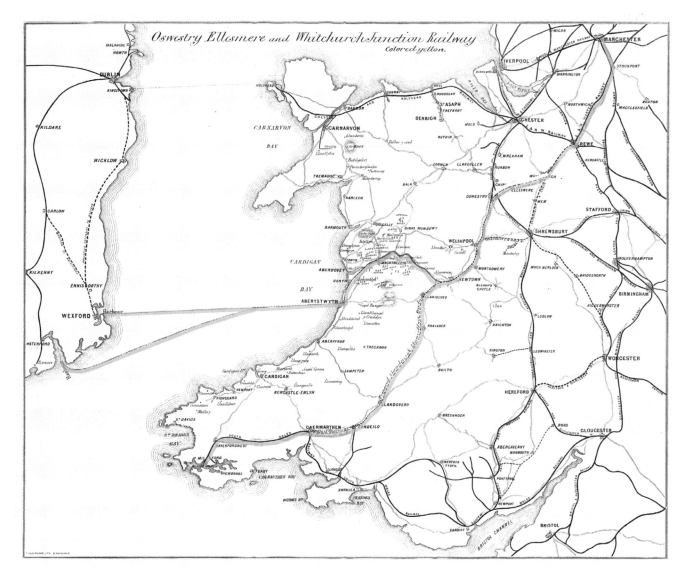

This 1857 map illustrates the ambitions of the original promoters, the through route from the English North West to Milford Haven and Ireland. The route between Llanidloes and Llandeilo is the proposed Llandovery & Llanidloes Railway, while the proposed Carmarthen & Llandeilo Railway makes the connection with the South Wales Railway at Carmarthen and Llandeilo. The later addition of the Wrexham & Ellesmere Railway made it possible to avoid using the LNWR completely.
*National Archives*

moved on to instruct Piercy to measure the works completed or in progress by 1 June, including verification of those already certified by Rice Hopkins.

By 29 June hopes of placing the LNR debentures had ended, the directors realising that there would be no interest in them until the line was completed and open for traffic. The secretary's appeal for shareholders to subscribe for more shares had little effect.

The cessation of work until funds could be obtained did not inhibit Piercy's appointment as engineer on that date; he was to seek a solution concerning the outstanding order for rail. At Piercy's request, 'Mr Cubitt' was appointed consulting engineer; Cubitt was, of course, already working on the ONR.

Piercy had reported a lack of progress on that line on 5 February 1858, regretting that, due to the lack of access to land at the Oswestry end, they were finished 'to a length not much exceeding three miles'. Permission was given to push on from Llanymynech towards Pool Quay, where the railway crossed the Oswestry-Welshpool road close to the canal, and Howell was to apply to the magistrates for authority to exercise the compulsory purchase powers.

Davidson's colleague Oughterson was joined to the ONR contract on 6 February, the same date that the directors accepted the arbitrator's award of £3,774 4s 4d due to Barlow, setting off £3,500 outstanding on his shares against it.

The location of ONR stations was discussed on 28 May. Llynclys, Four Crosses, Buttington, Welshpool, Montgomery and Abermule

were deemed to be worthy, in addition to the termini, although a site at Abermule had not been identified. The purchase of two plots for the station at Oswestry was approved.

Some Oswestry shareholders had long been dissatisfied with the ONR's office being in Welshpool and made more than one attempt to have it moved. The directors resisted the pressure, however, and in May had it relocated to 17 Buckingham Street, London, at a cost of £100. The former office was to be returned to its owner or let. Nothing was said about the employment status of Stephens's staff.

Reporting on 31 July, Cubitt said that the earthworks between Oswestry and Pool Quay had made considerable progress, the limestone cutting at Llanymynech was nearly complete and other cuttings well advanced. Several bridges had been completed, and the abutments of the Vyrnwy river bridge at Llanymynech were finished, the two river piers were above floodwater height and the wrought-iron girders were on site ready for installation. A 'considerable portion' was ready for track-laying and 2 miles of track had been laid. He anticipated having this 12-mile section ready for opening by Christmas. On 19 October he was instructed to complete the line from Oswestry to Llanymynech and to have it ready for traffic by 1 February 1859.

Earlier in 1858, the LNR directors accepted the shareholders' committee's proposal to extend towards Milford Haven, saying that the first step would be to have a fresh survey to determine the best and cheapest route. Noting, however, the committee's observation about the effort already expended on surveys, the directors resolved that before any professional appointments were made public meetings should be held to gauge opinion.

A route to Pencader was receiving favourable attention to avoid (Parliamentary) competition with the Knighton-Llandovery proposal. 'A line at a gradient of 1 in 80 will be able to reach Cwmystwyth and the Hafod valley with less than a mile and a half of tunnelling.' By the time the shareholders reported on 27 August the directors had decided that the project should be developed by a separate company.

There had been no progress with the NMR by the time of the shareholders' meeting on 10 September. They were told that this was partly due to the absence of Vane and Wynn, chairman and vice-chairman, from Wales, and Thruston's 'lamented death'. The directors hoped, they said, to make arrangements for the 'early commencement' of the works within six months. In their report they noted that the 'Corris Tramway Company' had obtained a new Act, 'this line is in course on formation and it will, when completed, form a junction with our railway and be an important feeder to it.' Vane owned the Corris-served Aberllefenni slate quarry.

Concerning the LNR, Davies had agreed to complete construction, re-starting in September and expecting to take three months. He would then operate it and pay rental on agreed terms. Piercy, in the same report, said that, because of the deviations, he anticipated completing the line for less than the authorised capital. Referring to 'the contractors, Messrs Davies and Savin', he made no comment about the inclusion of another party in the contract.

Thomas Savin was an Oswestry merchant anxious for improvements in communications; in 1856 he had been elected to the town council. It is said that he and Davies had known each other since 1850, having been introduced by George Owen, a friend or acquaintance of Savin's, when Davies was building the town's cattle market. In 1857, when work on the LNR had slowed down, Davies had made a contract to build the Vale of Clwyd Railway, which he and Savin carried out together. Resident in Oswestry since 1853, Owen had been born in Tunbridge Wells in 1827 and trained with Sir John Rennie and W. S. Moorsom on the Staines & Farnborough Railway, later working with Piercy in Montgomery, and marrying one of Mickleborough's daughters.

Nothing was said of the termination of Evan Hopkins's relationship with the LNR, but by 28 October 1858 a writ had been issued by Rice Hopkins's widow 'for recovery of the amount claimed to be due to her from the company'. The action was defended.

The financial position saw some improvement in October, when Whalley persuaded the North & South Wales Bank to make £2,000 available on the directors' guarantee, £3,000 shares being issued to Whalley and Lefeaux as security.

Thomas Savin

The Misses Hamer remained entrenched in their refusal to agree to the use of their land, so on 28 October the directors resolved to take possession compulsorily and appointed a surveyor to value it. They were prepared to take action against Mr Herbert as well. The Hamer land was to be valued at £318 12s 6d, that amount being paid into court.

Another attempt was made to extend the LNR to the canal at Newtown. On 10 November the directors resolved to apply 'for leave to extend railway to canal, for powers of leasing and such other powers as [the] chairman may think needful'. The published notice described a Bill seeking powers for the canal extension, to alter the levels between the terminus at Llanidloes and the Morfodion river bridge to accommodate an extension to Llandovery, to extend the time allowed to purchase the deviation lands, to lease the undertaking, and other purposes. On 17 December Piercy signed the estimate for £3,000.

Two other Bills were advertised at the same time. One was for the Manchester, Liverpool, Swansea & Milford Haven Junction Railway (Mid Wales Sections), a route from Llanidloes to Newbridge in Radnorshire and thence to Llandovery in Carmarthenshire, mountainous country, with little habitation.

The other was headed the Oswestry & Newtown Railway, the Llanidloes & Newtown Railway, the Shrewsbury & Welshpool Railway and the Newtown & Machynlleth Railway. The Bill's purpose was to enable the ONR and LNR to lease their works; to amalgamate; to construct branches at Llanymynech, Llynclys and Newtown; to substitute level crossings for bridges; to enable the four companies, or any of them, to enter into agreements; to make arrangements with each other, and with the GWR, the Birkenhead, Lancashire & Cheshire Junction Railway and LNWR, or any of them; for the use, working and management of the four companies, or any of them; for the apportionment of tolls and the renewal and extension of powers to purchase lands and complete works; the provision of capital; and other purposes.

The proposed branch at Llynclys would terminate at Porthywaen, 'at or near a lime kiln … in the holding of Thomas and John Savin'. That at Llanymynech was to serve the Carreghofa lime works adjacent to the Shropshire Union Canal and required authority to alter existing tramways to accommodate the ONR's stock. At Newtown, the branch would serve the canal. The Savin brothers often worked in partnership on railway construction.

The LNR directors must have known of these Bills but they made no recorded comments about them. Whalley even chaired the first meeting of the Manchester, Liverpool, Swansea & Milford Haven Junction Railway's provisional committee in London on 12 January 1859. Among those 'in attendance' at this meeting were the LNR solicitor, Piercy, Savin and Richard Samuel France. How the latter came to be there is not known; he was to become the secretary of the SWR and contractor of the Potteries, Shrewsbury & North Wales Railway. He was appointed secretary pro tem.

The offer from Davies and Savin to provide the £33,600 required for the deposit was accepted the next day, and Piercy was instructed to negotiate the contract with them. Whalley said that the LNWR was prepared to guarantee 4½% dividend against a rebate of 50% on charges due to the LNWR for traffic passing from the proposed railway.

On 12 November 1858 Davies had attended an NMR board meeting and offered to take the contract with Savin. Consideration was deferred for ten days, when the directors resolved to appoint Joseph Cubitt as consulting engineer and 'Messrs Piercy' as engineers. Their fees were set at £5,000 in total, payable as £1,000 already incurred, mainly by Piercy, £2,000 in paid-up shares, including £500 already registered to Piercy, and £2,000 in cash, payable in instalments as the work progressed. They had intended to charge £5,750, but Piercy had deducted £750 'in consideration of the present state of the share list'; he thought the company could not afford it. When the railway was opened to traffic they could claim the £750.

Davies and Savin were given the NMR contract for £130,000, to be payable as £102,000 in cash, £23,000 in paid-up shares and £5,000 as a loan. To save time they were to be allowed to start work as soon as access to the land had been obtained, starting between the junction with the LNR and the 'tunnel at Talerddig', that portion of the railway to be opened to traffic on or before 1 January 1860. On completion, the contractors were to work the railway with their own rolling stock, paying dividends of 3½% initially, then 5% when the ONR was opened to Newtown. 27 November was set as the date for cutting the first sod at Machynlleth, Countess Vane to perform the ceremony.

A public collection raised money to decorate the town with arches, flags and banners. Bells rang, cannons were fired and bands played. The arches carried exhortations in English and in Welsh. At 1.00pm the directors, shareholders and some 300 schoolchildren processed from the town hall to the ceremony site. In his speech Earl Vane alluded to the ONR's problems when he said that the NMR board was small and united. He explained that, although some shareholders wanted construction to start at Machynlleth, it would be better to start at the junction with the existing railway than at the terminus where there was no railway. They would be in a poor way if they made 5 miles to Gwastadgoed, instead of 9 miles from Caersws to Talerddig, 'for once we get there we will never stop until we get the line to Aberystwyth'. He concluded by asking director John Foulkes to speak in Welsh for the benefit of those who had no English.

Davies presented Lady Vane with a mahogany wheelbarrow and 'a unique spade' with which to perform the ceremony. Due to the short notice, reported the *Shrewsbury Journal* on 1 December, he had been unable to obtain implements suitable for presentation so they would be replaced by items of greater value, suitably inscribed for adoption as heirlooms. She was also presented with a pair of gloves to wear.

Afterwards, Foulkes presented Lady Vane with a purse of Maundy money as payment for the work done. Then several others, including Vane's four children, the directors, Davies and 'real navvies' also dug and moved earth before the party moved to the town hall.

Among the speeches, Davies said that this was the third such ceremony he had attended for lines that he had contracted to build and that he thought that the NMR had the best prospects, for it had more money subscribed as a proportion of capital required than the others.

The collection that paid for the decorations in Machynlleth had evidently been a great success, for it also paid for dinners for members of the Machynlleth Second Friendly Society, nearly 400 quarrymen from the Aberllefenni, Tyddynyberth, Geiwern and Braich Goch quarries, and navvies of the Corris & Machynlleth Tramroad. National School children were treated to currant buns while Lady Vane treated those attending the Vane Infant School to plum cake and tea.

When the NMR shareholders met on 26 February 1859, land had been purchased and was being fenced, construction of the Severn river bridge had been started and completion of the line from Caersws to Talerddig, 9 miles, was expected by the year's end.

Resumption of work on the LNR in December 1858 became conditional on an advance of £3,000 demanded by Davies and Savin to offset the same amount they were owed on the Vale of Clwyd contract. Although this was in complete contradiction to the undertaking Davies had made in September to complete the railway within three months, the directors did not dispute it. Perhaps they thought they had no choice. Not only did the contractors make the demand but they had also already obtained the bank's approval for it. Taking it as an alternative to the £2,000 borrowing arranged by Whalley in October, the directors agreed to it on the same terms, allocating 450 shares to Whalley and Lefeaux as collateral. They also asked for the Vale of Clwyd debt to be assigned to the LNR. This money-go-round was to be a feature of Savin's contracting career.

By a letter dated 4 January 1859, Davies and Savin made another demand, for £20,000 shares to be transferred to them as security for work to be carried out and for any rolling stock purchased by them for use on the railway. The shares were those already issued to, or due to be issued to, the Ebbw Vale Company as security for the rail purchases, and their transfer was linked to the contractors' desire to 'find the deposit' for 'the Llandovery line'. They wanted to place it under the control of two LNR directors; Whalley and Lefeaux were nominated 'although this board does not feel justified in recognising or taking part in the arrangements…'

Dealing with this on 5 January, the LNR directors agreed that the rail was to be paid for in five quarterly instalments, starting from 4 August 1859, against the security of debentures. A £5,000 debenture, repayable in two years, was issued to Davies and Savin as a payment for 'works done and to be done'.

Despite their reluctance to be involved in the Llandovery line, on 2 February 1859 the LNR directors agreed that it was 'material to the success' of the scheme to become a party to the proposed traffic arrangements, appointing the Shropshire Union Railway & Canals Company's solicitor to act for it.

Reporting to the LNR shareholders on 26 February, Piercy said that the works were progressing 'most satisfactorily'. Two locomotives were being used for ballasting and a night shift was being worked to complete 'the great cutting at Scafell' and track would be laid through it within a month. Rolling stock had been ordered and stations were being built. He forecast that the railway would be ready for traffic by 1 May. By 9 April he said that it would be ready for mineral traffic on 30 April and would be completed and compliant with Board of Trade requirements by 25 May.

Whalley told the meeting that the Board of Trade had been interested in the proposal contained in the 1858 Bill to lease the LNR to the contractors as individuals. While he thought that this could be overcome if Davies and Savin formed a joint-stock company, they got the powers they wanted.

Speaking at a public meeting called later to discuss the LNR canal extension, Whalley explained that it was required because the ONR was not finished. The only objections to it were from the turnpike trustees and Newtown residents. The latter had not complained before and, Whalley thought, the extension would make the carriage of goods through the town more convenient and relieve the pressure on the town's narrow streets. Responding to questioning, he said that the extension would be worked as a tramway, with wagons pulled by horses. The opposition seemed to be based on the expectation that locomotives would be used and perhaps that it would be the first stage to convert the canal into a railway. If the turnpike trustees would agree to laying rails in the road on a temporary basis, then the extension would only be needed until the ONR was opened and there would be no need for powers.

By 31 December 1858 expenditure on the ONR had reached £45,720, with £26,867 spent on land. The landowners were obviously striking hard bargains. With arrears on the share account of £12,883, several shareholders were sued to enforce their commitments. Barlow and others had issued a writ on 9 December, claiming that the forfeiture of shares was invalid and seeking to be relieved of the obligation to meet certain calls.

An extraordinary shareholders' meeting to authorise the use of ONR borrowing powers was held on 11 January 1859. A row broke out about whether it had been properly called, and the readership of the newspapers used to advertise it. Although the motion was put and carried, several shareholders were unhappy and sought to have it overturned or altered. Their clearly expressed view of distrust in the directors was probably aggravated by the circulation of rumours that the ONR would not be built beyond Welshpool, a matter of particular concern to Newtown shareholders. 'The meeting broke up in some confusion.'

Progress was slowed for want of money, Cubitt reported on 14 February, estimating that six weeks' work would see the line completed to Llanymynech and four more weeks would see it finished to Pool Quay. Track was laid to Llanymynech and the remainder was ready for ballasting. The Vyrnwy river bridge and the canal bridge at Llanymynech were nearly completed but arrangements for Oswestry station remained outstanding. Beyond Pool Quay the bridge abutments were almost finished. Given the land and finance the line could be extended to Welshpool in nine months and to Newtown in 12. On 1 January 467 men and 53 horses had been employed on the works.

Davidson and Oughterson introduced Savin to the ONR directors on 9 March, explaining that 'negotiations were proceeding between them as to carrying on the works'. Savin asked the board to exclude others while he was negotiating. After obtaining legal advice, Lloyds bonds for £900 and £2,780 were issued to the contractors as security on the outstanding debt on 13 March. This had not been mentioned previously but appears to have been consequential on Savin's involvement.

His proposals for completing the ONR contract were accepted by the directors on 9 May. The key points were that the existing contract be cancelled and replaced by one with Savin and Davies; the line be completed in exchange for the unissued and forfeited shares and £65,000 preference shares; the contractors to lease the line for 10 years from 1 January 1861, guaranteeing 3% dividend for the first three years and 4% thereafter; and the company to apply for powers to issue the preference shares and to lease the line. One of the founder directors objected to the agreement, arguing that if the contractors nominated the engineer then there was no one to protect the shareholders' interests. Barlow's written objection was 'received with considerable merriment' when it was read out at the shareholders' meeting on 5 June.

Reporting the meeting at length on 8 June, the *Oswestry Advertiser* also editorialised on the subject, expecting the adage 'when things are at their worse they mend' to be realised. While shareholders were split on the long-term objective of being taken over by the LNWR or the GWR, the paper tended to support the former, provided it abandoned its link to the SWR and built a line between Oswestry and Whitchurch. The outcome would be 'two distinct and tolerably direct routes to London, Liverpool and Manchester' and one could be played off against the other.

Under the heading 'The war in Montgomeryshire', the paper also published a set of spoof war telegrams, received 'not through Mr Reuter's office, but by the Queen's Head omnibus'. 'The earthworks are now in the possession of the popular party, who have placed Lieutenants Davies and Savin in charge, supported by a large body of the Army Works Corps,' is a typical example.

In its 11 June issue, the *Railway Times* commented on the involvement of a firm called Williams, Brace & Minshall, saying that it was about to take over from Davidson and Oughterson. Minshall was once a common name in Oswestry, so these were perhaps the people that Savin was keen to see excluded. There were similarities in the proposals: for example, the contractor was to operate the railway for 10 years from 1 January 1861 and guarantee dividends and interest. The paper was sceptical about the likelihood of any of the Welsh railways being completed.

There was quite a fall-out from the ONR's new construction arrangements, some of it immediate. At the adjourned shareholders' meeting that followed the Welshpool meeting, Stephens submitted his resignation, saying that as the company's policy had altered it was appropriate that he should retire. Savin supported a motion that he (Stephens) should be paid six months' salary, while some called for the resignation to be refused. The minutes of 13 June refer to a shareholders' deputation on 4 June, calling for his resignation. Although he had the chairman's support and agreed to remain in post for the time being, he was replaced by Benjamin Tanner on a temporary basis on 7 July and was paid £300; his request to be paid the income tax on this sum was refused.

Cubitt's resignation and replacement by Piercy had been approved on 28 June. On 20 July the resignations of the Earl of Powis and Richard Herbert Mytton as directors were accepted; the latter had been one of the founders. Wynn, the chairman, came to conclude that the directors had not acted in the best interests of the shareholders, his resignation being accepted on 17 December. Pugh was elected chairman on 11 January 1860.

The ONR's London office had been vacated on 24 June 1859, Stephens being instructed to make expedient temporary arrangements 'until the question of removal … be definitely settled'. On 20 July the directors resolved that the company's offices be at Oswestry until the line was opened to Welshpool.

The layout and station at Oswestry were the subject of negotiations with the GWR. On 24 August the ONR resolved that the GWR should have running powers over the ONR between the junction and the station in exchange for giving the ONR free use of the land it required. The cost of the station and its facilities should be shared equally and they would be joint proprietors.

On the LNR, Davies and Savin had repaid the £3,000 made available to them by 3 May 1859, applying for a further £4,000 on account of work done and offering to take payment in shares. The Vale of Clwyd Railway had been opened on 5 October 1858.

Piercy's predictions for completing the LNR still proved to be too optimistic, but on 17 June Davies and Savin carried 'without charge upwards of 2,000 of the inhabitants of Newtown to Llanidloes'. The train, reported the *Oswestry Advertiser* on 22 June, comprised more than 30 carriages and two locomotives. Prior notice of the intention to run the train having been given, factories and shops closed early. The beadle, in uniform, and the town band turned out to see the train off. When the train returned, 'some young vagabonds' threw stones at it, some of them receiving their deserts on the spot. On another date, possibly 13 June, 800 people had enjoyed a return journey from Llanidloes.

Colonel W. Yolland inspected the line on 28 June, reporting from London the next day. The LNR was 11 miles 49.5 chains long, with single track and stations at the termini, Dolwen and Llandinam. Land had been taken and overbridges constructed for a second track if required. The formation width was 18 feet. 70lb flat-bottom rail in lengths varying from 18 to 22 feet was fixed by iron dog spikes to transverse sleepers laid 3 feet apart. Joints were held by two wrought iron four-hole fishplates and rested on iron baseplates fixed to the sleepers by four spikes struck through holes in the plates. The sleepers were larch and the ballast rough gravel laid to a depth of 21 inches below the upper rail surface.

There were eight overbridges and 13 underbridges. The greatest span of the former was 26 feet on the square and 37ft 6in on the skew. Except for one that was built of timber, all had rubble masonry abutments and timber decks. The underbridges were mostly accommodation bridges of small span, but a turnpike road was crossed by an iron girder bridge 25 feet on the square and 34ft 3in on the skew. They also had rubble masonry abutments and, except the girder bridge, timber decks. There were five viaducts, of 150 yards, 232ft 6in, 159 feet, 60 feet and 285 feet span. The first four were of timber, the last using wrought-iron lattice girders on timber piles; the greatest span was 32ft 6in.

For about 2 miles there were no base plates under the joints, an extra sleeper being inserted instead, so the joints were not properly supported. Yolland was unhappy with the dog spikes and did not think that they were effective. He had been told that the company had insufficient funds to install the tie rods it proposed to use to keep the track to gauge. This was inadequate for the expected use of the railway as a through route carrying heavy traffic between Manchester and Milford Haven. He thought that baseplates similar to those used on the joints would make the track more suitable, and that the line should not be opened until all the joints had these fitted. Sleepers of less than average cross-section should be replaced. The timber decks on several overbridges should be strengthened – one was already sagging.

At Newtown, the turntable was on site but not installed, and the fencing and platform were incomplete. The station buildings at Llandinam and Llanidloes were incomplete and there were none at Dolwen; it was no longer intended to have a station there. The gates at a level crossing were being erected but there was no lodge. Hand rails were required on the viaducts for the protection of platelayers. Sidings were incomplete, and mile and gradient posts required erecting.

As it was quite evident that the line must be re-inspected, Yolland wrote, and the day being wet and unfavourable, he did not make a minute inspection of the structures. The company had previously asked for the inspection to be deferred until after 1 July, when the railway would be completed.

The railway was to be worked by the contractors for several years, continued Yolland. It had two locomotives at work, only one of which was fitted for passenger traffic. The line rose from Newtown to Llanidloes at an average of more than 15 feet per mile, and most goods traffic would have to be taken up this gradient; a second engine was therefore absolutely indispensable. Because the works were incomplete and the establishment insufficient, the LNR could not be opened without danger to the public.

The Board of Trade file is incomplete and contains only Yolland's report. There was no reference to it in the minutes, nor of the revised arrangements for the opening. On 8 August the directors made the statutory declaration that the railway would be worked with one engine in steam. The *Oswestry Advertiser* published on 10 August reported that following an inspection by Yolland and Colonel Ross, the line had been authorised to be opened for passenger traffic, whilst the 17 August issue said that 'the railway was duly opened on Thursday for passenger transit' – i.e. 11 August. The directors' report of 5 September explained that the Board of Trade certificate had been received on 9 August.

Incidentally, the *Chester Chronicle* of 30 July reported that on the 27th the ONR directors had travelled by special train to Llanidloes and that on their return to Newtown 'the church bells sent out merry peals'.

A fatal accident on 1 August had marred the completion of the LNR. A ballast train was approaching Penstrowed when a ganger attempted to remove a level lying across the track and was run down. The *Wrexham Advertiser* did not identify the victim.

A Mid Wales Railway share certificate dated 1859.

Celebrations to mark the opening took place on 31 August and 1 September 1859, detailed accounts being published in local newspapers. When planning for the opening anticipated on 25 May, the directors sought to avoid the embarrassment of the first sod ceremony by getting both Mrs Owen and the Earl of Powis to approve proofs of newspaper advertisements. On 31 August both Llanidloes and Newtown were decorated with much bunting and numerous banners, and decorated arches had been erected over the railway at the termini and at Llandinam.

Events started at Llandinam, where the Plas Madoc band led a procession that included 40 navvies wearing medals inscribed 'Commemoration medal, struck on the opening of the Llanidloes & Newtown Railway, 31 August 1859'; 350 were distributed to navvies, workmen and railway officers, and others were also given to those members of the public who paid the 1s 6d return fare to travel on this special day. The band played 'See the conquering hero comes' as the train arrived to a volley of exploding detonators 45 minutes late; it was a showery day.

The locomotives, named *Llewelyn* and *Milford* and decorated with evergreens, were turned on the turntable and another chorus of detonators signalled the train's departure. At Newtown the party processed to Newtown Hall, where Whalley extolled the virtues of the LNR and looked forward to the first sod ceremony of the Mid Wales Railway (MWR), due to take place at Rhayader on 2 September. After lunch, the party left for Llanidloes at 3.00pm.

One of the reports stated that the carriages had been made by Ashbury in Manchester and were similar to those supplied to the Oxford, Worcester & Wolverhampton Railway. The 1st Class were, it said, fitted up to the usual style of excellence, the 2nd Class seats were cushioned and more comfortable than the norm, and some of the 3rd Class were opens. Some wagons had been adapted to carry passengers on this day, too.

The return train apparently comprised 46 carriages that were hauled by three locomotives. Each carriage contained about 50 passengers, which would make 2,300 passengers in all – clearly this journalist was no mathematician. Some of the 46 carriages must have been adapted wagons. Arriving at Llanidloes, the railway was declared open and Mrs

Owen was first to speak, alluding to the Romans and referring to advancements in shipping as well as science, contrasting railway developments in Wales, favourably, with those on the continent. After the speeches and toasts, dinner was served in a marquee.

The second day of celebrations was centred on Llandinam, where Davies and Savin laid on entertainment for 'their friends and 600 of their workmen'. The party started at Newtown before joining the train for the journey to Llanidloes and back to Llandinam, where lunch was taken.

Davies and Savin were presented with a silver salver and cake basket each, the former inscribed 'This salver, together with a cake basket, was presented to [David Davies Esq/Thomas Savin] Esq by the inhabitants of the district through which the Llanidloes & Newtown Railway passes, as a mark of their approval for the energetic manner in which he and [Mr Savin/Mr Davies] have constructed the line. 1 September 1859.' As this silverware had cost 56 guineas it was a fine gesture from people who would have had very little.

Edward Woolley, a workman employed by Davies and Savin, made a greater gesture on behalf of his colleagues, presenting gold watches with the motto 'nid cariad am gais, on cariad am a ge's' ('Give not for what you might expect, but for what you have received') to their sons, aged five and six years respectively. The remainder of the day was given over to 'a variety of rustic sports, dancing, football &c.'

A timetable had been published in the *Oswestry Advertiser* on 17 August. The paper had been told that there would be five return trains each day and two on Sundays. Now, however, there were three each day and none on Sundays. It accepted that the original weekday service was too ambitious for the traffic, but could not understand why there were no trains on Sundays.

The service was based at Llanidloes, with 35 minutes allowed for the downhill journey to Newtown, and 40 minutes for the return. Trains stopped at Dolwen, despite what Yolland had been told, and Llandinam. Accommodation was provided for three classes, the 7.30am from Llanidloes and 4.00pm from Newtown being designated Parliamentary trains. On Newtown fair days there was a 6.00am departure from Llanidloes, taking 30 minutes inclusive of stops at intermediate stations.

Single fares had been set at 2s 6d (1st class), 1s 6d (2nd class) and 1 shilling (3rd class) – the last equated to the Parliamentary fare. Return fares were to be 3s 9d (1st) and 2s 6d (2nd), with no discounts for workers. Fares for the intermediate stations were set in proportion to the distance travelled.

Earlier, Savin had offered to redeem the £3,000 debenture due to the Ebbw Vale Company on 5 August on the company's behalf. A £1,610 5% debenture payable on 1 July 1860 and 139 paid-up shares were registered to him as security.

The Llanidloes & Newtown Railway (Canal Extension) Act had received the Royal Assent on 21 July and with it the leasing powers were obtained. The Newtown tramway was to be considered a part of the LNR and the existing capital could be used for it. As recently as 28 June the ONR had voted £200 to oppose the tramway.

As the figurehead behind the LNR and the company's chairman, Whalley received recognition at the events to mark its completion. In the community he was held in sufficient regard that on 30 August Llanidloes town council commissioned an engraved portrait of him. Within a few days he was receiving nationwide attention and was the subject of many critical column inches in newspapers.

The Manchester, Liverpool, Swansea & Milford Haven Junction Railway (Mid Wales Sections) Bill had been enacted as the Mid Wales Railway Act on 1 August, permitting construction only from Llanidloes to Newbridge, 22 miles. The promoters were lucky to get it through because their solicitor resigned just before the Bill was considered by the House of Commons committee. France and Piercy found witnesses and took statements from them before a new solicitor was found.

The committee rejected the Newbridge-Llandovery section, 23 miles, as not being compliant with standing orders, the promoters blaming opposition from the Central Wales Railway promoters. Thinking their case had been harmed by their inability to demonstrate local support for the railway by means of share subscriptions, the promoters arranged meetings to encourage residents in the locality to sign a subscription contract to present to the Lords, obtaining promises totalling £10,000. Davies and Savin agreed to take £60,000 and said that friends would subscribe £25,000. The friends were the Ebbw Vale Company (£15,000), John Ashbury (£5,000) and Sharp, Stewart (£5,000), who wanted the contract to be conditional on them supplying rail, carriages and locomotives respectively.

The capital was £170,000 and the LNR could subscribe up to £25,000. Subscribers included the Earl of Powis, Sir Watkin Williams Wynn Bt, Herbert Watkin Williams Wynn, Pugh and Whalley, and the first directors included Whalley and Jasper Wilson Johns. The MWR would provide any signalling required at the junction between the two lines. Whalley had been appointed chairman at the company's first meeting on 10 August.

The LNR lease had been discussed on 23 August. Rolling stock was to be provided by the lessees, 'the company to advance on the security thereon such a sum as they can afford, not exceeding two thirds [of its value]'. At the end of the lease, the company would take the rolling stock at valuation. Piercy was instructed to have the contractors' work measured for billing and settlement.

Vane's estates, settled on him in marriage, prevented him from assisting the NMR as much as he wished. On 26 May the directors had resolved to fund an application for powers to permit his trustees to raise £5,000 by mortgage, to become shareholders to that amount and to sell part of the settled estates to the NMR. The Bill was enacted on 13 August.

By 30 June the NMR had paid £6,000 for construction and £932 16s for land. The bridge over the Severn at Caersws had been completed and track was laid as far as Craigfryn. Excavations on to Talerddig were advanced and several bridges over the Carno had been started; a new course for the Carno had been excavated to drain the Talerddig bog. Work had been started on Talerddig cutting with the objective of completing and opening the line as far as the Wynnstay Arms at Llanbrynmair, 12 miles from Caersws, as soon as possible.

The first MWR shareholders' meeting was held in London on 27 August. Whalley paid tribute to the efforts of Piercy and France and explained that the MWR was of national importance, a link in the long-sought chain of communications between South Wales and the North of England, rather than just a local line. Supported by Piercy and others, Savin objected, saying that only an independent policy would benefit the Montgomeryshire railways. He proposed that France be paid a salary of £300, a considerable sum, especially for what was essentially a part-time position; the LNR secretary was paid half that amount.

Whalley's re-election as an MWR director went badly for him. Savin objected to his nomination, saying that the company could either have Whalley as a director or himself and Davies as contractors, not both. He nominated Pugh instead. 'A long and stormy discussion, of four hours duration, ensued' before Pugh was elected. The report from the *Shrewsbury Journal* of 7 September was distributed to shareholders as a part of the directors' own report. Davies was said to have told Savin that he would have nothing to do with the MWR if Whalley continued to be involved.

Despite heavy rain, on 2 September the MWR first sod party processed through Rhayader led by the Plas Madoc brass band. The mood must have been lifted by the flags, banners, streamers and flowers that accompanied the procession, the guests supported by navvies, children and tradesmen. Davies and Savin provided a ceremonial wheelbarrow and spade for Mrs Pyne, great-granddaughter of James Watt, to cut the first sod; she did so with the approval of her brother, Gibson Watt of Doldowlod, High Sheriff of Radnorshire.

Apparently at his request, Whalley chaired the event, about 300 guests sitting down to lunch in a Balaclava tent. Among the toasts, that to Whalley paid tribute to his efforts as chairman; the LNR had not cost much to build and its shares were selling at par. His reply made it clear that he was unhappy, to say the least, about the events of 27 August and how Davies and Savin were manipulating the situation to inhibit his strategic vision for the railways.

Informing the crowd that he was no longer an MWR director, he lambasted Savin, and Davies to a lesser extent. Savin was responsible for his defeat, but Davies and Savin 'acted in the most honourable and manly way possible'. His views differed from theirs. He thought that the railway should 'be perfectly free for traffic, and that no pettifogging interests of traders and monopolisers should interfere with the success of the line.' The line should not be made to enable railway contractors to carry their own coal and lime cheaply. They were not the men for him to work with. Contractors should keep to contracting and directors should do the directing. His position in the company was a matter of indifference to him.

He had known Davies for seven years and did not know a more energetic man. By his own unaided energies he had accomplished so much. With Savin, the LNR had been completed in a most efficient and satisfactory manner. 'It appeared that Mr Davies was the working contractor, and Mr Savin was the scientific one.' Urging the directors to keep an eye on them, he hoped there would be no hitches in their transactions with the MWR. His comment, 'When he said that he would not be the servant of those contractors he meant no imputation', was met with laughter. He also brought class into it, saying that he was not on equal terms with France and the contractors – he was an MP and a gentleman, while they were professional men.

France climbed onto a table to respond on their behalf, prompting the women to walk out. The *Shrewsbury Journal* wrote that 'The scene here ensued baffles description.' 'Chaos seemed to have come again.' Eventually given a hearing, France deplored Whalley's outburst, acknowledging his contribution to the LNR before vindicating the conduct of Davies and Savin. The LNR had been abandoned, the rails rusty and ballast wagons pushed off the track, it had been completed only because they had offered to take payment in shares and debentures. They had built the Vale of Clwyd Railway in 12 months despite that railway only raising £13,000 itself. The ONR was nearing completion because they worked with the original contractor and took payment in shares and debentures. Piercy had played an essential part to secure the ONR and MWR acts. The 'discussion' continued for some time, with Savin, Davies, Piercy and others all saying their piece.

Details of the proceedings were published at some length, both in Wales and in Peterborough, Whalley's constituency, generating considerable correspondence that continued for several months. The *Oswestry Observer* and *Shrewsbury Journal* were accused of bias in favour of the contractors, and several letters were sent to the *Llanidloes Telegraph* because they had not been published in the Oswestry paper. Some of the newspaper reports were collected together and published as a pamphlet. The latter might have been France's work, because when he distributed copies of the directors' report on 7 September 1859 he explained that 'the harmony of the proceedings was unfortunately interrupted … the directors, promoters … have nothing to conceal, and I therefore beg also to enclose copy of report [sic] of the proceedings'.

The essence of the reports and the letters was that Whalley's behaviour was undignified and unfair, although he did have some support.

The LNR lease had still not been completed by 5 September, but it was necessary to arrange for working the railway in the meantime. Whalley proposed that Davies and Savin should continue to work it with certain conditions applied; that the tariff of charges and the regulations and bylaws should be submitted for approval; that a weekly account of receipts, charges and current expenditure should be rendered; and the appointment, by the company, of 'a person to superintend on behalf of the company the working of the railway' to ensure its safe, efficient and economical operation – but he was outvoted.

Speaking to the shareholders later that day, Whalley described the negotiations concerning the LNWR traffic agreement in some depth. The LNWR wanted to use the LNR as part of the shortest route to Milford Haven and would guarantee 10% on its share capital for ten years in return for running powers. He wanted to protect the LNR's interests and to give access to other companies, including the GWR. The other directors had outvoted him and Davies and Savin also objected, to protect their train-operation revenues.

Some disagreement had also arisen between Whalley and the contractors over the status of the £20,000 shares they had been 'given' in January (see page 19) which he also covered at some length. He said the shares had been lent for the purpose of securing the deposit for the MWR. They said they were in part-payment for works on the LNR line and they were keeping them to protect their tenure on the line, which was only six months, claims that are partially supported by the minutes. Whalley said that he was happy for the contractors to operate the line and wanted them to have a ten-year lease, but he did not want them to have a monopoly on it.

They, however, had been buying shares to put themselves in a position of power when it came to negotiating the terms of the lease; they wanted to be both lessor and lessee.

Davies said that they had bought two lots of shares because the holders needed money. Only £30,000 of the company's share capital had been subscribed, the remainder being deposited as security for outstanding payments, of which the contractors had £20,000. He had established that the bank would lend the £30,000 at 5% so the company could pay what it owed. With the LNWR's 10% guarantee, the company would be in a good position. Davies said he and Savin had taken a line that was at a standstill 10 months ago, when the shares were worthless, and had made it, and the shares were valuable – Whalley was talking nonsense.

Establishing a shareholders' committee to advise on the principles on which the company's business should be conducted and to report on the proposed traffic arrangements and lease with Davies and Savin, the meeting closed after four hours.

The committee met immediately and passed a resolution that Whalley took to the board the next day. Davies and Savin were to return the shares or the lease would not be completed. If they refused, counsel's opinion should be obtained. The committee added a rider, that the directors should supervise the working of the railway to secure the company a fair return and to discharge their responsibility to the public.

Nevertheless, the resolution was rejected in favour of one proposed by Lefeaux, that when the claim by Davies and Savin was established it be liquidated by handing them shares or allowing them to retain shares already held, subject to them accepting restrictions on voting powers. With only Whalley voting against, this was accepted, and also accepted by the shareholders' committee.

Probably in a reaction to Whalley's outburst at the MWR event on 2 September, Piercy submitted his resignation as the LNR's engineer.

The directors unanimously refused to accept it, asking him to reconsider, which he did on 15 September.

Bills totalling £7,550 exclusive of payments to the contractors, estimated at £20,000, were outstanding. A North & South Wales Bank bill was due for settlement on 19 September, and it could be met by issuing shares or renewed until the contractors' demands were known.

When the half-year's accounts had been closed on 30 June, the LNR had received £52,018, including £18,290 of debentures, on its capital account. Expenditure of £52,549 4s 3d included £4,079 18s 2d on preliminary expenses, including the three Acts of Parliament, £3,791 0s 3d on land, £26,380 on works, £960 12s on carriage, £12,000 on rail and £1,046 17s 3d on wrought-iron girders.

£520 14s 8d had been spent on the locomotive, a purchase that appeared not to have been a success; an *Oswestry Advertiser* correspondent wrote in December that its remains were to be seen at Llanidloes, saying that it had been out of order for six months out of seven 'until at length it came to grief in endeavouring to bring Mr Whalley from Llanidloes'.

The LNR directors resolved on 10 September that Davies and Savin were to build the canal extension. The company would decide how they would be paid and would pay for the land.

The lease would not be executed until the accounts between the company and the contractors had been settled. The rent was to be 5% starting three months from 9 August as long as the extension land was provided by 10 October. The opening of the ONR, and the MWR to Newbridge and to Llandovery, would increase it to 6%, 8% and 10% respectively. Company expenses would be paid out of the rent and not by the lessees.

Even with rental income the company would still be in a tight position financially – £3,000, owed for rail, was due to be paid in November and there was no money to pay it. On 9 November Savin wrote to say that he had arranged for it to be covered by another £3,000 debenture, to mature in three years.

Lefeaux brought three of the railways closer together on 29 October and 26 November, when the ONR and MWR appointed him a director.

Piercy eventually submitted his account of the outstanding work carried out by the contractors, making it £18,629. Davies and Savin countered with a claim for £34,813. Considering the issue on 30 December, the directors accepted the first and appointed a committee to consider the second.

The LNWR traffic agreement was accepted on 31 December 1859. Lefeaux had negotiated a rebate for traffic transferred to the larger company that gave the LNWR the right to use its own locomotives if the LNR was unable to work its traffic for any reason. It was emphasised that the LNWR had no desire to work the LNR.

The transfer of ONR shares totalling £34,019 to Davies and Savin on 17 September had included £18,000 for 'certain materials' to be supplied by the Ebbw Vale Company. With regard to terminal stations, nothing had been heard from the GWR on the subject of the joint station at Oswestry since August, so Davies and Savin were instructed to make provision for a temporary station there. When, on 2 November, the GWR insisted on being given running powers to Newtown as a condition of completing arrangements at Oswestry, negotiations were terminated. At Newtown, the LNR was to pay rental for half of the site, make the railway on the Llanidloes side and 'bear half of the cost of the station'.

As the prospects of connecting the ONR with the Shrewsbury & Welshpool Railway at Buttington grew nearer, on 29 October Henry Tootal, an ONR director, had suggested that there would be many advantages to completing the railway between Buttington and Welshpool with double track; neither company would benefit from developing facilities at Buttington when Welshpool was more convenient. Although a committee was appointed to consider the proposal, the contractors started to implement it the next day.

Several Bills were deposited in December 1859, two by the ONR, for additional capital, to lease its line, to amalgamate, to invest in the MWR and to make a branch from Llynclys to Porthywaen, and to purchase and widen the existing tramway from the Shropshire Union Canal at Llynclys to Porthywaen.

The lack of funding to start its authorised line was no deterrent to the MWR, which wished to make a deviation at Rhayader; to link its Newbridge terminus to the Hereford, Hay & Brecon Railway (HHBR) at what became Three Cocks Junction; to connect that line to the Brecon & Merthyr Railway (BMR) line to Brecon at what became Talyllyn Junction; to connect the Central Wales Railway near Knighton to the Vale of Towy Railway at Llandovery, including a junction with the Three Cocks line; and to make a tramway from the Llandovery line to the Allt Dinas slate quarry. 'Mr [Alexander Thomas] Gordon' would find the £39,200 deposit subject to a satisfactory agreement, the solicitor informed the directors on 11 January 1860. Gordon was apparently introduced to the MWR by Savin; he had taken over the SWR contract in 1859. Savin had become the BMR's contractor and became the HHBR's contractor and lessee.

There was competition for access to Llandovery from the Central Wales Railway and the Breconshire, Radnorshire & Carmarthenshire Junction Railway, where both sought powers for a line from Llandrindod, the first also wishing to build a line to the Allt Dinas slate quarry.

Finally, the Manchester & Milford Railway wanted to connect Pencader on the Carmarthen & Cardigan Railway to Llanidloes, routed via Lampeter, Tregaron, Yspytty Ystwyth and Llangurig.

Welshpool was the right place for the ONR's offices, the directors decided on 11 January 1860, resolving that they should be relocated there immediately. Not less than three rooms were to be obtained. On 27 January, after the move had been completed, one month's notice was given to the company's policeman, Patrick Charles Fegan. After he died in April the directors ignored his widow's application for financial assistance but voted her £5 when she re-applied in August. The only payment for police services itemised in the company's accounts had been £17 5s 10d paid during the second half of 1858.

Herbert Watkin Williams Wynn's resignation was the last consequential on the ONR's decision to throw in its lot with Davies and Savin. He was replaced by Johnes on 12 January.

Piercy brought the case for supporting the MWR to the ONR directors on 23 January. The MWR was a vital part of the link between the North West of England and South and South West Wales, but required more capital than it could raise on its own account and would soon need to demonstrate its capability to Parliament. He proposed that the LNR and the ONR should each recommend to their respective shareholders the creation of £50,000 of new shares. If that turned out to be insufficient for the MWR's purposes, the SWR should make up the shortfall. On 11 February Piercy and France informed the ONR directors that the SWR was now intending to submit a resolution in support of subscribing £100,000. They, therefore, decided to match the larger figure subject to the SWR resolution going ahead.

During the first half of 1859 the SWR had made an agreement with the LNWR, which had agreed to work it for 52½% of receipts. It had also contracted with Gordon, who was to start on the MWR in 1860, to construct the line, replacing Thornton, one of the ONR's original contractors. The engineer was Edward Woods.

The LNWR's proposals for avoiding a Parliamentary contest over its canal conversion Bill by acquiring rights over the ONR between

Sharp, Stewart 0-4-2 *Wynnstay* was built in 1859 and delivered to the Llanidloes & Newtown Railway, transferring to the Brecon & Merthyr Railway in 1866.

Buttington and Welshpool and the option of using Welshpool station had been approved in principle on 12 January 1860. Negotiations to obtain better terms were concluded by 27 January, with the LNWR offering to pay £25,000 for the powers; the money was paid by 25 February.

The ONR's prospects were much more promising when the directors reported to the shareholders on 25 February; the change in chairman must explain a more detailed report. A year earlier funds had been exhausted and the works were on the verge of being suspended. There had been an impression that the only way Welshpool and Newtown would get their railway would be if the LNWR extended the SWR by converting the Shropshire Union Canal. Davies and Savin had taken over the contract and work had continued. Twenty miles of railway should be opened in the spring and the entire line by the end of the year. Most of the land had been paid for and the majority of the materials delivered.

The accounts to 31 December 1859 had shown that the ONR land had cost £26,892 18s, the works by Davidson and Oughterson had cost £53,800, and those by Davies and Savin £136,500. Incidental expenses of £514 15s 2d had been incurred in reaching a settlement with Davidson and Oughterson. The new contractors had arranged to pay the original contractors at their own risk for six months, the ONR shares being considered worthless.

Piercy reported that the line between Oswestry and Pool Quay was nearly ready for inspection. 'Extraordinary wetness' and frequent flooding had hindered the works between Pool Quay and Buttington. Locomotives were being supplied by Sharp, Stewart, and Ashbury was supplying carriages 'which will combine elegance with strength'.

When the NMR directors reported on 29 February 1860, effort was being concentrated on the 'great cutting' and masonry and embankments at Talerddig. Although track was already laid to Pontdolgoch, Piercy reported that heavy rain had delayed progress,

especially in the Pontdolgoch cutting, where the ground was already very wet. The river bridges were well advanced, the large culverts at Talerddig nearly finished and the 'high bridges' over the turnpike roads at Melin Talerddig and near the Wynnstay Arms were progressing quickly. With Davies and Savin anticipating that the line could be completed to Talerddig by the summer, he recommended making a start on the heavier works west of Llanbrynmair as soon as possible and forecast that the line could be complete to Machynlleth by the end of 1861.

The money available was not quite sufficient to complete the line to Llanbrynmair, where temporary facilities would attract worthwhile traffic. Having spent half of its capital the company could exercise its borrowing powers to raise £50,000 towards completing the line to Machynlleth – £14,000 was needed and £7,000 was already available or promised.

On 28 March the MWR's solicitor reported that after six days the Commons committee had found in favour of the Rhayader deviation and the extensions except for the Llandovery line. Operationally the MWR might have had the better route, with gradients up to 1 in 75 as opposed to the Central Wales having several miles of 1 in 60. The MWR directors were seemingly annoyed that their willingness to co-operate with the Central Wales was not reciprocated, and its route was laid out to exclude the MWR from any Llandovery traffic.

While in an incomplete state, the ONR had been used on 13 March 1860, when a judge, Sir William Henry Watson, collapsed during the Welshpool assizes. Savin 'went to Oswestry by special engine' and telegraphed to Shrewsbury for a surgeon, taking the doctor to Welshpool, where he arrived too late to save Sir William.

Sharp, Stewart 0-4-2 **Llanerchydol** had a varied history, starting with the Llanidloes & Newtown Railway in 1860 and being hired to work in South Wales and on the Carnarvonshire Railway before settling down on the Cambrian. *John Alsop collection*

Prospective surplus ONR property was considered on 17 March. A Mr Croxon was told there was no intention of selling Glanvyrnwy House, near the station site at Llanymynech, which he had owned. Savin, however, might be sold a house called Plas Fynnon, Oswestry, valued at £1,000.

Opening their line between Oswestry and Pool Quay on 1 May did not concern the directors sufficiently to warrant minuting. Colonel Yolland had inspected it on 18 April, submitting his report from Oswestry the next day. The line was single throughout, with sidings at the several stations. Except for the underbridges, it was constructed for a second track to be laid at a future date. The formation was 30 feet wide throughout.

The track comprised flat-bottomed, or contractors', rails in 21-foot lengths, weighing 70lb per yard and laid on sleepers 8ft 10in by 10 inches by 5 inches, 3 feet apart, the rails fixed by dog spikes, six in each sleeper next to joints, four elsewhere. Ordinary four-hole fishplates were used. Tie rods at 10ft 6in intervals held the rails to gauge. Ballast was stated to be 2 feet deep.

There were 14 overbridges and 19 underbridges together with two viaducts, one over a canal and the other over a river. Eight of the overbridges were built of brick with the arch in cement on masonry, five were built with brick or stone abutments and cast-iron girders, and one was timber-trussed. Nearly all the spans were 25ft 4½in on the square; the largest on the skew was 32 feet.

Three underbridges had masonry abutments and cast-iron girders, seven had brick or stone abutments and timber decks, two were entirely of masonry or brickwork, and seven were flood openings made of timber. The spans varied from 8ft 6in to 25ft 4½in on the square and 27ft 6in on the skew.

The canal viaduct comprised a single span of 37ft 6in on the square, 60 feet on the skew, with one centre and two outside wrought-iron plate girders resting on masonry abutments. That over the river had three openings of 47 feet on the square and 50 feet on the skew, with one centre and two outside continuous plate girders. Its abutments were masonry-built in cement, the intermediate piers formed of three 7-foot-diameter cast-iron cylinders resting on gravel foundations.

The ironwork appeared to be well executed, was sufficiently strong by calculation, and exhibited no unusual deflection. The masonry and brickwork was well executed and stable. There were no unauthorised level crossings. Turntables had been installed at Oswestry and Pool Quay, but that at the latter was not large enough to turn a locomotive and its tender at the same time. A turntable was being installed at Bank Pool [Welshpool?], a short distance away, which the company hoped to complete in two or three months. Until that portion of the line was opened the company undertook to turn locomotives and tenders separately to avoid running with the tender foremost.

Although the line was generally in good order, Yolland had noticed some items that required attention. The piles carrying the railway across the flood plain needed bracing. Some of the tie rods passed through a fishplate hole, leaving one side of the fishplate fixed by only one bolt; they should be moved away from the joints.

There were no lodges or houses at any of the level crossings, most being temporary wooden boxes. The gates should close the railway for the passage of cattle, as well as the road. The ballast hole at Four Crosses must be protected by station and distant signals in each direction as it was intended to cross trains there.

The method of working the repeating signal at Llanymynech also needed to be changed. Owing to the incompleteness of the works, therefore, the line could not be opened without danger to the public.

The *Shrewsbury Chronicle* of 20 April reported 'a run down the line … the other day' and commented on the inspection, but appeared to be unaware that Yolland had refused to sanction its use. The new carriages 'are exceedingly elegant, convenient and commodious; the locomotives are large and powerful,' said the paper.

Yolland returned on 28 April and found everything to his liking. The problem with the fishplates had been resolved simply by removing the tie rods. The company made an undertaking about its method of working the line, agreeing to erect lodges or houses at the level crossings within 12 months, to reinstate the tie rods within three months and to fasten the rails next to joints with fang bolts within two years.

In a brief report on 4 May, the *Shrewsbury Chronicle* noted that 'last Tuesday [1 May] the company commenced running four trains each way, daily'. There were no celebrations.

The four trains daily were Oswestry based, calling at Llynclys, Llanymynech and Four Crosses and taking 35 minutes. The 3.50pm from Oswestry and 4.30pm return, however, took 25 minutes and only carried 1st and 2nd class passengers. There were two trains each way on Sundays, one in the morning and one in the early evening. At Pool Quay a bus provided connections with Welshpool.

Reduced fare tickets were issued on specified trains for the market days at Welshpool (Monday) and Oswestry (Wednesday and Saturday). 'The Pant crossing', a locality near Llynclys, was also served on market days.

Although ONR trains were running to and from Oswestry, no agreement had been reached with the GWR over the provision or use of a station there and it was to be some time before arrangements were made. In his second report Yolland commented that he had not inspected the connection between the two lines.

The GWR's offer to lease the ONR between Oswestry and Welshpool was rejected on 10 May; in any event, the GWR shareholders' meeting required to approve such a measure would not be held in time.

Progress between Pool Quay and Welshpool was rapid and there was air of celebration on 22 May when the track was finally connected, 'a mile or two from the town'. The opportunity was taken to run a train, leaving Pool Quay shortly after 6.00pm. The *Shrewsbury Chronicle* on 25 May reported that a locomotive named *Montgomery* propelled 'about 18 open trucks', the last of which had planks on which sat Welshpool residents who had heard about the ad hoc excursion.

There were large crowds in the town and brief speeches were made before the train set off for Pool Quay, 'at a smart pace, considering the rails were unballasted' reported the *Oswestry Advertiser* on 23 May. Many townspeople joined the train for its return journey, disembarking at Buttington, or 'the Cefn junction'. Some, however, went all the way to Pool Quay, 'from which place they had to return as best they could'. In Welshpool the bells of St Mary's rang at intervals until about 9.00pm.

On 26 May the ONR directors ordered that free passes should be issued to the chairmen and deputy chairmen of the GWR, LNWR, SWR, LNR and to its own engineers, the secretary and their clerks. The appointment of the general manager, Robert Baker Elwin, who was to implement this instruction, appears to have been overlooked; he had previously worked for the Great Northern Railway in Manchester.

Reverting to the LNR, the construction account and lease by Davies and Savin had still not been settled on 29 February 1860, the directors told the shareholders. Rent was payable from 9 November and the first dividend was to be paid on 29 March.

Whalley explained that following Hopkins's death difficulties had arisen in the relationship with the contractors (the *Shrewsbury Journal* report had this as plural, but Davies was the sole contractor at the time) 'which had, to a great extent, placed the company in their power, as regarded work and prices, more that would otherwise have happened … they had … in no respect taken advantage of their position …'. The newspaper then commented on the controversy that surrounded the LNR and the MWR. Differences had arisen regarding that company's policy concerning its alliances: 'a small company like that could not stand alone'. The LNWR was interested in the area but should not be given powers that excluded the GWR. While the latter had interests that opposed the MWR's extension to the south, once built they would be good customers to each other.

The meeting closed with a resounding vote of support for Whalley, the *Oswestry Advertiser* of 7 March taking delight, and two columns, in reminding its readers of the controversy he had precipitated the previous year and clearly savouring the contrast.

The canal tramway and its strategic significance had also been discussed by the directors on 29 February. It was to be built before the powers expired because it would probably be of more value during the

**An 1891 dimensioned elevation of *Llanerchydol* from Oswestry Works.**
*National Archives*

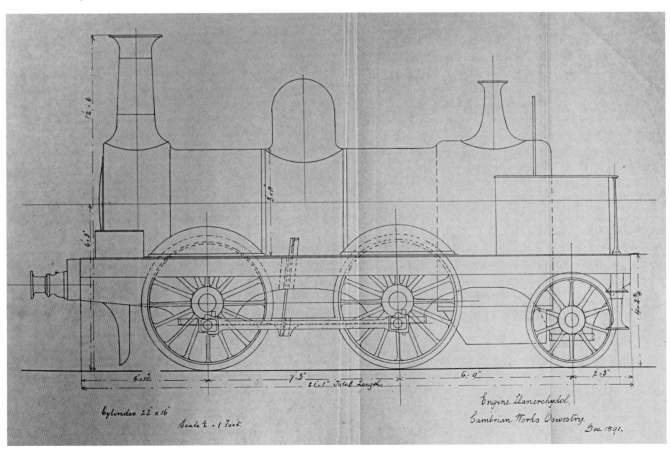

next 12 months than at any time in the future. In the longer term it might be useful in developing a separate route to Chester and Birkenhead via the canal. If the powers lapsed, Parliament was unlikely to give its assent again.

Additional LNR capital, £20,000 plus whatever the engineer thought would be required to make a double track, was needed because more was to be paid to the contractors and an extra charge was due to the ironmasters.

The creation of £25,000 LNR shares for the MWR investment was approved on 15 March. On 27 April the MWR directors resolved that each of the companies that subscribed to its capital – the ONR and SWR were the others – would have the right to appoint two directors to its board.

The LNR's office was in Llanidloes and the company's business was conducted there. On 3 April a proposal to participate in a London office established and shared by all the Montgomeryshire railways was approved. This would afford 'facilities of intercourse between the several companies', aid co-operation and financial and share transactions, and reduce costs while conducting Parliamentary business. Piercy was to make the necessary arrangements.

The LNR and MWR had made an agreement that at Llanidloes their interests would be better served by having a joint station on the MWR, and the short length of railway between it and the LNR terminus should be handed over to the LNR to construct. At the 3 April meeting Whalley had agreed to arrange a bank loan of up to £10,000 to pay for it and the canal extension, offering shares as security; the MWR directors decided that the cost of the Llanidloes works should be deducted from the LNR investment. Instructions to Davies and Savin, again, and Piercy to get on with the canal extension read as though the directors were frustrated by the lack of progress.

The MWR sealed its contract with Davies and Savin for the line to Newbridge on 5 May, although Gordon was going to carry it out. The *Shrewsbury Chronicle* reported on 22 June that it had been 'credibly informed' that the company's financial arrangements were complete and that the contractor was under penalty to complete by 1 January 1863. The newspaper had also been told that a route to Milford Haven better than that to Llandovery had been found. Subject to a satisfactory survey, powers would be sought to build a line from Rhayader that followed the Claerwen and reached the Teifi valley by a tunnel before taking 'easy country' to reach its target.

Rice Hopkins's executors were still pursuing a claim against the LNR. Having consulted Piercy and Davies, on 1 June the directors offered £400 in settlement, each side to pay its own costs. Following representation the offer was increased to £500 on 19 June, but Mrs Hopkins was determined that she was entitled to more and threatened to take action if she did not get £600. The directors thought they had a case worth defending, but instructed the solicitor to offer shares for as much as possible and to defer payment for as long as possible for any portion that had to be paid in cash, the company paying interest in the meantime. On 29 August Savin was asked to meet the claim for £600.

In contrast to the LNR and the ONR, the NMR had few problems gaining access to the land it required or in agreeing reasonable prices for it. Edward Allen's land, location unspecified, was an exception. The company had valued it at £604 and paid that amount into court. He wanted £1,327 15s. Not surprisingly, the company refused and on 19 June put the matter to arbitration. The example set by the other Montgomeryshire lines, approving the terms of an operating agreement to be made with Davies and Savin, was followed on 26 June.

The Mid Wales Railway (Extensions) Act gained the Royal Assent on 3 July, the MWR being empowered to build the Rhayader deviation and the extensions to the Hereford, Hay & Brecon and the Brecon & Merthyr railways. The clauses dealing with the connection to the HHBR were extremely detailed and it is quite clear which party had the upper hand during negotiations. The power to make agreement with the LNR concerning the transfer of a part of its authorised route and its station at Llanidloes was also given.

A prospectus issued earlier in 1860 described the likelihood of generating local traffic, the route's location along the banks of the Wye for a considerable distance and mineral springs in Breconshire attracting tourists, and minerals quarried and mined along it and, in Montgomeryshire, traversing it to reach smelting works in Swansea. Traffic in coal, pitwood, slate and lime for use locally would be considerable and the 'highly paid and hard-working population of south Wales will obtain ready access to the watering places on the Aberystwyth coast'.

Not everyone was blind to the practicalities of making a commercial success of railways in the remote areas to be served by the MWR and its competitors. As early as 1852 David Lloyd Harris of Llandingad House in Llandovery had written, in the *Carnarvon & Denbigh Herald*, that once Carmarthen and Milford were connected to the South Wales railway network 'no man in his senses will attempt any other line, particularly from this town to Builth and north Wales through a miserable country, without any chance of remuneration.' Someone thought sufficient of his objection to print it up, together with the supporting editorial, in a booklet, but sadly his words of wisdom were ignored.

The ONR and the ONR (Porthywaen branch) Bills deposited in December 1859 also received the Royal Assent on 3 July. In addition to authorising additional capital, the ONR Act sanctioned an additional level crossing and two overbridges. If the line was not completed when the two-year extension expired, the payment of dividends would be suspended until it was completed. Provisions for the line between the junction with the SWR at Buttington and Welshpool were quite complex. It had to be made double track by 1 January 1861 and the ONR had specifically to keep it in good order. The LNWR was allowed to make free use of it to a point near Welshpool, the £25,000 already paid commuting any fees chargeable.

The SWR, on the other hand, could make use of this section but had to pay as if for 3 miles, the distance being slightly less. The SWR receipts would be remitted to the LNWR, the whole charade a device to reimburse the LNWR its £25,000.

Welshpool station was covered separately, the LNWR and SWR having a 12-month option to use it subject to agreed charges. At Newtown an agreement could be made with the LNR over the siting and use of a station that could be used by both companies.

Davies and Savin were allowed to lease the railway for up to 21 years on terms similar to those approved for the LNR the year before. In this instance a clause also required them to maintain it. Other clauses confirmed that the lessees would be able to exercise the powers vested in the company, specified that rates already agreed could not be altered, and that companies with existing rights to use the ONR could continue to use them. In other words, the lessees could not increase rates to the SWR and LNWR or restrict or inhibit their access.

A hint of complications in the ONR's affairs appears in the minutes of 21 July. Three certificates totalling £20,960 10s 8d were due for payment. Davies and Savin had asked the directors to become securities for them for £5,000 upon security of £10,000 of the debt, and for the company to issue £10,000 in Lloyds bonds to them. The directors agreed providing the chairman, who was absent, joined them, that the solicitor and engineer were parties to the agreement, and that it was limited to two months.

The Manchester & Milford Railway Act received the royal assent on 23 July. None of the promoters or first directors had any obvious links with the Montgomeryshire railways.

At the shareholders' meeting on 2 August the ONR directors declared that opening the line between Oswestry and Pool Quay 'has more than realised our expectations'. The line onwards to Welshpool was ready for inspection and that between Abermule and Newtown was 'virtually completed'. With 21 out of the railway's 30 miles so well advanced 'we have every reason to believe that the whole line will be opened before the end of the year'.

Pugh's account of how 'last week' he had been, with his carriage, horses and servants, 'put into a railway carriage' at Euston Square and 'landed without unshipping at Welshpool' was greeted with cheers. Already, he said, the railway was bringing improvements to the district, with bus services being started from Montgomery and Llanfyllin.

Some ONR shareholders had questions. Ellis Jones, a Welshpool mercer, asked how the traffic arrangements were made. It cost more for his goods to come from Oswestry by train than it did by road from Shrewsbury, and there was no published scale of charges. His complaints to Elwin had been fruitless. He was told that until January 1861 the rates would be set by Davies and Savin; the latter hoped that better rates would be secured at a meeting due to be held with the GWR and said that the current train service was run at a loss for the benefit of local tradesmen. In contrast, a G. Parker said that he had got goods from Liverpool cheaper by railway than by canal.

The *Oswestry Advertiser* looked into this complaint and established that Jones had paid £1 4s 2d for five parcels, the GWR had charged 16 shillings, and the omnibus operator who had carried them between Pool Quay and Welshpool had charged 2s 6d, leaving 5s 8d for the ONR section, which the newspaper thought was reasonable.

Davies explained that he had tried to persuade Elwin to set lower rates and to be aware of the competition from the canal. He added that he had been reluctant to be involved with the ONR and, when Savin had pressed him, had said 'the dog he took out of the ditch would be the first to bite him'.

Timotheus Burd of Shrewsbury, Powis's land valuer, asked about the balance sheet, complaining that it did not show the liabilities to the contractors. Further, the highest estimate given to the shareholders' inquiry in 1857 had been £206,400, yet expenditure was already £40,000 more than that, there were three certificates unpaid, and the line was still incomplete. He had been a party to settling the compensation for half of the land required by the company for £40,000, but according to the balance sheet only £26,892 had been spent on land and compensation. Just £45,000 of debentures and the preference shares remained unissued; if they carried on at the same rate there would soon be no funds to finish the railway. He was told that Davies and Savin were owed about £90,000 and that his calculations were misfounded. The 1857 estimates were for the works only, while the contract with Davies and Savin included the stations, land and other items. Payment of £44,000 was still to be made for land.

Piercy strongly defended his own position and that of the current directors. As a shareholder, Burd was a latecomer who had got his shares from a former director who was also on the GWR board. Only the land had cost more than estimated, £70,000 instead of £38,000, and this was attributable to Burd. He, Piercy, had put the Bill through Parliament. His estimate comprised £250,000 share capital for the land and works and borrowing powers of £83,000 for rolling stock and general expenses. This assumed shares being issued for cash to pay the outgoings, a different proposition to 'having a line made for paper'. The original directors did not have confidence in him and he

did not acquire control until 'every halfpenny had been spent and the whole thing brought to a stand-still … when it had become a question of making the best of a bad job'. Now the line would be completed for 'just' £100,000 more than the authorised capital.

Burd did not dispute the claim that he had been responsible for inflating land prices. However, the only case cited had seen Powis accept the ONR's valuation in preference to Burd's slightly higher submission.

Particularly revealing was the explanation that the work undertaken by Davidson and Oughterson from January to July 1859 had been funded by Davies and Savin because the ONR shares were considered to be worthless. Between July and October Davies and Savin had been paid in shares and thereafter in debentures. So for nine months construction had been financed by Davies and Savin from their own resources.

At the extraordinary meeting that followed, the shareholders agreed to the company lending up to £3,000 secured on tolls to be collected on the turnpike, sanctioned by the 1860 Cilgwrgan, Bettws & Tregynon Road Act. Expected to feed traffic to the railway that might otherwise be diverted to the canal, the turnpike ran from the railway at Cilgwrgan, between Newtown and Abermule, to a junction with the Newtown-Llanfair turnpike at Tregynon. It would have been no coincidence that William Lloyd, who lived at Cilgwrgan, was a director of the ONR, the LNR and, later, the AWCR. Davies, Johnes, Johns, Lefeaux and Savin were among the first trustees.

Yolland compiled his report on the ONR between Pool Quay and Welshpool on 4 August. It was 4 miles 61 chains long, single track with sidings at Welshpool, the only station. Constructed for a double track, the formation was 18 feet wide throughout. The track comprised 70lb flat-bottom rail in 21-foot lengths, laid on sleepers with wrought-iron chairs fixed with dog spikes. Joint chairs required eight spikes, otherwise four were used. Four-hole fishplates were used at joints. Sleepers, 8ft 10in long with a cross-section of 10 inches by 5 inches, were laid at 3-foot centres on ballast said to be 2 feet deep. He was probably mistaken in identifying the chairs as made of wrought iron.

There was one occupation overbridge, built in masonry, and 17 underbridges crossing public or occupation roads or flood openings. Only one of these had brick abutments and cast-iron girders, the others being timber. The two bridges crossing the Severn, with 90-foot and 100-foot spans, were built with brick abutments and two outside girders and a central girder, all of wrought iron. The central girders were intended to carry half the load when the track was doubled, but he thought they would be inadequate for that purpose. Lateral stiffness was also required.

A turntable was provided at Welshpool. The Buttington level crossing required a permanent lodge, and the crossing at Welshpool station required a policeman's box. Mileposts had been made but not erected. On receipt of undertakings about the method of working and to install the lodge, Yolland recommended approval be given for the opening of the line to the public. He suggested that the company should be informed of his thoughts about the river bridges.

The opening to Welshpool on 14 August had been advertised in the *Shrewsbury Chronicle* the previous week. A special train would leave Welshpool during the morning, returning from Oswestry 'about midday', when the line would be formally opened. A cold collation on the Victoria bowling green at 3.00pm would follow a procession through the streets; dancing would start at 5.00pm. Tickets were 3s 6d for ladies and 5 shillings for gentlemen. At the Bull Hotel in Welshpool a public dinner would start at 3.00pm and a ball at 9.00pm. Admission for each was 2 shillings for ladies and 2s 6d for gentlemen.

Reporting the opening events in its 15 August issue, the *Shrewsbury Journal* stated that passenger trains between Oswestry and Welshpool

This Manning, Wardle 0-4-0, built in 1860, was used on Savin's Denbigh, Ruthin & Corwen contract before being moved to the Oswestry & Newtown Railway. *R. H. Bleasdale/John Alsop collection*

had been run for several days. In Oswestry shops were closed, cannons were fired and the church bells were rung. The train's arrival at midday was signalled by the sounding of whistles from the three locomotives hauling a 'large number of carriages', and the exploding of detonators. The crowd processed to Powis Castle and partook of a cold collation before returning to the station where it embarked in 'no less than fifty carriages attached to three engines' for the journey to Welshpool. (The *Oswestry Advertiser* of the same date said that this train comprised two locomotives, 28 carriages, 20 trucks and three vans.)

Crowds assembled at the intermediate stations, which were decorated with evergreens and flowers, and cheered the train on its way. At Welshpool barriers had been decorated with laurels sprinkled with artificial flowers. Numerous flags and streamers floated in the breeze. The goods station was enveloped in evergreens and banners inscribed 'Oswestry & Newtown Railway, may it prosper'.

Following a speech by Mrs Owen, the mayors and corporations of Oswestry and Welshpool, the directors, contractors, engineers and other railway personnel, including shareholders, were accompanied by three military bands as they processed through the town to Llanerchydol Lodge, by Raven Square, and back to the town hall. There, 550 workmen sat down to 'a good substantial dinner' on the ground floor and nearly 400 gentry and tradesmen partook of a cold collation in the assembly room. The latter had to endure more speeches until a 'late hour'.

It was the *Manchester Guardian*, on 16 August, that pointed out that the ONR was still not connected to the GWR at Oswestry. 'The stations closely adjoin each other, and difficulties which did exist as to making the junction are now believed to be overcome.'

On 21 August 1860 NMR shareholders were told that their line would be opened to Llanbrynmair in the spring of 1861 and completed in time to carry the summer traffic in 1862. The 'great Talerddig cutting … the heaviest work on the line … will be cut through by the end of February next year,' Piercy forecast. He added that he had been engaged in promoting a railway from Machynlleth to Aberystwyth that would pass near to Aberdovey and Borth. Consideration was also

being given to projecting a line 'up the Towyn coast'. Expenditure on works and land had reached £52,296 1s and £3,109 12s 1d respectively.

Not content with working simultaneously on the Montgomeryshire railways and their western and southern projections, Piercy was also engineer to the Denbigh, Ruthin & Corwen Railway. Its contractors were also Davies and Savin, and the first sod was cut on 4 September.

Working on so many sites simultaneously, including railways outside the purview of this book, required Davies and Savin to employ sub-contractors. The relationship with one of them, named Elkington, had resulted in a hearing at Chester Assizes on 9 August. Working on the NMR from March until October 1859 and employing 100 men, Elkington had asked for payment of £90 2s 6d, only to be met with a counter-claim for the same amount. Davies and Savin had eventually seized his possessions, triggering a claim, also for £90 2s 6d, from one of his creditors. The jury refused to hear the defence, saying they had decided on their decision, and the judge told the parties to reach an agreement between them. They did so, for £15 rent due on a house that Elkington had taken at Caersws.

A development concerning the LNR canal extension had occurred by the time the directors' reported on 29 August; the Shropshire Union, now leased to the LNWR in perpetuity, had offered to build it and a contract was being negotiated. Meeting on this date, the directors dealt with a claim from Davies and Savin for £12,000 for the purchase of rolling stock already in use, agreeing to £8,000 subject to a valuation confirming that it was worth £12,000 and to Piercy supplying an itemised list of the stock.

The LNR's new station on the MWR at Llanidloes was discussed on the same date. The MWR was to build the section concerned and the LNR would pay rent at 5% of its cost until its purchase was completed. When the agreement was put into effect the LNR would sign a subscription contract in the MWR for £25,000. 'With a view to the harmonious co-operation of the two companies the chairman of the Llanidloes company should be elected a director of the Mid Wales company and resume at that board his former position as chairman.' On 20 September the LNR agreed that the Manchester & Milford Railway should be allowed to use the station.

As ONR works progressed, the directors came under pressure concerning the facilities to be provided. In Newtown the residents wanted the ONR and the LNR to share a station on the Welshpool side of the town, a requirement that called for the ONR to permit the LNR to use a part of its line. They also wanted the LNR's canal extension to be replaced by a branch to the east of the town. Considering these requests on 8 September, the ONR directors made no commitment. The Welshpool board of health's request for the ONR to contribute half the cost of lowering the canal bridge on Severn Street, to improve communication between the town and the station, was accepted on 10 November.

The MWR had instructed Piercy to survey and produce plans for a line from Rhayader to Aberystwyth on 18 September. Six weeks later his proposal for a deviation of the MWR line near Builth was accepted. The first certificate, for £30,000, was approved on 28 November. A loan of £10,000 from Masterman & Company, the need for which had not been mentioned previously, was accepted on 12 December.

The LNR directors had, however, been concerned by newspaper reports to the effect that the MWR needed £800,000 more capital to be completed. Discussing the matter with great astonishment on 29 October, the MWR was to be asked about the reports and told that the LNR would not subscribe until it was assured that the financial position was satisfactory. The MWR did not reply and nothing more was said.

By 7 November £25,000 was needed to complete the LNR. Therefore the directors resolved to obtain powers to use the £25,000 authorised for investment in the MWR for the purpose, issuing the capital as preference shares.

Davies and Savin terminated their partnership on 29 October. Davies was to say that it was because he could neither approve nor stop the ruinous policy then pursued by the ONR and his co-contractor. The proposed line along the coast seems to have been the final straw.

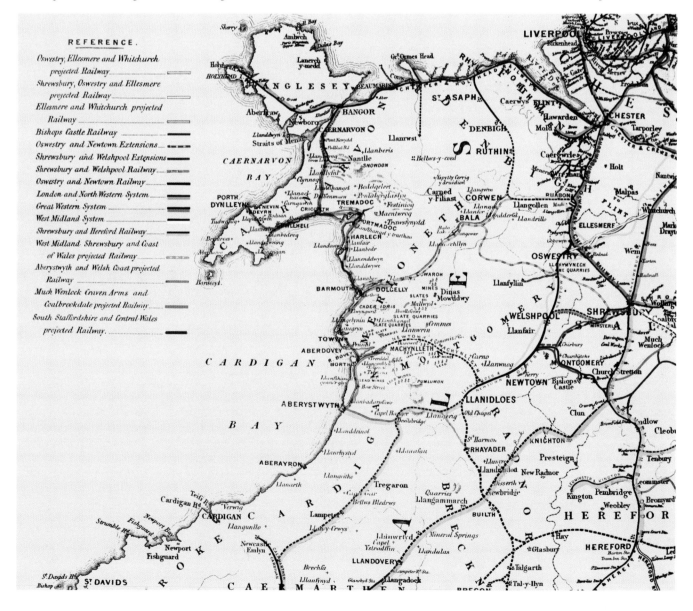

Extract from a map dated 1860/61 showing the Cambrian constituents, their neighbours and proposed railways. The pale pink line that runs to the west of the Oswestry & Newtown Railway is the Shropshire Union Canal. *National Archives*

# Interlude: Along the main line

Bettisfield was on the Oswestry, Ellesmere & Whitchurch Railway section, 6 miles from Whitchurch and 319 feet above sea level. *John Alsop collection*

12¹/₂ miles from Whitchurch, Frankton had a station that looks as though it was designed to impress the local landowner. It was on a rising gradient of 1 in 80 towards Oswestry. *Wilding/John Alsop collection*

Frankton Station, Shropshire.

Llanymynech Railway Station.

LEFT Llanymynech, with the source of so much traffic, the limestone rocks, behind. Located 6 miles from Oswestry, it was the junction with the Llanymynech branch. The Oswestry & Newtown Railway doubled this section of track soon after it was opened in 1860. *Park/John Alsop collection*

RIGHT A mixed goods train passes Four Crosses, less than 2 miles from Llanymynech, which had some very fancy bargeboards. *Park/John Alsop collection*

ABOVE Llanymynech was also the junction with the Potteries, Shrewsbury & North Wales Railway's main line to Shrewsbury and branch to Nantmawr. Abandoned since 1880, the main line was re-opened as the Shropshire & Montgomeryshire Light Railway in 1911. The Shropshire Railways' attempt to revive it had failed, although it leased the Nantmawr branch to the Cambrian in 1885. Standing in the down platform at the north end of the station, with the SMLR over the fence, the Llanyblodwel train obviously has a few minutes to wait before departure. No 15 was one of the Beyer, Peacock 0-6-0s ordered in 1915 but not delivered until 1918. *G. M. Perkins*

A passenger train hauled by one of the Sharp, Stewart 4-4-0s passes Montgomery station at speed.
Twenty-two miles from Oswestry, the station was nearly two miles from the town that it served.

Three constituents included Newtown in their names, and the one that put it first, the Newtown & Machynlleth Railway, did not actually have any tracks in the town, that privilege being shared by the Oswestry & Newtown Railway and the Llanidloes & Newtown Railway. Here, an eastbound goods train passes through the station. *John Alsop collection*

NEWTOWN FROM THE SOUTH.

Compared with the stations at Welshpool and Machynlleth, the facilities at Newtown were quite modest. No 14, seen here with a brake van, was a Sharp Stewart 0-6-0 built in 1875. *Park/John Alsop collection*

In charge of the station with the junction with the Mawddwy Railway, the Cemmaes Road station master clearly wanted to be sure that his status was recognised when a photographer called. No 73 was the first of five Neilson 0-6-0s built in 1894. The company only supplied two more locomotives to the Cambrian. *Park/John Alsop collection*

ABOVE Waiting for time at Cemmaes Road on 2 July 1909, No 64's driver takes advantage to oil round. The load comprises one bogie carriage, four six-wheelers and two four-wheeled goods vans. *Ken Nunn*

LEFT No 64, an 1893 Sharp Stewart 4-4-0, is seen again in this attractive scene at Talerddig, where its train has a more consistent appearance. Contrary to the date implied by the caption, the photograph must pre-date 1922. *J. M. Tomlinson/John Alsop collection*

TOP RIGHT With a load of ten carriages, this 4-4-0 is being banked on the climb out of Machynlleth towards Talerddig. The Dovey meanders on the right and the Machynlleth distant signal can be seen above the fourth carriage.

BOTTOM RIGHT A long goods train passes the goods shed at Machynlleth in 1919. The loco is No 14 again, an 1875-built Sharp Stewart 0-6-0. *H.W. Burman*

LEFT Dovey Junction, 60 miles from Oswestry, was known as Glandovey Junction until 1904. The main line is on the right of this postcard view. Apart from the trains its only access was by a footpath. *State Series/John Alsop collection*

BELOW Originally Glandovey, Glandyfi was also renamed in 1904. The two stations are less than a mile apart. The name was taken from a nearby house. *John Alsop collection*

The royal train passes Glandyfi as it carries the King to Aberystwyth in 1911. *E. O. Jones/John Alsop collection*

Compared with most of the Cambrian's resort stations, Borth was well provided with covered accommodation for passengers. *Park/John Alsop collection*

LEFT This 1906 platform view shows the attractive detail of the canopy ironwork. *Valentine*

BELOW The terminal platforms at Aberystwyth, 77 miles from Oswestry, and 19 feet above sea level. The Manchester & Milford Railway platform is on the left. One of the mobile gas tanks is stabled in the headshunt.

# 2

# The road to amalgamation 1860-1864

The amalgamation of the Montgomeryshire railways was started during the last quarter of 1860, the NMR calling a meeting in Welshpool to discuss it on 29 November. Each of the four companies was represented by its chairman, a director and its secretary or solicitor. A Bill was deposited but was later withdrawn by mutual consent, on the 'understanding that it was to be further considered before next session'.

Other relevant Bills deposited in December 1860 were:
* Aberystwyth & Welsh Coast Railway (AWCR): Aberystwyth-Porthdinlleyn with branches to Machynlleth, Dolgelley and Carnarvon
* Machynlleth, Aberystwyth & Towyn Railway: Machynlleth-Aberystwyth with branch to Aberdovey and Towyn
* Mid Wales Railway: extension from Rhayader to Aberystwyth: deviation between Newbridge and Builth, junction with Central Wales Extension Railway, agreements with West Midland Railway, access to the Hay Railway, arrangements with LNR at Llanidloes, additional capital

* ONR: branches to Llanymynech lime rocks, Llanfyllin, Chirbury, Minsterley, Shrewsbury and Kerry
* Oswestry, Ellesmere & Whitchurch Railway
* Llanfyllin Railway: branch from the ONR at Llanymynech
* Bishop's Castle Railway: branch starting from near the ONR's Montgomery station, the ONR to be authorised to subscribe to the capital
* West Midland, Shrewsbury & Coast of Wales Railway: Portmadoc-Shrewsbury via Dolgelley, the Tanat Valley and Llanymynech with branches to Corwen and Porthywaen; the engineer was Edward Wilson
* Portmadoc & Porthdinlleyn Railway, with branch to the Nantlle Railway from a location east of Criccieth to Penygroes
* Nantlle Railway: new line to Portmadoc, to the Festiniog Railway, change of gauge, use of locomotives, agreements with the LNWR and the Chester & Holyhead Railway

The four constituents resolved to support the amalgamation. On 11 December the LNR added a rider, that it was essential that the companies should unite in opposing the Shrewsbury-Portmadoc bill. Defeating that proposal and securing traffic that belonged to the Montgomeryshire railways, the companies should support the Welsh Coast Railway and grant it the same traffic arrangements that the SWR had obtained from the LNWR.

In London on 12 December, Whalley addressed a meeting on the subject of Welsh railways. The LNWR had control of the north coast, the GWR of the south, and after spending a great deal of money they

An Oswestry & Newtown Railway receipt.

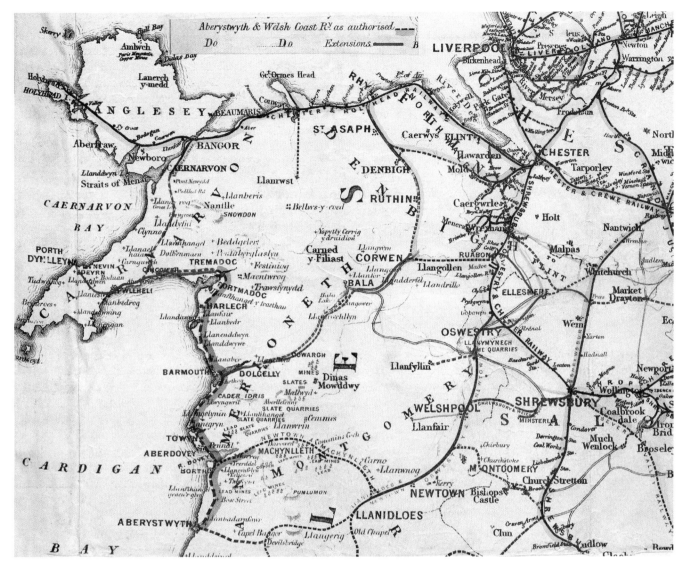

**Extract from a plan produced by the Aberystwyth & Welsh Coast Railway in 1862.** *National Archives*

had abandoned the rest of Wales. The Montgomeryshire railways should be connected to coast lines north and south of Aberystwyth and those should connect to the GWR and the LNWR. The Welsh lines would then be strong enough to be independent of the larger companies.

The *Merionethshire Herald*, published in Bala on 20 December, editorialised on the subject of railways as they would affect the town and, incidentally, set out the justification for the AWCR in the context of greater railway politics. There were two options. The West Midland scheme, routed from Shrewsbury to Bala via the Tanat valley and a 1½-mile-long tunnel under the Berwyns, depended on Porthdinlleyn and Carnarvon being served by independent companies, and an extension of the Denbigh, Ruthin & Corwen Railway to Bala being linked with the Montgomeryshire Railway from Bala to Dolgelley, the coast south of Barmouth being ignored. The AWCR started at Aberystwyth with a proposed connection from South Wales and would serve Borth, Aberdovey, Towyn, Barmouth, Harlech, Portmadoc, Criccieth, Pwllheli and Porthdinlleyn with branches to Carnarvon for the LNWR, to Dolgelley for the Montgomeryshire Railway and from Aberdovey to Machynlleth for the Montgomeryshire railways, collectively referred to as 'Mr Piercy's lines'.

Strategically the AWCR offered much more than the West Midland arrangement, although the latter was supported by the Earl of Powis, and therefore by the LNWR; France was its secretary. To preserve its Holyhead and Carnarvon traffic, the LNWR could take control of the existing 'weak' [Nantlle] railway and ensure that the GWR could not access Porthdinlleyn via the AWCR, the effect of recent storms on

Holyhead harbour making the LNWR sensitive to threats from that direction. The same threat of competition from the GWR reduced the significance of the West Midland's Corwen branch; it would not be built quickly and might not be built at all, the paper opined. It was quite clear that the interests of Bala and Wales would be best served by the AWCR.

Whalley had already been promoting the AWCR for at least three months. At a meeting in Criccieth on 24 September, reported in the *North Wales Chronicle*, he made it clear that its prime function was to be part of a north-south trunk route that would feed traffic to Porthdinlleyn from Milford Haven, Brecon, Merthyr Tydfil, Cardiff, Swansea, Hereford, Oxford and Worcester via Aberystwyth. The flow from Birmingham and the Midland counties via Machynlleth was secondary.

Unlike the Montgomeryshire railways, where several short lines were promoted with the long-term intention of amalgamation, the AWCR would be built by a single company he explained, adding that one of the key elements in keeping costs down was to prepare plans and submit them for public comment before a Bill was deposited. While this reduced Parliamentary costs, it did leave schemes open to 'speculative opposition', the promotion of other schemes that had to be bought off.

By 31 December 1860 the ONR had raised £76,711 18s 11d from its shareholders and spent £64,099 1s on construction and £3,612 18s 1d on land. Traffic revenue had averaged £300 per week over the previous three months, and 73,656 passengers had travelled. 'Unusually severe frost' had deterred the public from travelling and difficulties had arisen from the unfinished state of the line and the limited accommodation for goods traffic. Payment for land taken from the Earl of Powis and valued at £1,006 0s 3d was settled by issuing the £1,000 preference shares he had agreed to take on 12 January 1861; the contractor had paid the remainder.

Only the 10 miles between Welshpool and Abermule was incomplete, ONR shareholders were told on 9 February 1861. Except for the bridges, the formation was complete and track was laid throughout. Six miles had been ballasted. The Porthywaen branch should be completed in about six weeks. Johnes, an ONR director from 1855, had resigned.

The line between Abermule and Newtown, 4 miles, was finished. Under the heading 'the first trip', the *Oswestry Advertiser* had described an excursion the previous June; some 200 Newtown residents had travelled the short distance to Cilgwran by train, travelling in four 'freight cars,'; they were going to a tea meeting at New Mills chapel, so they still had a walk of more than 2 miles to reach their destination.

Commenting on the proposed amalgamation, Whalley referred to the 'Montgomeryshire or Mid-Cambrian system', the earliest recorded use of the word Cambrian to describe the constituents.

One shareholder thought that the ONR should be compensated by the contractors for their failure to complete the line by 1 January as contracted. Savin answered, saying that although they had had to contend with 'the most unfavourable weather', they also had a claim against the company. The completion date had been set in February 1859, but because the negotiations were protracted they were not given possession until November that year, 'when all the valuable season of the year was gone'.

The same shareholder asked about the commitments being made to other railways, wanting no steps to be taken towards extension until their own line was completed. Although he failed to gain support, the issue was to be raised again.

Land at Llynclys required for the Porthywaen branch was the subject of a dispute over its valuation with the farmer, a Mr Jennings, the only case to use the ONR's compulsory purchase powers, reported the *North Wales Chronicle* on 23 March 1861. He had claimed £3,661 15s for the land, less than 3 acres, and 'injury' to his property. The arbitrator awarded £685 for the land and compensation.

As the ONR approached completion, and its link to the LNR to take railway communication deep into Wales, in January 1861 Whalley started work on obtaining powers for the Oswestry, Ellesmere & Whitchurch Railway, a direct continuation of the ONR that would provide the shortest route between the Montgomeryshire railways and Crewe, Lancashire, Yorkshire, Cheshire and Staffordshire, developing local traffic and stimulating the extensions required to facilitate traffic for Merthyr Tydfil, Newport, Milford Haven, Swansea, Aberystwyth and the 'unsurpassed sea coasts of Cardiganshire, Merionethshire and Carnarvonshire'. The GWR objected to the proposal, saying that it was uncalled for and injurious to its interests, promoting its own line via Rednal in reaction. Bills for both schemes had been among those deposited in December 1860.

Ellesmere was keen to have a railway; being passed by the GWR's Shrewsbury-Chester route to the west and the LNWR's Shrewsbury-Crewe line to the east and convenient to neither, it did not benefit from them. On 27 March the *Oswestry Advertiser* claimed that the GWR had floated the idea of a line to Ellesmere in 1859 and had then dropped it because there was no opposition – implying that the GWR would only take the scheme forward to keep competition at bay, and that serving Ellesmere was not an adequate justification. The ONR

formed the view that the GWR wanted to prevent through traffic passing over the Montgomeryshire railways at Oswestry.

Whalley continued promoting the AWCR during the first months of 1861, addressing a series of meetings along the coast. In Aberystwyth on 28 January he explained that the Manchester & Milford promoters had lodged an objection on the technicality that the plans had been deposited late, by a matter of hours, adding that they were also unconvinced by any claim that their line would benefit from the link to Machynlleth.

Operated by the LNWR, the SWR was opened between Shrewsbury and Minsterley on 13 February. The western end of the line would take longer to complete, shareholders were informed on 28 February, because the embankment at Buttington was dependent on spoil being excavated from the tunnel at Middletown; due to the unstable ground, the tunnel was altered to a cutting after 63 yards had been dug.

Although Davies and Savin had ended their partnership on 29 October 1860, they do not appear to have told their clients for some three months. On 30 January they had attended an ONR board meeting to obtain consent to Davies withdrawing from their contracts, the arrangement being formalised shortly afterwards.

Similar requests were made to the other companies and, with the exception of the NMR, appear to have been accepted without any legal formality. Savin's application to become the NMR's sole contractor was 'partly considered' on 5 February and postponed for further consideration. On 11 March the LNR resolved to defer a decision until it had consulted with the ONR. Davies was to continue with the NMR on his own, and the company and Savin exchanged mutual releases on 19 June. This event might explain notices of the partnership's dissolution dated 28 June being published in the *London Gazette* on 2 July.

Writing on 26 February, Piercy had attributed 'unusually wet and otherwise unfavourable weather' for slips in the cuttings and delays on the NMR. From Caersws to Pontdolgoch the line was completed except for stations and lodges while the earthworks and bridges from Pontdolgoch to Talerddig were ready for track-laying. Talerddig cutting was producing stone suitable for use elsewhere on the line and should be ready for track-laying in June. Beyond Talerddig, works to Llanbrynmair were advanced. The contractors had forecast that the line could be opened to Talerddig in September, to Llanbrynmair by the end of the year and to Machynlleth by the end of 1862.

Completion to Carno, 7 miles, was marked by a dinner there on 3 May 1861. The main purpose of the occasion, however, was to pay tribute to Davies's locomotive driver, Richard Metcalfe, and to his gangers. Metcalfe had worked on the Vale of Clwyd Railway and the ONR before moving on to the NMR. Paying tribute to his energy and cheerful nature, Davies presented him with a purse containing £50. Presumably the gangers had a free dinner. Metcalfe's son, James, went on to invent the exhaust steam injector, a device that was to be manufactured and sold in partnership with Davies.

Early in 1861 the LNR, ONR and SWR made a working agreement with the LNWR without involving or consulting the NMR. Not wishing to be left isolated, the latter made an agreement with the GWR. In August the ONR explained to its shareholders that, in exchange for running powers and facilities at stations, the LNWR would give a rebate of up to 50% on all originating traffic until ONR dividends equalled those of the larger company. The NMR must have fielded the better negotiating team, or the GWR was keener to be involved, for the Swindon company agreed to work the line for 40% of the gross earnings. The MWR had made a similar agreement with the West Midland Railway.

At the LNR's general meeting on 12 March shareholders had been told that the Shropshire Union's requirement for sidings and other works deemed unnecessary by Piercy was responsible for the lack of progress with the canal extension. £3,150 rent paid by Davies and Savin up to 31 December 1860 was sufficient to pay the dividends, debenture interest and rent charges.

Savin's report that the ONR to Newtown would be ready for traffic 'within a fortnight' was submitted on 25 May. Yolland conducted his inspection on 4 June, the *Oswestry Advertiser* said; he reported from Birmingham the next day.

The line was 14 miles 21 chains long, single throughout with sidings at Forden, Montgomery and Abermule. Land and overbridges could accommodate double track. The formation width on embankments and in cuttings was 18 feet. Flat-bottom 70lb rail in 21-foot lengths had been laid on wrought-iron chairs or plates fixed to larch sleepers (8ft 10in by 10 inches by 5 inches) 3 feet apart; larger plates were used at joints. Four spikes were used on each sleeper except at the joints, where eight were used. The ballast was gravel, stated to vary from 1ft 9in to 2 feet deep. Again, the chairs were more likely to have been of cast rather than wrought iron.

There were 13 overbridges, 11 underbridges and 12 viaducts. Three overbridges had cast-iron girders, two were made of brick and stone, and eight had stone or brick abutments with timber decks. They were all of 25-foot span on the square, the largest being 32ft 6in on the skew. Nine underbridges had brick or stone abutments and timber decks, the other two had stone abutments and wrought-iron girders; the largest was 37ft 6in on the square and 40 feet on the skew. Eight viaducts had been built entirely of timber, one was of masonry and the other two had brick abutments and timber decks; all had small openings.

The 71-yard viaduct over the Severn, at Kilkewydd, had five spans and was well-constructed with stone abutments, cast-iron piers and wrought-iron piers supported on piles; one arch had a 60-foot span; the ironwork had apparently been supplied by Ashbury in Manchester. The 20-foot span of a timber viaduct was to be reinforced with struts to give it greater stability.

A road at Forden was identified as public in the deposited plans, but the engineer had treated it as an occupation road; it was gated and had the appearance of a private road. There was, however, an unauthorised level crossing of a turnpike near a timber bridge over the Severn at Kilkewydd at 18 miles 2 chains, which had been the subject of a complaint by the trustees.

Yolland had met the clerk and the county surveyor, learning that the crossing would be replaced by a bridge to be built in conjunction with the renewal of the dilapidated timber road bridge that crossed the river nearby. The railway company had undertaken to complete the work within 12 months.

He found the line in good order, adding that the company was installing signals to protect the ballast pit siding near Abermule at his request. Double connecting rods were required on all switches and the mode of working the distant and repeating signals south of Welshpool was to be changed.

The wooden boxes provided at the level crossings were to be replaced by brick lodges within six months. He had not seen the method-of-working undertaking but understood the line would be worked by train-staff and tickets like the remainder. He recommended that approval be given to its opening for public traffic. The crossing-keepers would have to wait a while for their brick lodges.

Nearly 1,500 residents along the route from Llanidloes discovered the delights of rail travel with a Bank Holiday excursion to Ruabon on 1 August, one of them being so moved by the occasion that she gave birth to a son in Sir Watkin Williams Wynn's hothouse, the grounds of his property being opened to the excursionists. Unfortunately, the *Wrexham Advertiser*, which described the day in some detail on 3

David Davies, left, conducting operations during the construction of the great cutting at Talerddig on the Newtown & Machynlleth Railway.

August, did not comment on the accommodation provided to transport the party.

The following day a celebratory dinner was held in Montgomery, apparently organised locally. Mrs Owen of Glansevern and Whalley were among the 350 guests at the town hall.

On 30 August the ONR shareholders were told that their line had been opened throughout on 10 June, a Monday, although *Bradshaw's Railway Manual* for 1867 recorded the date as the 19th. Construction expenditure had reached £415,164 13s 6d, including the £53,800 paid to Davidson and Oughterson.

Tribute was paid to Pugh, the chairman, whose death had been recorded on 4 May. He had been replaced by Whalley on 25 May, 'mindful of the important part which he took in the establishment of this company'.

In his report Piercy said that attention was being given to improving station accommodation, particularly wharves and sidings for mineral traffic. The surveys for the branches at Llanymynech, Llanfyllin and Kerry had been started but suspended until the harvest had been completed.

A shareholder queried the status of Whalley's shares. He had only paid the deposit and was in arrears with them, so was unqualified to be a director; in February Savin had transferred 50 fully paid shares to him. Whalley replied that he had started the company and was owed

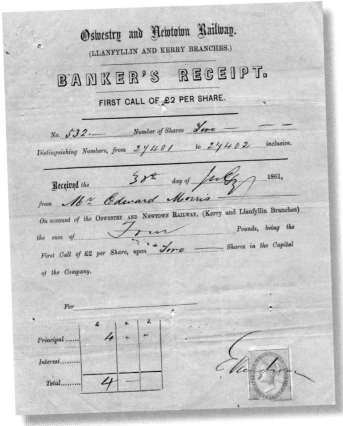

A receipt for a call on Oswestry & Newtown Railway (Llanfyllin and Kerry branches) shares in 1861.

more than the arrears for his expenses; he had threatened to sue the former directors for payment 'years ago'. He later claimed that he had received no favours from Savin and that he was allowing his director's salary to accumulate to pay for the shares.

After the meeting, the *Railway Times* (7 September) said that the ONR's original directors had been pushed out by inferior 'elements' as Savin's shareholdings had become larger and he had become more powerful. The paper was not impressed with the explanation about Whalley's shares, pointing out that ordinary shareholders in arrears had been prosecuted and saying that Whalley had got himself elected to the board to pay himself for the shares.

The paper pitied the shareholders, because having paid Savin £200,000 in shares they were outvoted by him and obliged to submit to his whims, especially in the election of directors. They in turn had not only paid Savin £200,000 more than the previous contractors had tendered, but had allowed him to use the company's credit to 'prosecute such wild-goose schemes as the "Welsh Coast"'. The paper also claimed that Whalley was held in 'unaffected contempt' in Euston Square [by the LNWR], landed gentry were refusing to meet him unless in the company of a third party, and he was held in contempt by Savin, 'a tool to be thrown aside when the dirty work he has undertaken is accomplished'.

Before the meeting it had become clear that some shareholders were nervous, probably because they could see that the dividends they expected once the line was opened were at risk. Signing himself 'Veritas' in a letter to the *North Wales Chronicle* published on 10 August, one wrote 'in place of some return from our money, we are called upon to become responsible for only about £130,000 towards other lines … and whose success is quite problematic. Are we to become railway makers to the world? … We are quite implicated enough without lending to other people.'

Another had gone to the trouble of publishing a small booklet setting out his concerns. He calculated that the ONR had liabilities of £821,333. With the LNR's liabilities of £181,000, because the two railways were so closely linked, the total reached £1,002,333. Including the unbuilt branches, annual income might reach £41,600. Assuming working expenses were 50% and directors' fees were £1,000, there would be a balance of £19,800 with which to pay dividends, interest and renewals. As more than half of the capital liability was entitled to interest in preference to the ordinary stock, the ordinary shareholders could not expect anything.

Even if the ONR stood on its own and did not subscribe to the other railways it had a capital debt of £288,000, requiring an annual interest charge of £14,400 at 5%. Assuming income of £29,120 and expenses of £15,560, there would still not be enough for the interest to be paid in full or for dividends. Concluding 'let retrenchment and economy be the order of the day', the writer's call for the subscriptions in other lines to be rejected and for an investigation into the company's position were ignored. The underlying complaint, that the company was overstretched financially, was valid and would cause problems for the Cambrian Railways for many years.

Whalley started libel proceedings against the *Railway Times*, saying that the decision to pay him had been made before his appointment. In that case, the paper observed, it was the Savin appointees, not the original directors, who made the award. The paper was equally unimpressed by the claim that the presence of Hanmer and others at a public dinner arranged by Savin undermined its assertion that the gentry avoided him.

On 26 August 1861 Piercy reported that, except for a mile at Talerddig, track had been laid on the NMR from Caersws to the Wynnstay Arms, Llanbrynmair, a distance of 12 miles, and ballasting was nearly completed. The earthworks between the Wynnstay Arms and Machynlleth were in hand. The gradients between Machynlleth and Talerddig required heavier track, so double-head rail and cast-iron chairs would be used instead of the flat-bottom rail used at the eastern end.

A consequence of the ONR's opening was a complaint from the Abermule turnpike trustees calling for the railway to be screened from the road. On 1 July Piercy had been instructed to arrange a site meeting to discuss the issue. In September general manager Elwin complained to the directors about the railway's fencing, 'casualties arising from its insufficient state'. Piercy was instructed to report on any necessary steps.

The Oswestry & Newtown Railway (Llanfyllin and Kerry branches) Act, enacted on 17 May, also sanctioned the construction of two lines to the Llanymynech lime rocks. Where the Shropshire Union's tramways were crossed by the latter their use was not to be disrupted.

The MWR's Newbridge deviation had been empowered on 12 June. Other clauses dealt with the transfer of the Hay Railway's property and the agreement with the LNR for the construction and use of Llanidloes station. The start of the MWR's construction had been delayed due to obstructive landowners at the northern end, forcing the company to use its compulsory purchase powers.

Powers for the LNR to subscribe up to £20,000 in the MMR were contained in the latter's Aberystwyth Branch Act, which received the royal assent on 11 July 1861.

Objections to the AWCR Bill were resolved to the extent that its Parliamentary passage was unopposed, assent being given on 22 July. Whalley and Lefeaux were among the subscribers and the nominated first directors. The capital was £400,000. The ONR was allowed to subscribe £75,000 and the LNR £25,000. Five railways were authorised: from Aberystwyth to Caepenmochno, on the south bank of the Dovey, thence to Towyn, to Barmouth, to Portmadoc, and to a junction with the NMR at Machynlleth. Objections from the Nantlle Railway had led to the withdrawal of the AWCR proposals beyond Portmadoc.

If the Aberystwyth-Machynlleth line was not completed within three years the company was not to inhibit an application from the NMR for powers to complete it. As drafted, this clause had been the subject of a letter that David Howell, the NMR secretary, had not only written to the Mayor of Aberystwyth but had printed for wider distribution. The Bill had made it imperative that the AWCR could not give priority to the construction of the Machynlleth line over the Towyn line, most likely to ensure that the river crossing was built. Howell, however, interpreted it to mean that once the coast line was built there would be no incentive to build the line to Machynlleth.

Howell was also concerned about the AWCR's ability to raise its capital beyond the £100,000 to be subscribed by the ONR and LNR. The ONR worried him, too, for he observed that, despite not having the funds to build its own permanent stations, it had either obtained or was seeking to obtain powers to subscribe a total of £225,000 in other railways, almost half of its own £475,000 capital. The LNR would soon be capitalised at £105,000 yet it was willing to raise a further £75,000 to subscribe in the MWR and the AWCR.

The Oswestry, Ellesmere & Whitchurch Railway Act received the Royal Assent on 1 August, having found favour, according to the *Railway Times*, in preference to the GWR proposal on the casting vote of the Commons committee's chairman. Whalley was the first subscriber named and was also identified among the first directors. Both the ONR and the LNWR were allowed to subscribe up to £30,000 towards the £150,000 ordinary capital; the LNWR later admitted that its purpose in making this investment was to secure access to Oswestry station; the *Railway Times* later reported the LNWR chairman, Richard Moon, as saying that the line passed through profitless country.

Unusually, the powers of construction west of Ellesmere were suspended until 1 September 1862 to give the promoters the opportunity to obtain fresh powers to make a deviation to facilitate a direct route from Ellesmere to Oswestry, Ruabon and Shrewsbury. The purpose of the delay, imposed in the Lords, was to reduce disruption in the town if the route was changed, the Bill's objectors having put great emphasis on the necessity of Ellesmere having direct communication with 'the mineral district of Ruabon'. Newspapers reported a requirement to avoid the property of landowner Sir John Kynaston, who did not want to see the railway from his terrace.

When the directors met for the first time on 17 August 1861, Ellesmere residents were still keen to get their railway, the town's bailiffs petitioning for the first sod ceremony, already set for 29 August, to be celebrated 'in the most public manner'.

That it certainly was. The town took a holiday, houses were decorated, arches spanned the streets, bells rang, cannons were fired and there was a procession. The ceremony was performed by Sir John Hanmer Bt, an MP who was making the land available for about 5 miles of the route, supported by John Stanton, a man of some years who did the work. More than 250 sat down to lunch afterwards.

Faced with a demand from Savin for £10,000, for 'Parliamentary expenses, purchase of land and works and Mr Piercy's certificate paid' on 2 September, the OEWR directors noted that it appeared that 'we have no balance available for such a payment' with an air of bewilderment, resolving to make a call of £2 per share and to request the £30,000 subscriptions that the LNWR and ONR were empowered to make.

Piercy was appointed OEWR engineer on 25 September and instructed to work with the solicitor to prepare a contract for Savin to build the railway for a fixed sum, to include all expenses, Parliamentary and otherwise. George Owen, Savin's friend from Oswestry (see page 18) was appointed local engineer on the understanding that he act as resident engineer and be paid by Piercy. The appointment of George Lewis as the OEWR's secretary went unrecorded.

Plans for lines from Ellesmere to Ruabon, Bettisfield to Wem and to Wrexham were produced by Piercy at the OEWR board meeting on 24 October. The GWR, asked on 31 October for its cooperation to give effect to the Parliamentary requirement that the OEWR have 'direct and unimpeded communication' from Ellesmere to Oswestry, Ruabon and Shrewsbury, was deliberately obtuse in its reply on 9 November, claiming not to understand what was required.

Not only did the GWR still want to make a railway between Oswestry, Ellesmere and Rednal, it also wished to take over the OEWR between Ellesmere and Whitchurch, repealing the OEWR's authority to build and operate that section, to make joint stations at Oswestry and Ellesmere, and to have running powers over the OEWR, the ONR and NLR.

Notices for two OEWR Bills were published on 11 November. The first was for a railway from Ellesmere to Ruabon with three short branches at the latter and a branch from Bettisfield to Wem, on the LNWR's Shrewsbury-Crewe line. The second sought approval to make deviations from the 1861 route to avoid Kynaston's estate, for changes to the line and levels at Whittington, and additional junctions with the GWR at Whittington station.

The LNR shareholders had been told when they met on 5 August that traffic had increased during the half-year, the directors promising that deficiencies in station accommodation required to meet traffic demands would receive attention. The extension to the joint station in Llanidloes was nearly complete. A 5% dividend was paid on 1 September.

The agreement between the LNWR and GWR not to support the construction of railways in mid-Wales was a 'matter of common notoriety'. To avert the isolation thus caused, the LNR and the ONR negotiated with the West Midland Railway to secure outlets to London and the south independently. Heads of agreement, which would have brought about the establishment of a 'great company entirely through Wales' had been signed when the WMR amalgamated with the GWR. Immediately afterwards the LNWR took control of the Shrewsbury & Hereford Railway, which, through its connection to the Central Wales Railway, formed a competing route with the Montgomeryshire lines to South Wales.

With the AWCR having gained its act, the LNR and the ONR were in a position to make a traffic agreement with the LNWR whereby dividends matching those of the LNWR would be guaranteed against a rebate on the traffic generated.

Savin submitted a bill to the LNR for extras amounting to £7,630. Most items were for additional facilities, but the list included £1,250 for one year's maintenance from 9 November 1859. Although Piercy said that the amount, roughly £100 per mile, was reasonable, the company noted, wryly surely, 'It appears that the contract did not include any maintenance of way.'

Savin also produced a list of rolling stock:

| | |
|---|---:|
| Engine *Enterprise* | £1,050 |
| Engine *Volunteer* | £2,530 |
| Engine *Milford* | £1,750 |
| Engine *Llanidloes* to be taken away | |
| Brake van | £200 |
| Wagons at £70 | £4,200 |
| Wagon truck | £150 |
| | £12,280 |
| Delivering this last month | |
| Wagons – lime £70 | £4,200 |
| Wagons – coal £70 | £4,200 |
| | £8,400 |
| **Total** | **£20,680** |

He held Lloyds bonds for £10,400. Being owed £10,280, therefore, he requested an advance of £6,000. The directors noted that 'Enterprise engine not included in inventory'. No reference was made to the carriages.

Another engine not on the list was Dove, the locomotive purchased during construction, which had made an appearance, metaphorically speaking, at the Montgomeryshire assizes on 16 July. Ann Owen, 'a respectable looking woman', had been charged with stealing brass belonging to the LNR. Evidence was given by employees of William Thomas, the Llanidloes ironfounder, that they had been working on an old engine named Dove in November 1860 when the pump had been stolen. A few days later Thomas was offered brass from the pump by a rag merchant and found the pump a few fields away. Owen had found the brass in the town and had sold it to the dealer. The case had already been dismissed by magistrates, and the policeman who dealt with it said that he knew Owen and her husband as respectable working people. The jury found her not guilty without retiring, the judge declaring that the case should not have been bought when it had been dismissed by the magistrates and that Owen was entitled to compensation.

Savin refused to be a party to any LNWR agreement until he had reached a settlement with that company concerning the transfer of the rolling stock. On 14 September 1861 the LNR directors resolved that if Savin did not reach an agreement with the LNWR, they would require the LNWR to accept the stock under the terms of Savin's agreements with the LNR. They were also concerned about any further delay to the completion and operation of the SWR beyond 1 January 1862, and decided to require the LNWR to surrender that line to the LNR if it was brought into use in a manner that hindered LNR traffic.

The concerned ONR shareholders would have been particularly troubled about their company's financial stability had they been aware of the first AWCR directors' meeting held on 2 September. The first item dealt with was Savin's request for £15,000 to disburse Parliamentary expenses, to purchase land and to pay for works certified by Piercy. Not having any money, the directors resolved to ask the ONR to exercise its power to subscribe £75,000. Piercy was not, incidentally, formally appointed the AWCR's engineer until 24 September.

The ONR dealt with the request on that date, when it handled a similar request from the OEWR. Both were approved, OEWR and AWCR capital was issued to Savin and then exchanged for the ONR capital, which could be used by him as security for his borrowing.

Arrangements between the MWR and the MMR at Llanidloes had been the subject of dispute during 1861. The MWR preferred an arrangement that transferred its line between Llanidloes and Penbontbren, the point of divergence, about 2 miles, to the LNR. Put into effect, this section became a part of the LNR, which built it, the MWR and MMR paying between them 5% of the outlay as rental and the entire cost of its maintenance, plus 5% on two-thirds of the cost of the station and two-thirds of its maintenance.

On 25 September France's role as secretary of the MWR was taken over by the company's solicitor on a temporary basis. No explanation was recorded. He seems to have terminated his relationship with the SWR at the same time.

Once more the ONR directors became dissatisfied with the location of the company's offices, resolving to transfer them back to London on 26 September. Rooms at 3 Storeys Gate were recommended by Savin on 25 October.

Also on 26 September, the ONR directors decided that the Llanfyllin and Kerry branches and other outstanding works should be carried out by Savin on 'similar terms', although the contracts had not been arranged. Savin was instructed to start work on the permanent station at Oswestry on 24 October.

The AWCR resolved to obtain powers to extend its line from Portmadoc to Porthdinlleyn on 25 October. The extension was to be in two parts, dividing at Pwllheli. By the time the notice was published on 11 November Porthdinlleyn was not included, although branches to Aberystwyth harbour and Dolgelley were. When the company held its first shareholders meeting on 21 January 1862 Piercy had been setting out the line and preparing plans and Savin had obtained 'a large quantity of material on the ground ready to commence'.

Although no land had been acquired at this date, earlier in the month the NMR had agreed to a request from Piercy for the AWCR to make cuttings on NMR land so that soil for the embankment west of Machynlleth could be taken away.

On 9 November Henry Baker and Herington Kerr, the driver and fireman of a goods train, were killed when it derailed on curves between Abermule and Montgomery and fell down the embankment. A third man on the engine and the guard escaped with bruises. Accused of 'furious driving', Baker was held responsible.

Notwithstanding the advanced state of the NMR's agreement with the GWR, on 27 November the NMR directors decided to take steps to protect the company if the agreement was not made by seeking a contribution towards the Parliamentary expenses and support for the additional £20,000 capital required, including the return of rolling stock to be contributed to the GWR pool. Piercy's plans for sidings were to be approved by the GWR and that company was to supply plans for the permanent stations.

Sharp, Stewart's bill of £4,890 for the locomotives, named The Countess Vane and Talerddig, was paid the next day. Davies was to erect sheds for them at Caersws, 'the same to be available for other purposes at a future time'.

On 26 December 1861 Davies was instructed to erect a shed for 'the new carriages'. John Ashbury had been paid £306 for a 3rd Class carriage on 18 October and was to be paid £336 for a 2nd/3rd Composite on 6 February 1862. One 26 February he was paid £1,070 for 'remainder of bill for rolling stock'.

The amalgamation Bill took a different form when deposited in December 1861. Powers for the union of the ONR, LNR and SWR, or two of them, were sought, together with powers to confirm the GWR's use of Oswestry station. In February 1862 the ONR and the LNR completed an agreement whereby the former would operate the latter under the terms of the ONR's 1860 Act.

The NMR and the Nantlle Railway also deposited Bills. The first was to give effect to the agreement with the GWR and to enable traffic to pass between them via the intervening railways. The desire to give Earl Vane and his successors, 'owners for the time being of Plas Machynlleth', the right to appoint a director was not in itself unusual, although its devolution to 'the husband and guardians of any such owner', which may be taken as planning for the eventuality of the lack of a male heir, was not usual.

The second Bill sought powers similar to those wanted the year before, except that the Portmadoc terminus would be a junction with the AWCR. The Nantlle Railway was a 3ft 6in-gauge horse tramway dating from 1825, when it was built to carry slate from the Nantlle quarries to Carnarvon via Penygroes, Llanwnda and Bontnewydd. It carried passengers, too, despite not being authorised for that purpose.

There was some scepticism about its intentions. A resident of Clynnog, writing to the North Wales Chronicle on 27 January 1862, stated that she had always doubted that it ever 'really' meant to build the Portmadoc line and now she was convinced that it did not. Piercy also had doubts about the Nantlle's objectives. Speaking in Pwllheli on 5 March, he said that the effect of the 1860 Bill, and its voluntary withdrawal, had been to keep out competitors. With the company

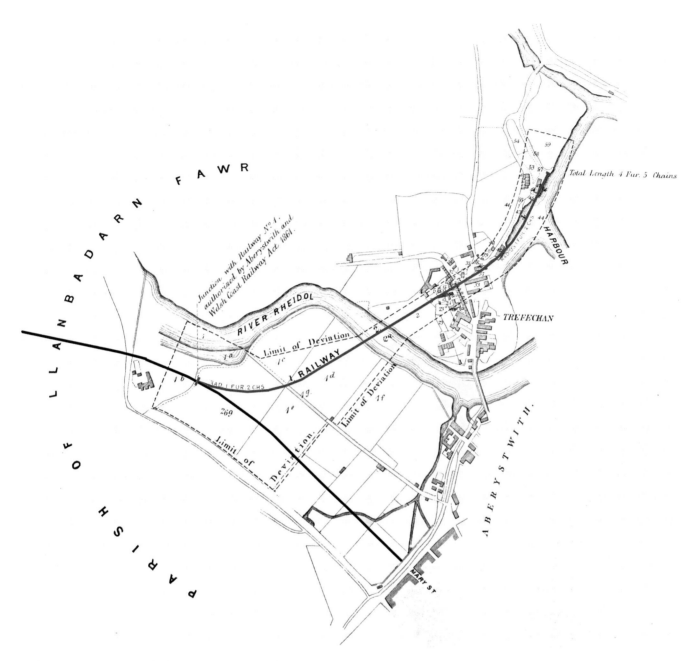

The Aberystwyth & Welsh Coast Railway's proposed Aberystwyth harbour branch, 1862. *Parliamentary Archives*

paying 7 or 8% it was in its interest to maintain the status quo; spending £200 or so a year on Parliamentary activities was a worthwhile expense, he thought. It was around this time that Savin acquired control of the Nantlle.

The AWCR directors were uncertain about their scope for objecting to this Bill in view of an agreement made to secure the withdrawal of the Nantlle objection to their Bill the previous year. Obtaining counsel's opinion, on 20 February they decided to petition against it, but it was to fail on a technicality.

A few weeks before, the *Railway Times* had described the AWCR as a 'successful adventurer', seeking to expand before its capital had been subscribed. Although the local press had been fed with stories about the progress of work, 'when it is remembered that the speculation is merely one of a series got up by Mr Savin, it will not be wondered that no detail of subscription or actual payment has yet been made.'

The Carnarvonshire Railway Bill had been deposited in December 1861. This was a development of the previous Nantlle schemes, a route from Carnarvon to Portmadoc with a branch to Pwllheli and a line between Portmadoc and Pwllheli, with new promoters. Nothing was said of it at the time, but the three promoters included Savin and Piercy; the latter had signed the estimate for £200,000. The *North*

*Wales Chronicle* of 12 April 1862 reported that the Nantlle had been taken over by the CR, while in 1865, referring to the change in ownership, the chairman of Carnarvon Harbour Trust referred to Savin as 'the embodiment of the Carnarvonshire company'. In 1867 Savin was to tell Major Fredric Henry Rich, the railway inspector, that he had operated the tramway for two years from 1862.

Savin's contract for building the AWCR had been agreed on 20 February 1862. For a fixed price, the railway would be built to meet Board of Trade requirements, complete with stations and lodges. On 15 January the *Oswestry Advertiser* had noted progress at Aberdovey, with an accumulation of plant and 1,000 tons of rail in transit from the Ebbw Vale iron works. Since the beginning of the year boring had been carried out to determine the nature of the river bed for the viaduct's foundations. On 12 March the same paper reported that Savin was living in Aberdovey.

The small ceremony that marked the start of AWCR works in Merionethshire on 3 April was reported in the *Oswestry Advertiser* on the 9th. With Savin and Piercy and a crowd of 'a few score', a Mrs

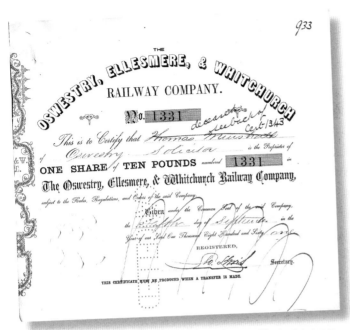

An Oswestry, Ellesmere & Whitchurch Railway share certificate dated 1861.

Foulkes of Aberdovey performed the honours on the green near the town's Corbett Arms Hotel. Land for nearly 7 miles of route from Aberdovey to the Dysynni river crossing had been obtained from the Ynysmaengwyn estate. Large amounts of timber were being obtained for use in the works.

The disagreement between the OEWR and the GWR had reached the pages of the *Oswestry Advertiser*, with both sides briefing the paper; on 15 January 1862 it published the correspondence. The 1861 Bill had been assessed on its merits, the OEWR's supporters having made a better case than those of the GWR. The 1862 Bill was being assessed on its technicalities, the engineers going head-to-head. The OEWR's offer to compromise, 'as a defeat on technicalities would scarcely lead to a proper settlement', was refused. The newspaper supported the OEWR's position, 'for to fight on technicalities, is at best but a foolish expenditure of money that might be much more judiciously spent.' The GWR would have been aware that it had deeper pockets than the OEWR. It transpired that the GWR had misunderstood the OEWR's suspension clause and thought that no powers had been granted for the Oswestry-Ellesmere section.

On the ground, sufficient effort had been made for the line between Ellesmere and Whitchurch to be well advanced. A mere six months after the Act had received the royal assent, the shareholders were told on 27 February that the line over Whixall Moss had been completed, and a party of directors had ridden across it on a locomotive that morning. Progress would have been better had Earl Brownlow's estate managers been cooperative and not forced the company to use its compulsory purchase powers. Three miles of the route was over the moss, a peat bog.

In a rare example of any comment being made about the train service, on 19 February the ONR directors had noted 'that the attention of the lessee be called to the necessity of continuing from Welshpool to Llanidloes the 2.45pm train from Euston.' No doubt this requirement followed the opening of the SWR to traffic on 27 January.

The latter did not, incidentally, bring the advantages that might have been expected, as two letters published in the *Shrewsbury Chronicle* on 7 February had testified. One writer explained that the 12.50pm from Welshpool took 70 minutes to cover the 19 miles to Shrewsbury, missing the Paddington train by 8 minutes and imposing a wait of nearly 4 hours for the next train. From Newtown, a journey

to London using the indirect route via Gobowen took 7hr 20min; the same journey using the 'direct' route took more than 10 hours. The other writer said that every train from Welshpool missed the connection by 10 minutes and wondered if it was 'paltry spite against a rival company'.

Oswestry residents were also complaining, about the time it took to get to London or Shrewsbury. An *Oswestry Advertiser* correspondent, on 5 March, said that they only had themselves to blame, for choosing to travel on the GWR. Travel by the early ONR train and change to the LNWR at Welshpool, he wrote, to arrive at Euston at 2.45pm, instead of Paddington at 5.40pm. When he visited the International Exhibition later in the year he did not intend to spend a whole day in getting to London 'just to enjoy the "splendid" journey promised on the Great Western'. As for Shrewsbury, he continued, if the ONR would add a 3rd Class carriage to the early train, 3rd Class passengers would have 2 hours longer in the county town. With identical fares by either route, time saved would be money.

On 18 February the SWR shareholders were told that the company expected the March timetable to make better connections. A Bill had been deposited for powers to make a second track and that would improve the situation. France's efforts in getting the railway completed were acknowledged. It must have been a close-run thing, with the contractor going bankrupt at the end of 1861; Yolland had inspected the line on 14 January.

On the MWR, Piercy had reported a lack of progress with the works on 23 January 1862, prompting one of the directors, John Edward Campbell Koch, to make an offer. If the ONR and LNR exercised their powers of subscription he would provide the rest of the capital and ensure that the line was completed. With his address given as 1 Threadneedle Street in London, Koch had the air of a successful banker, but in 1846 he had been a bankrupt East India merchant. In 1865 he was a director of the Belfast & Bangor Railway and in 1878 was to be involved in the financing of the Alexandra Palace development. He also became something of an inventor, in 1875 securing a patent for a device 'applicable to imitation or false neck ties', and in 1877, with William Durham, for an improved steam engine regulator. He was to put his offer in writing while the MWR asked the other companies for their views on his offer.

Piercy's report is the closest the MWR directors get to recording that there was a problem with the contractor, Gordon. Two suppliers approached the directors directly, seeking payment for materials supplied to his order. In October 1861 a Mr Morton had argued his case for payment in respect of 76 miles of wire fencing, saying that materials for 28 miles were then in stock at Llanidloes. After he refused an immediate payment of £2,000 for the material at Llanidloes, he accepted the offer of £2,060 in cash and £400 in debentures made in November. Then, in February 1862 the Ebbw Vale Company's representative claimed £7,235 for rail and fastenings. A 5% Lloyds bond was issued, payable in August 1863. The *London Gazette* records that Gordon's bankruptcy was registered on 17 December 1861. Koch was one of his trustees.

At the MWR shareholders' meeting on 21 February, 'the directors regret the works have been suspended, in consequence of the inability of the late contractor to carry out his contract.' The line between the junction with the LNR and the 'present' Llanidloes station had been completed and the LNR was in possession. The dispute with the MMR had been ended, with the LNR building the contentious section of railway. A few days later the LNR shareholders were told that the new Llanidloes station had been completed.

The prospect of work on the MWR resuming was within sight on 26 March, with the completion of a contract with Messrs Watson and

Overend. They would execute the works to the satisfaction of the company's engineer and the Board of Trade inspector, purchase the land and pay all expenses from the date of the contract until the opening of the railway. The contract price was £540,000, including an allowance of £50,000 for land. Payment would comprise £223,000 in ordinary shares, £117,000 in debentures and £200,000 in Lloyds bonds to be redeemed by preference shares at par. The company would be responsible for Parliamentary expenses and various other commitments entered into by Gordon on its behalf. Three days later Overend said that he was willing to work with Savin 'in the most amicable manner' on the line to Brecon, but required more information. The shareholders were told that the contract had been let to John Watson.

The *Railway Times* looked upon the MWR as favourably as it did the ONR, saying on 13 September that its balance sheet was 'neither trustworthy nor intelligible'. In three years only £70,442 had been received on the share account and there was nothing to tell how much of this had come from the shareholders and how much represented payment for work carried out.

Landed proprietors had delayed construction of the ONR's branches, shareholders had been informed on 25 February 1862, when Piercy reported that work had started on the Llanfyllin branch. The proposal that the ONR operate the LNR, to avoid the risk of traffic from Llanidloes being transferred to the canal at Newtown, was accepted.

On 26 February NMR shareholders were told that the GWR agreement would not be put into effect until the line was complete. Attempting to run services earlier would hinder the contractor, and the GWR's commitment to pay the 5% dividend was not effective until the line was complete in any case. Nearly 20 miles of track had been laid and ballasting was well advanced. Works to be completed were opening Talerddig cutting to its full width and three 'heavy' bridges over the Afon Twymyn, near Commins Coch.

The first locomotive to travel the length of the NMR coincided with the opening of the International Exhibition in London on 1 May. An *Oswestry Advertiser* journalist accompanied the party, his report being published on 7 May. The other participants were a Mr Jones from the GWR; Davies's secretary, a Mr Webb; the traffic manager, a Mr Richards; and the driver, a Mr Charlesworth. They all squeezed on the locomotive, 1861-built Manning, Wardle 0-6-0ST *Llandinam*. It had fallen into the Afon Twymyn the week before and the repairs had been completed just before the journey started.

At Talerddig five wagons loaded with stone for bridge testing and three or four more loaded with navvies were coupled on. Davies himself joined the party before Commins Coch. Because there were still a

number of temporary bridges, the passengers disembarked and walked to the Afon Twymyn bridge, half a mile beyond and the site of *Llandinam*'s encounter with the river; the bridge, a temporary structure, had collapsed as the locomotive crossed and its driver had been killed. Satisfied with the loaded wagons test, Davies gave the instruction for the locomotive to cross, a sight that was greeted with cheers.

As the ensemble approached Machynlleth crowds started to gather. Howell, the secretary, and his dog joined the train at Abergwydol. Close to the station a ceremonial arch had been erected. Davies was carried in a chair shoulder-high through the streets to the Wynnstay Arms, where a welcoming party greeted him. It was around 5.00am the next day before the train set off to return to Caersws.

The ONR's suggestion that two public sidings be provided on the Porthywaen branch for use by the quarries' lessees in substitution for the existing siding on the main line at Llynclys was accepted on 25 June. The quarry owners' benefited by being relieved of a £20 annual rent charge, and the railway benefited from not having to screen the railway from the quarry tramway.

At the LNR meeting, also on 26 February 1862, some shareholders were unhappy about the prospect of being involved with the ONR. Whalley tried to convince them that they only had to be satisfied with the offer of 5% that the ONR would guarantee, but they were not persuaded. The source of ONR shares being offered at £5 10s could not be identified, but one cited a broker in Llanidloes saying they were not worth £6.

For three years or more the *Railway Times* had been critical of Whalley and his railways, describing them as a 'combination of daring enterprise and unscrupulous speculation'. On 10 May it subjected them to scrutiny, saying that, 'In undertakings in which we find the munificent Mr Whalley elevated to the post of chairman, wherever we trace the energetic Mr Savin grubbing as a contractor, with Mr Benjamin Piercy as his valet-engineer, there we do homage to the mighty confederacy of Whalley-cum-Savin.' Including the Bishop's Castle Railway, of which Whalley had been invited to be a director, and omitting the NMR, six companies were chaired by him and had Piercy as engineer. Savin was contractor to all except the MWR.

The paper listed the railways, together with their directors, their capital, their borrowings, agreements and commitments to other companies before commenting that, with their approval to the AWCR extensions and Carnarvonshire Railway Bill, the Lords had given the confederacy 'another two inches of rope whereby to strangle itself'. The CR had no directors identified, but Piercy and Savin had been allocated their customary roles.

The mileage, capital and borrowing of the Whalley-cum-Savin railways is shown in the table below.

**Mileage, capital and borrowing of the Whalley-cum-Savin railways**

(A calculation of average construction cost per mile has been added to the *Railway Times* data.)

| Line | Miles | Shares | Loans | Average construction cost/mile |
|---|---|---|---|---|
| AWCR | 106 | £400,000 | £133,000 | £3,773 |
| AWCR extensions | 27 | £250,000 | £83,333 | £9,259 |
| BCR | 19¼ | £180,000 | £60,000 | £9,350 |
| Carnarvonshire | 27½ | £200,000 | £65,500 | £7,272 |
| LNR | 12¼ | £85,000 | £20,000 | £6,938 |
| MWR | 39 | £410,000 | £136,000 | £10,512 |
| OEWR | 20 | £150,000 | £50,000 | £7,500 |
| ONR | 30 | £450,000 | £141,300 | £15,000 |
| | **281** | **£2,125,000** | **£692,133** | **£7,562** |

This Sharp, Stewart 0-6-0T had a diverse history, starting in 1860 on the Oswestry, Ellesmere & Whitchurch Railway with the name *Whixall* before being renamed *Green Dragon*. It was used on the Carnarvonshire Railway contract and also spent some time on the Brecon & Merthyr Railway, becoming No 13 with the Cambrian.

The paper rejoiced in the Parliamentary decision to clip the wings of Savin and Piercy by rejecting Bills for the Bala (from Corwen) and Merionethshire (Bala-Dolgelley) railways, which were probably speculative ventures on their part. According to the paper, Savin put his shares on the market when a railway was completed, but could only sell them if the dividend was guaranteed. It did not believe his claim that 'his' railways were open to all that wished to make use of them. It cited the Denbigh, Ruthin & Corwen Railway, which Savin had controlled; his dealings with the LNWR had led to that company taking over the DRCR and thereby preventing Corwen traffic from being routed to England via Llangollen.

Whalley's libel claim seemed to be taken in good spirit, the paper saying that it had been accused on four counts of 'contriving and unlawfully, wickedly and maliciously intending to hurt, injure, vilify and prejudice … and to deprive him of his good name, fame, credit and reputation and to bring him into great contempt, scandal, infamy and disgrace.'

The account of an *Oswestry Advertiser* journalist, who had inspected the OEWR works from Ellesmere to Whitchurch, had been published on 14 May. From a point 3 miles east of Ellesmere, the track had been laid and ballasted for 5½ miles, and a locomotive named *Green Dragon*, a Manning, Wardle 0-6-0ST delivered earlier in the year, passed over it regularly.

The same issue contained a brief report on progress with the AWCR. William Edwards' contract at Aberdovey was nearly ready for track, while near Towyn a Mr Jones' contract was finished and ground at Penbryn marked out for the station. Despite the large number of navvies employed, there had been no disputes. A property boom was expected after a Mr Beddoes sold Brynymore, near the beach at Towyn, for development, obtaining more than £3,000.

The AWCR was concerned about Savin's plans for the Carnarvonshire Railway, for it duplicated the AWCR route between Afon Wen and Portmadoc. On 12 July its solicitor reported that Savin had asked for that section to be left in his Bill, otherwise Parliament would probably reduce the authorised capital. On the same date it was reported that Savin had paid the deposit for the AWCR's own Bill.

The Bills designed to secure the ONR, LNR and SWR amalgamation and to authorise the LNWR agreement were lost because the Commons committee ran out of time and the Lords would not suspend its standing orders. The NMR's GWR agreement Bill was lost for the same reason. Learning this on 23 July, the ONR reacted by instituting a review of its financial commitments because its anticipated capital would not be available.

The AWCR and OEWR extension Bills were enacted on 29 July and 7 August respectively – the AWCR got its extensions and the OEWR its Wem branch. Despite the GWR, the latter could now make the 1861 route between Oswestry and Ellesmere. The Carnarvonshire Railway Bill was also enacted on 29 July, revealing that Savin had been accompanied by Piercy and a Thomas Haywood to promote it. When directors were appointed on 19 May 1863 they included the familiar names of Johns and Lefeaux. Only the Carnarvon-Portmadoc line had been approved; Pwllheli was excluded. The route description was vague enough to obscure the route shared with the AWCR between Portmadoc and Afon Wen. On 1-inch-scale maps they appear to be identical.

By 28 August Piercy reported that track-laying on the NMR was complete except for about half a mile, and the bridges were nearly complete. Expenditure on construction had reached £118,328 8s 6d.

Most of the land required for the AWCR between Machynlleth and Aberystwyth and Aberdovey and the Afon Dysynni had been obtained by the time the company's shareholders met, also on 28 August. A further 4 miles between the river and Llwyngwril was the subject of negotiation and steps to take possession of the remainder required to reach 'the junction opposite Barmouth'. Only 2 miles were incomplete between Machynlleth and Borth and the portion from Aberdovey to the Dysynni was complete.

With the powers recently given for railways in Carnarvonshire and Merionethshire, the AWCR would have contact with the LNWR at Carnarvon via one, and with the GWR via the other.

Savin turned the movement of the first locomotive to run over the coast line, on 1 September, into an event of some proportions. At Towyn placards were posted, ceremonial arches erected, flags were hoisted, bells rung, and children and a brass band processed. The *North Wales Chronicle* estimated that some 800 people travelled on the train from Aberdovey, to be greeted by a crowd in excess of 2,000, and 109 sat down for dinner in the town hall. There were also entertainments for the crowd, fireworks and a ball. The purpose of the exercise, according to the paper, was to show respect to the heir to the Ynysmaengwyn estate.

The agreement by which the ONR operated the LNR, the product of several months' negotiation, was completed by 24 September. The LNR had sealed it on 27 June, the Board of Trade gave its assent on 4 July, and the ONR directors signed it on 27 August. One immediate consequence was the resignation of the LNR's secretary, Mr Hayward, due to the transfer of the company's offices to 9a Bridge Street, London, already occupied by the ONR, and his replacement by the ONR's Tanner on 27 June. The LNR directors paid tribute to Hayward's 'valuable services' in the 'organisation and incorporation of the company, construction of the railway and in the conduct of its affairs through its eventful career up to the present time.' In practice, the operating agreement had little effect because Savin was running both railways.

Employed as secretary by the ONR on a temporary basis in 1859, on 24 October the company decided that Tanner should be 'considered to be an assistant secretary' on the same salary. No explanation was given for the designation, which seems for have been an afterthought; the decision was recorded in different handwriting from the other entries.

The passenger accommodation at Welshpool station was giving cause for unspecified criticism, dealt with on 24 October. Savin was instructed to take 'such temporary improvements as are practicable for the removal of the complaint'.

The NMR had been nearly completed when the *North Wales Chronicle* published its report on 4 October. At Machynlleth the platform had been completed, a turntable installed and sidings laid for slate, lime and general cargo. Captain Henry Whatley Tyler submitted his report from Shrewsbury on 25 November. He had not completed his inspection because of a commitment to inspect the Stockport & Woodley Railway the next day.

The line was 22¾ miles long. Its junction with the LNR at Caersws, near Moat Lane, was single 'but it will eventually be important and it would be better at once to double it'. A good junction station had been erected that would be improved by glazing the exterior. Some rock at the western end of the Talerddig cutting that had been moving was being removed.

The steepest gradient was 1 in 52.87 and the sharpest curve had a radius of 10 chains; that curve, and a 15-chain one, should have check rails fitted. A footbridge over the railway should be erected to 'afford communications' to the old chapel and British School at Llanbrynmair; residents had petitioned the Board of Trade about it.

Eight miles of the route was laid with flat-bottom rail, the remainder with bull-head rail, weighing 70lb per yard in 21-foot lengths in both cases. Timber sleepers, 8ft 10in by 10 inches by 5 inches, had been laid at 3-foot intervals. The flat-bottom rail was supported on wrought-iron soleplates fixed to the sleepers using dog spikes. The rail was kept to gauge by wrought-iron tie bars, two per rail length. He recommended that through fastenings replace the spikes at the rail joints within six months. The double-head rails sat in 24lb cast-iron chairs fixed by spikes.

Bridges were numerous, variously constructed of iron, timber, brickwork and masonry. The iron and timber structures were substantially constructed. In some cases masonry bridges had given trouble under heavy earthworks, requiring some of them to be rebuilt. They would need to be watched for evidence of settlement. Some of the bridges required fencing. Point signals needed some modification and a water tank was too close to the track. Several stations had only temporary accommodation and all required conveniences.

Due to the outstanding works, Tyler could not recommend the opening of the line and the NMR was asked to defer it for one month.

After the ONR's solicitor had attended a meeting at which the 'harmonious action' between the Montgomeryshire railways and other companies was discussed, on 6 November the ONR directors agreed to be parties to another amalgamation Bill. The other participants were the LNR, OEWR, AWCR, NMR, Bishop's Castle, Carnarvonshire, MWR, MMR, Brecon & Merthyr Tydfil Junction, Hereford, Hay & Brecon, Kington & Eardisley, and the Wrexham & Connah's Quay. By the time the Bill was deposited, only the ONR, LNR, OEWR and NMR were involved, although powers were sought to make agreements with the LNWR, GWR and 'ten other Welsh railway companies'.

Other Bills of interest deposited in December 1862 were for the AWCR, NMR, the Oswestry & Llangynog Railway, the MWR, the MMR, the Corris, Machynlleth & River Dovey Tramroad, and the West Shropshire Mineral Railway. With a main line from Llanymynech to Shrewsbury sanctioned in 1862, the WSMR was a precursor to the Potteries & Shrewsbury & North Wales Railway. The 1862 Bill sought powers for branches serving Moat Hall, Llanyblodwel and Nantmawr, the latter quite close to the terminus of the ONR's Porthywaen branch.

The AWCR Bill sought powers for extensions to Aberystwyth harbour and Blaenau Ffestiniog, to make a junction with the MMR's Aberystwyth branch, to make a deviation, to divert the Dovey, and to adapt its estuarial bridges to carry road traffic. The deviation was on railway No 5 at a location referred to by the directors as Garreg. The Blaenau Ffestiniog branch had some similarities with the later Merionethshire Railway, and was intended to terminate at Dolgarregddu.

Savin's AWCR workforce appears to have caused the Cardiganshire police some extra work. On 27 November the company refused the chief constable's request to defray the expense of keeping additional constables in the county during the construction, saying it had no funds for such a purpose. On 6 December the *Hereford Times* reported that the locomotive *Cardigan*, a Manning, Wardle 0-6-0ST, had been running between Borth and Garreg and that 11 miles of rail had been laid.

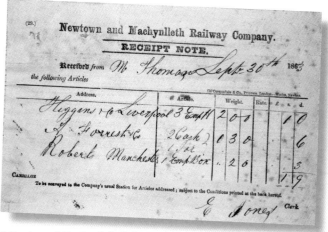

A Newtown & Machynlleth Railway receipt dated 1863.

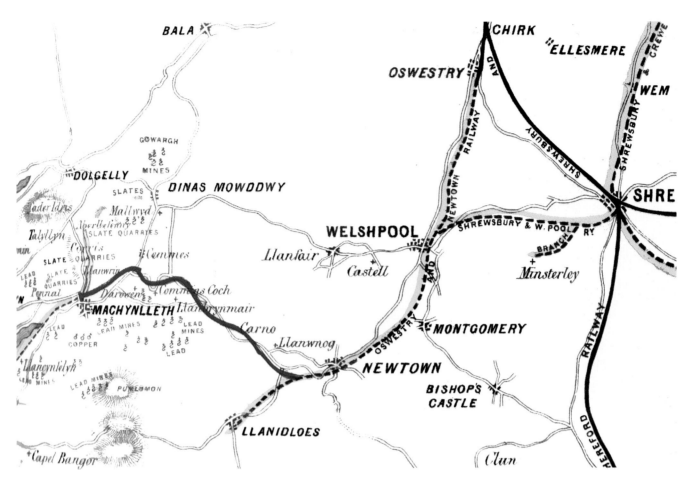

Extract from a Newtown & Machynlleth Railway map. *National Archives*

Whalley's libel suit against the *Railway Times* was called before the Lord Chief Justice and a special jury on 29 November, but the paper changed its plea to guilty and apologised. Strangely, Whaley appears to have made no claim for damages and there was no award for costs.

Tyler's second inspection of the NMR seems to have been made on 31 December 1862, the date of his report submitted from Shrewsbury. His requirements had been met, although he still thought that the masonry bridges showed symptoms of failure under the weight imposed upon them, especially that at Cwmbychan, and required close supervision. He thought that the line could be opened, adding a rider that due to the severity of the gradients the company should install a system of continuous brakes on its passenger trains.

On 2 January 1863 Davies was given responsibility for working the NMR, and was also authorised to order rolling stock to the value of £20,000. Twelve months' maintenance and the construction of stations were also to be undertaken by him at a cost of £2,000 and £6,000 respectively. The architect's name, Mr Poundley, was written into the minutes later; he was probably John Wilkes Poundley (1802-72) of Kerry.

The formal opening took place on 3 January. The streets of Machynlleth were decorated and a procession made its way to the station ready for the train of 22 carriages hauled by two locomotives to depart at 9.00am; Davies had brought the carriages up the day before. Some 1,500 tickets had been sold, according to the *North Wales Chronicle*. Features of the route noted by the paper included the cutting at Talerddig, 115 feet deep and nearly a mile long; the 85-foot-high embankment on its western side, with a culvert nearly half a mile long carrying a stream through it; a brick-arch bridge 65 feet above the turnpike road nearby; and the three-arch bridge 80 feet above the river at Gwastadcoed, east of Cemmaes Road.

Departing at 12.30pm, the return journey was made in the company of 600 Newtown residents, the load made up to 36 carriages and the journey taking 2 hours. During speeches at Machynlleth,

Davies presented Countess Vane with a silver spade to replace the iron one she had used to cut the first sod. He reckoned that the delays due to bad weather had cost him £10,000. The celebrations lasted until the early hours. On 5 January the Countess entertained 200 children from the National Schools to tea and plum cake at Plas Machynlleth.

The *North Wales Chronicle* had commented that the NMR was not a speculative line, but one originated, carried on and completed by its promoters for the benefit of the community it served. By 31 December 1862 it had spent £117,328 8s 6d on construction, financed by £93,529 from the shareholders and a £50,000 loan. Considering the effort required in excavating the great cutting at Talerddig, Davies deserves credit for completing the NMR for less than the £130,000 contract price, at approximately £5,000 per mile. If the other Montgomeryshire railways had been constructed for such a low rate their financial futures would have been much brighter.

Not everyone engaged in Welsh railway contracting found it as rewarding as Davies, who apparently could afford to write off £10,000 in extra costs on the NMR. On 26 January 1863 Thomas Robinson, railway contractor of Llanidloes, was discharged from bankruptcy, having owed £800. The *North Wales Chronicle* reported the commissioner as saying that had any creditor appeared to oppose the petition for discharge he would have had no hesitation of dismissing the petition 'on account of the bankrupt having so immediately prior to his bankruptcy denuded himself of his estate'.

The GWR seems to have had second thoughts about its agreement with the NMR, and in October had made the guarantee conditional on the stations being complete, when it knew they could not be because the NMR had lost its capital bill. The NMR's view was that the intention was for the guarantee to be payable when the line had been inspected and opened for public traffic.

## Summary of Llanidloes & Newtown Railway capital

| Debentures | Preference | Ordinary | Total | |
|---|---|---|---|---|
| Ordinary stock, LNR 1853 | | | £60,000 | £60,000 |
| Debentures A, LNR 1853 | £20,000 | | | £20,000 |
| Preference stock A, MWR 1860 | | £10,000 | | £10,000 |
| Preference stock B, LNR 1861 | | £25,000 | | £25,000 |
| Preference stock C, AWCR 1861 | | £25,000 | | £25,000 |
| Preference stock D, LNR 1862 | | £25,000 | | £25,000 |
| Debentures B, LNR 1862 | £8,000 | | | £8,000 |
| | **£28,000** | **£85,000** | **£60,000** | **£173,000** |
| Deduct subscribed to AWCR | | £25,000 | | £25,000 |
| | **£28,000** | **£60,000** | **£60,000** | **£148,000** |

On 28 February the shareholders were told that one of the reasons the Bill had been lost was because it had contained contested clauses at the GWR's insistence. The NMR had warned that they could cause trouble but the GWR had not budged. The NMR was also irritated that the GWR had had four shareholders' meetings and several extraordinary meetings without putting the agreement to its shareholders as required. It might be considered that the GWR's purpose in making the agreement was not to run the NMR but to stop the LNWR from doing so.

The NMR therefore decided to join with its neighbours and amalgamate with the ONR. The terms were similar to those agreed with the GWR except that the dividend would be 4½%. The directors had not felt the need to comment on their railway's completion in the minutes and only made the briefest mention in the shareholders' report. Telling its shareholders of the NMR's opening on 25 February, the ONR said that the two railways worked in harmony.

The ONR's second track from Welshpool to Buttington was inspected by Yolland, who reported on 17 January that the only difference from his 4 August 1860 report on the line from Pool Quay to Welshpool was the addition of two wrought-iron tie rods to each length of rails in both tracks; he understood that the remainder of the ONR was to be modified similarly. The wrought-iron bridge over the Severn had been strengthened and stiffened laterally. At Buttington the facing points at the start of the single line were worked at a 'considerable distance', 240 yards, by the means of rods, indicators showing the pointsman which road the points were set for. Recommending that the installation should be watched, he said that the use of the second line could be sanctioned.

The ONR's review of its financial commitments ordered in July 1862 was not delivered until 9 January 1863. Robert Piercy had been in Sardinia and was then ill after he returned. The figures are shown in the table below.

Informed of this calculation, Savin said that there were omissions, and that he was owed more than £30,000. He had not had time to consider the detail, having been given the information just before the meeting started, and the engineers had not issued their final certificate. Savin thought that while the companies owed him money they ought not to insist on such a high level of retention. He asked for £30,000 – £20,000 from the ONR and £10,000 from the LNR – to which the directors agreed, subject to the restrictions placed upon them by the loss of the capital Bill.

The LNR had its solicitor conduct a similar review, submitted on 12 February 1863. First, it described the Acts relating to the company with particular reference to capital, as shown as the table above.

To put it another way, at 5% this 12¼-mile-long railway had a commitment to pay £4,400 interest a year and an expectation from its shareholders of up to £3,000 in dividends.

After a settlement had been made with Savin, the LNR had a balance on its capital account of £3,563 10s 5d when opened in 1859. However, additional work was required on the main line, and when it was re-surveyed on 8 January 1863, adopting the same rates as applied on the ONR, it was determined that Savin was owed another £1,600. The full list of debts is shown in the table below. On 27 August the LNR asked Savin to meet its outstanding commitments, issuing Lloyds bonds to him as security, the ONR being asked to approve the arrangement.

## Financial review of the ONR, January 1863

| | |
|---|---|
| Owed to Savin by ONR | £42,813 11s 3½d |
| Lloyds bonds issued to Savin | £32,000 |
| | **£10,813 11s 3½d** |
| Owed to Savin by LNR | £9,511 1s 6d |
| Advance to meet payments now due | £5,000 |
| ONR rolling stock | £48,000 |
| LNR rolling stock | £20,680 |
| | **£68,680** |
| Retained as security | £22,893 |
| | **£45,787 12s 9½d** |

## Owed to Thomas Savin

| | |
|---|---|
| Extra on main line | £14,444 17s 9d |
| MWR transferred to LNR | £3,045 7s 11d |
| Joint station | £17,183 0s 4d |
| Joint line | £16,584 13s 0d |
| Maintenance, first year | £1,754 12s 1d |
| Payments | £16,950 |
| | **£69,962 11s 1d** |
| Preference shares | £60,000 |
| Debentures | £8,000 |
| 1859 balance | £3,563 10s 5d |
| | **£71,563 10s 8d** |
| Balance in favour of LNR | £1,600 19s 7d |
| | |
| Other liabilities | |
| LNR land | £720 |
| MWR land | £475 |
| Joint line land | £3,313 10s |
| | **£4,508 10s** |

Piercy submitted a detailed report on the progress with the MWR on 24 February 1863. Track laying had started on 8 miles of formation between Llanidloes and Rhayader. Seventeen river and eight road diversions had been completed, and 23 culverts had been built. Three viaducts, over the Tylwch, the Marteg and the Wye, were nearly completed. At the Rhayader tunnel, a shaft had been sunk, the north cutting excavated and tunnelling started from the south end. Development of station sites at Tylwch, Pantydwr and Rhayader were well advanced. Saying that work had started between Rhayader and Builth, he forecast that the line to Rhayader would be ready to be opened in July.

Tanner, secretary to the ONR and LNR, was sacked for unspecified reasons in March. A committee was appointed to examine the books before they were handed over to his replacement, the OEWR's George Lewis, appointed by the ONR on 25 March and by the LNR on 27 August. On 26 March the AWCR had deplored the appointment, its secretary, William Roberts, being more experienced than Lewis; it would support his appointment if there were any further amalgamations of Welsh railways. The ONR refused to consider a request from Tanner's solicitor for the payment of one year's salary on 22 April, but had settled for £200 by 24 June. Subsequent comments suggest that Tanner's record-keeping had left something to be desired.

On 24 April the ONR directors declared that workshops at Oswestry were now an urgent necessity. Piercy showed them a plan of the Shrewsbury & Hereford Railway's workshop at Shrewsbury and recommended its adaptation to ONR purposes.

By the time the AWCR's Bill had been in committee, in February, the company had persuaded the Aberystwyth harbour commissioners, corporation and improvements commissioners to withdraw their support for the MMR's proposed harbour branch in favour of the AWCR proposal.

Unspecified legal issues with the ONR rolling stock became an issue in April, causing Savin to propose transferring it to the company and paying for its use, providing the company with stock equal in quantity and quality at the end or determination of the lease.

Amalgamation of the Montgomeryshire railways moved a step closer on 1 May, when the NMR was leased to the ONR for 100 years on payment of £12,698 18s 6d per annum, that sum covering rents, interest on borrowing, 4½% dividend on the ordinary shares, and £300 to meet current expenses. There is no evidence, incidentally, in the surviving original documents seen by the author of a 'joint committee' taking charge of operations until the 1864 amalgamation, as stated in some publications.

ONR traffic had increased, shareholders were informed on 27 August, mainly due to the development of the ONR itself. The directors looked forward to the development of through traffic from the MWR, MMR and OEWR, and looked back to the opening of the OEWR between Ellesmere and Whitchurch on 1 May, the AWCR from Machynlleth to Borth, and the branches to Llanfyllin and Kerry on 1 July; *Bradshaw's Railway Manual* (1867) recorded 11 July for the last two. A commemorative dinner had been held at the Pavilion in Llanfyllin on 17 July.

Rich had submitted his report on the ONR branches from Chester on 28 June. The Llanfyllin branch was about 8¾ miles long, the Kerry branch about 3 miles 5 furlongs long. Both had separate passenger platforms at their respective main-line stations. No junctions for passenger traffic had been arranged.

Double-head 70lb rail in 24-foot lengths was used. Rail joints were fished, the chairs weighed about 24lb. The larch sleepers were 9 feet by 9 inches by 4½ inches, laid at 3-foot intervals except at joints, where the spacing was 2ft 3in. Broken stone or gravel was laid to a good depth.

Between Llanymynech and Llansantffraid, 3 miles, the formation and structures had been made for a double track. The Kerry branch was single-track throughout.

Both branches had a vertical deviation of about 12 feet, at 1 mile 4 chains on the Llanfyllin and at 3 miles on the Kerry, required by the nature of the ground and made with the landowners' consent. A private tramway that crossed the line near Llansantffraid required a box and gatekeeper. There was one public level crossing. Llanfyllin station was unfinished and had temporary facilities.

The Llanfyllin branch's 12 overbridges and 18 underbridges were variously constructed of stone, brick and timber. Five had wrought-iron girders, the largest span being 27ft 3in. There were seven viaducts, two with stone abutments and wrought-iron girders, the widest span being 45 feet on the skew. The other five had stone abutments and timber decks or were completely of timber. One of the latter had 13 openings of 17 feet each. They appeared to be substantially constructed and of sufficient strength. Piercy had agreed to complete the facing point indicators.

The Kerry branch was a short line with heavy gradients and sharp curves throughout. The steepest gradient was 1 in 42 and the sharpest curves were of 5 chains radius. There was one public level crossing. Six bridges and eight viaducts were all of small dimensions, and appeared to be substantially constructed and of sufficient strength. There were turntables at Abermule and Kerry. The line wound through a narrow glen and should be worked with care and at low speed.

Two deep cuttings near Abermule needed loose material and rubbish cleared away. A quarry hole at the back of the deepest cutting should be filled in and clear runs made in the embankment for the small mountain stream so that water would not lodge in the cuttings. Piercy had promised to attend to this and to keep a watchman in the cutting.

Rich had not received the undertakings about the method of working and he thought that the Kerry branch should be worked by one-engine-in-steam rather than the train staff. On receipt of the undertakings, both branches could be opened for passenger traffic.

When on 28 August Piercy produced plans for workshops at Oswestry which would cost £28,000, he was told to produce something capable of being executed for £5,000. Another building dealt with at the same time was Welshpool station. The plans of the architect, J. M. Penson of Chester, had been approved by the Earl of Powis on behalf of the SWR, and Savin was instructed to carry them out under Piercy's and Penson's supervision 'with the least possible delay'.

Penson became the ONR's architect of choice, for on 24 September, when the NMR was informed that it was to proceed with the construction of its remaining stations, he was to prepare the plans for Machynlleth station, 'not to be inferior in appearance or accommodation to the plans supplied by Mr Poundley'. Considering the companies' poor financial positions, these buildings were much grander than they need have been.

Tyler had inspected the OEWR and submitted his report from Edinburgh on 2 May 1863. The line was 10¾ miles long and the land taken and bridges built allowed for double track. The steepest gradient was 1 in 80 and the sharpest curve had a 20-chain radius. The track was laid with 70lb double-head rail in 24-foot lengths set in cast-iron chairs weighing 24lb 9oz. The timber sleepers were 9 feet long and an average section of 50 inches, laid transversely 3 feet apart. Chairs on bridges were of a different section to allow them to be fastened more securely. All the chairs were fixed by wrought-iron spikes.

The track on Whixall Moss needed to be straightened and packed in places, he reported, and would require careful attention for some time, but was generally in a firm condition and in good order. There were 11 bridges under and 13 over the railway, all with spans of less than 30 feet. They were variously constructed of brick, wrought-iron and timber. A

An engraving showing the Newtown & Machynlleth Railway's buildings at its western terminus. A horse-drawn Corris Railway train is about to cross the Dovey, left of centre.

turntable had been installed at Ellesmere and the LNWR had undertaken to install one at Whitchurch within three months. An undertaking to work the single line in compliance with the Board of Trade train staff regulations had been given. Although Tyler omitted to say whether or not he recommended that the line could be operated safely, the Board of Trade office decided that was what he intended and informed the company to that effect on 5 May. The shareholders were told that the line had been opened on 1 May, a Sunday and the day before Tyler reported; Bradshaw's 1867 *Railway Manual* gives the date as 4 May.

Earlier, on 27 February, the OEWR had been trying to finalise its contract with Savin. The cost was still unknown and his attempt to remove some items from the draft was rejected. The company expected him to complete a similar contract for the line between Ellesmere, Ruabon and Wrexham. Regarding the station at Whitchurch, on 26 March he produced an agreement between himself, on behalf of the OEWR, and the LNWR. The OEWR would pay for the land, widening a bridge and sidings on the brook side of the station, and rental and maintenance would be on the same basis as agreed with the LNWR at Welshpool.

Whalley had property that would be affected by the Ruabon extension; he stated his views and left the room while Piercy explained the implications. Piercy was instructed to drop a connection to the Vale of Clwyd Railway and to reduce the length of the Ellesmere-Ruabon line to 10 miles 7 furlongs. On 27 May 1863 a deadline of 1 July 1864 was set for completing the Oswestry-Ellesmere line, and the contract was finally sealed on 23 July.

A cessation of work at Ellesmere station for unspecified reasons was reported on 29 October 1863. Piercy was instructed to see that it was constructed and completed in accordance with the plans. The purpose of an agreement sealed with Watson and Overend on 13 January 1864 was also unexplained.

The first few months of 1864 brought changes to the constituents' direction and saw Savin dispel the myth that he was merely the contractor. In fact, the shares he had been issued gave him control, and Henry Gartside and Jasper Wilson Johns helped him to exercise it. Before the first quarter was out Whalley had been ousted as chairman and Piercy sacked as engineer. The *Railway Times* took pleasure at reporting the shareholders' meetings at length.

A division among the OEWR directors was first manifest on 28 January 1864, when Johns objected to the minutes of the previous meeting, handing in a note protesting about the expenses of extensions being charged to the company. He also tried to stop Whalley being reimbursed his expenses incurred in promoting the extension Bill.

The committee examining the ONR's books (see page 54) was given additional work on 24 June 1863, to ascertain the liabilities and the amount required to be spent in order to put the capital account on a proper footing, and to do the same for the LNR, taking into account the ONR's liabilities to it.

Rich inspected the AWCR from Machynlleth to Borth, submitting his report from Oswestry on 26 June. The line was 12 miles 12 chains long, and enough land had been taken for a second track at a later date. Rail of 70lb in 24-foot lengths had been laid in 24lb iron chairs and fastened to sleepers 9 feet long by 9 inches by 4½ inches. Ballast was gravel and broken stone about 1 foot deep under the sleepers. Intermediate stations were located at Glan Dovey and Ynys Las. There were six underbridges, the largest having stone piers and wrought-iron girders with a 33 foot span. The largest span of the 11 timber viaducts was 18 feet; all appeared to be of sufficient strength although one, about 3 miles from Borth, would be firmer if the piles were braced. Piercy promised that this would be done and that indicators would be fitted to all facing points. Turntables had been erected at the terminal stations. On receipt of the company's undertaking as to the method of working, Rich recommended that the line could be opened for passenger traffic without danger to the public.

The MMR's solicitor had written to the Board of Trade on 29 June, objecting to any part of AWCR Railway No 1 being opened before Railways Nos 2 and 3 were completed. Opinion was obtained that the opening could not be postponed on any basis not cited in the Act, but the directors should understand that if the opening did contravene the Act they would be responsible, which sounds like a fine civil service get-out! Whalley had signed the undertaking to work the line by train staff on 26 June.

*De Winton*, an 0-6-0 built by Manning, Wardle in 1862, was one of the locomotives transferred to the Brecon & Merthyr Railway in 1866.

Some 70 guests, including Savin, Piercy, Whalley, the directors of all the constituent companies and their Welsh neighbours and some of their officers, attended a banquet at Borth on 30 July, travelling thence by special train from Oswestry. In October, Whalley told the shareholders that, despite the station being unfinished, a Mondays-only tourist train from Oswestry had been started on 13 July. A four-horse coach made a connection with the trains and Aberystwyth.

The MWR's 1862 Bill had been enacted as the MWR (Capital) Act and received the Royal Assent on 4 May, authorising it to raise up to £200,000 in 5% preference shares. In a separate Act, assented on 22 June, the company could make a branch to the MMR at Llangurig and other works, raising up to £75,000 in ordinary shares for the purpose.

The NMR's 1862 Bill of 8 June enabled it to raise £40,000 new capital, and £70,000 new capital in lieu of the same amount of original capital that had not been fully paid.

A short branch to Aberbechan from Cilgwrgan, to the east of Newtown, was authorised by the ONR's 1863 Act on 29 June. £200,000 new capital was also approved. The loss of the Bill the previous year had left the company indebted to Savin by £140,000, including two-thirds of the cost of the rolling stock; he subsequently claimed 7½% compensation for the delay in settlement.

Opposition by the Festiniog Railway Company, Lord Newborough and Colonel Tottenham was obviously responsible for the AWCR losing the Blaenau Ffestiniog branch from its 1862 Bill when it was enacted on 13 July.

The amalgamation Bill having failed, on 20 July the LNWR wrote to the ONR and LNR complaining that although it, and other unspecified Bills, had not been promoted by them but by their lessee and others, the LNWR thought that they were not consistent with agreements already existing between the companies and that their refusal to promote Bills confirming the agreements was 'entirely at variance with … good faith'. It is now, said the LNWR, for your companies and for your lessee to consider whether it would not be more advantageous to the companies and to the public that the lines already authorised should be made available for the development of traffic and fairly remunerative to their owners by cooperation under friendly arrangements than that the parties should expend their energies and money on hostile contention respecting duplicate and unnecessary lines.

The LNWR was still willing to deal with the companies, the letter continued, on the understanding that the 'spirit and good faith' of the

agreements be observed and that the companies and Savin agree to their confirmation by Parliament. Counsel's opinion was to be obtained before a reply was sent, the ONR resolved; the LNR did not discuss the letter at all, but it was not mentioned again.

Unspecified problems with the Admiralty had prevented the AWCR from finalising a construction contract to complete the coast line. The difficulties overcome, on 23 July 1863 Savin told the directors that he would undertake the work for a fixed price to be determined, inclusive of all expenses, until the railway had been approved by the Board of Trade. He subsequently agreed to be responsible for the purchase of the land required.

On 12 August he proposed that the contract price be calculated at £15,000 per mile, producing a price of £1,297,000. However, with £1,066,300 authorised capital, there was a deficiency of £230,700. He also suggested that the Carnarvonshire Railway be 'united' with the AWCR by lease.

The AWCR also decided on 12 August that the roads authorised to be constructed with the Dovey and Mawddach viaducts would be for pedestrians only. Two weeks later Piercy reported that the masonry was complete between Borth and Aberystwyth, 'with some trifling exceptions'. Problems with constructing the embankment on the marsh near Borth had delayed the earthworks; a solution having been found, they were now in a 'satisfactory state'.

On 4 March the *North Wales Chronicle* had reported that the first locomotive to run between Aberdovey and Llwyngwril had been the Manning, Wardle 0-6-0ST *Merion*. On 18 April the paper reported that guests from Towyn and Aberdovey attending a society wedding at Llwyngwril on the 8th had travelled there by train.

An unfortunate accident befell a horse at Friog on 27 May. Edward Humphreys, the sub-contractor, had bought a new horse to pull wagons out of the cutting with two others. Reaching the point where the horses were unhitched, the new animal refused to move from the track and was run down by the following loaded wagons running under gravity. Falling over a 40-foot precipice, the animal pulled the other two horses with it, one of which survived the drop.

The LNR dealt with the MMR's request for it to operate the latter's line to Llangurig on 27 August. It would work it at cost but would not subscribe the authorised £20,000 in the MMR until it had received a report on the practicality of making the MMR in the direction suggested.

The MWR had received £2,260 from the LNR for the land between Llanidloes and Penbontbren by 25 March. In May 1862 Savin had been allowed to use MWR materials stored at Llanidloes to lay the track on this section; a year later Piercy was instructed to report on the materials used and to arrange for Savin to replace them. A £904 2s 9d bill for transporting rail via the ONR and LNR was passed for payment at the same time.

Piercy reported on 11 August that the decision to line the MWR's Rhayader tunnel, despite it being cut through stone, prevented the fulfilment of his prediction that the line would be ready for opening in July. A locomotive had been put to work between Llanidloes and the tunnel and he now expected the line to be ready in October. In expectation of the July completion date, in February Piercy had been instructed to 'ascertain by communication with lessee of Oswestry & Newtown company on what terms he will work the line'.

Rich inspected the AWCR between Aberdovey and Llwyngwril on 11/12 September, reporting from Welshpool on the 13th. The line was 10 miles 24 chains long, single throughout, with sidings. Land had been taken for a double track and the overbridges and wrought-iron underbridge at Towyn had been constructed to accommodate a second line. The formation was 18 feet wide. There was a space of 6 feet where two tracks had been laid. The double-head rail weighed 70lb per yard in 24-foot lengths, and 24lb chairs were fixed to Baltic fir sleepers 9 feet long by 9 inches by 4½ inches with iron spikes. The sleepers were laid at 3-foot intervals except at joints, where they were 2 feet apart. There was about 1 foot of broken stone or gravel ballast under the sleepers.

There was one wrought-iron overbridge of 35-foot span, and one of stone and brick. There were two stone and brick underbridges and one of wrought iron with a 35-foot span. The latter was close to the only intermediate station at Towyn, and carried part of the platforms as well as the railway. However, the outside girder was not strong enough for both purposes and, as the timber beams that carried the remainder of the platforms were also too weak, Rich recommended that the platforms be carried independently.

The largest of three timber viaducts had 17 openings of 18 feet and two of 20 feet, all on the skew, the last in the centre of the stream; the structure was of adequate strength but could be improved by the addition of iron straps or bolts. Rail chairs next to joints should be fastened with fang bolts.

The distant signal on the Aberdovey side of Towyn required raising and point indicators were required at Aberdovey and Llwyngwril. No turntables had been provided. Vertical deviations of more than 3 feet at 6-6¼ miles and 6½-8½ miles had been made with the landowner's consent. There were six unauthorised level crossings, four to the north of the large viaduct at 6-6.40 miles where the same road crossed the railway four times in half a mile – they could be reduced to one by diverting the road. The other two were at 4 miles 10 chains and 5 miles 78 chains. Fencing was incomplete at several sites, including the wing walls of the underbridges.

'By reason of the incompleteness of the works' Rich could not recommend the line being opened. He had been given an undertaking as to the method of working, although it was unsealed. The company was instructed to postpone the opening for a month.

He re-inspected the line on 12 October, reporting from Welshpool. The signal and platforms at Towyn had been altered, fencing completed, point indicators provided at facing points, and the installation of fang bolts would be completed in a day or two. Two of the crossings had been eliminated and two provided with gates and lodges. Turntables and chock blocks to the sidings were still required. The undertaking had still not been sealed.

Completing his report without making a recommendation, the next day Rich telegraphed the Board of Trade to say that the railway could still not be opened because it was still incomplete, following it with a note explaining that he had written the report in the middle of a lot of people talking, and had rushed to hand it to a train guard as the mail had left by road before he had reached Welshpool. The error was not important, he said, 'as they have no intention of opening 'til they settle about the level crossings.'

Receiving the news in London the same day, Roberts, the AWCR secretary, attended the Board of Trade and secured an agreement to the effect that providing the chock blocks were installed, and an undertaking given to install turntables within two months, using tank engines only in the meantime, and constructing bridges over the unauthorised crossings before 1 November 1864, unless Parliament should authorise them to be retained, approval for opening would be given.

Whalley and Roberts gave the required undertaking on 15 October and the letter of approval to open was dispatched on the 16th. The *Wrexham Advertiser* of 31 October reported that the line was opened on 24 October, amid great rejoicing with stations and lineside buildings decorated with flags, bunting and ceremonial arches.

On 29 October Piercy reported that Savin's proposal to build the AWCR for £15,000 per mile was reasonable. Accepting this, the directors reserved to the company the obligation to meet management, engineering, legal and Parliamentary expenses, reducing the mileage sum to a rate to be agreed. Consequently the company would also retain so much of its capital as would be necessary to defray the expenses. The directors also made it a condition that the works agreement and amalgamation of the Carnarvonshire Railway with the AWCR should be completed and form part of the arrangement with Savin.

With a view to diversifying their business, the AWCR directors also resolved to apply for powers to raise £100,000 additional capital to build hotels at stations, and for £50,000 to buy steamers to trade on the Irish coast.

Savin apparently did not approve of the conditions to be attached to his AWCR contract and failed to tell the directors the revised price. Therefore, on 11 November the directors instructed the solicitor to prepare a fixed-price contract, Piercy advising on the price to be inserted. This move brought Savin back to the table, and on 26 November he accepted the terms subject to an arrangement protecting the price of shares, restricting their sale before the line was completed.

In determining the clauses to be included in the contract, the AWCR showed a measure of resolve in dealing with Savin not seen in the other constituent companies. As Whalley and Lefeaux, in particular, had been engaged with him since his entry into railway construction, maybe this demonstrates that they had come to understand his methods and thought that he should be constrained.

Clauses were inserted to prevent him from using his shares to vote on any matter in which he had an interest, and to prevent him from selling or transferring any shares without the associated voting rights. As the line from Borth to Aberystwyth was subject to forfeiture to the ONR if it was not completed before 1 August 1864, a penalty would be imposed on Savin if it was not completed by 1 March. Another penalty would be imposed if the Dovey viaduct was not completed by January 1865.

The company reserved the right to carry out the works if they were not started and prosecuted with 'all adequate vigour'; the company's interest in the line between Afon Wen and Portmadoc, shared with the Carnarvonshire Railway, was to be protected; the CR was to be transferred to the AWCR as soon as practicable; the AWCR was to have an option to purchase the 2ft 3in Corris Tramway at valuation and Savin was not to sell it elsewhere until the option had been exercised.

Calculating that over five years the costs would be £186,000, the construction mileage rate was reduced to £13,000.

In response to a request minuted on 29 October 1863, the ONR had offered to work the AWCR's Aberystwyth line for 45% of the traffic receipts, later offering to work the coast line at cost.

The NMR appears to have decided that the AWCR would not complete the Aberystwyth line in time, so deposited a Bill to obtain powers to complete and maintain it and to make provision for its 'speedy opening throughout'. The AWCR resolved to oppose it on 17 December.

Despite an earlier decision to the contrary, the AWCR also deposited a Bill for a Ffestiniog branch. At 8¾ miles long, it would have started from the Minffordd side of Penrhyndeudraeth and crossed the Festiniog Railway near Ty Fry and in front of the northern end of Moelwyn Tunnel, to terminate at Duffws. Others bills were deposited by the MMR (extension of time, new lines), the ONR (amalgamation, arrangements and working arrangements (three bills)), the LNR (capital, additional land), the MWR (junction with the Central Wales Extension Railway, diversion and level crossing), and the OEWR (extensions and deviation).

There were those who despaired of ever seeing the Carnarvonshire Railway built. An unnamed correspondent to the *North Wales Chronicle* wrote on 1 January 1864 that there was nothing to show for it but a pile of sleepers stacked in a field at Ynys Galch, opposite the present Queen's Hotel in Porthmadog. The writer had heard that there was a disagreement between the directors and a 'large landed proprietor' whose land was needed. There could well be something in this as the CR required both an extension of time and almost 5 miles of deviation before it was completed. On 8 March the shareholders were told that the problem was a disagreement with the AWCR directors on policy; large cargoes of sleepers and timber had been imported with a view to starting at Portmadoc.

The sleepers had been delivered by ship from Danzig in October 1863, the ship-owner winning a claim against Savin for demurrage because the harbour was so busy it had not been able to reach the wharf to unload for a week.

Two letters dealt with by the AWCR in January and February 1864 concerned the possibility of building a branch or tramway to serve the Bryn Eglwys slate quarries, near Towyn, or terms for carrying slate from Towyn to Aberdovey. The board was willing to help but required more details. The quarries were shortly to be served by the Talyllyn Railway.

Savin still refused to sign the contract, and by 14 February was refusing to pay for land; a payment of £6,575 was approved on that date, and Savin had instituted proceedings against the AWCR. There was a split in the board, too, with Johns and Gartside regularly putting motions that were rejected. Gartside also submitted a written objection about £10,000 paid to Piercy on account, claiming that it was unjust to the shareholders and illegal.

On 6 February John Williams, a man working at Ynys Las, was killed in a shunting accident; the locomotive involved was a Manning, Wardle 0-6-0ST named *Nant Clwyd*. However, the *North Wales Chronicle* of 13 February, which recorded the incident, gave more space to reporting John Savin's marriage to 'Miss Jones' of Ruthin in Aberdovey two days before. The navvies had a holiday, while Aberdovey and, to a lesser extent, Towyn were adorned with flags, bunting and banners. A locomotive was decorated and detonators marked the arrival and departure of the trains. A committee organised and paid for 300 women and children to have tea and plum cake at the Corbett Arms Hotel.

On 20 February the paper was sceptical about the likelihood of the railway reaching Dolgelley in the near future. Progress had slackened since Christmas, it observed, due to the high state of the money market.

The split between Savin and Whalley became public at the AWCR shareholders' meeting on 25 February. Whalley started by reading a statement describing the arrangement the company had with Savin and the legal action he, Savin, had brought against it. The state of the share list was peculiar, he explained – no calls had been made and the only shares issued for money were those held by the directors and £100,000 contributed by the ONR and LNR. Savin had been paid with £239,000 in fully paid shares, and the directors believed that he would use them to obtain such terms on his contract to enable him to proceed free of directorial or shareholder supervision.

Whalley also claimed that Savin was using his influence to secure the election of his nominees to the LNR and ONR boards, and pointed out that Gartside and Johns, who supported Savin, were also directors of those companies. Although Savin's shares had been used as security for his borrowing, he had retained the voting rights attached to them. The division between Savin and his clients had started on 17 December 1863, when the ONR had resolved to reject his policy vis à vis the LNWR. Because the latter's guarantee and rebate was important to Savin, they maintained the share value, he had stopped work on the Bishop's Castle Railway, which would divert traffic from the LNWR, and said that he would not allow anyone else to make it.

Gartside objected to being called Savin's representative, saying that his appointment had actually been made by Whalley to represent investors in Lancashire. He also explained that the objection to Piercy's payment was because he had not submitted a bill. Whalley was happy to accept that Piercy was owed £53,000 based on the contract price. When the cheque had been stopped by the court Piercy had been given a debenture for £10,000 instead.

Johns also denied being a Savin nominee, explaining that he had become involved in Welsh companies when he had raised the £60,000 that enabled Davies and Savin to take on the ONR contract.

Lefeaux resigned as an AWCR director on 2 March and, in response to a shareholders' requisition to call an extraordinary meeting to reduce the number of directors, Whalley and two others resigned the next day. On 4 March the remaining directors decided that, as Piercy had been so closely aligned to Whalley, he should go as well. G. B. Bruce was appointed as an 'independent and competent engineer' to investigate the state of the accounts between Savin and the company, taking as his starting point the provisional contract of 20 February 1862 and assuming a lump sum on the basis of £15,000 per mile.

Piercy protested against his dismissal on 8 March. The only cause for disagreement between him and either the old board or the current one, he wrote, 'could' be his refusal to certify some of Savin's claims. The directors rejected his assertion that his appointment was 'co-extensive' with the construction of the authorised works and his assumption that an arbitrator would be appointed. They seemed to be particularly aggrieved by his practice of claiming considerable sums for work done without submitting any details, and on 5 April appointed Henry Conybeare (1823-92) to replace him.

Piercy issued a writ against the company by 22 April. The reason that he had refused to approve some of Savin's claims was because the two men had argued over the original route across the Dovey, the contractor baulking at the cost of it and wanting it changing. With a crossing of some 2½ miles and a 60-foot depth of sand to reach ground suitable for foundations, that was perhaps no surprise.

On 5 April the AWCR agreed to take the Corris Railway from Savin 'at par', providing that he made an agreement to that effect, resolving to withdraw its opposition to the Corris Bill then in Parliament. Savin accepted the offer and on 25 April the AWCR resolved to complete the purchase, paying for it with Lloyds bonds, but on 26 April decided to reconsider the acquisition. A working agreement between the two companies was ordered to be drafted on 15 December.

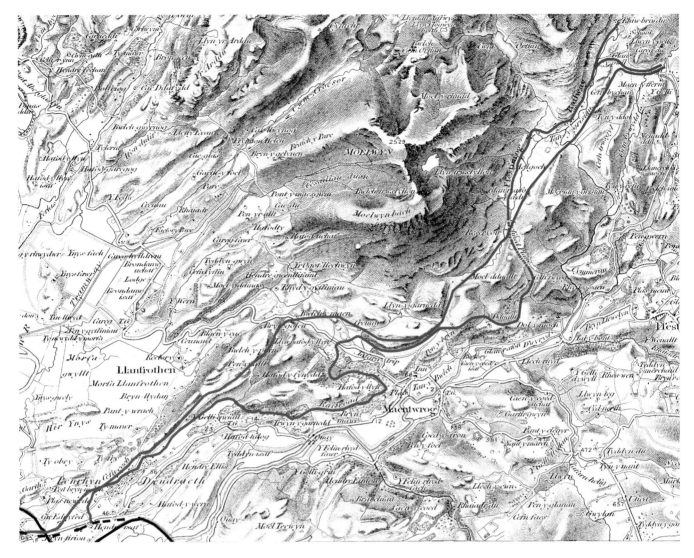

The Aberystwyth & Welsh Coast Railway's Ffestiniog branch traced onto a map of slightly later vintage. The broken black line is the AWCR's 1861 authorised route; the solid black line is the railway as built. The Festiniog Railway is shown in blue.

William Bage, Savin's Aberdovey-based resident engineer, was evidently a popular man. On 15 April 1864 he was presented with an engraved silver salver and tankard by Savin's employees because he was leaving for a new job in London.

A few weeks later, on 22 May, 100 residents of Aberdovey petitioned the Board of Trade, complaining that the AWCR's route would interfere with shipping. They were referred to the deposited plans to see if construction was on the agreed alignment.

Tyler inspected the AWCR from Borth to Aberystwyth, reporting from the latter on 26 May. The single line was 8 miles 54 chains long, the steepest gradient was 1 in 60 and the sharpest curve had a radius of 27 chains. The track was laid with 70lb double-head rail at an average length of 21 feet. Cast-iron chairs weighing 26lb were fastened to the sleepers by wrought-iron spikes. Laid transversely, the sleepers measured 9 feet by 10 inches by 5 inches. A large proportion of the fish bolts were too short and required replacing.

Additional post-and-wire fencing was required at Bow Street, around Aberystwyth station and at some other places. Extra drainage was required in some of the cuttings. A water crane was required at Aberystwyth in place of a temporary tank nearby, which should be removed.

There were nine bridges under and six over the railway, the largest span being 51ft 6in. He had asked for the joints of the wrought-iron girders to be improved. Continuous angle-irons were required under the cross-beams of a bridge at 3 miles 76 chains (measurements from Aberystwyth), and cover plates or angle-irons under the cross-beams of other bridges. Cross ties and transoms were required in some cases and through bolts to connect the longitudinal timbers with the wooden platforms in others. The abutments of the bridges at 1 mile 32 chains, 3 miles 31 chains, 7 miles, and 7 miles 48 chains had settled or bulged and would require watching. Screw bolts in some bridges were too short.

The bridges, mostly of timber, were not as strong as Tyler would have liked. One of them, for a public road, and another like it, had permanently deflected and needed strengthening.

At Aberystwyth station a cross-over road, siding, supports for a signal, and level crossing lamps were needed. At Llanfihangel, the level crossing gate-posts were too close to the rails. The quadrants for working the distant signals required improved catches and notches. Indicators were wanted on some of the switches.

There were two unauthorised level crossings on public roads, one at 1 mile 5 chains, the other at 8 miles. Authority for the first was being sought in a Bill before Parliament, while the other was on a minor road near Borth; it would be impossible to build a bridge under the railway for want of drainage, and steep approaches on soft ground would be required to carry the road over the railway. Parliamentary approval should be obtained and suitable gates with a lodge should be provided. In view of the incomplete works Tyler could not recommend the railway be opened.

On 7 June Savin, who had recently built an additional platform and two long sidings at Borth, 'to meet urgent requirements', assured the AWCR that the deficiencies were being put right, and on 13 June Roberts

THE OPENING CEREMONY AT MACHYNLLETH.

asked for the re-inspection to be carried out as quickly as possible 'as we are most anxious to have the line opened for the summer traffic'.

Tyler submitted his second report from Aberystwyth on 22 June. The requirements of his first had been attended to, but three road overbridges were still unsatisfactory, although some work had been done on them. He recommended that they be propped and have their superstructures replaced at an early date.

A culvert at 4 miles had partially failed. Originally made too short, it had been lengthened in a substantial manner, and Tyler had been told that it had not moved in eight or nine months. It should be watched.

The level crossing at Llanbadarn, 1 mile 5 chains, had received Parliamentary approval [actually, the authority came into effect a few days later] and a footbridge had been erected. Improved gates and a wooden cabin had been provided at the unauthorised crossing at 8 miles, and a lodge for the gatekeeper was being erected.

The undertaking concerning single-line working was dated 28 May and had been delivered to the Board of Trade on 21 June. Approval to open, dated 24 June, was conditional on the bridges and culvert being dealt with. Services had started on 23 June, with the celebratory junketing following on 22 July.

On 16 December 1863 Savin had been chased by the ONR for his estimate for undertaking the outstanding works on the NMR. Over the years there were several such requests from his clients and, taking into account that he built the ONR and the OEWR without completing the contract (see pages 55 and 61), the impression is left that he preferred not to be tied down to details, leaving the companies without any choice when dealing with his payment claims.

Earlier, on 3 December, he had asked the ONR to be relieved of his responsibilities for supplying the rolling stock, saying that it was difficult to comply with the existing arrangement satisfactorily and suggesting that the stock of the ONR and the railways operated by it should be owned outright by the company. Instead, he would manage

**Opening the Newtown & Machynlleth Railway at Machynlleth on 25 February 1863.** *Illustrated London News*

the railways, collect the income and discharge the obligations to the other companies. He enclosed a draft agreement that included a requirement for the ONR to take over the locomotives and carriages ordered from Sharp, Stewart and Ashbury for the NMR and to reimburse him £10,000. Both had been accepted on 16 December, Piercy and the solicitor being instructed to ensure that the stock was henceforth identified as the ONR's property.

It took three adjournments of the ONR board on 17 December to agree a strategy over the Bill dealing with the LNWR agreement. The solicitor advised the directors to accept an LNWR amendment, but Whalley declared his intention to vote against it. Eventually a vote was taken and the proposal was lost without him having to vote. Afterwards, for unrecorded reasons, the directors resolved to withdraw the amalgamation Bill. There were more signs of dissent among the ONR directors that continued into 1864, when Johns and Gartside objected to the minutes of several meetings, claiming irregularities in their conduct.

'This small but exceedingly sulphurous volcano indicates a speedy eruption,' the *Railway Times* said of the situation on 23 January 1864. The rebate agreements with the LNWR that were to be included in the Bill 'by which the Oswestry and other lines are sought to be amalgamated under the name of the Cambrian' were to be rejected and a grand alliance established with the MWR and other lines suggested by Piercy to attack the LNWR's Welsh interests.

The paper thought this was suicidal, explaining that the LNWR had offered the rebate, and the £30,000 to the OEWR, when it was competing with the GWR. Now, however, the two great companies had reached an accord and Whalley was determined to break the agreements. He and three other directors controlled the board despite holding only £2,100 stock between them, against the minority directors' holding of nearly £1 million.

Savin, the paper said, was 'heartily sick of these heartless and selfish proceedings', as well he might, it continued, because it was claimed that Whalley, as chairman of the MWR, was deluded if he thought that the MWR's contractors would be able to fulfil a promise to send £15,000 of traffic over the ONR if the rebate agreement was set aside.

The long-awaited report in the ONR's financial affairs was delivered on 27 January 1864. Consisting of 38 printed pages, it started by setting out the arrangements with the various contractors. It appears that when Davies and Savin took over the contract they had enhanced the prices by an amount equal to a discount of 50% on the ordinary shares, 20% on the preference shares and 10% on the debentures; they had also added £12,800 for contingencies. The discounted shares would have given room to manoeuvre when negotiating their use as security for loans.

Although the contract with Savin was not executed, construction was undertaken in accordance with its terms. No contracts were completed for the Llanfyllin and Kerry branches, either. Including £105,000 subscribed to the OEWR (£30,000) and the AWCR (£75,000), the ONR's capital was £944,898 15s 11d. Expenditure, including payments to Savin (£613,696 19s 8d), the original contractors (£117,364 1s 1d), and on rolling stock (£92,809) had totalled £942,517 14s 5d. Current assets, mostly unissued capital, included £26,000 owed by the NMR and £10,000 by the LNR, and the £105,000 subscribed to the OEWR and the AWCR, totalling £170,935 11s 6d; only £25,000 of this was available.

Savin claimed that he was due £15,557 plus £3,889 if paid in preference shares. He also wanted 10% on the cost of the main line as compensation 'for having push on the works … and for overcoming difficulties … which … would have ruined the company'.

Outstanding works, including locomotive sheds at Llynclys (for the Porthywaen branch), Llanfyllin and Kerry, and permanent stations at Llanymynech, Welshpool, Montgomery, Abermule and Newtown, were estimated to cost £42,000. £12,500 was allowed for uncompleted land purchases, and miscellaneous debts were calculated to be £4,749 1s 10d. The company had no information available to it regarding net receipts or working expenses.

The LNR had liabilities of £36,500, although Savin had not submitted his final account. Fixed annual outgoings were £8,816 6s 9d. The working agreement had the ONR meeting all outgoings and paying 5% of ordinary capital. The NMR had fixed outgoings of £12,698 18s 6d. Rolling stock valued at £5,628 12s 5d had been handed over to the ONR.

The report concluded with a recommendation that the ONR's offices should be in London and that its accounts should be audited. The authorised capital had been spent, leaving no reserve to meet outstanding claims. No further capital expenditure should be made until the capital required had Parliamentary approval, and no contract should be let until approved by the board, the engineer having submitted plans and estimates that had been examined by two directors.

There was doubt about the validity of Savin's claims and they required 'the most serious and grave consideration'. On 29 January the directors rejected all of Savin's claims, and attempts by Johns and Gartside to put the matter to arbitration. By 12 February Savin and his London agent, James Fraser, had lodged a claim against the ONR and four of its directors. Savin's request for arbitration was refused because accepting it would give credence to his claims.

Whalley's reign over the constituents came to an end at the ONR shareholders' meeting held on 29 February. In a four-page printed report, the minority directors explained that they were in dispute over the direction of the company. The majority directors wished to pursue the original strategy, of developing a network independent of the LNWR,

GWR and other companies, while wishing to establish 'harmonious co-operation' with existing companies, using existing lines for mutual benefit and public convenience, avoiding unnecessary expenditure on duplicate lines and Parliamentary conflicts, inconvenience from obstructive and disjointed working and constant litigation.

In common with the compilers of the 26 January report, the ONR's auditors also called for the accounts to be examined by a 'professional accountant', in their case drawing attention to £257,696 7s 5d of new expenditure. Only £8,651 capital remained outstanding after all the available stocks and debentures had been issued.

Whalley claimed that the reason the amalgamation Bill had not been deposited was an LNWR threat to object unless approval was given to its Bill to lease the SWR, with a consequential loss of traffic worth £15,000. He also explained that Savin's contract allowed him to appoint two directors but not to exercise the voting powers on the shares he was awarded. Now, however, he insisted on the right to vote his shares, claiming to control £140,000.

Savin's actions were, Whalley continued, explained by his dealings with the LNWR. He had obtained a guarantee of 4½% on the Brecon & Merthyr and Hereford & Brecon railways at the expense of diverting north-south traffic away from the MWR, ONR and OEWR. It was galling to the Montgomeryshire lines to have created the route only to lose the traffic by the efforts of their contractor.

The shareholders eventually adopted the minority report and replaced two of the retiring directors, including Lefeaux. Whalley resigned immediately afterwards. After 7 hours, the meeting ended at 10.10pm.

Assessed by the length of its *Railway Times* report, the OEWR shareholders' meeting on 27 February had been the shortest and was reasonably good-natured. Despite Whalley's ejection from the board, the meeting closed with a vote of thanks to him, seconded by Savin. While they had differed, the contractor said, it had not been on personal grounds but on policy.

So concerned were the ONR directors about their internal wrangling and other matters that they overlooked the inspection and approval of the second track between Oswestry and Llanymynech. Instructed to make the inspection on 16 December 1864, Tyler reported from Newtown on 15 February. This section was 6 miles long, and the track materials were the same as before.

There was only one platform at Oswestry, the layout was to be 're-arranged immediately' and a second platform built with a footbridge connecting them. Lockable stop blocks should be fixed to the sidings at the Oswestry cattle dock, at the mineral line junction at Llynclys and at the Llanymynech connection to the Shrewsbury & North Wales Railway, then under construction. The distant signal north of the western siding should be placed further from it, and the signalman's stage at Llynclys should be glazed at the sides and have doors provided. The second platform at Llanymynech was 'destitute of shelter and conveniences', which should be added; there would be more need for them when the PSNWR, which would run to the east of the platform, was opened for traffic.

The fence around the old platform at Pant should be made higher and a portion of the rock cutting next to the siding there should be removed. A bridge beam that had been damaged by the tramway traffic below should be replaced and the tramway lowered to prevent a repeat of the damage. Better wall plates should be inserted under the girders of a cast-iron bridge near Llanymynech.

Tyler enclosed a letter from George Owen dated 13 February stating that, except for the waiting shelter at Llanymynech, the works had been carried out, so he recommended that the second line could be opened.

Earl Vane was appointed as a director and chairman of the ONR on 10 March. Whalley's future was determined with a decision to support

Supplied in 1864 by Sharp, Stewart for the Oswestry & Newtown Railway, 2-4-0 *Plynlimon* lasted long enough to be taken over by the GWR in 1922. *Ted Talbot collection*

the withdrawal of Savin's claims against him and the company, providing it was made clear in court 'that all imputation of or implying any corrupt motives to the defendants are withdrawn'. Savin, who was present, assented to this, and the resignations of Whalley and the last 'majority' director were handed to Vane.

No doubt Savin's enthusiasm for having 'his' railways associated with the LNWR had to do with the guarantees. The value of his holdings of the various shares and debentures would have been enhanced by them, strengthening his position whether he wanted to sell them or use them as collateral for borrowing.

Reviewing the process of 10 Bills deposited in 1863, the ONR was informed that although the amalgamation Bill had been withdrawn on 18 December, it had been re-deposited by the NMR in order that it could be dealt with jointly if desired. The ONR's own Bill seeking to confirm its agreements with the LNWR had also been withdrawn and re-deposited, by the LNWR in this case. It was subsequently claimed that the Bills had been 'improperly and summarily' withdrawn in breach of sealed agreements with the NMR and the LNWR.

The *Railway Times* had commented on this situation on 30 January 1864, explaining also that the 1862 amalgamation Bill, which included several smaller Welsh companies, had failed because not only had several of them not started their works, but there was little probability of them ever being able to do so. Cambrian, it had explained, was the name by which the companies 'which have had affixed upon them the euphonistic cognomen [resounding nickname] of Whalley-cum-Savin' would be united. The measure would bring a better working of the disjointed system for, although the boards had 'nearly the same directors', there were differences between them.

They were united on one point only, the paper declared, the impolicy [inexpediency] of fusing the companies and the boards together, for the first outcome would be to terminate the duplicate salaries paid to Whalley and his associates. This explained the Bill's withdrawal, the paper declared, adding that it was almost certainly calumny (defamatory).

Savin's case against the AWCR about the validity of the £10,000 cheque issued to Piercy (page 58) was reported by the *Railway Times* on 27 February, the argument centring on whether the money was for engineering services, which should have been paid by Savin, or to promote Parliamentary Bills for new lines, in collusion with the directors who approved the payment. The judge observed that it was a very curious case and the directors' conduct most singular. The case, and two others of a similar nature, was withdrawn by agreement on 17 March, probably a consequence of Whalley's ousting from the AWCR, LNR, OEWR and ONR.

Locomotive builder Sharp, Stewart had dispatched four 2-4-0s to Oswestry on 8 March. Ordered by Savin, he took advantage of his

presence at the ONR board meeting to request reimbursement of £10,000 for them, immediately assigning them to the ONR once the directors had acceded to his request. Recorded in the minutes, the locomotives carried the works numbers 1485 to 1488 and bore the names *Cader Idris*, *Glandovey*, *Plynlimon* and *Rheidol* respectively.

Owen, the OEWR's resident engineer, was appointed the ONR's engineer provisionally, without comment, on 24 March 1864. Piercy's dismissal by the AWCR on 4 March must have been a contributory factor to this. On 19 June he was instructed to supply the measurements of works up to the date of his last certificate, the last occasion that he figured in the company's transactions.

Reverting to the MWR, by the end of 1863 the line from Rhayader to Builth had been so close to completion that the directors had decided to defer opening the Llanidloes-Rhayader section, despite it being ready for traffic. An agreement with the ONR completed on 29 January 1864 provided for mutual running powers and facilities with the MWR, guaranteeing through traffic to the ONR valued at £15,000. On 19 February the shareholders were told to look forward to an opening in May.

Tyler inspected the LNR between Llanidloes and Penbontbren, reporting from Shrewsbury on 6 January. This was a portion of single line, about 1½ miles in length, a second line having been built for the MMR. The lines diverged at Penbontbren, the LNR extension running forward as the MWR to Rhayader to the south and the MMR taking a more westerly course. There being no accommodation for passengers at Penbontbren, the extension could not be opened until a portion of the MWR was ready for opening. It had been intended to open them at the same time to Rhayader, but the MWR had withdrawn its notice because movement in an embankment had affected a bridge.

The steepest gradient between Llanidloes and Penbontbren was 1 in 75 and the sharpest curve had a radius of 26 chains. There were two bridges, constructed with cast-iron girders on masonry abutments, with spans of 28ft 9in and 25ft 2in on the skew.

The track was laid with 24-foot 69lb double-head rail, fishplated with suspended wrought-iron plates. The sleepers (8 feet by 10 inches by 5 inches) were placed about 3 feet apart. The rails were laid in cast-iron chairs weighing 21½lb each.

A good deal of fencing was required at Llanidloes station and some at other paces on the line. The wall-plates on which the chairs rested at the side of several drains across the line needed changing for others of more suitable dimensions.

Straining posts of the wire fencing had been used as gate-posts and some gates did not shut properly, so suitable gate-posts needed to be supplied. Shelter and conveniences should be provided on the platform constructed for MWR traffic at Llanidloes. The works were incomplete, so he could not recommend that the line be opened.

On the MWR, opposition to Whalley first manifested itself on 19 February, when Johns made a counter-proposal to his reappointment as chairman. Johns then also tried to restrict his expenses claims.

The LNR shareholders' meeting held in Llanidloes on 26 February was as exciting as the AWCR meeting the day before. Whalley made excuses for refusing Johns's request to exclude non-shareholders from the meeting and sealing the register, preferring to adjourn it. According to Johns, the £25,000 capital that had been created for the MWR investment in 1860 (page 28) had been issued on a deposit of 10 shillings per share in an attempt to create the votes needed for Whalley to control the meeting. The outcome of a court hearing being held in London the same day was awaited to determine if the strangers could stay or should leave.

Why, asked Johns, was it necessary to invest £25,000 just now, when the line was nearly ready to be opened? It was, he said, with £75,000 from the ONR, to finance the Llangurig branch for the benefit of

Whalley's property there, 'a pretty little scheme' that would take South Wales traffic to Aberystwyth without bringing any traffic to the LNR.

He claimed that Whalley opposed the proposed amalgamation to maintain his income. The directors were paid £5 for each board meeting attended, or £1 1s if it was adjourned. By March there had been 94 board meetings; on one day there had been 16 adjournments. Whalley pointed out that as the directors were paid from an allowance voted by the shareholders it made no difference how many meetings were held, but Johns's contention was supported by the secretary. Johns and Gartside also complained of meetings being called at short notice when they could not attend, and of resolutions being altered.

After extensive deliberations, Johns brought the meeting to a close with a set of motions calling for the replacement of Whalley and Lefeaux and the resignations of the other pro-Whalley directors. He had sufficient proxies to get his way and Gartside became chairman.

Nearly a year after Piercy had been asked to report on the MWR materials used by Savin and to arrange for their replacement (page 57), on 27 April the directors were still waiting. They were also waiting for outstanding materials due from the Ebbw Vale Company.

Yolland re-inspected the line from Llanidloes to Penbontbren, reporting from Stoke on 11 August. It was in good order but the gate-posts had not been dealt with. Some fencing at the ends of the station platform was too close to the edge and the wire fencing required intermediate posts. He had informed the resident engineer that providing these small items were dealt with the line could be opened when the MWR was ready. He also required an undertaking that 30lb chairs would be installed on the rail joints within six months.

When the MMR single line was opened it would be better to establish a double junction, he continued, and work the two lines as a single railway rather than work them as single lines by different railway companies. He understood that the Cambrian was precluded from working the line, but the Board of Trade would have to decide which company should provide the undertaking regarding the method of working to be used.

The OEWR had a problem with a legal deadline to deal with when the directors met on 30 May. The solicitor informed them that the two years permitted to purchase the Wem branch land would expire on 7 August. Notices needed to be served on owners and occupiers before that date, yet no plans had been prepared and it could take two months to make them. The branch was included in Savin's contract and the company had an obligation to prepare the plans and acquire the land when required.

Wem branch capital had already been issued and the deposit had not been released. Some of the directors were personally liable for the deposit and there might be other consequences if the powers were allowed to lapse. Savin should arrange for the deposit to be returned and its guarantors should be indemnified against any loss. The amalgamation Bill, the directors thought, should not be allowed to pass the Lords until the deposit had been returned. The surveys should be undertaken and plans prepared, but no notices served until directed.

Legal proceedings against the OEWR were threatened because the purchase of land belonging to a Mr Smith remained incomplete. Savin was responsible for its purchase and on 24 June was told to settle it. The solicitors were instructed to arrange for land currently vested in Savin to be transferred to the company. He was present at the meeting, and was also reminded that the directors' fees had not been paid since December. It sounds as though Savin's financial edifice was creaking. On the annual reports, incidentally, his addresses were given as 40 Hyde Park Square in London, and Plas Fynnon in Oswestry.

ONR dividends due to the OEWR had not been paid. The former's solicitor said that as the amalgamation Bill was awaiting the Royal Assent the matter could be left until the first board meeting of the amalgamated companies. The ONR was told that OEWR shareholders were entitled to the dividends and that the response was unsatisfactory. The reason that the ONR had not paid the dividends would be that Savin had not provided it with the funds to do so.

Tyler inspected the OEWR between Oswestry and Ellesmere, reporting from Shrewsbury on 12 July. The single line was 7¼ miles long with works suitable for a double line. The steepest gradient was 1 in 80. The sharpest curve, near the junction with the ONR at Oswestry, had a 10-chain radius. The track was laid with 70lb double-headed rail in 24-foot lengths. Wrought-iron spikes fixed 24lb 9oz chairs to the sleepers, which were of a minimum section of 9 feet by 40 inches, laid 3 feet apart. A peat bog had given a good deal of trouble in construction but the embankment upon which it was crossed appeared to be in good condition.

There were 15 bridges under and five over the railway, constructed with masonry, brickwork, wrought-iron and timber, the greatest span being 35 feet. There were a few settlement movements in the brickwork and masonry, which would require to be watched, particularly in the cattle creep 2 miles 64 chains from Oswestry.

At the Oswestry junction, the further end of the main-line crossing and both ends of the siding crossing to the main line should be connected with the junction signal box. A short signal with two arms and a lamp was required near the clearing house box to be worked from the junction box to protect the main line from the branch and the sidings during shunting operations. The signalman needed a clock and a desk. No shelter had been provided at Whittington.

A distant signal should be provided in each direction to protect the points and crossing at the Gobowen road bridge near Whittington. The point indicators required adjustment and some of the signals slight improvements. Some fencing was incomplete. Tyler could not therefore recommend the line being used.

Owen submitted an undertaking that the works had been carried out on 20 July and approval was given two days later. On 30 July the *Wrexham Advertiser* reported that the first regular train for Ellesmere and Whitchurch had left Oswestry at 8.10am on 25 July (Monday) with its engine 'gaily dressed'. It arrived back at Oswestry at 10.30am, setting off detonators and carrying passengers bound for the market. The line was the last link in the chain connecting Whitchurch with Aberystwyth and would in future be known as the 'Cambrian Railway'. 'The line was opened for general traffic on Wednesday,' the paper concluded. In a newspaper notice dated 25 July, George Findlay, the general manager and a former Savin employee, announced the opening of the line from 27 July. So, did any trains run on the Tuesday?

According to the *Wrexham Advertiser* on 21 May, the formation had still been incomplete a few weeks before, an embankment at Hardwick taking time to cut through and a pit consuming large quantities of stone before it was stable. Construction activity was close enough to Ellesmere, though, that residents could hear the locomotive whistle. The same paper also reported that on 13 June Job Horton, a construction worker, fell off a wagon on the OEWR near Oswestry and was run over; he was taken to Oswestry for medical intervention, but the outcome was not recorded.

Between May and July, several of the 1863 Bills had been enacted. The LNR's Act of 13 May extended its compulsory purchase powers by a year, repealed its 1859 obligation to subscribe £25,000 in the MWR without invalidating the £10,000 already subscribed, and authorised £25,000 additional capital. The OEWR's Act, of 23 June, merely authorised a further £100,000.

The AWCR's General Act, 30 June, authorised the acquisition of additional land at Ynys Las, level crossings at Llanbadarn and Towyn, £300,000 capital, £100,000 additional investment by the ONR, imposed an obligation to install a pedestrian footbridge over the railway at

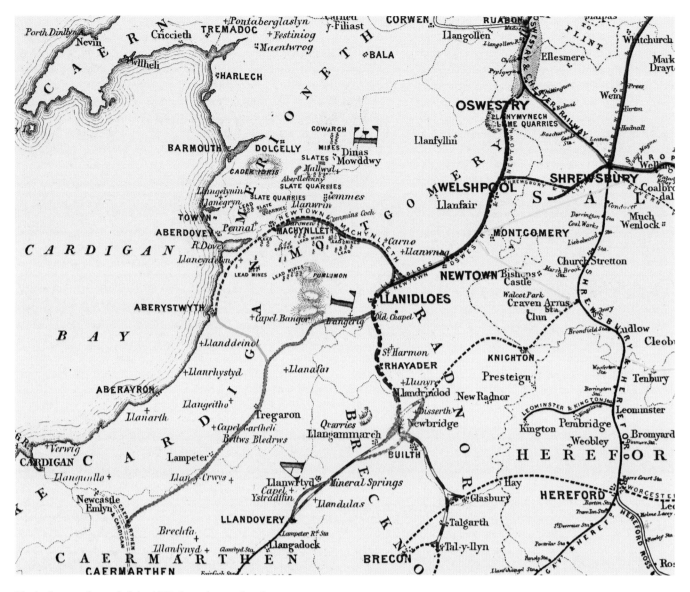

Llanbadarn, and repealed the 1861 clause instructing the company not to build railway No 1 more expeditiously than railways Nos 2 and 3.

The MWR's Act, also 30 June, authorised a junction with the Central Wales Railway, road diversions and crossings, the erection of hotels on surplus land sold by the company, and a 21-year lease by Watson and Overend.

The ONR's first Act, dated 14 July, authorised the company to invest up to £50,000 in the Bishop's Castle Railway. The interest in the BCR stemmed from a strategy intended to make a route from the ONR near Montgomery to the Shrewsbury & Hereford Railway that avoided the LNWR. The BCR's promoters included Whalley, Lefeaux and two other ONR directors. Savin was its contractor; he had already stopped work on it (page 58).

The ONR's second Act, the Oswestry & Newtown and other railway companies (arrangements) Act of 25 July, sanctioned the ONR's agreements with the LNWR and allowed the LNR, OEWR, NMR, Hereford, Hay & Brecon Railway and Brecon & Merthyr Tydfil Junction Railway to be party to them.

The SWR's transfer Act also received the Royal Assent on 14 July, whereby the LNWR or the LNWR and GWR jointly were allowed to lease or purchase it. Notwithstanding the leasing powers, the LNWR had agreed to purchase the SWR for £300,000 4% perpetual preference stock. If, however, the lease or sale was completed with the LNWR, the GWR could become joint lessee or owner within 12 months. Article 36 protected the ONR's LNWR rebate if traffic was diverted to the GWR because of the change of ownership.

Extract from a map retained with Mid Wales Railway papers. The lime-green lines indicate proposed routes from Montgomery that upset Savin because they put the LNWR rebate at risk; they were sketched in in pencil on the original document. The Manchester & Milford Railway route between Strata Florida and Aberystwyth is shown in green.
*National Archives*

The Cambrian Railways Act received the Royal Assent on 25 July. The ONR, LNR, NMR and OEWR companies were immediately dissolved and constituted in a single undertaking, and the existing shareholders of those companies were united and incorporated under the name of the Cambrian Railways Company. The AWCR shareholders had been told that their railway had been excluded from the amalgamation because their line remained incomplete.

The existing capital, tabulated at £1,275,000, was designated preference stock in the amalgamated company, but the holders would only receive their interest if the railway in which they had originally invested had earned it.

Provision was made for the mutual exchange of traffic with the MWR, MMR and GWR. If the combined company ever took over the management of the MWR, the joint line and station at Llanidloes would be jointly vested in the company and the MMR.

The Cambrian Railways directors met for the first time in Welshpool on 29 July, and the first proprietors' meeting was held in London on 13 August.

# Interlude: Into Mid Wales

ABOVE Like much of the Mid Wales Railway, Tylwch served a thinly-spread rural community. It is best remembered for the accident that occurred on 16 September 1899. An up excursion train overran the home signal and collided with the down mail that was standing in the loop. One passenger was killed and five were slightly injured. The driver said that his brakes had failed and the station master said that it had been his practice to set the up facing points for the down road when accepting down trains, because he thought he could not lower the down home signal unless he did so. Colonel Yorke blamed the driver for assuming that the home would change when the distant was against him, so braking too late, and the guard for being unaware of what was happening and not being in a position to apply the handbrake. The company, he suggested, should provide an extra man at the station on the rare occasion that passenger trains crossed there. *John Alsop collection*

BELOW Some idea of the grandeur of the Mid Wales Railway can be had from this view of the line to the north of Tylwch; the home signal is in the lower left corner. The gradient is falling at 1 in 111 towards Penbontbren and Llanidloes. *John Ellis*

ABOVE Pantydwr was, at 941 feet, the highest station on the MWR/Cambrian, and 6 feet below the summit. Situated 7 ¼ miles from Llanidloes, its bay window was obviously designed to enable observation without going outside. *Wallace Jones/John Alsop collection*

BELOW Fourteen miles from Llanidloes, Rhayader was kept busy with Birmingham Corporation's Elan reservoir traffic. Locomotive water was provided to both platforms. The goods yard, to the left, was connected at both ends. *J. Roberts*

ABOVE South of Rhayader, the MWR joined the Wye valley, sharing it with the river and the road, seen here at Glaslyn.

BELOW By the time it had reached Newbridge-on-Wye, 21¼ miles, the MWR was 407 feet closer to sea level. The station was adjacent to the village it served. *A. Pritchard/John Alsop collection*

ABOVE Aberedw, 30¾ miles, was south of Builth Wells and barely rated the station appellation given to it, the traffic only warranting a small office and waiting shelter. A level crossing justified the employment of staff to work the signals if a train was required to stop. *John Alsop collection*

MIDDLE Three Cocks, 40 ½ miles, was the junction with the Midland Railway's route from Hereford. The publisher of this busy scene thought that some explanation was required, but while the trains were heading in the general direction of the places indicated it is unlikely that the Midland train was going to Birmingham, that the northbound Cambrian train was going to Aberystwyth and that No 68 was going beyond Brecon. *John Alsop collection*

LEFT Unlike other MWR stations, Talgarth was built of stone. As at Rhayader, a large water tank enabled locomotives to take water in each direction. Like Newbridge-on-Wye, the station was also convenient for the village.

RIGHT Talgarth was also the subject of a humorous postcard. The product of a Liverpool publisher, the backdrop appears to be on the Wirral Railway. *Everton Series*

*Arrived Safely at Talgarth*

# 3

# The collapse of the contractors 1864-1869

Twelve years after Whalley had called the meeting in Llanidloes, his dream of connecting the English North West with the port of Milford Haven via Montgomeryshire under a single operator was almost fulfilled. The north-south railway from Whitchurch to Llanidloes was open and would soon be connected to the south by an associate. On the east-west axis the newly formed Cambrian combined with its Aberystwyth & Welsh Coast subordinate and the nominally independent Shrewsbury & Welshpool Railway linked the English Midlands with the Welsh coast. Having got so far, and been a driving force behind the development of the Montgomeryshire railways and their associates, it is no small irony that Whalley himself had been kicked out.

Of the amalgamation, the *Railway Times* said on 20 August 1864 that investment in Welsh railways would not become general and popular until Whalley had been perpetually banished from the slightest interference with their management. The Cambrian had done its duty in this respect, and the AWCR had spoken out; it remained for the MWR and 'one or two other adventurers to do likewise… The process of purgation is not yet complete.'

The Cambrian Railways crest.

The greatest problem to be faced by the Cambrian was the overwhelming debt it had inherited. It was never going to be completely eliminated and the company's options were always to be constrained by it.

The Cambrian's first shareholders' report, on 23 July, had been a substantial attack on Whalley and the 'majority' directors. Engineers'

reports were submitted for three of the constituents. For the ONR, Owen said that water tanks and columns had been erected at the principal stations and that satisfactory progress was being made with Welshpool station. For the OEWR, Piercy said that sidings, turntable and station accommodation had been provided at Whitchurch, Bettisfield station had been finished and a goods shed provided, and at Ellesmere two platforms and extra sidings had been built. The permanent stations had yet to be built at Whittington and Welshampton, and Savin was still required to build two cottages in the yard at Ellesmere. The telegraph was still to be erected. For the NMR, Owen added that additional wharves and sidings for mineral traffic had been added and permanent stations with residences erected 'at all places along the line'.

No attempt had been made to combine the finances of the four companies. Only the ONR submitted audited accounts, with the auditors expressing concern about items in the capital account that should have been in the revenue account and vice versa. Rent charges should be capitalised as they reduced the company's borrowing powers. The revenue account was under Savin's control, of course. The LNR and OEWR submitted simple balance sheets, while the NMR submitted an account of capital and income as guaranteed by the ONR.

Whalley was confident, when the MWR shareholders met on 2 August 1864, that the inspection scheduled for 8 August would be successful and that soon afterwards traffic would be flowing between

Crewe and Merthyr Tydfil. He paid tribute to the contractors, saying that since he had been chairman there had been no dispute, either with them or at board level, conveniently overlooking the furore he had himself caused at the first sod ceremony. He forecast great things for the company. If the ONR could pay up to 7% competing with a canal to Newtown and a railway to Welshpool, then the MWR should do at least as well, for it had no such competition.

At this point construction had cost £638,777 4s, including £37,060 18s 8d spent on Parliamentary expenses, £64,838 7s on land and £15,000 paid to Savin for procuring the Parliamentary deposit. The company was heavily in debt, its share capital of £401,114 being outweighed by borrowing totalling £409,500. Watson had been asked to submit his proposal for working the line and, in the meantime, he and Overend were appointed managers; a lease was to be completed on 22 March 1865, when a Frederick Broughton was proposed as the contractors' general manager.

Yolland made his inspection on 8-9 August 1864, reporting from Stoke on the 11th. The distance between Penbontbren and the junction with the Brecon & Merthyr Railway at Bryn y Derwyn was 46 miles 66 chains. The line was single-track throughout with sidings or portions of double track at stations. Land had been purchased and overbridges built for double track.

The Mid Wales Railway crest.

The formation was 18 feet wide, except in rock cuttings where it was 15 feet. The rail was 70lb double-headed in 24-foot, 21-foot and 18-foot lengths, except on bridges and viaducts where flat-bottom rail was used. The chairs weighed 22lb, fixed to larch and Baltic pine sleepers (9 feet by 9 inches by 5 or 4½ inches) with iron spikes. The sleepers were spaced at 2ft 2in at joints and 3ft 2in or 3ft 3in elsewhere – one gets the impression that Yolland had a tape measure with him on this inspection – although broken stone or gravel ballast was 'stated to be' 10 inches deep below the sleepers.

There were 19 overbridges and 42 underbridges in addition to 30 viaducts and two tunnels, 369½ and 70 yard in length. The bridges and viaducts were almost entirely constructed with masonry abutments and with masonry or brick arches. Wrought-iron girders were used on the underbridges and viaducts.

The most important structure, Yolland reported, was a lattice girder bridge with a clear span of 191 feet above the River Wye at Boughrwd. The next largest structure was a wrought-iron girder with a 59-foot skew span, also crossing the Wye.

The whole of the works were fully executed, especially as regards the ironwork, although on the lattice bridge the strain on the iron with a load of locomotives covering the whole of the 191 feet somewhat exceeded the 5 tons per square inch maximum weight it was designed to carry. The bridge was a good one, however, and deflected about 1½ inches when loaded with more than 200 tons of rolling stock.

Although the line was well executed there were many outstanding tasks. He mentioned fences, signal levers, distant signals, platforms, clocks, tunnel drainage, facing points, facing point indicators, a catch siding and chock blocks. Station buildings and platforms were incomplete. Tie rods were required to restrain the baulks on timber bridges, and the 12-inch baulks installed on a bridge with a 12-foot span needed to be replaced with 14-inch timbers. Modifications were needed to two of the iron viaducts.

The track was too light for some of the gradients, he thought, and 30lb chairs should be installed at joints and in the middle of each rail.

He was prepared to allow 12 months for this to be done providing the company gave an undertaking to carry it out. South of Builth the track seemed to have been laid more quickly than elsewhere, and needed lifting and packing. Throughout the line the transitions between rails laid on transverse and longitudinal sleepers, used on plain line and bridges respectively, required attention.

The steepest gradient was 1 in 60 and the sharpest curve 18 chains; there were many curves of 21-chain radius. After the line was opened the track would need to be closely watched as the ballast in some parts was not good. Speed would need to be moderated until the embankments had consolidated.

A turntable had not been installed at Three Cocks, and one would be required if trains terminated at Bryn y Derwyn. Finally, repeating signals that rang a bell at the station were objectionable, as the bell could ring without the arm rising to danger.

As might be expected with such a long list of requirements, Yolland was not prepared to sanction the MWR's opening.

He conducted his second inspection on 9 September, reporting from Sandown, Isle of Wight, the next day. John Wade, the MWR's secretary, had given him an undertaking, dated 6 September, regarding fences, crossing gates and heavier chairs. The first two were to be completed by the end of the year, the last within 12 months of opening. The junction signals were complete except for about 24 hours' work at Talyllyn; some of the distant signals still required moving. In 1872 Wade became secretary of the Potteries, Shrewsbury & North Wales Railway.

Heavy rain was said to have caused a wing wall on an underbridge at Newbridge to collapse the previous night. The stability of the arch was unaffected but it would need watching. The junction with the Brecon & Merthyr Railway should be altered to a double line if it was to be used regularly.

Because of the steep gradients, the MWR should not use staff-and-ticket working, where a second train was allowed to follow the first 5 minutes later. Yolland recommended, however, that the railway be allowed to open using this system provided the telegraph was installed and used to report the arrival of the first train at the next station. The old system would have to be abandoned and traffic controlled by the telegraph on the block system within two months. He required an undertaking to this effect, and for the installation of a turntable at Bryn y Derwyn.

Yolland found nothing amiss with the connection to the Hereford, Hay & Brecon Railway at Three Cocks. It was 36½ chains long and could be opened as soon as approval had been given to the opening of the HHBR extension. The Three Cocks turntable was ready for use. Wade gave all the required undertakings on 12 September.

The first MWR public trains ran on 21 September 1864, a Wednesday, apparently without ceremony. A timetable notice published in the *Manchester Guardian* on 19 September was signed by the general manager, J. A. Jebb. Three trains each day were advertised, with connections from as far away as Liverpool and Dowlais. The shareholders were told on 27 February 1865 that the line was initially worked at a disadvantage owing to the difficulty in obtaining sufficient locomotives, although there was 'an abundant supply of rolling stock'; £60,091 16s had been spent on rolling stock, presumably including locomotives, by the end of the year.

There were soon complaints, a clergyman, Reverend Hugh Bold, writing about late running on 8 October. Wade was instructed to obtain further information about the causes and obtain 'statements as to the officers or servants responsible when delay originates on Mid Wales line, and in case of other companies, which.'

The first Cambrian directors' meeting minuted had been held on 13 August. Vane was elected chairman and Johns his deputy. Gartside and Tootal were also present, together with Robert Davies Pryce of Cyfronydd, near Welshpool, a founding director of the NMR. George Lewis was appointed company secretary.

The seals of the constituent companies were to be destroyed with the exception of the NMR's, which was given to Vane. William Watkin Edward Wynne (1801-80), MP for Merionethshire, had voluntarily submitted a design for a combined seal that was accepted and engraved.

The corporation and inhabitants of Welshpool, having submitted 'memorials' calling for the company's workshops to be established at that place, were informed that arrangements had already been made for them to be at Oswestry. Savin was instructed to produce plans, a specification and estimates.

After a board meeting on 2 September, Piercy was told that his services were no longer required on the OEWR and that he was to hand over all plans, sections, drawings and other documents relating to the constituent companies that he had worked for.

A flag station at Bryngwyn on the Llanfyllin branch was accepted as the price to pay for a Mrs Williams, presumably a landowner, withdrawing her claim for a permanent station there; Owen produced plans and an estimate of £145 6s 2d for it. Works in progress were Welshpool, Moat Lane and Machynlleth stations and the road bridge at Welshpool.

On 14 September the directors met at the Cambrian Hotel at Borth, an enterprise designed to bring business to the railway. They were inclined to make a contract with Savin to build the workshops according to Owen's plans and to his estimate of £35,000, the equipment to be supplied on the same basis as the rolling stock, but they decided to employ a consultant to assess if the expenditure would meet the company's requirements and if the works could be undertaken for the estimate.

Appointments and salaries were set for officers: Lewis (secretary) £700; David Howell (solicitor) £1,000; Owen (engineer) £600. The directors' salary was reduced to £2,000 from the constituents' £2,550.

Savin's claim for £45,000 for work carried out on the ONR up to January 1864 was settled with preference shares and debentures on 13 October. He undertook to indemnify the company against any claims made by Piercy in respect of his ONR work. Piercy's claim for £1,677 19s incurred on NMR work was accepted by the company on 17 December, providing he handed over all plans and documents in his possession.

Meeting on 26 October 1864, the general purposes and parliamentary committee resolved to seek new powers: to lease the undertaking to Savin, the LNWR or the GWR; to abandon the Wem branch; to construct wharves at Aberdovey, Cerrig y Penrhyn and Ynys Las, and to operate steamboats between them and Ireland; to purchase the ferry tolls at Aberdovey and Barmouth; to purchase the Corris Railway; to amalgamate the AWCR; and to alter advertising provisions relating to the placing of legal notices.

When it came to it, the Bills were slightly different. Under the heading 'Coast Extension', powers were sought for a line called the Morben Railway, from a junction at Morben, on the south bank of the Dovey, nearly 4 miles from Machynlleth, to a junction at Penhelig, near Aberdovey, and for another called the Mindovey Railway, from a junction by the Corbett Arms at Aberdovey to the proposed Penhelig junction, and for an embankment with wharves and quays with a railway or tramway thereon at Aberdovey. Both lines would be in addition to the existing AWCR, including the bridge, not in substitution to it.

The designer of the Cambrian's crest, William Watkin Edward Wynne MP, was sent this impression of it.
*Sara Eade collection*

A second Bill, for additional powers, dealt with the Wem branch, leasing agreements and additional capital, while a third dealt with the AWCR amalgamation.

The AWCR's main 1864 Bill, No 1, dealt with deviations at Aberdovey, Barmouth and Penrhyndeudraeth and extensions to Portmadoc harbour and Aberdovey, and Cerrig y Penrhyn, on the southern shore of the Dovey. It also wished to use the Traeth Bach embankment for ordinary road traffic; to purchase ferries, the Corris Railway and the inner harbour at Portmadoc, and to construct wharves and a swing bridge there; to construct a quay at Aberdovey and wharves at Ynys Las; and to carry passengers on the Corris Railway using locomotives. It required additional capital and approval for the Cambrian to appoint two directors.

The Aberdovey deviation was in substitution of the original bridge, the result of Savin's objection to its cost; just over 5 miles long, it included three tunnels of 141, 187 and 182 yards in length. The Corris, Machynlleth, Aberdovey & Towyn Railway's Bill, deposited in 1852, would have taken a similar route along the bank of the Dovey had it come to fruition. The civil engineer Thomas Elliott Harrison (1808-88) was appointed to give his opinion on the replacement bridge. The AWCR also wanted a line from the Corbett Arms at Aberdovey to Penhelig, which it called 'a railway or tramway'.

The AWCR also resubmitted a steamboats Bill, an 1863 Bill having been withdrawn because there had been a feeling in Parliament that railway companies should not run shipping services; second thoughts now prevailed.

The apparent duplication by the AWCR and the Cambrian probably arose from the knowledge that sooner or later they were to be amalgamated, the outcome of the amalgamation Bill influencing the Bills that went forward. The Barmouth and Penrhyndeudraeth deviations were the result of Conybeare's appointment.

Other Bills deposited during the same session were for the Talyllyn Railway and the Mawddwy Railway. As a narrow-gauge line, the former was always a client of the Cambrian, but the latter, branching from the Cambrian at Cemmaes Road, had a tortuous and impecunious history before it came under the Cambrian's wing. A Bill for the Croesor & Portmadoc Railway, to sanction the maintenance and public use of part of a 2-foot-gauge tramway that connected the Croesor quarries with Portmadoc harbour, the line having been built earlier in 1864, was also deposited.

Earlier, the AWCR board had been unhappy with Conybeare's application for payment of £1,000 for three months' work. Agreeing to pay it on 26 August, the directors also decided to give him one month's notice to terminate the contract in order to rearrange its terms. On 14 September payments already made to him were deducted from payments due to Savin, whose contract had still not been settled.

Proposed lines affecting the AWCR prompted a meeting between two directors, Savin and Charles Easton Spooner, the Festiniog

Railway's secretary and engineer, on 14 October. The routes were Bala to Festiniog and Portmadoc; Carnarvon to Beddgelert and Portmadoc; and Portmadoc to Beddgelert and the South Snowdon slate quarries. Bills for the Beddgelert Railway and the Carnarvon, Beddgelert & Port Madoc and Carnarvon, Pen y Groes & Pwllheli Direct Railways were deposited in December.

The MWR also deposited a Bill for new lines called the 'western extensions', from Marteg to a point on the MMR 8 miles from Aberystwyth, in the Ystwyth valley, a spur to the MMR at Llagurig, and a line from Rhayader to the Central Wales Railway near Cross Gates. It also wanted to abandon the 1863 Llangurig branch in its entirety.

While all this legal activity was in progress, the first sod of the Carnarvonshire Railway was dug by William Roberts, the AWCR's secretary, at Penygroes on 14 December 1864. The *North Wales Chronicle*, reporting the occasion on 17 December, did not think to mention that he was also the CR's secretary, or that he performed the same function for the Beddgelert Railway come to that. Spooner and John Savin were among the guests.

Appointed the CR's engineer on 19 May 1863, Piercy was dismissed on 23 March 1864 and replaced by Spooner on 29 October. Under the CR heading, the *North Wales Chronicle* had noted the letting of the first contract on 9 November, when John Savin had appointed

Portmadoc contractors named Mackenzie and Williams to construct the low embankment from the Glaslyn to Ynysgalch, the site of the station. 100 men were working on the contract by the end of the month but on 4 February 1865 the Welsh navvies forced their Irish counterparts to leave the site, because they were Irish. The contractors were inclined to take action against the culprits. Construction of the CR from Afon Wen towards Pant Glas was reported as starting on 6 January 1865 and there was activity at Wern, between Portmadoc and Pentrefelin, by February.

The Beddgelert Railway was another Savin venture in Portmadoc. The first sod ceremony was performed in the Traeth by Allen Searell, manager of the South Snowdon quarry, intended to be served by the railway, on 23 February 1865.

On 24 February Cambrian shareholders were told that receipts since the amalgamation were nearly £10,000. Effort had been directed towards unifying the defunct companies' accounts. In modern

A plan of the Aberystwyth & Welsh Coast Railway's Morben Railway and Mindovey Railway, 1865. Piercy's intended Dovey crossing is shown between Ynys Las and Aberdovey. The Mindovey Railway took the railway between the town and the foreshore; it was to be taken behind the town, requiring three tunnels. *Parliamentary Archives*

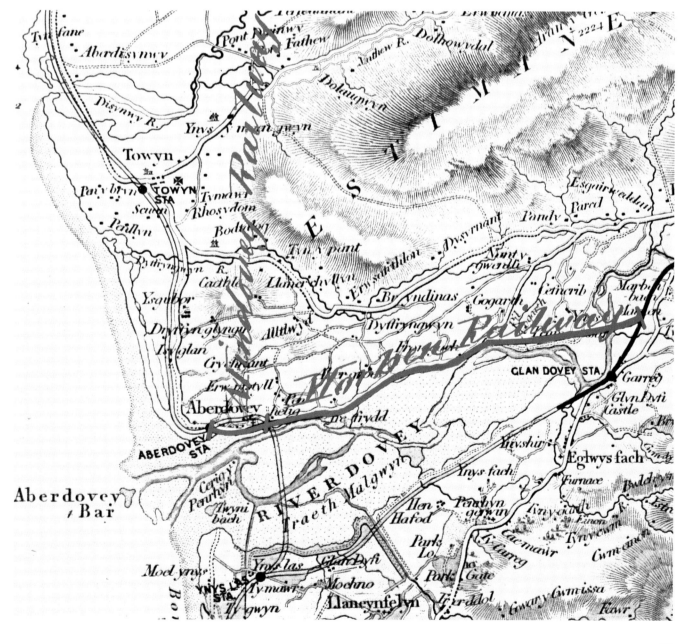

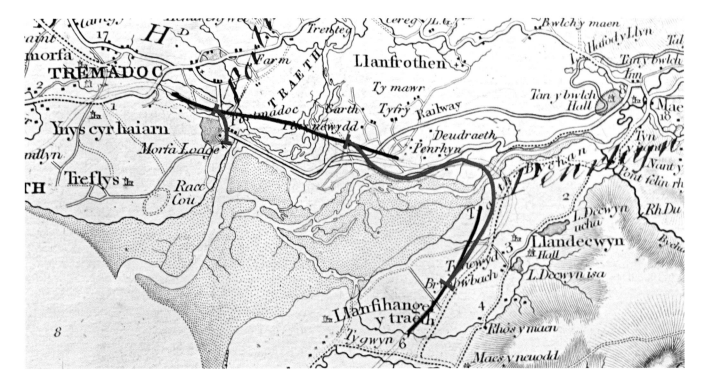

language, systems were being standardised across the company – it took four lines to say that in 1865.

The expense, delay and inconvenience of sending rolling stock away for repair had induced the company to erect the workshops at Oswestry. A station was proposed for Newtown. The 'extension' from Machynlleth to Aberdovey would improve the connection to the coast.

Savin's 10-year lease, backdated to 1 July 1864, guaranteed a 5% dividend instead of the variable amounts of the previous agreements. The auditors, however, pointed out that the agreement had still not been completed and signed. They also observed that Savin had not paid £1,405 5s due to the ONR for payments made on the revenue account six months previously, and that he now owed another £1,100 5s 7d on the same account.

One of the shareholders, a former director, complained about the preference being given to a station at Newtown. His station, Montgomery, was likely to be a junction [with the Bishop's Castle Railway], yet it had the most miserable accommodation, and ladies often complained about it. Was there any possibility of having a station built there? The workshops, he thought, should have been at Welshpool or Newtown. Was there any guarantee that Savin would honour the dividend guarantee? The promised link with the LNWR dividend had already been broken.

At the AWCR meeting the day before, shareholders were told that the Aberystwyth line was joined and worked in connection with the Cambrian and Corris railways – how many of them knew that the latter was not the same gauge? The isolated section was expected to be extended to Friog and Penmaenpool within a few weeks. Most of the land required between Barmouth and Portmadoc had been obtained and work was already in progress between Portmadoc and Pwllheli. Conybeare added that the Mawddach viaduct was 'in progress and under contract to be finished in April next'. Of the section at Friog, where the railway ran on a ledge cut into the cliff, he merely remarked that it was the heaviest work on the line.

More detail of the progress of works around Barmouth was published in the *North Wales Chronicle* on 28 February 1865. The bridge had been started from both ends and W. Owen of Tremadoc was engaged in making the rock cutting in the town. Four miles of track had been laid on the town side of the estuary and a locomotive

*The Aberystwyth & Welsh Coast Railway's deposited plan shows the deviation at Penrhyndeudraeth and the Portmadoc public wharf branch in 1865. The Penrhyndeudraeth deviation appears to have reduced the length of the river crossing and the need for a tunnel under the Festiniog Railway at Minffordd. Parliamentary Archives*

had been put to work. On 4 April the paper reported the arrival of the first steam locomotive at Penmaenpool on 18 March, when the Manning, Wardle 0-6-0ST *Cardigan* hauled a wagon-load of Ruabon coal for delivery to the Ship Hotel. Savin accompanied the train and no doubt arranged for the band and the crowd that greeted it.

Despite previously having agreed to purchase the Corris Railway, on 27 January the AWCR had still not received the draft working agreement. Given Savin's reluctance to complete agreements, this may not be too surprising. By 23 February the construction contract was still awaiting the schedule of prices for extra works.

Working its way through a list of Bills passing through Parliament, on 22 March the AWCR decided to petition against the Beddgelert Railway Bill until protective clauses had been inserted. It also decided to offer both the Beddgelert and Croesor companies the 'privilege' of running into its Portmadoc station, its motive being to monopolise non-Festiniog traffic to the harbour.

Clarification of the AWCR's position regarding the Corris Railway was recorded on 26 April. A resolution of 23 February, guaranteeing debenture interest and dividends, was rescinded in favour of a decision to purchase the railway for £21,000 in preference shares, rolling stock put on the line by Savin to be taken at valuation.

Tyler reported on the Llwyngwril-Penmaenpool section from Aberystwyth on 29 June. The railway was 9 miles 32.8 chains long, comprising 3 miles 65 chains continuation from Llwyngwril to the junction of the line to Barmouth with the branch to Dolgelley, and 5 miles 47.8 chains from the junction to the temporary terminus at Penmaenpool. A greater part of the line between Penmaenpool and Dolgelley was already completed but work had been stopped until a dispute over land had been settled.

Some of the works were very heavy, particularly the rock cuttings winding round the sides of the hills. The cutting sides seemed very solid although Tyler drew attention to some loose pieces that should be removed. The steepest gradient was 1 in 58 and the sharpest curve had a 13-chain radius. The company should use continuous brakes on its passenger trains.

The brick arch built on the skew at 2 miles 2 chains (from Llwyngwril), which crossed the turnpike road from Friog to Barmouth Ferry, was considerably out of shape but was stated to have been in its current position since February 1863. It should be watched to assess the effect of regular traffic. With the exception of one span of 40 feet crossed by wrought-iron girders, the bridges and viaducts were principally of timber. He recommended that more transoms and cross ties should be inserted to connect the longitudinal sleepers together on some of these bridges as a precaution, and that in one case pieces of boiler-plate 4 feet long and connected with screw bolts should be added to both sides of a scarfed joint in the timber that had a corbel under it.

The permanent way and fencing was similar to those already used in other portions of the line. The track would require extra maintenance over certain parts, where it crossed a peat bog. Some of the rails should be straightened. If Llwyngwril should become a crossing place, which was not contemplated, he said that a second platform would be required.

The Dolgelley branch junction had been supplied with locking apparatus and the usual signals. It was at present a single-line junction only, but a triangle was to be formed in connection with it, with a double line on all its sides. A distant signal should be installed on the Barmouth side immediately as it would be used for the conveyance of materials to the new works.

Subject to the conditions mentioned, the line could be brought into use. The single line working undertaking was given on 30 June.

The AWCR directors had recorded nothing about work having stopped on the Dolgelley branch, nor did reports on legal issues concerning land give any information about the location. The notice sanctioning the opening was dispatched to the AWCR's London office on 5 July and the extension was opened on the same date. Tyler must have intimated that his report would be positive because, reported the *Chester Chronicle* on 8 July, crowds had started to gather at 3.00am to see the first departure at 6.30am.

Two Cambrian Acts received the Royal Assent on 5 July. The key points of the additional powers Act were the Wem branch abandonment, the agreement for working the AWCR transferred to Savin, and the lease of the undertaking to Savin.

The Cambrian/AWCR amalgamation Act dissolved the AWCR one month after the assent, when its undertaking would be amalgamated with the Cambrian. AWCR stock would become part of Cambrian stock with the same status, but was to be kept separately.

The AWCR general powers Act was also enacted on 5 July. The branch that it sanctioned to Cerrig y Penrhyn, opposite Aberdovey, had already been made by Savin without approval and had been the subject of complaints. Among other powers, the Traeth Bach bridge was to be made accessible to pedestrians.

The inner harbour at Portmadoc could be acquired and completed and the 'existing stone bridge' at the entrance to the harbour converted into a swing or draw bridge. Clauses protected the rights of Charles Capper and Alfred Brett, owners of the Frongoch quarry near Aberdovey, and the Festiniog Railway. The Aberdovey deviation's bridge over the Dovey was to include an opening span of not less than 35 feet.

Section 14 of the Corris Railway's 1864 Act, which prohibited the carriage of passengers and speeds greater than 10mph, was repealed. By agreement with their owners, the Dovey and Mawddach ferries could be purchased.

A few days before, on 27 June, the locomotive *Merion*, a Manning, Wardle 0-6-0ST, had been delivered to Barmouth from Aberdovey by

sea. The locomotive was erected and made its first trip towards Portmadoc the next day, driven by George Gutheridge, with Savin and others, including the *North Wales Chronicle*'s reporter, on the footplate. Written as though the locomotive was the first at Barmouth, this report contradicts that of 28 February cited earlier (page 75).

Faced with the imminent dissolution of the company, on 29 July the AWCR directors decided to do something about Savin's contract, deferred at their request. Having consulted with Conybeare, they decided that the mileage rate should be fixed at £17,500, including all legal and Parliamentary expenses and the completion of the authorised works up to Board of Trade approval.

The last business conducted by the AWCR was an extraordinary meeting held on 1 August, when authority was given to create £120,000 5% preference stock and £40,000 loan stock. In March it had spent half of its capital and had only been able to continue by calling on the Cambrian to exercise its right to subscribe £100,000, £75,000 in preference stock being subscribed. Roberts, the secretary, remained in post until 6 October, when Lewis took over.

Owen's Cambrian report on 24 January 1865 had highlighted one of the problems arising from inter-operability before standards on rolling stock and clearances had been settled. The LNWR had sent a cattle truck, larger than those of the Cambrian, to a fair at Welshpool. When it was being pulled out of the Smithfield siding it struck a large iron entrance gate and pulled it away, demolishing a length of iron railings and copings as it did so. The gateway had been made in accordance with Piercy's plans and would cost £36 to repair.

Rail between Oswestry and Weston wharf, the oldest on the ONR, had been replaced by 11 February because it was delaminating. Owen planned to relay between Weston and Llynclys during the spring, but on 9 March he informed the board that it would be necessary to replace it as far as Buttington, 11½ miles, before the summer traffic started or it would quickly become unsafe.

This extract from the detailed plan for the Portmadoc public wharf branch shows the extent of the proposed expansion of the inner harbour. The routes of the Croesor Tramway, Festiniog Railway and Gorseddau Tramway have been added in blue, yellow and green respectively. *Parliamentary Archives*

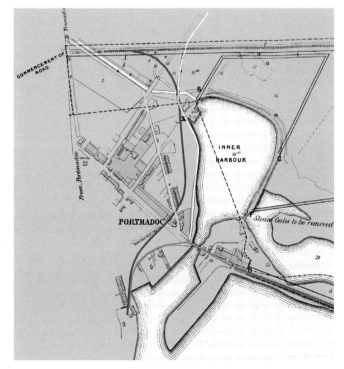

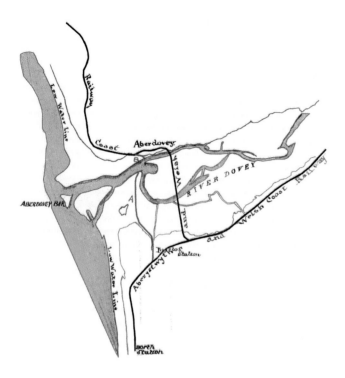

A sketch showing the lines built by Savin on either side of the Dovey that were the subject of complaints because they were beyond the limits of deviation. *National Archives*

Recommending doubling the track between Llanymynech and Buttington and between Newtown and Moat Lane, Owen quoted for doubling to Pool Quay, £12,500, and thence to Buttington, £14,382 6s 7d; the former was cheaper because the bridges would not need altering and the embankments would not need much work. The timber bridges were in good condition and he recommended leaving this section until the bridges needed renewing.

Owen thought that doubling between Newtown and Moat Lane should have a higher priority, although his estimate for the 4½ miles was £26,859 5s, the greater expense due to two river crossings and other bridges; material for widening the embankments could be taken out of the cuttings. The directors approved both sections on 29 August, instructing Owen to proceed with doubling the OEWR section as well.

Earlier in the year, Findlay had left to work for the LNWR. More than 600 people contributed to a testimonial, raising £180 to present him with five oil paintings at an event held in Oswestry on 30 January.

Ardleen station was destroyed by an arsonist on 3 February. Discovering that the stations were not insured, the secretary was instructed to take appropriate action.

An ongoing issue concerned the rolling stock agreement that Savin had not completed. Considering his request for payment of £11,816 0s 9d due to him on this account on 24 March, the Cambrian resolved to make the payment conditional on him executing the working agreement and giving security for £45,000 on certain property. This did the trick, and by 30 March Savin had completed both agreements and given the security.

Owen reported the arrival of three new locomotives on 24 April: 2-4-0s No 47 *Usk* and No 48 *Wye* were for passenger work and cost £2,491 each, while 0-6-0 No 49 *Snowdon*, £2,719, was 'a heavy goods engine'; all had been built by Sharp, Stewart; Owen was to have them marked with the company's name and registered in the rolling stock register. No instruction was issued in respect of Owen's report that No 4 *Wynnstay*, an 0-4-2 passenger locomotive built for the LNR in 1859,

was unsuitable for the Cambrian's curves and gradients and that the Brecon & Merthyr Railway was interested in buying it; its book value was £2,555. *Harlech*, another goods engine, had been delivered via Savin by 27 June.

After some badgering, Piercy handed over the constituent companies' plans and documents that he had held by 26 May, releasing £1,677 19s owed to him for NMR work.

Settlement of the constituents' affairs continued for some time, mostly related to land purchases, but Savin's claim for £86,032 1s 4d for OEWR work required an investigation that took until 28 July to complete. Johns and Gartside, as former OEWR directors, thought that £78,407 1s 4d in full settlement up to 26 May was a fair sum. By 24 November Savin had only £3,500 of OEWR liabilities to settle.

Summarising the company's position for the shareholders at Borth on 29 August, Vane observed that it had a continuous railway 106 miles long from Whitchurch to Aberystwyth fully operational, together with 20 miles opened of the 62-mile route from Morben to Porthdinlleyn and the branches to Porthywaen, the Llanymynech rocks, Llanfyllin, Kerry and Dolgelley adding another 23 miles, 191 miles in all. Works on the line between Barmouth Ferry station and the viaducts over the Mawddach, Dwryd and Glaslyn were sufficiently advanced for him to forecast the line being opened in the spring of 1866. The Aberdovey deviation had been started.

Conybeare added that the foundations and superstructure had been fixed for 2,200 feet of the 2,420-foot waterway length of the Barmouth viaduct, the principal work of the line.

By 30 September eight locomotives had been hired to what Owen called 'the South Wales lines'. They were *Wynnstay*, *Montgomery*, *Glansevern*, *Llanerchydol* and *Leighton*, all LNR Sharp, Stewart 0-4-2s, *Hercules* and *Vulcan*, ONR Sharp, Stewart 0-6-0s, and *Cyfronydd*, an NMR Sharp, Stewart 0-6-0.

Two days before, Owen had been asked to explain why the company's rolling stock had been seen at work on other lines. On 6 October Savin was told that hiring stock out was contrary to the terms of his agreement with the company and that its use should be confined to the company's lines. He explained that any company would hire stock to its neighbour; he was hiring it out for his benefit, of course, not the company's.

*Llanerchydol* had been returned when Owen reported on 21 October, and *Wye* and *Usk* had been transferred to the Hereford, Hay & Brecon Railway. Owen continued that they had been replaced by 'two new first class passenger engines named *Gladstone* and *Palmerston*'. These had arrived in Oswestry on 3 October and 12 October respectively and were 'fitted with all the most recent improvements'.

Carriages had also strayed, the Denbigh, Ruthin & Corwen Railway using three composites, six 3rd class, a passenger van and a goods brake. Ten wagons were also in Denbighshire. Owen had arranged for plates reading 'Hired only to the Denbigh, Ruthin & Corwen Railway' to be fitted in addition to the company's ownership plates.

Extension of the system by means of further amalgamations had been proposed by 28 October 1865, the projected constituents being the Carnarvonshire, Nantlle, Beddgelert and Corris railways. The same Bill also sought running powers over the LNWR from Whitchurch to Crewe. It was withdrawn in May 1866.

A second Bill covered further track doubling, acquisition of land at Portmadoc (for the harbour), Oswestry, Newtown, Welshpool and Caersws, the last for ballast, a line to Carreghofa, Llanymynech, quays and wharves at Pwllheli, and a floating dock at Ynys Las. Steamboat powers were to be obtained in a third Bill.

When construction of the Shrewsbury & North Wales Railway (whose contractor was Richard France) approached Llanymynech, a

Sharp, Stewart 0-6-0 *Snowdon* was one of two of this type delivered to the Cambrian in 1865. *John Alsop collection*

dispute developed over the nature of the junctions with the ONR. Rich, deputed to adjudicate, had reported on 1 August that they should be 'on two lines of rails, commonly known as a double junction', 115 and 156 yards south of the road overbridge and on curves of not less than 10 chains radius. France took some persuading, eventually proposing combining the platforms to make the required space, to the advantage of passengers changing trains and the general convenience of the Cambrian, Owen thought.

The Oswestry workshops had been nearly completed when Owen reported on 18 November, with the steam engines recently started for the first time. Most of the fitting shop gearing had then been installed. Equipment for the works had been supplied by Sharp, Stewart.

The locomotive builder delivered 2-4-0 passenger locomotives *Treflach* on 18 December and *Whittington* 10 days later. They cost £2,491 each.

Owen ended the year with suggestions for improving the working of Oswestry station. Writing on 31 December 1865, he said that the goods shed was in the wrong place and too small, and should be relocated. When the new running shed was complete the old one should be adapted to house the 'saloons and spare coaches', creating space for goods sidings. Rearrangement of the goods lines would leave three lines for passenger purposes, with an arrival and a departure platform. They would need a footbridge and covering over.

Another footbridge would give access to the shops and sheds to the east of the railway, saving the men concerned from having to cross the line at a dangerous point and 'keeping them entirely away from the traffic department ... as during the unloading and removing of goods many temptations are placed in the way of the company's servants.'

He mentioned his ideas now, he reported, to help counter GWR proposals in a recently deposited Bill. In addition to connecting its Shrewsbury-Chester line to the Cambrian on either side of Oswestry station with double junctions, the GWR sought to have use of the Cambrian between the junctions and for running powers from Buttington to Welshpool without payment of fees. The works, estimated to cost £9,897 15s 3d, were approved on 25 January 1866.

On the MWR, the December 1864 Bills had received the Royal Assent on 29 June 1865 (eastern extension) and 5 July (western extensions). The company had defeated a Bill for amalgamating the Vale of Neath Railway with the GWR, had secured running powers to Hereford over the Hereford, Hay & Brecon Railway, and extended its

running powers over the Brecon & Merthyr Railway to reach the aforesaid Vale of Neath Railway.

On 2 October Piercy submitted a certificate for MWR rolling stock supplied by Watson, as shown in the accompanying table. On the same date the solicitor had objected to some £5,000 of expenditure claimed by the contractors, saying they were not entitled to it – £2,113 9s 8d was 'charged in error'.

Including land purchases, a total of £253,786 10s 4d was due to the contractors, who were asked, on 6 October, how they wished to be paid, 'having regard to the present financial position of the company'.

| Mid Wales Railway rolling stock 1865 | | |
|---|---|---|
| Locomotive engines | 12 | £45,425 |
| 1st class carriages | 8 | |
| 2nd class carriages | 14 | |
| 3rd class carriages | 24 | |
| 1st and 2nd composite carriages | 4 | |
| 2nd and 3rd composite carriages | 4 | |
| Passenger brake vans | 4 | £21,275 |
| Goods wagons | 200 | |
| High-sided goods wagons | 150 | |
| Covered goods wagons | 50 | |
| Goods brake vans | 6 | |
| Lime wagons | 50 | |
| Timber wagons | 30 | |
| Cattle wagons | 40 | £49,392 |
| | | **£116,092** |

On 12 October Watson informed the company that the state of the money market made it much more difficult to extend credit than it would have been a few days earlier. He could not, therefore, allow a year's credit on the same terms as previously offered verbally. He would, however, accept Lloyds bonds for £239,400 payable in 12 months without interest, in exchange for the securities already held. The offer was accepted.

As the end of 1865 approached it was clear that the MWR's contractors were in difficulties, even to the extent that on 9 November one of the directors gave a personal guarantee for £8,000 on being told that they could not meet bills to that amount.

By 12 December the National Bank had issued a writ for £2,000 and the National Discount Company had requested immediate payment of £17,000 that was overdue. A writ had been issued for the latter by 15 December, when the London Financial Association wrote to demand that as 'large holders of ordinary and preference shares' the company should not issue any Lloyds bonds 'without communicating with us'.

Whalley appeared to be concerned that the MWR was not doing as well out of traffic from its neighbours as it might have been, and on 14 December he made a formal proposal that the contractors should obtain a report on the railway's traffic and prospects from Broughton.

Facing the prospect of being unable to pay debenture interest amounting to £5,773 19s due on 31 December, on 22 December the solicitor was instructed to do what he could to raise the money, pledging or selling surplus rail or other material as necessary. As the lessees were not prepared to pay the rent, Broughton was instructed to retain the receipts and remit the net balances to the company's bank.

The solicitor reported arranging for the London Financial Association to advance the interest, the association buying the surplus materials as security, on 28 December 1865. On the same occasion Wade reported receiving writs from Overend, Gurney & Company, the discount house, for £20,000, and from a Benjamin Bateman for £29,000; several more had been received by 17 January 1866. Earlier, on 22 December, the solicitor had reported that the Llanelly Railway had refused to return MWR rolling stock that had been loaned.

On 5 January 1866 Savin proposed that the Cambrian should work the MWR, but it was to be another 20 years before the Cambrian controlled MWR operations, long after he had ceased to have any influence.

Some 18 months after its legislative creation, on 13 January the Cambrian was now the subject of compliments from the *Railway Times*, 'proceeding regularly, but perhaps too rapidly, in its work of consolidation'. Whalley's 'unfortunate reputation' had prevented it from obtaining financial facilities but it had a great work to accomplish and could be excused in its efforts to recover as much of the past as possible.

*Hercules*, a Sharp, Stewart 0-6-0, was supplied to the Oswestry & Newtown Railway in 1862. *John Alsop collection*

Having become one of the 'chief prominences' in Wales, the paper continued, and relieved from obstruction on account of other undertakings being unwilling to deal with its 'renovated and now respected management', it was no surprise that other undertakings should wish to be associated with it – referring to the amalgamation Bill then in Parliament.

Despite this goodwill, the financial edifice upon which the Cambrian was built began to collapse on 1 February. Meeting to discuss the dividend, the board considered the position 'in the event of Mr Savin not being prepared'. The meeting, and two others, was adjourned without a decision. Meeting with Savin in attendance on 7 February, the directors were informed that 'in consequence of the high cost of money' he was obliged to suspend payment and had placed his affairs in the hands of his creditors.

'He also made a general statement of his affairs and liabilities he had incurred as lessee of the company especially with reference to those of Messrs Sharp, Stewart & Company and Messrs Stevens and to the clearing house in respect of the traffic account.' He had instructed his staff to pay traffic receipts from 6 February into the company's bank at Oswestry. What the directors thought about this, beyond asking the bank if the traffic takings had been deposited, they did not say.

The *Manchester Guardian* had announced the day before that Savin had 'requested the temporary forbearance of his creditors', adding that although his liabilities were about £2 million, his assets were valued at £3.5 million. Summarising the year's events on 31 December, *The Times* was to state that it had been announced on 1 February that the contractors were in trouble, which may explain the Cambrian minute of that date. The total debt between them was £4 million.

Overend, who had no connection with Overend, Gurney, was able to continue on the MWR for a time, reporting on 8 February that he had repaid £3,000 of a £5,000 loan to a particularly insistent creditor. The MWR board could not have realised how serious the situation was, for it instructed Piercy to start work on the western extension and to consult with Overend concerning it.

Although Overend, Gurney had succeeded with a claim against the MWR, the company was at liberty to have the judgment set aside, the solicitor reported on 13 February. According to the *Railway Times* the case related to four £5,000 bills sealed by the company but repudiated by the directors. The paper thought that matters between the finance house, contractor and railway were 'approaching to something like a crisis.' There was no connection between the contractor and the finance house but, as will be seen, the collapse of one did nothing for commercial confidence in the other.

By 27 February, when its shareholders met, the MWR had lost its contractor/lessee as well. Broughton's report on the traffic was included with the accounts. Such are rarely seen, especially from contractor-worked railways.

From his office in Brecon, Broughton explained that traffic revenue for the half-year to 31 December 1865 had been £11,312, and working expenses had been £6,550, 58% of receipts. Mileage operated had been 49,455 for passengers and 32,760 for goods, producing 2s 3½d and 3s 6d per mile respectively. Because the line was new and connecting lines incomplete, traffic was undeveloped and expenses therefore out of proportion to the receipts; the UK average receipts/expenses ratio was 46%.

Receipts per passenger and per passenger train run compared well with the UK average, but goods traffic was less remunerative. Revenue per mile for both passenger and goods workings was nearly half of the UK average.

Three passenger trains and two goods trains were run daily, carriages being added to the latter. The total of 93,018 passengers comprised 5% 1st class, 10% 2nd class and 85% 3rd class, and earned £5,703. Some 5,000 passengers had been tourists visiting Aberystwyth and the coast.

For goods, 12,000 tons had produced a quarter of the gross receipts, although volume had been hindered by the lack of through booking facilities. Improved facilities for handling timber traffic would be beneficial.

Three-quarters of the gross weight carried had been 36,000 tons of minerals, a third of it being Northamptonshire iron ore carried over a short distance of the MWR by the Brecon & Merthyr Railway. Broughton anticipated carrying coal for export from South Wales, routed via Ynys Las on the Dovey, and iron ore from North Wales and possibly Cumberland destined for Dowlais and Merthyr. He was unable to compete with GWR rates for coal traffic to Birkenhead despite the GWR route being longer. Could he have seriously expected South Wales coal to be exported via Ynys Las?

Some 8,000 tons of lime had been carried. Complaints about the adequacy of supply should be ameliorated by Savin leasing the Tylerybont lime quarries to a company that intended to develop the trade.

Rolling stock maintenance costs would be lower if the MWR had its own facilities, Broughton continued. Some carriages were unused and would benefit from undercover storage. Despite protests, the Brecon & Merthyr Railway continued to damage wagons by spragging their wheels on steep inclines instead of using adequate brakes. Mr Thomas, at the Llanidloes Foundry, repaired the stock as required.

Referring to 'this wretched concern', on 3 March the *Railway Times* reported another case concerning £46,000 of bonds. 'As a matter of course a verdict was entered against Mr Whalley and his co-enterprisers,' it said, adding that this case and the earlier one would be dealt with on appeal.

The Cambrian's Oswestry Works had been completed by 12 February 1866, when Owen reported that most of the machinery had been commissioned; the whole was in accordance with the specification originally submitted.

After seeking legal advice, the Cambrian formally terminated Savin's contract on 16 February. Although it was not stated explicitly, Savin actually continued with the coast line construction under the supervision of his inspectors in bankruptcy. Four days later their request for £5,300 due on the coast section was accepted. The half-yearly meeting was deferred until 6 March to give time to obtain a loan to cover the debenture interest.

The meeting took place without any recorded comment being made about Savin's suspension and termination. The directors said that 'the engine' ran along a considerable length of the railway under construction, and they forecast its completion in time to carry the summer traffic.

Conybeare added that bad weather had caused the temporary suspension of work on the Barmouth viaduct and six weeks delay in delivering castings for the Morben bridge over the Dovey. The contractors, Cochrane, Grove & Co at Barmouth, and Rankin at Morben, had said that their works would be complete by 1 June, when he anticipated the lines to Pwllheli and Dolgelley being opened. The dividend was declared; the North & South Wales Bank at Liverpool had agreed to advance £30,000.

Another 1865 delivery from Sharp, Stewart was this 2-4-0, the first of a batch of four. Originally named *Gladstone*, by the time it was photographed in 1891 it carried only the number 53.

As might be expected, the fallout from Savin's suspension continued for some time and was manifest in different ways. Two of 'his' railways proved difficult to deal with. The Denbigh, Ruthin & Corwen Railway, when asked to pay hire fees due from 6 February, replied that it had no knowledge of any Cambrian stock on its line, while Conybeare, as engineer of the Brecon & Merthyr Railway, handed in a list of BMR stock that Savin had given him in September 1864.

On 7 March the solicitor was instructed to have Savin's power of attorney revoked so the company could receive payments due from the GPO for the carriage of mail. Two weeks later, Elijah Elias, the traffic manager, requested a cheque for £1,690 7s 2d in order to pay two weeks wages. Sharp, Stewart wanted to know how the locomotives that were on order were going to be paid for; the company intended to apply for powers to issue more capital.

The company first took steps to manage its own undertaking when the board met on 5 April. Savin was present, raising several issues concerning the line's management and objecting to changes made since the company had taken over. Vane told him that the board was in a painful position but had a duty towards the shareholders that compelled him, with the unanimous concurrence of his co-directors, to request Savin 'to be good enough to cease from attending the boards in future unless specifically summoned'.

He remained in attendance, however, and later said that his inspectors wanted to call a special meeting to elect three directors, a requirement that had been discussed by the respective solicitors previously. New contracts were to be made and the notice of the meeting to elect the directors would be published after they had been completed. Owen was instructed to report on the state of the line and the station furniture and to make a return of the individuals occupying company land.

On 13 March, at Montgomeryshire assizes, a Cambrian engine driver was sentenced to eight years' penal servitude for the criminal assault of a young female passenger. Unfortunately the *Liverpool Mercury* gave no details of the background to the incident in its report.

Three appointments were confirmed on 6 April: Elias as traffic manager, £300; A. H. Coulson, accountant and cashier, £200; and Mr Shepherd, audit clerk, £150. Savin's audit clerk, Noble, was told that his appointment could not be continued at the salary paid by Savin and was given a gratuity of £50 in lieu of notice.

Elias requested direction on certain matters. Workmen 'engaged at the Aberystwyth and Borth hotels should be charged 3rd class for the double journey' – half fare? Hotel development on the coast was expected to bring increased traffic to the railway, and several board meetings had been held at the Cambrian Hotel in Borth. No one engaged on coast-line construction was to be allowed to issue Cambrian passes. Repairs or additions required for traffic purposes to the value of £100 could be ordered by the traffic manager with the engineer's agreement.

The cost of timber trucks, ordered from Ashbury by Savin, and of station cranes was to be established. Tenders submitted for 1,000 tons of rail were not satisfactory.

Savin's inspectors attended the board on 26 April, applying for £40,000 in Lloyds bonds as payment on account of work on the coast. A discussion reduced the claim to £10,000, the remainder being paid on 4 May.

Two of Savin's employees had to wait until they were released by him, or his inspectors, before they could apply for their jobs with the Cambrian. Alexander Walker, the locomotive superintendent, combined the post with that of Oswestry works manager, and Charles Mann was confirmed as storekeeper.

The Bill seeking powers to amalgamate with the Carnarvonshire, Nantlle, Corris and Beddgelert railways was abandoned following a decision taken on 26 April. The first two lines were to come under the

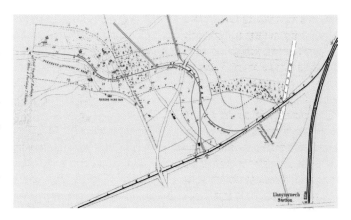

ABOVE This 1866 scheme for a line to Carreghofa off the Llanfyllin branch was lost in Parliament. The blue lines indicate the private tramways that connected the Llanymynech quarries with the Shropshire Union Canal. *Parliamentary Archives*

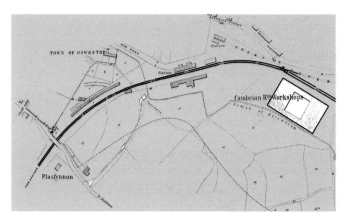

ABOVE An 1866 plan of Oswestry, showing the location of the then proposed workshops. *Parliamentary Archives*

control of the LNWR, the third to remain in limbo for several years, and the fourth was abandoned. In 1872 Lefevre, its engineer, complained that the Cambrian stole sleepers he had certified for it; perhaps he was unaware that Beddgelert Railway equipment had been sold to Savin's inspectors for £400 on 10 January 1868.

Conybeare submitted a claim for £15,673 17s 6d in May, saying that he was prepared to accept Lloyds bonds providing they were chargeable on the 'Cambrian proper', a distinction that was to cause problems, particularly with the shareholders, for some time to come.

Piercy's claims totalling £103,236 for work on the ONR, AWCR, LNR and OEWR were countered by an offer of £54,000 on 18 May, the debt to be payable in Lloyds bonds at 5% for three years, providing he dropped all claims and suits.

Owen had been trying to get locomotives and rolling stock back from the Brecon & Merthyr Railway since March, even visiting that company's solicitor. *Wynnstay, Montgomery, Glansevern* and *Leighton*, the ex-LNR Sharp, Stewart 0-4-2s built in 1859 and 1860, with a combined book value of £10,220, were claimed by the BMR. Not in dispute were *Green Dragon* (last seen on the OEWR contract) and the Sharp, Stewart *Hercules* (0-6-0, ex-Savin, ex-ONR), *Mountaineer* (0-4-0ST, ex-ONR), *Cyfronydd* (0-6-0, ex-NMR), and *Usk* and *Wye* (2-4-0s, Cambrian). Savin also had a locomotive named *Usk*, a Manning, Wardle 0-6-0ST.

The claim for 150 wagons, including a horse box and a carriage truck, was accepted and Owen billed them at £12 per annum each; he had got all the wagons back by 24 May. Some wagons, he thought about 70, were being used on the Carnarvonshire Railway contract.

Regarding the locomotives, the BMR traffic manager's claim that an exchange had been effected 'by some comparatively worthless engines now in use in Mr Savin's brickyard and in construction' led Owen to recommend that the solicitor should start proceedings against the BMR. The Denbigh, Ruthin & Corwen Railway wanted to keep *Llanerchydol* until the repair of its own No 2 had been completed at Oswestry, a reference to contract work being carried out there.

The *North Wales Chronicle*'s 17 March 1866 report described a journey from Bontnewydd, on the Carnarvonshire Railway, to Pwllheli the week before, the party travelling in a locomotive-hauled wagon from Dinas. At Glandwyfach there was a 'splendid new engine and tender, of beautiful construction and great power', named *Castell Deudraeth*; this was a Sharp, Stewart 0-6-0 built for the NMR in 1861 and originally named *Countess Vane*, so it had probably been renamed and repainted for its work in Carnarvonshire. 'The portion between the junction and Pwllheli is quite finished, so that it permitted the engine to be driven at the rate of 60 miles an hour', a claim that seems quite unlikely.

This same report also claimed that the railway between Portmadoc and Criccieth had been opened 'three or four months ago'. If this were so, then it was without the knowledge of the directors or the Board of Trade. The Carnarvonshire Railway board had resolved not to 'take any cognizance for or responsibility with respect to the line between Portmadoc and Afon Wen' on 13 December 1865, and had no rolling stock suitable for operating a regular service.

When Tyler reported on the fatal accident that happened to a Carnarvonshire excursion train at Brynkir on 6 September 1866, where the passengers travelled in ballast wagons with plank seats, he said that the unopened lines of the Carnarvonshire and the Cambrian were in Savin's possession. Although they had been used 'for the accommodation of people living in the district on certain occasions, and to some extent for goods traffic', there was no suggestion that there had been anything like a regular service for most of the year. One more fatality had been dealt with by the Aberystwyth coroner on 9 June 1866. Thomas Finchett, an off-duty guard, was on the platform at Aberystwyth watching an Oswestry excursion depart when he tried to stop two men from jumping on to the moving train. He succeeded but fell under the guard's van as it passed; he had been the guard of the train that derailed near Abermule in 1861 (page 46).

A part of the Manchester & Milford Railway from the junction with the Cambrian and the MWR at Penbontbren towards Llangurig had been built and was not connected to the MMR, that company having had, since 5 July 1865, powers to build a line from Alltddu to Aberystwyth and to abandon its line to Llangurig. On 11 August 1866 the traffic committee considered a request from a George Farmer to have coal and clay conveyed along it. Owen and Elias were to report on the feasibility, but their reports, if made, were not retained.

Progress on the coast was manifest on 18 April 1867, when Elias reported that he had been asked to provide a carriage to work passenger traffic over Barmouth bridge instead of forcing passengers to use the ferry. It could be worked by John Savin or Mr Davies of the Gorsygedol Arms Hotel, he said. On 12 October the *Merionethshire Standard*, in its report on the ferryman's claim for damages, said that the 'carriage which now runs across the bridge was put on in April of the present year'. The same report stated that the company 'began to carry [goods] across the bridge in June 1866'. It seems that Davies dealt with the passengers.

The Cambrian began advertising excursions to Barmouth on 3 June 1867, noting that 'Arrangements have been made to enable passengers to proceed from Barmouth Junction to Barmouth (over the bridge instead of over the ferry as before). The bridge is half a mile in length with a footpath for passengers, and from which one of the most magnificent views in Wales can be obtained.'

Passengers came from far afield, the North Staffordshire Railway advertising excursions to Aberystwyth, Borth, Towyn, Aberdovey, Barmouth and Dolgelley on Tuesdays, for example. Passengers from Derby, Burton and Ashbourne changed at Crewe for a special train that reached Aberystwyth at 6.40pm; the return working was at 8.00am on Wednesdays, so participants either had a two-day trip or an eight-day adventure. The Aberdovey ferry fare was included for those visiting the coast. A guide was published, a booklet with descriptions of the attractions and advertisements; it was free at stations and sent by post in exchange for a postage stamp.

The Cambrian ran another excursion from Oswestry to Aberystwyth on 25 August, carrying 700 employees and their families in 17 carriages free of charge. The *Wrexham Advertiser* identified the locomotive as *Cambria*, a Sharp, Stewart 0-6-0; the staff excursion became an annual event. At the resort, the Cambrian had been joined by the MMR on 12 August, sharing the same station.

Owen had been instructed to keep a watching brief on the incomplete coast line. On 16 June he reported that if the works continued with the same vigour the line should be ready for opening 'about' September. He was concerned that no quickthorn had been planted along the boundaries, however; if it was not planted the fencing would soon need replacing. The solicitor was told to see what the contractor had to say about it. Many miles along the boundary were to be planted from 1871 onwards.

It is difficult to tell from what was recorded whether or not there was conflict between Savin's inspectors and the Cambrian. Because Savin held so much Cambrian capital and debt, the inspectors wanted to appoint two directors. At the same time that this was agreed, 20 June, the inspectors were informed that unless the company received money to pay dividends and interest before 1 July, property held as security for Savin's performance would be sold.

In Parliament, running powers were obtained in exchange for withdrawing the objection to the Bala & Dolgelley and Llangollen & Corwen railways' amalgamation. The branch to Carreghofa proposed in the 'new works' Bill was withdrawn due to opposition; the property designated for its terminus, Burntfield House, was owned by Savin.

On 5 July Owen submitted an estimate of £127 17s 6d to install a 470-yard-long 3-inch cast-iron water main into Oswestry works. Until the main was installed, water was being carried 4 miles in locomotive tenders, 'a process expensive in itself, detrimental to the permanent way and obstructive to traffic'.

On the same day the tenant of the Welshpool refreshment room was given permission to occupy the old station on payment of £5

2-4-0T locomotives were delivered by Sharp, Stewart in 1866. *Maglona* was No 57. *John Alsop collection*

annual rental; nothing had been recorded about the 'new station' replacing the old.

The *Wrexham Advertiser* reported that the coast railway was sufficiently advanced for Savin and Ward to take Sir Watkin and Lady Williams Wynn on a trip to Pwllheli on 10 July. When Tyler investigated the Carnarvonshire Railway derailment in September he was told that several excursions from Barmouth and Portmadoc to Carnarvon had been run during August using wagons. He was also told about a trip to Carnarvon for Vane that ran at the end of August, when the party had travelled in a train of two carriages and a van.

For something slightly different, the *Chester Chronicle* told how, on 14 July, men working on the Barmouth bridge had caught a 3-foot 50lb shark, one of the men losing the end of a finger in the process.

Savin drove the first train across the bridge at 2.00pm on 23 July; it comprised two carriages and sundry trucks. *Mazeppa*, a Sharp, Stewart ONR 2-4-0 that had also been taken over the bridge, was added to the train and the ensemble set off for Carnarvon. The *Oswestry Advertiser*

*Prometheus*, one of the same batch as *Mountaineer*, spent most of its time on the Porthywaen branch. Photographed at Llynclys in 1891, the designated branch brake van is just visible behind. *R. H. Bleasdale/John Alsop collection*

*Mountaineer* was one of three Sharp, Stewart 0-4-0STs supplied to the Oswestry & Newtown Railway in 1863. Savin used it on the Brecon & Merthyr Railway and it was hired to the Dowlais Iron Company circa 1866. Later giving it the number 37, it was no wonder that the Cambrian attached a combined ownership/number plate to it.

reporter said that in the bridge Savin had given Wales an 'eighth wonder' and the public 'the most attractive promenade pier in Great Britain'.

Having inspected the coast line, on 25 July Owen was concerned about the cutting at Friog. The wall had already been washed away during the previous winter's storms and, unless replaced by something of a more substantial nature, the line would inevitably fall into the sea. 'This is most important as in the event of an accident occurring at this point it would be of the most fearful kind and would be injurious to the interests of your line for years.' How very prophetic.

The available engine power would be inadequate when the coast line extension opened, he reported. *Mountaineer*, No 37 in the asset register, was much needed for the Kerry branch, but the Brecon & Merthyr Railway had hired it to the Dowlais Iron Company. He also needed another 300-400 tons of rail to renew the line between Four Crosses and Pool Quay.

A claim against the company for taxes owed on Savin's arrears was considered on 26 July. The amounts were £487 3s 5d (1864) and £1,823 18s5d (1865), which may give an indication of how long Savin had been in trouble before his business collapsed. The special commissioners of taxes were threatening to remove the company's property unless the tax was paid immediately. An offer of payment by instalments was made, the payments to be debited against Savin's estate.

Few of the engineers or contractors escaped the contagion. France, formerly secretary of the MWR and SWR and secretary and contractor of the Shrewsbury & North Wales Railway, had also gone bankrupt, owing the Cambrian £710 10s 3d for haulage. Piercy was bankrupt, too, to the extent of around £500,000, his assets comprising mostly 'worthless' railway shares and debentures.

Still in July, the solicitor was to deal with outstanding claims for rolling stock hire against the Brecon & Merthyr and Denbigh, Ruthin

& Corwen railways, amounting to £7,525 and £1,107 respectively. Owen had despaired of getting them to settle, the BMR claiming to have purchased the locomotives from Savin. The company also had to deal with the owners of coast-line land that Savin had not paid for, several having issued writs.

The Cambrian Railways (new lines) Act was given the royal assent on 6 August. The authorised works were a deviation on the line to Porthdinlleyn at Pwllheli, a road across the Traeth Mawr from Portmadoc to a point between Minffordd and Penrhyndeudraeth, a road from Penrhyndeudraeth and Llandecwyn, and various improvements to the stations at Oswestry, Welshpool and Newtown. The first road, had it been built, might well have avoided the need for the recently opened (2011) Porthmadog bypass. In addition, £142,000 of additional capital was authorised for the inland section and £300,000 for the coast section.

Conybeare informed the Board of Trade that the Aberdovey deviation and the remainder of the coast line were ready to be opened on 15 September 1866, asking for each section to be treated separately in order that a problem with one did not prevent the other from being opened. His optimism for an early opening proved unfounded as damage caused by gales and high tides forced him to ask for a postponement as soon as the 18th.

Tyler submitted his report on the Aberdovey deviation from Aberystwyth on 25 September. It was a single line, 5 miles 77.55 chains from the junction with the Aberystwyth branch to Aberdovey station. The steepest gradient was 1 in 60, and there were curves with radii of 12, 13, 15 and 16 chains. It should, therefore, be worked with caution and at moderate speed.

Double-headed 70lb rail was laid in 26-27lb chairs spiked to sleepers laid 3 feet apart. It required a good deal of adjustment, especially on the marsh a mile from the junction. The large stones used as ballast in most places required breaking up. Post-and-wire fencing required improvement in places.

There were 14 bridges under and one over the railway, and all appeared to be standing well. The maximum span was 58 feet. There was a viaduct 140 yards long, comprising 17 18-foot timber spans and three iron-girder spans of 29, 36 and 37 feet across the estuary. The 37-foot span opened to allow vessels to pass. The woodwork was well made but the ironwork needed reinforcing. The rolling beam should be strengthened to prevent deflection on the rollers. The connections between the shifting and the stationery rails on the bridge would be improved by the addition of internal fishplates and keys. The longitudinal timbers carrying the rail and chairs should be extended beyond the ends of the viaduct.

Use of the moving bridge would be improved by a telegraph between Aberdovey and the junction and some improvements made to the interlocking between the bridge-controlling levers and the signals. Cross-bracing needed to be added to the timber piling of a bridge 'near Messrs Brett and Capper's quay' – this served the Frongoch slate quarry and was immediately adjacent to the western portal of the first tunnel.

There were sea walls or cuttings over a considerable portion of the line; the former would need to be carefully maintained and already required some attention in two places. Tyler noted that his remit actually did not extend below the high-water mark and he could not therefore resolve a complaint from Brett and Capper about the sea wall near their quay, which was on soft ground and had given way. They had also complained that the bridge over their tramway was lower than agreed.

There were four tunnels with an aggregate length of 1,139 yards, the longest being 530 yards. As the train staff system was to be used, the telegraph already mentioned would be useful to protect the traffic through the tunnels. The tunnels were partly lined, and both lined and unlined looked sound, but the clearances were insufficient in places and one of them had poor drainage.

At the junction the arm of the distant signal should be moved because it was not visible to drivers. Self-adjusting levers were required on the rods that worked the distant points. The nomenclature of the points needed improving. Some of the locking required adjustment to make the points lock closer, and the notches in the quadrants in which the levers worked should be filled in, except those required for use.

Where the single and double lines met, the rails needed adjusting. The

Cambrian Railways No 2 was a Kitson 0-4-2 built for the Mid Wales Railway in 1864. No 2 on the MWR, it was photographed at Llanidloes.
*C. Thomas/John Alsop collection*

junction was necessarily a staff station but was not, he understood, to be used for the interchange of passengers – no platforms had been provided.

He could not, therefore, recommend that the line be opened until his requirements had been dealt with. The Board of Trade consulted with its harbours department over the works below the high-water mark.

On 15 October Owen reported that ticket platforms at Oswestry would cost £30 each. He thought, however, that the work could be more usefully done during station stops at Llynclys and Whittington. There were practical reasons for not having such platforms at Oswestry: on the one hand it would require stopping the trains on a 1 in 80 gradient, and on the other it would be easy for someone intent on defrauding the company to leave the train on the offside.

Because of delays in finalising arrangements with Savin's inspectors, the shareholders' meeting to adopt the accounts for the first half of 1866 was deferred until 25 October. Revenue had been affected by 'the stoppage of the cattle trade' and the financial crisis.

The crisis had followed the collapse of Overend, Gurney & Company on 10 May. The *Manchester Guardian* reported that it was believed that the company's assets were good, but for weeks there had been a run against it by speculators and its credit had been damaged. The final straw had been a court declaration that some MWR bills were invalid. The Bank of England had refused to bail it out.

*The Times* explained that the limited company had been formed in August 1865, adding, 'The frequent recurrence of disasters affecting the assets of the old firm affected the reputation of the new one; the notorious failure of Overend, Watson & Company, the railway contractors, operated injuriously from the similarity of name; the heavy fraud of Pinto, Perez & Company [£500,000, a £40,000 loss for Overend, Gurney], the general break-up of the finance companies and the hourly expectation of a European war were all calculated to try them to the utmost.'

The English Joint Stock Bank collapsed on 11 May, and on the 16th John Ashbury, the carriage builder, petitioned for the winding up of the Financial Corporation Ltd, another discount house. On 11 May the Governor of the Bank of England had written to the Government explaining that it had loaned £4 million to banks, bill brokers and merchants, an unprecedented sum to lend in one day.

Quoted in the *Manchester Guardian* on 12 May, the *Economist* had said something to the effect that it had thought that the Overend, Gurney partnership had been, through reckless mismanagement, one of the 'most losing' firms in Europe, but had been unable to say so

Sharp, Stewart 0-6-0 *Rhiewport* was also built for the Cambrian in 1864. It became No 45 in the Cambrian fleet and by the time it was photographed it had acquired a number and ownership plates above the leading wheel splashers. *John Alsop collection*

because of the fear of litigation. The prospectus was subsequently found to have been misleading, the guilty party being dismissed shortly after the limited company had been formed. Unusually, the creditors were paid in full, with interest, although the shareholders lost £32 1s 10d, plus any premium, per £50 share.

This aside into banking history will sound familiar, although its relevance may not be immediately apparent. It shows that Savin's collapse was not a consequence of Overend, Gurney's failure as some, including the present author, have said, and has parallels with recent events.

The year's chaotic events seem to have been responsible for the Railway Companies Securities Act, which came into effect on 10 August. One of its key features was a requirement for railway companies to make half-yearly returns of their loan capital.

Reverting to the Cambrian's October 1866 report, the directors had no information regarding receipts and expenses. Working arrangements were continued as before with attention given to reducing working expenses. Although the priority had been to settle outstanding claims on the capital accounts, the board thought that it would still be able to pay the dividends and interest. At the date of the meeting, the company, including its constituents, had issued £3,340,727 of the £4,345,890 authorised capital. Debenture interest owed by Savin from 1 January until 6 February was £8,695 17s.

During the period from 6 February to 30 June, traffic revenue had been £54,396 17s on the inland section and £8,251 13s 3d, including £994 14s 10d from the Aberdovey ferry, on the coast section; working expenses had been £22,882 9s 3d and £7,841 6s 8½d respectively. The inland revenue included £13,622 16s 10d from hire of rolling stock to Savin and other companies.

Aberdovey ferry expenses of £1,329 8s 11d included items relating to train operation, for the branch line from Ynys Llas to the ferry wharf at Cerrig y Penrhyn. The ferry was worked by the 'iron steamer' *Elizabeth*, built by Lewis & Stockwell in 1865. The vessel was 126 feet long, had a beam of 20 feet, weighed 86.95 tons and had a draught of 31 inches. Powered by Watt 30hp engines with oscillating cylinders and 2-foot stroke, it was to be sold to a Mr Green of Londonderry for

£500 plus £45 for the cast-iron ballast and commission in December 1869.

With the Aberdovey deviation works coming to an end, another presentation was made on 13 October. On this occasion the recipient was T. H. Hankinson, the cashier, who received an engraved gold watch, guard and ring valued at £37 from workmen and townspeople. Presumably to distract the workforce from drink, he had run a series of 'penny readings' and had contributed to other civic activities in the town.

Tyler re-inspected the deviation on 10 November, reporting from London. The ironwork on the rolling bridge was improved but still with more deflection over the rollers than was desirable as the bridge was lowered. The connection between the shifting rails and the fixed rails was improved but the work had not been completed. The telegraph had not been installed.

The embankment at Frongoch appeared to have sunk some 18 inches since his last visit. The wall that contained it was built on soft ground without foundations, and needed reinforcing with 'heavy stuff' to check its tendency to sink towards the sea.

The points at the junction still did not lock closely – one set only half-locked. The tunnel clearances were still inadequate. Although the design profiles were always too small, they had not been adhered to and the tunnels had been built irregularly. Once again he could not recommend opening. Having read and discussed the report, the traffic committee instructed Conybeare to attend the next board meeting to explain; however, the matter was not discussed then and he was not recorded as being present.

The apparent lack of interest in Conybeare's failure to have the Aberdovey deviation completed for its second inspection might be because an attempt had been made to place the company in receivership. The relevant entries, in November and December 1866, were deleted before the minutes had been agreed, but it appears that ONR and NMR debenture holders had, separately, made applications to try and secure their interest.

An outline of the problems was given to the shareholders at the adjourned general meeting held on 3 January 1867. Brett and Capper, the quarry owners affected by the Aberdovey deviation, had secured an *ex parte* sequestration order on the company's assets because the bridge over their tramway was 6 inches lower than specified in the Act of Parliament. In a letter published on 26 December, the company's solicitor explained to the *Manchester Guardian* that the contractors had breached an injunction, defining how the railway should relate to their property, which the quarry owners had obtained within a few weeks of the AWCR 1865 Act being enacted. The claim that the injunction had been obtained *ex parte*, without the defendant being notified or present, was repudiated by the plaintiff's solicitors on 3 January.

An early view of the promenade and the lifting section of Barmouth bridge, looking towards the town and showing the tunnel mouth.

The solicitors also disputed the claim that the order had been lifted as soon as the company knew of it, saying that it had merely been suspended until the company complied with the Act. News of it had frightened some of the creditors, one of whom had instructed bailiffs to pursue a debt of £900, and the debenture holders, who could not be paid with the order in place, a situation aggravated by the bank's seizure of £5,600 of a loan that had been earmarked for the purpose. The engineer (Conybeare?) had also obtained an attachment for £2,000 for work done, some of which had only been done a few days before. The debt was paid and arrangements made to pay the debenture interest.

The sequestration case also seemed to involve an authority given to the AWCR solicitors in August 1865 to complete the compulsory land purchase. They were informed that as soon as the damages and costs had been ascertained the Cambrian would expect to be indemnified. On 22 January Owen reported that it would cost £900 to make alterations to accommodate Brett and Capper's requirements and suggested offering £500 as a compromise to leave things how they were.

Owen subsequently met Brett, who threatened to restart proceedings unless the company paid £800 costs by 27 January. Meeting the day before the deadline, a Sunday, the board approved the immediate issue of a cheque for that amount. Another £300 was to be paid on 22 March and £200 more on 6 April.

The shareholders' meeting, which had been adjourned several times since 25 October 1866 (page 84), came to a climax on 21 February, as explained by the *Railway Times* two days later. Acting on legal advice, dividends could not be paid until debenture debts had been settled. LNR and NMR preference holders claimed that protection given to them in 1864 took precedence over provisions concerning the division of revenue granted in 1865.

Johns, the deputy chairman, complained that the directors' report contained inaccuracies and was approved by an incomplete board at a hastily convened meeting. He also complained about the solicitor not informing the directors about a Bill deposited by a group of shareholders intended to enfranchise the preference shareholders. The company took over the Bill and withdrew it.

The retiring directors, appointed by Savin's inspectors, were replaced by James Bancroft, representing the LNWR, and Davies, the contractor, after some argument. Ashbury, the carriage builder, had proposed them and France spoke against them. Bancroft replaced Johns as deputy chairman.

Meanwhile, work on the coast was not without setbacks, several incidents making the pages of the *North Wales Chronicle*. On 10 October 1866 a man had been returning to Barmouth from Arthog by walking across the bridge after dark when he realised that some planks were missing. Savin's foreman decided that the guilty party was John Wall, a recently discharged labourer, and ordered him to leave town on the next train. Fifty navvies were sent to 'politely' escort him across the bridge to Barmouth Ferry station when he did not appear at the station voluntarily.

Wall did not agree that he had been treated politely and complained about five men who, he said, had carried him across the bridge, tied him to a piece of timber and made various threats against him. The magistrates found them guilty, fining them between £1 and £2 and costs. No action seems to have been taken over the allegation that Wall had damaged the bridge.

Two other cases involved the theft of timber, although they had very different outcomes. At the Dolgelley petty sessions on 5 November, Richard Williams of Llwyngwril was charged with stealing 27 lengths worth more than 5 shillings. He was bailed for seven days. Five more men brought before the Merionethshire quarter sessions on 2 January 1867 were also charged with stealing timber from the bridge.

It had been washed away from the site and up onto the river bank, one log being sold at a third of its value and used in the roof of a new house. The jury found them not guilty, probably because it was the habit of residents to take any timber that was washed up.

Despite the jubilation that had greeted the first train to cross the bridge, it was January before it was considered complete. It transpired that the iron components had been manufactured to tolerances that were too fine for it to work. On 2 February the *North Wales Chronicle* credited Savin's manager and agent James Evans, formerly employed by Thomas Brassey, with sorting it out – 'the iron drawbridge can now be worked easily by two men'. The paper also thought that the 2d charge to use the promenade was too expensive.

The goods service appears to have been extended northwards straight away, but was soon suspended. On 19 February a steamboat ran into the bridge, breaking some of the piles. Reporting the incident on 2 March, the paper added that goods trains had not been able to proceed to Barmouth since.

Whalley's association with Welsh railways ended with his resignation from the MWR board at the shareholder's meeting on 26 February. The *Railway Times* was jubilant. Claims had been made, it said, that the MWR was the only railway with which he had been associated that had not been 'taken out of the hands of its board of directors', i.e. put into receivership. This was not strictly accurate, it continued, but it had to be admitted that the MWR board was the only one that condescended to the drudgery of doing the work of jobbers and speculators under colour of independent action; they had for some time been the mere creatures of certain dominant creditors. Now all hopes of foisting the worthless adventure were at an end, and Whalley's influence and talents were no longer needed. Surprisingly, John Overend remained a director; others included Lefeaux and Johns.

The MWR was, of course, facing serious financial problems. A J. H. Lee of Derby demanded payment of £5,000 due to him by 23 February, but the company could not pay. The Joint Stock Discount had started proceedings for repayment of £20,000 secured on Lloyds bonds. The Contract Corporation laid claim to 'certain plant and materials'. The Cambrian had issued a writ. By 26 March a debenture holder had applied to put the company into receivership; the debenture holders were asked to approve of Broughton's appointment to this position. Wade was called as a witness to a case in Liverpool for non-payment of dividends, where judgment was given for the plaintiff for £408; payment of the dividends was approved on 24 October.

A request from Agra & Masterman's Bank for repayment of loans totalling £9,500 was met with an instruction to the solicitor to pursue shareholders in arrears with their calls. This bank was to collapse on 6 June.

On 30 March Broughton reported having identified three 1st class, eight 2nd class and five 3rd class carriages as surplus to requirements and proposed selling or hiring them. Instructed to obtain an offer, he was also told to identify any surplus land.

On 29 June he was instructed to dispose of three locomotives and tenders. By 25 July three locomotives were on hire to the Manchester, Sheffield & Lincolnshire Railway; their sale for £7,500 was approved on 29 August.

Broughton became receiver during July. On the 30th the board accepted his suggestion that a £505 19s 7d claim from the Brecon & Merthyr Railway be settled by withdrawing the toll for horses carried in cattle trucks and handing over a 3rd class carriage.

Another court appearance occurred because Piercy had issued a writ for £38,000. On 24 October Lewis was to find out how much the contractors had paid for his services.

On 17 November, following an approach from the Carnarvonshire and Nantlle railways, the Cambrian board decided that it would be 'desirable' for the company to work them. At the same time it decided the time was not right to participate in the Union of Welsh Railways, a scheme of amalgamation.

Dealing with the same matter on 11 December, the MWR took the opposite view, listing the participating companies as the Brecon & Merthyr, Cambrian and Potteries, Shrewsbury & North Wales, in addition to itself.

On 5 January 1867 the *Railway Times* opened the year with a commentary on the Cambrian's position. There were three parties pulling in opposite directions, it said. Savin's inspectors were trying to get out of the company as much as they could, the preference shareholders were claiming the revenue for themselves, and the ordinary shareholders were seeing their claims and expectations indefinitely postponed. The last group was creating distrust, without benefit to itself, while starting to exercise an adverse influence on the debenture holders.

On 9 January Owen reported that a landslip at Friog had breached the Llwyngwril-Dolgelley turnpike and deposited a 'large mass' of debris on the line. Fortunately the railway's watchman had noticed a fissure in the ground and was able to stop the trains. It took two days to clear the rubbish, passengers walking between trains on either side in the meantime. He had made arrangements to repair the road but hoped to avoid the £500 cost of rebuilding the wall, a structure 80 feet high, from the bottom by using sheet piling. Sooner or later a tunnel would have to be built. Extreme weather or severe frost would always put this location at risk.

Heavy tides on 12/13 January washed over the sea wall, with irresistible force, and demolished another portion of the original wall. A new wall would be needed as the present one was 'quite a mistake in engineering'.

In contrast to the efforts being made to complete and open the coast line, on 26 January the board considered closing the Kerry branch and instructed the solicitor to ascertain the company's obligations. Elias had reported that the branch had cost £368 8s 1d to run during the second half of 1866. Revenue for the same period had not been audited, but in 1865 it had been £374 11s 11d; he predicted that the 1866 figure would be greater. The subject was not mentioned again.

The *North Wales Chronicle* described two incidents on the deviation. On 12 January it told how Robert Green, 'manager of the deviation line', was severely injured and others slightly hurt when tunnel centring collapsed. Then on 28 January two men were killed when the plug in a temporary shaft fell after a thaw and heavy rain; they were in the process of strengthening the lining as the plug had already dropped 15 inches. Jenkin Evans, a carpenter, was extricated alive after 6 or 7 hours but died soon afterwards; Richard Morris's body was not recovered for five days. Four others were seriously injured.

Nothing in either the board or committee minutes explains the lack of progress beyond Penmaenpool on the Dolgelley branch. Writing on 5 February, Owen described several mitigation measures required at Penmaenpool and Arthog. Some of them, he thought, could be resolved by diplomacy, while the contractors had committed to others. On 9 July 1864 the *North Wales Chronicle* had said that a dispute over the valuation of land owned by the Hengwrt estate had stopped the work; Tyler had referred to a dispute in 1865.

On 11 February 1867 Owen reported that the coast line was ready for inspection, 'but I must call your attention to the fact that not a single shed has been erected or a siding put in to carry on the goods or mineral traffic, consequently an outlay of some £10,000 will be necessary before the line can be considered complete for the working

of the general traffic.' A landslip caused by the 'sudden and recent thaw' at Penhelig meant that the Aberdovey deviation was not ready to be re-inspected. On 21 February Conybeare had a member of his staff send Captain Tyler extracts from the shareholders' report, 'as an answer to why the coast lines are not inspected'. The letter was filed without comment.

Progress on the coast line may be illustrated by reference to expenditure – the six months to 31 December 1865 it was £242,300, to 30 June 1866 £146,307 9s 3d, and to 31 December 1866 £3,161 3s 8d – which suggests that the works were substantially complete by 30 June 1866. The figure of £146,307 9s 3d for the first half of 1866 should include expenditure incurred by Savin before 6 February.

Reviewing 1866 for the Cambrian shareholders on 18 February, the picture was by no means as rosy as it had been the previous October. The embarrassment, the report started, caused by Savin's suspension has been increased by the difficulties encountered in dealing with his inspectors.

An amended revenue statement for the previous half-year was included, to take account of payments not received. £12,281 4s 11d due for haulage and rolling stock hire was countered by claims for £4,920 7s 10d deductions, which were eventually accepted, but the balance remained unpaid. Neither the Brecon & Merthyr Railway or the Denbigh, Ruthin & Corwen Railway debts had been paid either, despite agreeing to deductions in both cases. On the positive side, the company looked to obtain around £5,000 to cover the first five weeks' revenue of 1866 from the sale of Savin's securities, but there remained nearly £9,000 of unpaid hire fees from the second half of the year.

Savin's inspectors had offered to complete the coast line under the terms of his contract, taking payment by means of certificates of indebtedness payable in three years instead of by shares and debentures. The company had approved the contract and put it into effect, but the inspectors then refused to complete it. They had borrowed £200,000 to complete all of Savin's railways, allocating £110,000 to the coast line; that was all they were prepared to spend on it, regardless of outstanding obligations, which included £50,000 for land.

During the second half of 1866 £6,413 4s 10d had been spent on renewal of the permanent way, subject to adjustment with Savin's estate. Tourist traffic no doubt explained the small profit generated by the Aberdovey ferry. Savin's inspectors had been issued with certificates of indebtedness to the value of £38,333 7s 8d and £4,558 for the coast and inland sections respectively, taking their total to £122,333 6s 8d and £71,658; neither the certificates nor the work they represented had been included in the accounts.

Being bankrupt did not prevent Savin from proposing deals. The company's inability to sell the property that it held as security against his performance had compelled it to obtain an overdraft. His offer to take on the overdraft, transferring the property to his mortgage and to erect shops on company land near Oswestry station and on other company property was considered on 8 March. The valuer was consulted over the Oswestry property; his other proposals were not acceptable.

The company had hardened its line against its debtors by 22 March, having started actions against the Brecon & Merthyr, Denbigh, Ruthin & Corwen, and Potteries, Shrewsbury & North Wales railways, the MWR and the MMR. Two locomotives had been recovered from the first, a settlement reached with the second, and the third was before a judge; settlements would be attempted with the last two.

Because the sales of Savin's securities had failed, the solicitor was instructed to start proceedings against the inspectors to compel performance of the contract. In a related action, Waterlow the printer had taken action against the company to recover a debt incurred by Savin as lessee. As the outcome would be a precedent for similar cases, the appointment of a QC to defend the action was approved.

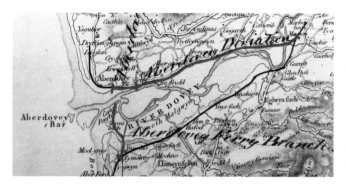

The Cambrian Railways' Aberdovey deviation and ferry branch, 1865.
*Parliamentary Archives*

A claim by Conybeare had been set for a court hearing before a settlement was reached for £1,125. The details were not recorded, but it seems likely that the claim should have been the responsibility of Savin's inspectors.

Tyler eventually re-inspected the Aberdovey deviation, his report being compiled in London on 27 March 1867. The line was much improved, he wrote; among other things the tunnel linings had been taken down and rebuilt. Although they were still too narrow he did not think any more could be done.

Some work was still required on the interlocking at what he now called Glandovey Junction, previously referred to as Morben. On the Frongoch embankment rock had been tipped but it would want watching. Some tidying up on the slopes was needed at Penhelig. On the opening bridge the rail joints and telegraph connections should be improved.

Tyler was satisfied that Owen would attend to his requirements, except the tunnel linings, but he was still unable to recommend that the line was safe for public use. Precedents, however, he cited the Metropolitan Railway, would allow it to be opened with narrow works providing a 'light bar' was placed across the carriage windows. These were made of brass, and were intended to be broken in the case of an accident.

The previous December Conybeare had informed Tyler that he had arranged for the tunnels to be opened out according to a gauge mounted on a truck, and that the clearance so created would be one-third greater than existed on the Metropolitan Railway and equal to that on parts, if not all, of the London & Birmingham Railway. The Board of Trade considered the precedent and thought it appropriate but made no comment to Conybeare or the company about it.

Owen had reported that track repairs on the deviation had been completed by 21 March, adding that if the goods and mineral traffic over it were to be resumed he needed resources to maintain it. 'Otherwise from the marshy state of the ground over which … the line passes a few weeks will see it in as bad a state as ever.' He wanted 13 men, two gangs of four and one of five, to deal with the marsh.

Tyler's report on the remainder of the coast line, including Portmadoc-Afon Wen, was also submitted on 27 March. It was 33½ miles long and the steepest gradient was 1 in 56; the sharpest curve, on the viaduct at Barmouth, had a radius of between 8 and 9 chains. On no account should the speed on this curve exceed 5mph.

He noted that absence of AWCR plans had made his inspection more difficult, and sounded particularly anguished that the plans borrowed from the Board of Trade by Conybeare in November 1866 had been returned in his absence. However, there were still no drawings of the Barmouth viaduct, 'the most important work on the line'.

The permanent way comprised 24-foot lengths of 70lb double-headed rail laid in 26lb chairs secured to the sleepers with wrought-iron spikes. The sleepers were half-round Baltic fir with a minimum section of 10 inches by 5 inches placed 2 feet apart at joints and 3 feet elsewhere.

There were some heavy cuttings and a number of timber viaducts, with an opening bridge near Barmouth, and various bridges of masonry, timber and wrought iron.

In many places fencing and guard rails needed improving. The track needed lifting and packing at many places, especially near the ends of bridges. The wrought-iron straps on the longitudinal beams on a bridge at Plas Canol, near Llanaber, should be moved to cover the scarfed joint, and one of them needed repairing.

The ladder of the down distant at Dyffryn should be properly secured at the ground and two short bolts that secured it to the stage should be replaced by others of suitable length. The slopes on the deep cutting at Harlech should be trimmed and drained and the permanent way below them improved. When they were in better condition he wanted to inspect the cutting sides more closely.

At the Traeth Bach viaduct vertical wrought-iron tie rods should be added to the wooden truss on both sides of the 30-foot span. Short bolts and distance pieces should be added to the portion of the truss that was in compression. Some soil should be removed from the sides of the summit cutting near Penrhyn, and accommodation should be provided for the gateman at the public road level crossing near Penrhyn, as at all level crossings.

Similar accommodation was wanted for the level crossings of the Croesor and Gorseddau railways. Locked chock blocks should be provided on either side of the level crossings across those railways and distant signals were to be worked in each direction.

The Traeth Mawr viaduct had been constructed with only three piles in each pier. The plans were said to have been approved by the Board of Trade but it would have been better if four piles had been used. The work would need to be carefully watched.

At Portmadoc station fencing was required at the back of the platform, chock blocks to the sidings, a distant signal to be worked from the points to the west, a water tank, with crane and water supply, for the engines, and an approach for passengers.

There was an unauthorised level crossing by the old Criccieth public road, which appeared to be used for little more than fetching seaweed from the shore. Criccieth station required an approach road to its parking ground.

At the Afon Wen junction the branch line from Pwllheli should be run into a siding at the back of the south platform and a second siding should be provided for the engine to run round its train. The points leading to this passenger siding should be worked from the junction stage with a lever connected with the locking apparatus. A clerk should be placed in the signalman's box. (Rich had noted the existence of a turntable here when he had reported on his first inspection of the Carnarvonshire Railway on 15 October 1866.)

At Pwllheli wrought fencing was required at the back of the platform and buffer stops at the ends of the passenger and goods sidings. There was no other place for goods trucks but the passenger line and the line by which the passenger engine would run round its train. He seemed to be contradictory about the number of sidings here. A water crane and water supply for locomotive use was required at Pwllheli or Afon Wen, and an access road was needed at Pwllheli. A telegraph should be installed between Pwllheli and Barmouth, it not being desirable or practical to attempt to work so great a length of single line without – there were no passing places.

He regretted that wood screws had been used to fix the bridge rails to the longitudinal timbers on the viaducts. He recommended their replacement by fang bolts in the course of maintenance as rapidly as possible.

No goods sidings or sheds or loading docks had been provided at most stations and passenger accommodation was limited. He would make no further comment as the goods traffic was not relevant to the public safety.

There was a long timber viaduct south of Barmouth with an opening bridge and several spans near it carried by wrought-iron girders on cast-iron cylinders or columns. It took two men 37 minutes to open and close the rolling bridge – means should be adopted to reduce this time, as a train might be delayed by three-quarters of an hour if a vessel approached the bridge shortly before it was signalled.

Another defect in the opening portion of the bridge was that cross-girders hung on the heads of rivets in the main girders. The counter-balance girders connected with the machinery for moving the bridge were closer to the rails than desirable. The cast-iron columns on which the girders south of the opening bridge were carried should be protected by fenders. These columns were placed together in the form of a tripod and the fracture of any one of them might cause part of the structure to fall. They were in an exposed situation, when a ship could be driven against them and a much smaller object might break them. The wooden piles might also be protected. Three of them, he understood, had been broken by a steamer a short time before. Tyler wanted to make a further visit, when staging could be erected on the viaduct and instruments provided to test the deflection of the girders and the stability of the columns.

At the Barmouth junction station shelter was much required and a second platform should be provided on the west of the line. The additional works required meant, of course, that he was unable to recommend opening the line.

Receiving Tyler's report on 29 March, the Board of Trade was puzzled by the status of the railway between Portmadoc and Afon Wen, which appeared to belong to the Carnarvonshire Railway yet both it and the Cambrian had issued notices of intent to open. The remainder of the CR had been inspected by Rich in October and

December 1866 and authorised for public use on 28 December. It is interesting to note that the last date was that on which Spooner signed the estimates for the CR's deviations, and the Act authorising them was not enacted until 25 July 1867.

A civil servant asked to report on the matter went to the trouble of producing a sketch map to accompany his notes. No provision had been made in either of the 1862 Acts that gave effect to this conundrum, or in any subsequent Act, he reported, to cover either the joint construction or operation, although the Carnarvonshire Railway did have powers to make working agreements with the LNWR and the AWCR. Both companies were asked to explain the anomaly, the CR replying on 25 April that the matter was intended to be resolved by an arrangement to be inserted in a forthcoming bill.

There was more confusion when the Cambrian withdrew its notice of intention to open on 11 May but the Carnarvonshire Railway did not. The CR, including the line to Portmadoc, had been built by Savin under Spooner's supervision.

The resignation of Coulson, the accountant, on 11 April had brought with it an application for the post from John Conacher, Coulson's clerk. A decision was deferred, but it was not the last the Cambrian would hear of Conacher.

On 15 April Owen reported on the number of men under his control. On the permanent way there were 242, including three inspectors and three in the Moat Lane workshops. The length covered per gang varied between 2 and 3 miles. There were seven stone-breakers and roadmen covering the line between Whitchurch and Llanidloes, Llanfyllin and Porthywaen. John Clare, the carpenter bridge repairer, led a gang of four, soon to be reduced to two, and the mason Thomas Davies, bridge and general repairer, had an assistant. Thomas Morris led the ballast gang of 18 men and a boy.

Sharp, Stewart 2-4-0 *Lady Elizabeth* was one of two locomotives delivered to the Manchester & Milford Railway in 1866, the year before that railway was opened to Aberystwyth, where the photograph was taken.

The Barmouth bridge when quite new – only one pair of the iron tripods is protected by the fenders required by Captain Tyler. *John Owen*

Out of his own £600 salary Owen had to pay for three assistants and his office expenses, together with travel expenses for the four of them when away from home, nearly half the time, leaving little for himself. He did not ask for an increase – it was not the right time – but he was sure the board would reward him 'adequate to my responsibility' when the circumstances were right.

Elias produced a similar report on 17 April, comparing 1866 with 1867 and showing posts at each station with weekly wages. There were 291 men and boys in 1866; wages included £10 15s for the crew, captain, mate, five seamen and carpenter of the steamer *Elizabeth*, the Aberdovey ferry. Overall Elias had already saved £33 0s 8d weekly and expected to save £12 more in the next two weeks. He pointed out that if the company owned the horses it hired for shunting and deliveries at Newtown, Llanidloes and Aberystwyth, as he had suggested previously, it would make an annual saving of £200.

Owen informed Tyler on 20 April that the Aberdovey deviation was ready to be re-inspected. On 7 May he wrote again, saying that he 'begin[s] to despair of ever completing the additions and alterations required by you … owing to money being so scarce, more especially if you insist on the fenders round the columns of Barmouth bridge as the fact of many thousands of tons of stone have been placed round them will render the pile driving a very expensive and difficult operation. Will you kindly write me whether this is with you a sine qua non [essential].'

Tyler would not budge and suggested withdrawing the notice if Owen was not ready. Notwithstanding Tyler's response, on 8 May Major Charles Scrope Hutchinson was appointed to inspect both the coast line and the deviation. He found that no works had been carried out on the former since Tyler's visit.

The Aberdovey deviation was a simpler matter, Hutchinson's report being submitted from London on 13 May. With the exception of the tunnel lining, Tyler's requirements had been complied with, but Hutchinson still considered the works to be incomplete.

A draft agreement on the joint use of Cemmaes Road station with the Mawddwy Railway was dealt with on 11 June. The company had refused an invitation to work the MR on 8 March.

An auction of railway plant was held at Aberdovey on 18/19 June. Items included a 12hp Hornsby portable steam engine, 60 tons of 'temporary' rails, a 40-foot turntable, a 16-foot turntable, a wagon weighbridge, and 1,500 'permanent' sleepers. Return tickets were offered at single fares.

On 25 June a directors' committee discussed the company's position, financially and generally, making a number of observations and recommendations. The Acts of Parliament were unintelligible, and the interests of the different sections were conflicting; there was no way of satisfying them all, so the only remedy would be to repeal the amalgamation Act and relevant parts of the other Acts and restructure the company, combining the receipts.

It would be expedient to reduce the nominal capital, which had been increased by improvident arrangements. Priority must be given to protecting the value of the LNR and NMR guarantees. The debenture interest must also be protected, although it might be necessary to extend the repayment term. The accounts needed overhauling and a statement prepared to illustrate the situation with regards to Savin and his inspectors. Powers to effect these and other changes should be obtained with a consolidation Bill.

The directors' concerns were partly addressed by the Cambrian Railways (Finance) Act, enacted on 15 July. The preamble explained that the company was unable to exercise its 1866 borrowing unless certain restrictions were removed to prevent litigation by debenture holders and other creditors. Further clauses extended the compulsory

In this later view of the bridge, from the west, all the tripods have been protected by fenders. The small shed erected on the structure was presumably used for maintenance purposes. *Graystone Bird*

purchase powers for the Penmaenpool-Dolgelley land by six months and the time for building it by 12 months.

Acting on instructions, by 5 July Owen had reduced track maintenance to an average of four men per 3 miles, the minimum he thought safe. The Penrhyn branch for the ferry, opposite Aberdovey, caused problems daily because the course of the River Lerry, running into the Dovey, changed with each flood tide. If the deviation was not opened before the winter gales more piling would be needed.

Tyler's comment of 27 March about the Metropolitan Railway precedent of using carriages with barred windows in tunnels of sub-standard width finally sank into the Cambrian's subconscious on 1 August. Asking the Board of Trade for the precedent to be applied, the solicitor offered an undertaking that only carriages with barred windows would use it because the coast line would be worked as a separate branch. This was accepted on 12 August, and the deviation was opened on 14 August. Announcing the opening in advertisements dated 5 August, the Cambrian said that it was for a limited time, with the landowners' permission, and the opening was not to prejudice existing rights or be deemed to dedicate the railway to the public.

There were still problems with the neighbours, though. On 6 August 1867 Elias reported that the LNWR was refusing to pay more than £600 due for Buttington Junction, saying that it had been omitted from the list of liabilities when it had taken over the SWR and it could only pay if the Cambrian had some authority from the SWR, which could not be obtained because the SWR had been dissolved… At Llanidloes the MWR wanted to pay only one-third of the costs of running the station instead of half, presumably because it had agreed to meet a one-third share when the MMR was expecting to use the station. Elias proposed that the Cambrian should refuse to do MWR work unless it came to terms.

Elias returned to the subject of horses, saying that the company paid 5 shillings per day providing the drivers, except at Machynlleth where a horse and driver was hired for 6 shillings per day. Savin, he continued, had offered to sell the Corris horse for £15; if the Cambrian took it it could do the Machynlleth work as well.

Hutchinson made his coast-line inspection on 30 August, submitting his report from London on 5 September, saying that Tyler's various requirements had 'to a great extent been complied with'.

He had tested and examined the Barmouth viaduct and found it satisfactory except in regard to the cross girders on the opening section being suspended from the main girders by rivets; these should be watched and iron straps added during maintenance. Substantial fenders had been added to the columns.

He drew attention to incomplete fencing in some places. The telegraph connected to the opening bridge was not connected at Barmouth Junction and there was no down distant signal there. The iron straps had not been relocated over the scarf joints on the Plas Canol bridge. The centre truss of the Traeth Bach viaduct required distance pieces and bolts adding. A projecting rock in the Penrhyn cutting should be removed. At Afon Wen, the up starting signal should interlock with the down main signal. Afon Wen and Barmouth Junction signal boxes required clocks and none of the stations had name boards. The track required lifting throughout.

The Harlech cutting had been much improved but there was still a likelihood of slips or large boulders falling on the line; the company must undertake to keep a watchman constantly patrolling it and not to allow any train to pass without his permission. He should not be removed without the Board of Trade's permission.

For the second time, the coast line was not approved, but the company wasted no time. Another inspection was requested on 9 September, and Hutchinson returned on the 14th, compiling his report

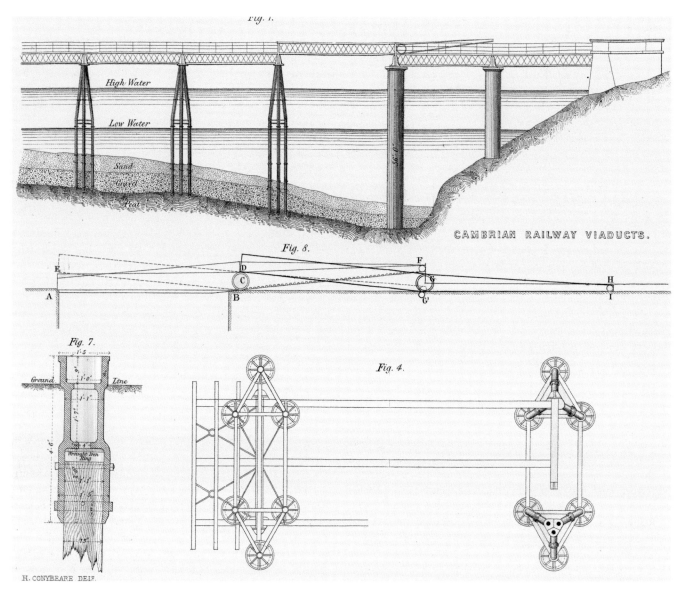

*Fig. 1.*

High Water

Low Water

Sand

Gravel

Peat

CAMBRIAN RAILWAY VIADUCTS.

*Fig. 8.*

*Fig. 7.*

Ground          Line

Wrought Iron
Ring

*Fig. 4.*

H. CONYBEARE DEL.ᵗ

Conybeare's plan for the iron spans and the opening bridge at Barmouth.

in London four days later. His requirements had 'to a great extent been complied with'. The track works were incomplete but in progress. His suggestion that block instead of speaking instruments be used on the bridge telegraph was being adopted. On receipt of undertakings regarding the Harlech watchman and the method of working the single line 'their lordships need no longer withhold their consent to this portion of railway being opened for passenger traffic'. The undertakings were dated 17 September and approval was given on the following day.

Owen claimed expenses totalling £8 2s 10d for the inspections: £4 10s for Tyler's, £2 0s 4d for Hutchinson's first, and £1 12s 6d for his second. It is not clear if the services of Mr Campbell, two drivers, two firemen and two fitters were required on each occasion or just on the first. Because Hutchinson had set a target for improving the track, threatening not to pass the line unless he saw an improvement while he was there, and Savin did not have the resources, Owen had put his own trackmen on to it, paying £30 6s 6d out of his own pocket until it could be approved.

John Savin had arranged for 200 children from Barmouth's National School to have their annual treat by riding to Portmadoc in 'railway trucks' on 31 August, the day after Tyler's inspection.

It is appropriate to say something about the distinctive bridges built to carry the Cambrian across the estuaries of the Dovey, Mawddach (Barmouth), Dwyryd (Traeth Bach) and Glaslyn (Traeth Mawr). These notes are based on Conybeare's paper presented to the Institution of Civil Engineers in 1871 (see Bibliography).

Timber was used because the estuaries were shallow and generally dry at low water, and it was cheaper, an earlier design using wrought iron on cast-iron piers being rejected. Importing the timber direct to site from the Baltic reduced the cost considerably; on 26 March 1864 the *North Wales Chronicle* had reported the presence of three German brigantines, chartered by Savin, at anchor off Aberdovey.

On the low-water sections, not more that 3 feet deep at spring tides, 14-inch-square piles were driven into the sand to a point just below the lowest low-water level and cast-iron splices attached before the piles were driven home. The design allowed all timber that was not constantly immersed to be seen and readily replaced when found to be defective. Several feet of rock was tipped onto the sand around the piers, the tides washing out the sand so that the rock stabilised the piers.

The opening span of the Dovey bridge was 35 feet, that at Barmouth 36 feet. Here, rock on the north shore quickly gave way to a channel 54 feet deep during spring tides; to the south of the rock a layer of sand up to 8 feet deep overlay a gravel layer 6-8 feet deep; underneath was a peat bog of unknown depth.

This geological situation made the site unsuitable for a swingbridge, Conybeare explained, adding that he was therefore forced to adopt a drawbridge. Of these there were two types, the under-drawbridge and the over-drawbridge. James Brunlees had devised the first, using it in Morecambe Bay, and this had been used on the Dovey. In this arrangement the roadway was drawn back beneath the roadway of the adjoining superstructure and had to be lifted into position and supported by eccentrics for the passage of a train. At Barmouth such a structure would have interfered with the integral promenade.

The only over-drawbridge that Conybeare knew of was a double installation in Rhyl, carrying the turnpike over a river. Conditions at Barmouth made the foundations simpler and supported its adoption. When the bridge was lifted it was pulled back out of the way on four 4-foot-diameter wheels carried on rails mounted outside the main running rails.

The deep-water channel at Barmouth was spanned in two sections, by the moveable bridge mounted on four columns and by a fixed section using iron piers, each comprising six piles in two groups; the spans were of 40 feet. The depth of the channel was reduced by tipping stone.

In a similar manner to the timber piles, the screw piles, 10 inches in diameter in shallower water, or 14 inches, were driven to just below the lowest low-water level and cast-iron splices used to interface between them and the above-surface structure. They were designed to take a weight of 2½ tons per square foot. The load was taken by the gravel using 3-foot-diameter discs fitted to the piles driven 8 feet through the gravel into the peat. Cast-iron collars with a diameter of up to 4ft 6in were fitted to the piles to bear on stone tipped onto the sand, with more stone tipped onto them. This sand was also washed out, the rock making the structure very stable.

The piers for the opening bridge each comprised two 6-foot cylinders placed on 18ft 6in centres, making the base 24 feet in the direction of the current. The No 2 pier was 56 feet high, bedded on rock by divers and filled with concrete. Work to position the first cylinder from barges had started in the autumn of 1865, but on 27 November work had been stopped for the winter because it had proved impossible to keep the cylinder in position.

Resuming in the spring of 1866, progress had been much better, using a staging projected from the abutment. The two cylinders of No 1 pier had been sunk by 17 March, and by 26 April both had been fixed and filled with concrete to the high-water mark. No 2 pier had been completed by 30 June.

A problem with building in this manner, Conybeare observed, was that while the structure was sound when complete, the unbraced piles had little strength. There were several incidents at times of high tides and stormy weather when damage was caused. On 24 March 1865 the temporary staging around pier No 4 was washed away, together with its unbraced piles, losing a month on this pier as a result.

In ideal circumstances he would have preferred the longer tubes to have been of 10-foot diameter but the ground conditions prevented that. Having experience of installing both types of drawbridge, he thought the over-bridge was better. He accepted that it had been a mistake to start work in the autumn.

The opening width was 47 feet between the points of support, Tyler's fenders reducing it to 36 feet. 'As the harbour was free from worms, timber supports were used in the fenders…,' he remarked; it was not the fenders that required major repairs as a result of an attack by teredo marine worms more than 100 years later.

Brunlees, present during Conybeare's presentation, complained about the lack of credit given to his friend Piercy, who, he said, had designed the viaduct using drawings that he, Brunlees, had lent. Conybeare replied that he had designed it from first principles and described a number of significant differences.

Returning to operating matters, on 7 September the board agreed to negotiate terms for the Carnarvonshire Railway's use of the line between Pwllheli and Portmadoc. The CR also wished to hire two Cambrian locomotives, *Llanerchydol* (Sharp, Stewart 0-4-2, built 1860) and *Seaham* (Sharp, Stewart 2-4-0T, built 1866). The rate was £4 per locomotive per day in steam, payable in advance, and the agreement was dated 14 September. *Llanerchydol* had been transferred three days earlier, and *Seaham* was required from 16 September. Three months' notice to terminate the hire of the first was given on 4 June 1868.

Davies had negotiated a settlement with the Brecon & Merthyr Railway. Each company would have two of the four locomotives concerned – *Wynnstay*, *Montgomery*, *Glansevern* and *Leighton* – with the locomotive superintendents casting lots for them. The BMR would hand over *Mountaineer* and *Green Dragon* to the Cambrian and the claim for hire would be settled by the BMR paying £2,500 within 10 days. The BMR did quite well out of this – the Cambrian's claim had been for £13,260 8s 5d. Only *Mountaineer* and *Green Dragon* moved to Oswestry, the BMR paying £2 per working day for the use of *Leighton* and *Montgomery*.

On 14 September the shareholders were told that, having been in possession of the undertaking for two complete half-years, the board now had some idea of how the company should perform in the future. Using the Railway Companies Act, effective from 20 August, and the company's own Finance Act, further litigation by debenture holders and creditors should be avoided. On 25 October the board decided to file a Railway Companies Act scheme 'as expeditiously as possible'. The *Railway Times* 21 December issue described the purpose of the Act: 'to prevent the undertaking from being torn to pieces by a mass of competing judgment creditors swooping down in one general scramble to enforce execution against the property and effects of the company'. In particular, article 4 protected a railway's rolling stock and plant from seizure by creditors.

A temporary arrangement with landowners had enabled the Aberdovey deviation to be opened, expediting the traffic and avoiding the inconvenience and expense of the ferry. The remainder of the coast section could not be opened, however, until land purchases and other charges that totalled £80,000 had been satisfied; 21 landowners had obtained injunctions. Meetings with the debenture holders, in whose interest it was to open the line as soon as possible, to encourage further investment had not borne fruit.These meetings had been held in Crewe and were reported in the *Manchester Guardian* on 13 June and 21 August. At the first Davies explained that Savin had paid the dividends from 1863 until 1866, very likely out of the money the

| Aberdovey ferry revenue | | | | |
|---|---|---|---|---|
| | June 1866 | December 1866 | June 1867 | December 1867 |
| Passengers, parcels | £479 8 3 | £829 8 11 | £517 14 3¾ | £265 5 8 |
| Merchandise, minerals | £515 6 7 | £816 16 1 | £654 12 3½ | |
| Livestock | | | £0 3 9 | |
| | £994 14 10 | £1,646 5 0 | £1,172 10 4¼ | |
| Expenses | £1,329 8 11 | £1,433 9 7 | £1,410 2 8 | £325 3 5 |
| Profit/(loss) | (£334 14 1) | £212 15 5 | (£237 12 3¾) | (£59 17 9) |

debenture holders gave him to make the line, a claim that Savin never disputed, and the only published suggestion seen by the author that he had been corrupt.

The second meeting considered a report into the company's affairs produced by Waterhouse of Price, Holyland & Waterhouse, the London accountants. Savin had been paid a total of £1,390,884, including £52,000 due at the time of his suspension, on the coast line. The contract price of £17,500 per mile for 80 miles 1 furlong 7 chains amounted to £1,386,218, so he had already been paid more than he was contractually due for the complete line. His inspectors had been given £130,321 in certificates of indebtedness due in three years and £50,000 in debentures and preference shares on account of the £52,000; this amount was thought to be greatly in excess of the amount really due.

Most of the 1861 and 1862 ordinary shares had been subscribed by Savin and registered to his nominees. No calls had been made so they might be forfeited for non-payment; it would be impracticable to re-issue them. The same applied to £300,460 preference shares. Savin's security had been property stated to be worth £45,000; the company also had a lien on all horses, materials or plant found on the works at the time of his suspension. The company had settled £203,513 claims that Savin should have met.

Director James Bancroft explained that the 180 miles of railway would have cost around £4 million when the original capital should have been less than half that. £850,000 of debt, nearly £1 million when the line was finished, would cost £50,000 a year to service. He advised writing off questionable assets as bad debts and starting again. The board thought that if all parties, except bond, debenture and rent-charge holders, who must be paid, would agree to reducing their nominal holdings, to bring the capital down to £2,250,000, they would inspire confidence in the company. Then it could be run without the board being worried and harassed by questions of financial and legal expediency.

All parties would be asked to make some sacrifice: the debenture holders might have to defer their interest, and the LNR and NMR holders might have to settle for a reduced interest. No decisions were wanted then, but the shareholders should consider the situation and prepare to decide at a future meeting.

A short item in the *Carnarvon & Denbigh Herald* of 21 September reported the opening of the Carnarvonshire Railway 'as far as Penrhyndeudraeth and Pwllheli' on 'Tuesday last', 17 September. The strange acknowledgement to the two companies' managers and auditors 'for supplying the public convenience at the present time' suggests an element of co-operation, but what the auditors had to do with it will never be known. Both companies' minutes are silent on the issue.

When the CR had opened from Carnarvon to Afon Wen on 2 September, the *North Wales Chronicle* commented that the terminus was inconvenient and 'nowhere', so maybe the 'extension' was opened in response to public objection to these features; no doubt the hire of locomotives from the Cambrian approved on 7 September was also relevant.

A CR timetable published in the *Carnarvon & Denbigh Herald*'s 28 September edition was dated 1 September and effective from 20 September, offering a weekday service of three return trains between Carnarvon and Portmadoc and six on 'the Pwllheli branch'. A later timetable, effective from 1 October, included a Sunday service of one return journey on the main line and two on the branch. If the Cambrian directors knew about this they said nothing, the shareholders' report issued on 14 September declaring that '40 miles of the line … remain unproductive'.

However, having taken legal advice, on 8 October the directors decided that services between Barmouth and Pwllheli should start on the 10th. They also recorded the circumstances under which the line

was being opened, to avoid prejudice and preserve the rights of the various interests of the several sections of the railway: the land had not been purchased in accordance with the contract, the contractor creating rent charges without making provision for the associated reduction in capital to redeem them; the works were generally defective, especially the timber viaducts, at Friog and the Aberdovey tunnels; and the securities given to Savin or his inspectors were 'largely in excess' of the work done.

Goods services beyond Barmouth had probably been started by the contractors as soon as the rails were down, Elias having reported on 7 July that John Savin had refused to pay for the hire of a locomotive and had returned it to Aberdovey. Elias had proposed running a service three days a week, arranging for local carriers to deliver the goods and collect charges. 'This could be done by the engine now working the goods on the Aberdovey side and we should not incur any extra expenditure… There is at present a considerable traffic arriving daily at Barmouth.' Neither the board nor the traffic committee commented on the proposal and Elias did not return to it. From casual remarks made in the reports, it is obvious that a goods service had been operated over the Aberdovey deviation before Hutchinson approved its use by passengers.

Elias produced a timetable poster on 8 October, announcing a 'new route to Carnarvon via Barmouth', stating that 'the line between Barmouth Junction and Pwllheli will be opened for passenger and goods traffic.' The Carnarvonshire Railway's timetable effective from 11 October included a sub-heading, 'Opening of Cambrian extension between Pwllheli and Barmouth Junction', and its weekday services were restricted to its own line; the Sunday trains had been discontinued, having been run only once.

Elias had also drawn the board's attention to several issues affected by the opening. There were 180-200 wagons awaiting repair at Oswestry, traffic was already hindered by the shortage they created, and the opening of the coast line would make the situation worse. He had been unable to have the telegraph installed at Barmouth because the Electric Telegraph Company had not given the company credit facilities. John Savin wanted to erect refreshment rooms at Portmadoc, Afon Wen and Pwllheli.

The *North Wales Chronicle* of 19 October declared the 'last remaining link' to be as important as the accession of King Henry VII to the English throne in 1485, 'when Wales became really, as well as nominally, a part of England. The opening of this railway will mark a new era in the social and material history of Wales. It has added another and stronger tie connecting England and Wales.' Summarising British railway history and the development of the coast line, the paper paid tribute to Savin's contribution before noting that there were no stations and that the line terminated on the Abererch embankment, outside Pwllheli.

The board was right to be concerned about the land. The first (7.00am) train from Portmadoc was greeted by a solicitor serving injunctions on behalf of three landowners owed £1,212 19s 7d, reported the *Liverpool Mercury* on 11 October. The paper's claim that services between Pensarn and Barmouth were suspended was mocked as being erroneous by the *North Wales Chronicle* on 19 October, although the *Cheshire Observer* claimed that the train had been seized by the sheriff's officers. So much for the Railway Companies Act.

Despite his forecast in February that £10,000 expenditure would be required on the coast line, Owen made do as best he could. On 21 October he reported on the necessity for engine sheds at Portmadoc and Pwllheli. Damage was being caused to locomotives stabled without protection, from 'sand and wind on the one hand and the wet and dust on the other'. There was an old shed at Ellesmere that could be moved at 'a trifling cost' and 'another portion' of the old Oswestry carriage shed could also be used.

Details of the Aberdovey deviation landowners' agreement had not been minuted, but it was extended by a month on several occasions. It entailed monthly payments related to traffic, £119 4s 0d for October and £112 6s 9d for November 1867.

Nothing was recorded about the incomplete Dolgelley branch, and the decision to seal the contract with John Ward, Savin's former partner, to complete it on 29 October did not even merit its own heading in the minute book.

Two months after the Aberdovey deviation had been opened, the *North Wales Chronicle* published an item deploring the dull state of trade in the town: 30 houses were empty and shipping trade much diminished.

To accommodate coast-line traffic, Elias changed the timetable, requiring passengers to change at Glandovey Junction, where there was no shelter. On 30 December Owen asked for permission to extend the platforms and to relocate the old waiting shed from Ynys Las.

Several items of rolling stock were sold in the last months of 1867. A Mr Buckley bought the 3rd class carriage used on the Penrhyn (Aberdovey ferry) branch and a 1st/2nd composite in November. The Manning, Wardle 0-6-0ST named *Borth*, No 24 in the asset register, was sold to the Llynvi Iron & Coal Company, Maesteg, for £775, valuation £750, by 17 December. The sale of 0-4-0ST *Lilleshall*, No 21, built by the Lilleshall Company in 1862, for £850 was completed by 15 January 1868.

Meanwhile, on the MWR Broughton's proposal to provide a station at Aberedw, between Builth and Three Cocks, was accepted by the board on 2 May 1867. He thought that he could raise £100 locally to pay for it. Traffic agreements between the MWR and the Brecon & Merthyr, Neath & Brecon and Cambrian companies, in various combinations, were sealed on 28 May.

A long and severe winter, depressed money market and stagnation in trade had not been good for railways, MWR shareholders were told on 27 August, the situation made worse by the Neath & Brecon Railway, and the portion of the Brecon & Merthyr Railway that would connect the MWR to the Vale of Neath Railway, not being opened as expected.

Revenue was slightly increased but, Broughton explained, passenger traffic had fallen off at several stations. At Builth, in contrast, a big increase in numbers, to some 5,000, had not produced a corresponding increase in income because they had been transferring to the Central Wales Railway. An experiment with the Brecon & Merthyr Railway had seen BMR locomotives hauling MWR trains between Brecon and Three Cocks, reducing costs and locomotive mileage. Two locomotives had been overhauled and 10 locomotive tyres had been renewed. On the track 2,094 sleepers had been replaced – 40,000 would need renewing – and 11,802 of the heavier joint chairs required by Yolland three years before had been installed, with 6,254 more in stock. Sixteen carriages had been revarnished and the tops (roofs?) and ironwork repainted during the half-year.

The *Railway Times* reported that one of the shareholders thought that Broughton should forego a part of his salary. Replying, Broughton said that he had been solicited to take charge of the line, and it would not be right for him to be the first to give up his entitlement. He had given a security of £18,000 to act as receiver, and the company would have been much inconvenienced had he not done so, the chairman explained.

On the Cambrian, a locomotive crew was killed when an embankment adjacent to the river bridge at Caersws was washed away during a 'fearful hurricane and storm … unprecedented in severity in Montgomeryshire' on 1 February 1868. Owen submitted his report to the directors on 18 February. The train, the No 1 down mail, left Newtown at 6.30am, comprising *Castell Deudraeth*, four loaded

trucks, six empties, a goods van, two passenger carriages and the mail van. The driver was Samuel Daniels, his fireman was John Davies, and the guard David Jones. The only other people on the train were two timber loaders employed by the company.

The locomotive and tender, a loaded wagon and two empty cattle trucks fell into the flooded void, trapping and killing the locomotive crew. Arriving on site at 11.20am, it took until 3.45pm for Owen's crew to recover Daniels's body and until nightfall to recover Davies's. Recovery was suspended until 3 February and was not completed until 9.00am on the 9th. Daniels and Davies had worked the previous eastbound train and, finding the water up to the bridge, Daniels had walked across to check it with a lamp, while Davies drove the train after him.

Owen explained that he had had the embankment reinforced with stone previously and that the bridge itself had been undamaged. The bridge at Pontdolgoch, however, was damaged and its north abutment collapsed on 2 February, despite its substantial nature. The section ganger, having been to the Caersws site and realising that he could nothing there until more help arrived, had decided to inspect the remainder of his section, noticing a deflection in the rails before establishing that the abutment had settled. He continued to Carno, putting down detonators as he went, and arranged to stop the trains. Elias reported that his action almost certainly stopped the 8.00am up passenger train from going into the river with an 'appalling' loss of life.

Tyler's report added that the breach was 48 feet long and up to 8 feet deep. He made no comment about the embankment being built of gravel and silt from the river, which knowledge must go a good way towards explaining why it was so easily washed away. Some larger stone had remained in situ. Reinstating the embankment, the company proposed to include a spillway to reduce the pressure on the embankment in any future flooding. The company's rules required the entire line to be inspected before 8.00am in winter and 7.00am in summer, but Tyler called for a more rigorous routine to be devised to cover flooding situations. He made no comment about the collapse of Pontdolgoch; perhaps the knowledge had been kept from him.

The storm had been wide-ranging in its effects. Another trackman noticed that an embankment near Llanymynech was in danger of being breached, and had the wit to fetch and dump a load of stone already loaded and stabled at Pant. The bridge over the Severn nearby also sustained some damage.

With engineering advice from Davies, who had built it in the first place, the first train was run over the reinstated Caersws embankment on 7 February and over a temporary bridge at Pontdolgoch three days later. Elias had arranged to run a replacement bus service until the repairs were completed. Owen's estimate to repair all the damage was £502, and Pontdolgoch bridge had been repaired, without interrupting traffic, by 29 June. On 31 March the board contributed £10 to the fund for the widows and families of Daniels and Davies.

More bad weather was to follow, Owen reporting that heavy rain had caused the Ellesmere goods shed to subside and that high tides on 10/11 March had damaged the Traeth Mawr and Traeth Bach embankments. One train had been delayed 52 minutes.

Elias regularly submitted details of staff changes, injuries and fatalities to the traffic committee. On 31 March his list of staff changes included the resignation of W. Vaughan as station master at Penrhyndeudraeth; he had been incompetent, and his replacement, J. G. Bevan, had been too slow for his previous appointment as station master at Pwllheli.

On 5 June Elias reported two fatalities that had occurred on 21 May, at Kilkewydd and Criccieth. At the former, a man was crossing the line when he was run down by the 8.00am up train. At the latter, a woman was using the level crossing when she was run over by the 11.20pm goods. Inquests recorded both deaths as accidents, the jury at Criccieth adding the rider that the crossing was dangerous and should be provided with a pedestrian route that either crossed over or under the line. The crossing still has no pedestrian route and has been the site of many accidents and fatalities since 1868.

Elias's report of an accident that had occurred to the east of Welshpool on 3 April brought him an unexpected rebuke. At 8.00pm the 7.20pm down passenger train ran into a special LNWR goods train that was standing on the main line opposite the down goods through siding. When the goods had approached Welshpool its driver had whistled at the distant signal, which had been lowered in response. The signalman, however, thought he had lowered the signal for the passenger train because he had not been notified about the goods. The LNWR, it transpired, had not sent the usual written notice about the goods and no one knew about it at Welshpool except the wagon examiner, who heard of it while chatting to an LNWR passenger guard. The passenger train driver did not see it until it was too late to avoid a collision. Elias thought that the shunter, who had seen the goods arrive and should have known that the passenger was due and taken appropriate action, was most to blame. As he had ignored the rule about removing obstructions from the main line 15 minutes before a train was due, he was sacked.

Seven passengers were slightly injured. In compensation Elias gave one of them a three-month pass for travel between Newtown and Welshpool. This was 'highly objectionable', the directors thought; in future he must not arrange compensation without consulting Pryce. The incident appears to have escaped the attention of the Board of Trade.

Reporting on 25 January 1868, after there had been shareholders' meetings to discuss the Railway Companies Act scheme filed the previous October, the *Railway Times* called the Cambrian a 'stupendous imposture [deceit?] which grew out of the most contemptible scheme ever sanctioned by Parliament (the Llanidloes & Newtown Railway), embracing as it does a nominal capital of at least £3½ million, is now at a dead-lock…' and linked its situation to earlier behaviour by the LNWR. 'The wild projects of which the Cambrian is made up would never have reached their extravagant extent had the LNWR been animated, 10 years ago, by the commercial integrity which now regulates its conduct. The delusion culminated to its ruin-producing point when Captain Huish [General Manager 1846-58] was permitted to exercise his folly in encouraging extensions in Wales in opposition to the GWR…' The meeting was a melancholic spectacle, its misery enhanced by LNWR director Bancroft's presence in the chair, the paper claimed.

Perhaps seeing the chance of redress or recovery disappearing if the scheme had been finalised, 'Robinson and others' had put the company into receivership, with Pryce appointed receiver on 15 February, which the board did not feel obliged to mention to the shareholders in its 28 April report.

A lot of effort was put into the Railway Companies Act scheme but ultimately it failed under the onslaught of opposition by counsel representing some 70 suits against the company and a ruling that the court could only accept or reject the scheme, not amend it to reach a settlement.

Fortunately, the board had hedged its bets by depositing a Bill with the same objectives which was enacted on 31 July. Receipts from both the inland and coast sections would be fused into a common fund from which working and maintenance expenses, except rent charges, interest and dividends, would be paid, the net surplus being divided between the two sections. The unexpended coast capital was to be used to equip the coast railways with stations, sidings and other works. The number of directors was to be increased to ten, four representing

each section; Jasper Wilson Johns, David Williams and two others were to be elected for the coast section, and James Bancroft, David Davies, Robert Davies Pryce and Henry Gartside for the inland section, with two permanent directors. The latter were Vane, as owner of Plas Machynlleth, appointed under the NMR's 1863 Act, and an appointee of Powis, as owner of Powis Castle, appointed under the ONR's 1855 Act. The preference shareholders received voting rights.

The unissued capital, totalling £147,300, could be issued as preference stock, taking the first charge on the undertaking, its purpose being specified in some detail. Excluding the company's activities as a carrier of goods or passengers or new liabilities, no actions against the company or its property could be continued or commenced without court approval for five years. Section 35 brought the receivership to an end.

The MWR *did* succeed with its Railway Companies Act scheme, which was made on 12 June and enrolled on 31 July. The existing debt was covered by the issue of £10,600 5% B debenture stock, the western extension would be funded by the issue of new ordinary shares or C debenture stock, and the existing debentures were grouped together as A stock. On 11 August the board instructed Broughton, no longer receiver, to apply the court-held surplus to the payment of debenture interest.

Facilities for MWR rolling stock were limited. A shed for storing up to 12 carriages had been erected at Rhayader early in 1868, and the 'old sheds' from that place used to make a shed for two locomotives at Builth a year later. On 30 January 1869 Broughton reported that 'two engines had been thoroughly overhauled and two others partially'. One of these repairs used a set of locomotive driving wheels with crankpins and tyres obtained from Kitson, but the facilities for installing them must have been quite primitive. Nine carriages had been varnished and 20 low-sided wagons converted into timber trucks.

Savin's affairs continued to cause problems for the Cambrian. On 22 February 1868 the secretary reported that he had received a writ from the Plas Kynaston Colliery Company in respect of £868 11s owed for coal supplied while Savin was lessee. His freight account was £2,081 14s in arrears, reduced by £1,000 after he had been threatened with having his traffic stopped otherwise. On 4 August the board demanded payment of £2,000 within a week, adding that if it were not paid property belonging to him or his brother would be seized and that in future their traffic would only be accepted if prepaid or charged forward.

The company had no funds available in the capital account to meet the last instalment of £826 10s 11d due to Sharp, Stewart for the 2-4-0s *Gladys* and *Seaham* on 18 April. The money was raised by selling Manning, Wardle 0-6-0ST *Nant Clwyd* to a James Taylor for £800, the sale being completed by 4 August 1868. *Nant Clwyd* had been supplied to Savin in 1862 and is said to have been used on the construction of the Vale of Clwyd Railway and the Llanfyllin branch. It was No 14 in the Cambrian register.

An agreement negotiated by Elias for the carriage of mail brought good news. The GPO would pay £39 per mile for use of the railway between Aberystwyth and Welshpool and £12 per mile for the coast line, a total of £3,591.

Elias reported on 18 August that the opening of the Bala & Dolgelley Railway had placed the company at a disadvantage as goods were being delivered free of cartage, whereas the Cambrian charged for delivery from Penmaenpool. He recommended that the company should pay the cartage, 5 shillings per ton for about 90 tons per month. He was allowed to do this after the opening of the BDR for goods on 1 October 1868 saw its operator, the GWR, ignore an earlier agreement on the issue.

The MWR started running its own trains over the Hereford, Hay & Brecon Railway during 1868, and from 1 October started a 12-month trial period of running that line; Broughton hired 25 timber wagons at

16s 8d per month for use thereon. The move, therefore, by the HHBR to deposit a Bill seeking powers, inter alia, for running powers over the MWR between Three Cocks and Talyllyn was not well received. The MWR intended to return to Parliament for additional time to construct the western extension and to abandon the eastern extension.

The HHBR action appeared to be part of a move to give the Midland Railway access to Dowlais and was also the subject of objections by the GWR and LNWR. The MWR was accused of preventing HHBR traffic from reaching the Brecon & Merthyr Railway. The Commons committee gave the Midland running powers to Talyllyn and refused to give the HHBR power to make agreements with the Midland or any other company. The Midland did, however, take over the operation of the HHBR from 1 October 1869, when the MWR's 12-month agreement expired.

On 26 July 1869 Broughton reported that locomotive expenses had been increased on account of the stock being overworked. The increase showed mostly in wages (£201 15s 9d), coal (£241 1s 4d) and hire of a locomotive (£179 7s 10d). Loco repairs and renewals increased by a mere £45 7s. In the second half of the year another £170 18s 6d was spent on locomotive hire.

The Cambrian's half-year report of 22 September 1868 had included the first report signed by the locomotive superintendent, Alexander Walker. Costs had increased because more work had been done and some stock was older, requiring heavier repairs. A travelling crane had been built. The company owned 42 locomotives, 107 carriages and 1,235 goods vehicles.

Six tenders for the construction of a station at Newtown were considered on 24 November 1868. That of John Ward for £1,697, not the cheapest, was accepted, the amount including the transport of materials. The station was to be completed by 27 May 1869, costing £1,725 2s 8d in total. Extras of £28 2s 8d for the erection of steps at the approach instead of raising the road were also allowed.

Salt vans were removed from mixed trains following consideration of Hutchinson's report into a broken axle that had occurred at Abergwidol bridge, west of Cemmaes Road, on 12 December 1868. The van in question belonged to the Cheshire Amalgamated Salt Company, and was the ninth of 18 wagons in the train from Oswestry that also included a guards van, a composite carriage and a 3rd class carriage at the rear. On a downward grade approaching the bridge at a speed estimated at 15-18mph, the guard saw a wheel fly off. He and the locomotive crew brought the train to a stand 200 yards beyond the bridge. The wagons following the van derailed, three of them falling into the river. The van and the passenger carriages were both derailed on the bridge. Several chairs were broken and the bridge decking sustained considerable damage.

Hutchinson, reporting on 30 January 1869, was sceptical of the claimed speed – the gradient favoured the late-running train and the average speed for the section was 22mph. The two passengers were uninjured. One of the van's axles was broken under the seats of both wheels; one break was smooth and probably caused by saline solution dripping onto it, while the other break had probably occurred during the accident. The Cambrian did not inspect private owners' wagons before allowing them in its trains and only checked the tyres during the course of a longer journey. Hutchinson recommended the discontinuance of 'these mixed trains', adding that if they were used the passenger stock should be coupled next to the locomotive to avoid the risk of them being derailed in the event on an incident involving the wagons.

A landslip occurred at the eastern end of the long tunnel at Penhelig on 17 December 1868, immediately after the passing of the 11.15am from Pwllheli. Fortunately the man in charge of the tunnels discovered it straight away. Starting immediately and working all night, the line was cleared in time for services to be resumed the next day.

The offer of £147,300 preference capital at 5% prompted the *Railway Times* to go on the attack on 19 December. 'The deplorable condition into which the Cambrian has been dragged by its originators – by the faction immortalised under the designation of Whalley-cum-Savin – has at length brought forth its fruits.' The Cambrian stood alone, it continued, in the special powers it had obtained on the basis that its capital could be protected not only by a pre-preference stock but by a pre-debenture charge. It appeared to be the most secure stock on the market, thought the paper.

On 31 December a fishing smack, the *Margaret and Jane*, ran against pier No 5 of the Barmouth bridge, damaging the fender. The watchman had been in position and the lamps were lit. The captain and owner, A. Jones of Barmouth, had ignored shouted requests to let his anchor go and the collision was inevitable. Had it not been for the fenders protecting the iron columns, Owen reported, the consequences would have been most severe. The damage was valued at £5 4s.

The board's expectation that the 1868 Act would remove the threat of legal action proved to be ill-founded. By January 1869 Frederick Adolphus Fynney, a Manchester stockbroker, had issued a writ for the interest due on certificates of indebtedness since 31 July; holders of LNR and NMR priority stock and others also petitioned the court to establish their position. Opinion was obtained on the interpretation of article No 36 of the Act, whereby proceedings could only be brought with court approval, and in respect of liabilities incurred after 31 July.

Fynney was one of a three Manchester stockbrokers determined to get the interest due on the stocks of the Cambrian and its constituents in which they had encouraged their customers to invest. The railway's finance committee suggested converting all of the certificates of indebtedness to debenture stock and 'expunging from the accounts … the documents bearing the objectionable term of "Lloyds bonds".'

Progress on completing the line to Dolgelley was the subject of Owen's report on 7 January 1869. The pile bridge over the Afon Wnion, the most important work on the section, he explained, was nearly complete. The piles had all been driven, but the superstructure remained incomplete. Between Penmaenpool and the river the line had been sufficiently complete to carry goods traffic 'for some time', but the sleepers had perished, and should never have been approved. On 11 March approval was given to Ward's request to hire a locomotive (No 2 ballast) at £1 12s per day and 12 wagons at 1 shilling each per day.

The Aberdovey quarry owners had complained about the shortage of wharfage there, and the sidings in the lower yard being covered in drifting sand. Owen said that he could build a new wharf to the east of the landing stage and access it via the existing high-level siding. Timber from Penrhyn could be re-used, but more would be needed. Elias reported that only the landing stage was accessible, and only to one vessel at a time, when three daily were expected. Loads included guano from London.

Payment for the use of shared facilities was one of the topics Elias covered in his 7 January report. The MMR had not paid its dues for the use of Aberystwyth station because it thought that the agreed portion, half, was too much, proposing one-third instead. In November, Elias said, the Cambrian's receipts had been more than £400, while the MMR had only taken £127. At Llanidloes the MWR would not make any agreement despite his best efforts, so he proposed giving three months' notice. Both items were deferred to a committee.

At Portmadoc, Messrs Green of Bedford and the Diphwys Casson Slate Company wanted a wharf 'at the junction between the Croesor and the Beddgelert siding', estimated to cost £15; the traffic committee agreed on 21 January.

Elias's special report of 16 January had dealt with a problem that was

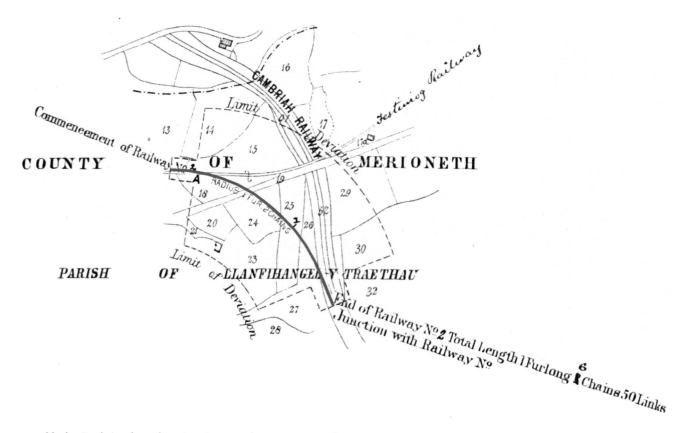

**The Cambrian's proposed branch for connecting with the Festiniog Railway at Minffordd in 1866.** *Parliamentary Archives*

to trouble the Cambrian throughout its existence – the management of the single line. On this occasion the driver of the 6.15am goods train from Ellesmere to Whitchurch did not take the staff. There was contradictory evidence from the personnel involved, but Elias said that it did not exonerate the driver, for whom it was a repeat offence; he had done the same thing between Cemmaes Road and Moat Lane 'recently'. Elias asked the locomotive superintendent to sack the driver.

The Potteries, Shrewsbury & North Wales Railway, about to be re-opened after a period of enforced closure, asked if the Cambrian would do its work at Llanymynech on payment of half of the station running costs. The agent, a boy and three porters should be shared, the traffic committee decided on 21 January, the PSNWR paying half of their wages, and the Cambrian making no charge for the use of the station. Rates were set for PSNWR traffic passing through the junctions. Earlier, on 7 November 1868, the Cambrian had agreed that the PSNWR could also hire a locomotive, providing it guaranteed payment.

Considering Parliamentary matters on the next day, the board decided to petition against the Festiniog Railway's Bill, which 'interferes with the interests and property of the Cambrian Company'. The Cambrian was concerned about the siding that became the exchange facility at Minffordd, despite Owen having reported on 21 October 1868 that a connection with the Festiniog Railway would be 'manifestly essential'.

The company also petitioned against a GWR Bill, whereby that company sought to build a railway between Dolgelley and Penmaenpool jointly with the Bala & Dolgelley Railway and the Cambrian, to obtain property adjacent to the Cambrian in Barmouth, and to have powers over the Cambrian between Penmaenpool and Barmouth. Presumably the GWR wanted to be certain of access to Barmouth in case the Cambrian failed.

More bad weather affected the railway on 31 January 1869, with several locations washed out. The worse wash-outs were at Ynys Las (36 yards), on the deviation (1,000 yards), at Towyn (500 yards) and at Friog (cutting side). Damage at Criccieth, Penrhyndeudraeth, Harlech and Llanaber was sufficiently repaired for trains to run by midday the next day. It took two days to repair the breach at Ynys Las and four

days before trains were run through Towyn and over the deviation. At Friog passengers had to walk around the damaged section for several days longer. 'Our receipts this week will in consequence be very much reduced,' concluded Owen.

Walker and Elias recommended the removal of the window bars from the through Composite carriages, 'which we know as the metropolitan', Elias arranging that the vehicles would not be worked through the tunnels. His 5 February report was annotated 'to be done'.

In February the threat of competition forced the Cambrian to amend its coal rates. The MMR had informed Aberystwyth traders that it would introduce a lower rate despite the mileage being greater, a move that prompted Elias to point out that rates for coastal destinations were not competitive with sea freight.

On 23 March the GWR gave notice that it intended to make use of Welshpool station from 1 April, using powers contained in its 1867 Act. Acknowledging the notice, the Cambrian asked the GWR how it proposed to implement the powers, and a copy of the notice was sent to the LNWR. The GWR had powers to use the ONR as far as Welshpool that required the Cambrian to render facilities and provide convenient accommodation for GWR personnel based there. It could be that the LNWR interpreted the GWR's activities as in contravention of their non-compete agreement, for nothing came of the proposal.

Relationships with the MWR at Llanidloes seemed fraught. Without notice, the MWR had sought an injunction to prevent the Cambrian charging 3d per ton for coal unloaded at the upper siding there in March 1869, when it also wanted a ruling that it could use the wharf for stacking coal. Broughton told his board that the Cambrian wanted the coal to be stacked at the old station site, causing inconvenience to the public, some of whom had to pass through a toll gate to get there. The injunction was held over, neither company making any comment on the eventual outcome.

In May the MWR decided to install a clerk to handle its own

bookings. Elias met Broughton and tried to persuade him that his actions caused inconvenience and expense for both parties and that the two companies should not compete.

The MWR's 1869 Act received the royal assent on 12 July. Further time was given to build the western extensions, the eastern extension was abandoned, and running powers over the Neath & Brecon Railway between Brecon and the NBR's junction with the Brecon & Merthyr Railway were granted.

Wade, the MWR secretary, doubled as secretary for the PSNWR, collecting £50 a year for the use of his office for the MWR. On 10 November 1869 the MWR agreed to his appointment as secretary to the Mold & Denbigh Junction Railway, charging that company one-third of the cost of the office space.

Reverting to the Cambrian, the directors' report for the half-year ended 31 December 1868 was issued on 28 April; the first to comply with the Railways Regulation Act of 1868, it revealed more about the company's financial position. Under the heading 'capital raised by loans' was the revelation that £849,876 had been borrowed at rates that ranged from 4½% to 10%, £8,100 being borrowed at the highest rate. During the half-year, £40,800 borrowed at 4½%, 5½% and 6% had been refinanced at 5% and redeemed.

Running at speeds of 75mph caused an engine to derail into a field near Abererch on 31 May, according to several newspapers. The 6.00pm from Pwllheli carried the mail for Carnarvon, but on this date had left it behind. An engine was sent back from Afon Wen to fetch it and was returning when the incident occurred. The crew, being uninjured, collected the bags and ran with them to Afon Wen, the connecting train still making its connection with the English mail. Nothing was said about the recovery of the locomotive from the field, and neither company secretary George Lewis nor Owen thought to refer to it in their reports.

Low tides allowed Owen to inspect the Barmouth bridge in June. The timber and ironwork below water level was encrusted with a 'small spiral fish'; they were to be scraped off and the whole of the works gas-tarred. In other respects the structure was in a good state of preservation. The channel marker buoys had moved out of position during the winter; they needed scraping to remove the black shellfish that covered them, and painting.

Rich inspected the line between Penmaenpool and its junction with the Bala & Dolgelley Railway on 11 June. It was 1 mile 64 chains long and single except for sidings at Penmaenpool. The track comprised 24-foot lengths of 70lb double-headed rail laid in 27lb chairs on 9-foot-long half-round sleepers. It was ballasted with gravel.

There were two timber viaducts, one with seven spans of 16 and 17 feet, the other with three 11-foot spans. Two small underbridges had brick abutments and timber girders. The works appeared to be satisfactorily constructed.

The only station was at Penmaenpool. The Cambrian had powers to use the Bala & Dolgelley Railway station at Dolgelley and the new line had been built with that objective. However, a vertical deviation beyond the Parliamentary limits was required to connect the railways; the landowner did not object.

The turntable at Dolgelley had been removed to enable the station to be rearranged, so Rich recommended approval be given to opening the line subject to the Cambrian undertaking to use tank engines until the turntable had been reinstated.

However, Elias reported on 24 June that the GWR refused to allow Cambrian goods trains into its station at Dolgelley because there was insufficient accommodation. Therefore a temporary platform had been built at the junction between the two lines, and had opened for passenger and goods traffic on 'Monday last', 21 June. Despite the

dispute, the GWR had advertised excursions from Liverpool and Birkenhead to Borth and Aberystwyth via Llangollen, Bala and Dolgelley from 12 June. A draft agreement for the use of the station, including the Cambrian's goods, had been reached by 21 July. Ward was paid £6,579 14s 2d for the works.

With some of the railway's structures now having been in use for 10 years, and some longer than that, Owen regularly reported on renewals and strengthening. In June he reported weakness in the viaduct at Llandinam, deflecting more than it ought, and recommended, in consultation with Davies, strengthening at an estimated cost of £150-180. A month later a five-span timber-pile bridge near Pool Quay was found to be rotting; Owen recommended replacing it with a twin-span girder structure carried on stone abutments at a cost of £207 14s 8d – renewing it like-for-like would cost £125 17s.

Owen's reports regularly included proposals and estimates for enhancements to the railway's infrastructure. In 1869 items included 11 level crossing gate houses built to a standard design by Ward for £85 each, improved facilities at Pwllheli (the present station was too small and in the wrong place, and a new one could be built for about £350), and a station at Afon Wen, where some shelter should be afforded, as it was a very bleak place. Another 'level crossing house' was built to the same specification for the Talerddig watchman.

In August Whalley was found to be travelling on an old director's ticket; returning to Llanidloes, he was made to pay for his journey. Elias asked the board to get Whalley to surrender the ticket as it should have been handed in when he ceased to be a director.

The NMR stockholders considered themselves above the other priority stockholders, but on 24 August their solicitor wrote that they were prepared to waive their priority provided they were ranked equally with the debenture stocks. They would not, however, agree to the Lloyds bonds, LNR preference stocks and coast-section debt being ranked in the same class, nor to a reduction in interest.

Arbitrators appointed under the terms of the 1868 Act made their award on the division of the net surplus on 5 November 1869, 65.43% to the inland and 34.57% to the coast. Landowners were undeterred from attempting to obtain court orders, and by December two were successful in obtaining permission to retake land on which the railway had been constructed, which would stop the railway operating if put into effect. Not having the capital to pay for the land, and being unable to issue the pre-preference debenture stock while the court cases were outstanding, the board obtained counsel's opinion on whether it could use the debenture interest fund to pay for the land, then pay the interest when the pre-preference stock had been issued. The opinion was that payment could be made from income, but that notice should be given of the intention to do so to give those concerned an opportunity to object. Damned if it did and damned if it did not!

A head-on collision east of Carno on 1 November was again caused by the mismanagement of the single line. Rich, Lieutenant-Colonel since 1867, reported on 23 November. Knowing that the 7.10pm up goods would be late, the Machynlleth station master decided that it should cross a down passenger train at Carno instead of Moat Lane, sending a written order to those stations with an earlier train. He made no arrangement to inform the driver of the change, but did inform the guard. The foreman porter, deputed to handle the token, delegated the duty to an assistant guard; the driver was not told that he would cross the passenger train at Carno.

The double-headed train comprised 36 wagons, mostly loaded, and one brake van with two guards; the company's rules required two brake vans with such a load. At stations where he was not due to cross, the driver was in the habit of throwing the token onto the platform and collecting that for the next section from the station master on the move. On a falling gradient of 1 in 149 to the west of the station, the distant signal lamp had been lit but had gone out, and the home signal was at danger. Running through the station, the goods collided with the passenger some 438 yards to the east.

The passenger train comprised a locomotive, five carriages of different types, and a brake van. The locomotive and first carriage were derailed. The two carriages at the end of the train became uncoupled and ran away until they were barely half a mile from Moat Lane. The goods locomotives sustained some damage, but remained on the rails. One wagon in the centre of the train was derailed. Injuries were confined to the passenger train locomotive crew, its guard and two passengers. One of the latter was Earl Vane, travelling in a composite saloon in the runaway portion, who sustained a cut to his head.

Rich attributed the accident to the carelessness of the Machynlleth station master, but also acknowledged the negligence of the goods train drivers for not being able to stop when the signals were against them. He also took a swipe at the passenger train driver for not noticing that the goods train had not stopped at the station sooner; what he expected him to do is not clear.

The Machynlleth and Carno station masters lost their jobs, the latter for his failure to manage the signal lamps properly, despite the petitions submitted by the respective communities. The goods train drivers ought to have lost their jobs, too.

The railway could be re-opened very quickly after an incident. On 1 December the 6.00am from Portmadoc to Pwllheli ran into and killed two horses in Penamser cutting, a mile from Portmadoc. Two carriages and a van were derailed, yet the delay to trains was less than 2 hours. Elias thought that the horses had got onto the line unnoticed at Portmadoc before the station gates had been locked the previous night. A claim for compensation from the animals' owners was declined because they had been trespassing.

During the same month a goods train from Welshpool ran onto the PSNWR at Llanymynech and collided with a van after a PSNWR brakesman had not restored the points for a train to Nantmawr after its passing. Elias refused to repair the van, telling the PSNWR that in future the signal box would be manned at its expense.

Still in December 1869, Elias sought fresh opportunities for traffic, drawing attention to the Festiniog slate handled at Portmadoc. Up to 140,000 tons was delivered to the port annually, 10% of which was transferred to the Cambrian via the Croesor Tramway. With proper facilities, and conversion of the tramway to standard gauge, the Cambrian should attract a third of the traffic and, getting its wagons onto the wharves, the company could import as well as export. The tramway's proprietors were prepared to countenance the laying of a third rail, he said. It would be a good feeder to the Cambrian, and independent of the proposed junction with the Festiniog Railway, especially as that company had taken no action since obtaining powers on 26 July. Owen estimated that the work could be done for £1,500-1,600 – only the conversion of the tramway in Portmadoc was involved, not the entire route to the quarries.

On 6 January 1870 Elias reported that the toll was 1 shilling per ton, of which the Tremadoc estate took 3d. As the Croesor wanted the Cambrian to do the haulage, Elias thought the Cambrian should have 6d. He thought the work could be done with two men and two horses. The present traffic bound for the Cambrian was 350 tons per week, £8 15s at 6d per ton; the men and horses would cost £3 8s. He foresaw traffic doubling even if the Festiniog Railway junction was built.

Elias seemed to have overlooked the facilities required to load standard-gauge wagons. Some rough arithmetic suggests that at 2 tons per wagon there would be seven or eight four-wagon trains daily, six

days a week. Put 8 tons into a standard-gauge wagon that a horse might be able to cope with and the number of movements would be about the same.

The tramway's owner, Hugh Beaver Roberts would accept £13,000 if the Cambrian bought it, Elias reported on 8 June, submitting the prospectus of a company being formed to take it over. By this time the traffic was 100 tons per day. However, in the end the Cambrian neither bought nor operated the Croesor.

By end of 1869 the Cambrian's core network was complete. Although it had cost much more than it should have, there are indications that, with the early track renewals and storm damage sustained, the materials used had not been of the best quality and that some of the structures had not been well made. Yet without the determination of Whalley, Piercy and Savin, and the bankers' willingness to load debt onto the ONR, when the slightest scrutiny would have revealed that it was incapable of fulfilling its obligations, it is unlikely that most of the constituents would have been built.

Consider the LNR, which was incomplete and penniless before Savin appeared on the scene. Had he not offered a way out, the LNR's failure would have been a deterrent to the development of other railways radiating out of Montgomeryshire, and the Welsh railway map would have looked very different.

Porthdinlleyn remained a dream that would be taken forward by others but never achieved. There would be no expansion on the Cambrian's own account for nearly 40 years.

OPPOSITE TOP No 17, a Sharp, Stewart 0-4-4 of 1875, runs along the Dovey estuary with a good load on 17 June 1912. *H. W. Burman*

OPPOSITE This 1898 view may look like the coastline, but the railway here has completed its crossing of the Dovey and is following the northern bank of the estuary to Aberdovey. *Valentine*

# Interlude: Along the coast

*The Terrace, Aberdovey*

**ABOVE** Viewing this 1908 picture, the residents' enthusiasm for pushing the railway to the back of Aberdovey can be understood, but they still had to endure the industrial atmosphere of the wharf and its ancillaries. The sheds were usually rented out, although one of them was used for wagon repairs for a time. *Valentine*

**BELOW** The original station building at Aberdovey. *Park/John Alsop collection*

Aberdovey. The Railway Station.

ABOVE One of the three 0-6-0s built by Vulcan Foundry in 1895 passes Aberdovey wharf siding. *H. W. Burman*

BELOW *Cambria*, an 1863-built Sharp, Stewart 0-6-0, stands next to the South signal box at Towyn circa 1894. *C. J. Young*

Towyn Station

52536. ⓙⓥ

**ABOVE** The North signal box at Towyn is seen in this 1906 view. After the Grouping the GWR concentrated all the station's signalling in a single box. *Valentine*

**BELOW** A train hauled by one of the GWR 2-4-0s acquired in 1921 drops down the 1 in 55 gradient on the cliff between Llwyngwril and Fairbourne. Over the years much more work was required to stabilise the cliffs. *John Alsop*

Friog Cliffs
Fairbourne

Fairbourne

JV72166

ABOVE Fairbourne and Friog, c1912. Fairbourne was developed as a resort by Arthur McDougall, a businessman who had made his money from self-raising flour. The station cost £576 13s 3d and McDougall paid £500 towards it; it was opened by 1 February 1899. A 2ft gauge horse tramway used in the development became a tourist attraction and was rebuilt as a 15in gauge steam railway in 1916. *Valentine*

BELOW Barmouth Junction, looking towards Barmouth. A selection of well-travelled empty wagons is stabled on the east-south curve, in the bay platform and on the siding on the Barmouth side. There are at least 50 wagons in the picture. Was the Cambrian taking advantage of their common-user status to hide them away for a rainy day? *D. George*

ABOVE The Barmouth East signalman offers up the tablet to a Dolgelley train, circa 1918. No 3 was a Nasmyth, Wilson 0-4-4T built in 1895. *H. W. Burman*

BELOW A steam boat bound for Penmaenpool is about to pass under Barmouth bridge as a train crosses overhead. The archway over the promenade entrance has been removed.

Barmouth Viaduct

84638

ABOVE A goods train crosses Barmouth bridge in 1920. The short viaduct on the left was subsequently renewed in concrete. *Valentine*

BELOW No apologies are offered for including this well-known photograph of 0-4-2 *Llanerchydol* at Barmouth – it is such a splendid photograph! Nine railway personnel are to be seen, seven of them from the traffic department. Is it any wonder that the railway struggled to make money?

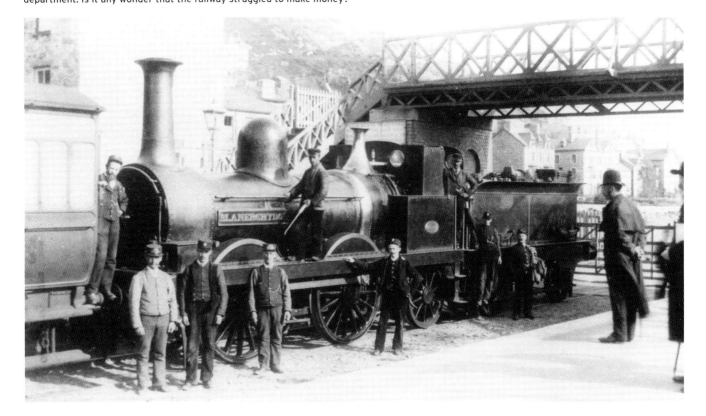

Station and Llwyncadwgan, Dyffryn Mer.

ABOVE Twenty-six miles from Dovey Junction, Dyffryn was the first passing place north of Barmouth and served one of the larger communities along the coast. As the railway headed north from Barmouth the alignment was mostly straight with easy curves. At 64 feet, Dyffryn was the second highest station on the coast. *John Griffith/ John Alsop collection*

BELOW Located between Dyffryn and Llanaber, the halt at Talybont was established for seasonal use following a petition submitted to the board on 11 June 1912. By 30 July the petitioners had raised £10 to pay for it and a short platform had been erected. The company reserved the right to close the halt if it was not justified, refunding £5 if it did so. It looks as though Captain Tyler would have recognised the overbridge. *John Alsop collection*

Railway Halt and Bridge, Talybont

ABOVE A goods train arrives at Llanbedr from the south. The train is hauled by No 48, a Sharp, Stewart
0-6-0 built for the Mid Wales Railway in 1873. *John Alsop collection*

BELOW Sharp, Stewart 4-4-0 No 50 was built in 1891 and rebuilt in 1915. It was photographed leaving
Pensarn with an up train circa 1921. *H. W. Burman*

ABOVE This location, approaching the cliffs to the south of Harlech, was one of several places where the Cambrian posted watchmen (Friog and Talerddig were others) in case of rockfalls. No 20, a Sharp, Stewart 4-4-0 built in 1886, is captured passing. *H. W. Burman*

LEFT Located midway between Harlech and Penrhyndeudraeth, Talsarnau was a mere 19 feet above sea level; Abererch, near Pwllheli, was 1 foot lower. A siding accommodated a small amount of goods traffic. *Park/John Alsop collection*

LEFT Like many other buildings on the coast line, Penrhyndeudraeth station was probably built by John Ward, Savin's former partner. The loop was for goods, with no provision made for passing passenger trains.

BELOW This is the level crossing at Portmadoc before the loop was extended across the road. Some of the fenced land in the foreground was once occupied by the Gorseddau Railway. In the 1860s Charles Easton Spooner, engineer to the Festiniog and Carnarvonshire railways, lived at Tuhwnt i'r bwlch, the house on the hill on the right of the photograph. *Pritchard's Series*

BOTTOM The 1909 station at Pwllheli, shortly after it had been opened.

# 4

# Emerging from receivership 1870-1872

Four years after Savin had collapsed, the company's settlement with his estate warranted the briefest of notes in the directors' and auditors' reports published in February 1870. The final payment due had been made by the issue of Lloyds bonds for £10,000 drawn on the coast section on 27 October 1869. The accompanying table shows the stocks and shares that he had held. Proceedings to determine the priorities of the various classifications of debt still remained outstanding, though. The board knew that whatever judgment was made, there would be an appeal, so the matter was not going to be resolved quickly.

'The conflict between the shareholders and the directors of the Cambrian Railways is growing more fierce,' the *Liverpool Mercury* had declared in October 1869. Led by the Manchester stockbrokers (page 97), the 'indignant' shareholders also had the support of Savin's inspectors. On 20 October their call for a vote of confidence in the directors had been refused for want of advance notice. Instead, an extraordinary meeting would be held in Oswestry. Refusing requests for the meeting to be held in Crewe, more convenient for Manchester shareholders, the chairman adjourned the meeting and left the room, whereupon the meeting elected a new chairman and changed the venue.

Nevertheless, the meeting was held in Oswestry on 27 October, when the confidence motion was withdrawn in favour of appointing a committee to reconstruct the board. On 17 February 1870 the committee asked for the resignations of all the directors except Vane and R. C. Herbert to be given to the chairman of the shareholders' meeting to be held on 28 February.

At the adjournment of that meeting, on 4 March, the Manchester contingent secured sufficient proxies to declare that it was entitled to reconstruct the board and carried a vote of no confidence in it.

| Cambrian Railways stocks and shares held by Thomas Savin, 7 January 1870 | |
| --- | --- |
| Cambrian Railways - Debentures (Inland & Coast) | £80,170 |
| Cambrian Railways - Ordinary - Inland | £307,165 |
| Cambrian Railways - Ordinary - Coast | £147,140 |
| Cambrian Railways - Preference capital: | |
| Oswestry & Newtown 1855, 1860 | £1,100 |
| Oswestry & Newtown 1863 | £149,400 |
| Oswestry & Newtown 1864 | £157,850 |
| Llanidloes & Newtown 1864 | £23,600 |
| Oswestry, Ellesmere & Whitchurch 1864 | £76,100 |
| Cambrian 1864 | £29,300 |
| Newtown & Machynlleth | £6,010 |
| Aberystwyth & Welsh Coast 1863 | £61,425 |
| Aberystwyth & Welsh Coast 1864 | £169,050 |
| Aberystwyth & Welsh Coast 1865 | £99,000 |
| Cambrian Railways (Coast Section) - Ordinary | £169,040 |
| Preference 1863 | £828 |
| Preference 1864 | £66,770 |
| Preference 1865 | £7,000 |
| Debentures 1862 | £1,000 |
| Debentures 1863 | £1,000 |
| Debentures 1864 | £3,000 |
| Debentures 1865 | £2,000 |
| Lloyds bonds | £7,874 13s |
| | **£1,565,822 13s** |

However, the board seemed to consider that it was not bound by the vote, probably because no advance notice had been given of it, but some of the board's subsequent decisions were certainly influenced by it. On 29 April the board agreed to pay the committee's expenses, to hold future general meetings in Crewe, and to appoint S. E. Bolden, the vice-chairman, to supervise the company's affairs at a salary of £1,500 in lieu of his director's fees.

NMR-guaranteed stockholders still had grievances, and had petitioned against the 1868 Bill. In brief, alone of the Cambrian constituents the NMR had been fully independent and had built its railway from its own resources, working it with its own rolling stock – and it was profitable. Keen to control the link with its AWCR client, the ONR made the operating agreement with the NMR in 1863 (page 54), but the amalgamation Act did not include the exact words of the agreement, leading to disputes over interpretation. For four years the guaranteed interest had not been paid and efforts to obtain it had been resisted. The stockholders were prepared to compromise if their stocks were treated the same as the mortgage stocks, on which interest had been paid.

On 20 January 1870 landowners whose property had been taken in 1862 sought leave to take action against the company. The conveyance had been completed in 1867 but the agreed price, £475, had not been paid. The judge ruled that leave to proceed under the 1868 Act should not be granted unless it was shown that the company was in a position to pay.

The early renewal of the track was not only confined to Savin's work. On 28 April Owen reported that he was relaying the NMR, rails and sleepers, at the rate of half a mile a week. Considering that the work was being carried out manually, and in between trains, this seems to be quite an achievement. By the end of October 9 miles (ONR 2 miles, NMR 4½ miles, LNR 2½ miles) had been renewed using 1,000 tons of new rail. On 9 June Owen had requested 25 tons of steel rail to lay in the middle (shunting) road at Oswestry station, where it would last much longer that the 'ordinary' rail used hitherto.

Coast-line trains were marshalled at Machynlleth, Owen reported on 12 May, recommending expenditure of £350 on a carriage shed as a means to avoid the damage done by exposure to the weather. There was ample room in the yard, he said, and it could provide accommodation for Vane's private saloon, a privilege for which the earl was prepared to pay. If Rich's description of the stock involved in the Carno accident (page 97) is correct, it seems unlikely that Vane was travelling in his private carriage on that occasion.

A month later Owen explained that he had improved level crossing safety by linking the gates to the distant signals so they would come off if the gates were opened. The modification had only cost a few shillings and did away with the lever, which was 'too heavy for a woman [crossing-keeper] to work'.

Considerable damage had been done at Aberystwyth, he reported in June, when the MMR carelessly shunted 12 loaded wagons into the Cambrian siding, running through the buffer stop before colliding with the refreshment rooms. The MMR repaired the damage without prompting.

On 10 June, under the heading 'Croesor & Portmadoc Railway', the vice-chairman was instructed to arrange 'for the purchase of a portion of the land on which the Beddgelert line is laid'. Construction of the Beddgelert Railway had ceased with Savin's insolvency in 1866. Purchase of the land in question facilitated the exchange of traffic with the Croesor Tramway.

The LNWR acquired the Carnarvonshire Railway under the terms of its additional powers Act, which came into effect on 4 July. On 16 September the Cambrian's traffic and works committee decided to provide facilities at Afon Wen, rather than let in the LNWR as joint owners.

The details and timing of Elias's resignation as traffic manager were not recorded. Candidates had been interviewed on 15 July and Henry Cattle, manager of the Cockermouth, Keswick & Penrith Railway, was appointed, taking up the post on 1 August. The MWR's Broughton had applied for the post but was not considered.

Making his final report on 13 July, Elias had either been very upset or angry by an accusation that he had been carrying Savin's traffic at a loss, taking seven pages to explain how profitable it was and finishing by saying that if it was still felt that the traffic was insufficiently remunerative, he would find 100 wagons and send it via the PSNWR, when the Cambrian would only get 6d per ton for carrying it from Porthywaen.

A serious accident that could have seen a train falling off the Dovey bridge was, it seems, narrowly avoided on 9 August. The bridge had been opened to allow a sloop, the *Mary Jane* from Liverpool, to pass up-river, but the bridge-keeper had failed to secure it properly afterwards. When the 8.10pm from Barmouth passed over it the moving section sank 5½ inches at the Aberdovey end. The locomotive crew felt their steed roll but the train was not derailed. The cogs in the apparatus were sheared off and a half-inch cast-iron pillar was broken. The bridge was packed up overnight, delaying the next morning's down mail by 34 minutes, but the first up train from Pwllheli went through on time. It was four days before the sloop could be released from the river. The bridge-keeper was sacked and £4 compensation was paid to the sloop's owner.

Notice that the LNWR intended to charge Railway Clearing House mileage rates and demurrage on its cattle trucks led to the traffic and works committee instructing the locomotive superintendent to build ten such vehicles on 16 September 1870. The Midland Wagon Company's offer to supply timber wagons on a seven-year purchase lease for £9 each per annum was also accepted.

Honesty of personnel was a regular issue. One case in 1870 involved a shortfall of £5 19s at Towyn, but it could not be determined if the booking clerk or the agent had taken the money, so the former was asked to resign while the latter was sacked. Another case involved a purse lost by a passenger, which came into the possession of Mr Baily, a clerk in the manager's office. Baily decided to investigate it privately with the objective of soliciting a reward; found out, he resigned, the company paying him a month's salary in lieu of notice, suggesting that maybe he had been well regarded. The purse was reunited with its owner.

Paid 10 shillings or less per week, Cattle was concerned that some of the clerks and boys who worked for the company did not receive enough to live on and were thus more liable to be tempted to misappropriate any money they handled. He increased some of the wages and proposed that in future boys should only be employed if supported by a reference from a clergyman or similar in the community where they were to work. He made savings in the wages bill, too, dismissing a boy paid 8 shillings a week at Whittington, whose services were not required; his work was done as well by the man in charge, saving £20 16s annually. He also unilaterally reduced the timber loaders' rate to 10d per ton, considering that 1 shilling was too much; the loaders accepted the reduction, doing the work as well as they did before. The saving was £115-120 per annum.

Cattle reported on 15 September that facilities at Pwllheli were inconvenient and insufficient. There was no shelter for goods traffic except for two box wagons that had been there for about a year and which should have been in traffic. The booking office was small and had to deal with left luggage. The waiting room was also small, and half full of items that should be elsewhere. 'It is not at all adapted for the class of people who use the station.' The LNWR had been canvassing for traffic, attempting to encourage traders to cart their goods to Chwilog, which would not succeed if Pwllheli had better accommodation. With a budget of £2,000, plans for a new station were approved the next day and Ward's tender was accepted. Obviously no action had been taken when Owen had raised the issue the year before.

On 13 October Cattle reported that the 11.50pm goods train from Oswestry had divided on the 1 in 80 gradient between Frankton and Ellesmere. Twelve wagons and the van were detached, neither the guard nor the driver noticing the division until the latter missed the former on arrival at Ellesmere. In thick fog he set off to look for the rest of his train, colliding with it on the level near the distant signal. One wagon was smashed considerably and five others were damaged. The line was blocked for several hours, one goods train was cancelled and another was delayed. No explanation was given for the wagons becoming uncoupled. As the train was going downhill and the detached portion did not catch up with the front portion, the guard must have applied the van brake for the gradient.

On the MWR, ownership of the 'Builth curve' had been transferred to the LNWR under the terms of that company's additional powers Act of 4 July. Sanctioned by the MWR's 1862 Act, shareholders were told on 10 August that the principal outlay on the curve had been made by the Central Wales Railway. A balance of £750 had been received and allocated to the capital account.

Following complaints from the MWR about the working of Llanidloes station, on 17 November 1870 Cattle recommended that the station master's position should be a joint post and that the present incumbent should be sacked. The traffic committee agreed in principle but wanted the station master removed to another station.

The Cambrian's habit of attaching carriages to goods trains had not impressed Cattle when he joined the company – he thought it was dangerous. On 17 November he sought the board's approval of the practice, adding that he would prefer to be instructed that it should cease. There had been no passenger stock on the goods train involved in the Ellesmere breakaway, but on 25 October a goods train involved in a 'serious accident' at Cemmaes Road had carriages attached; happily there were no passengers or 'we might have been brought in for a considerable amount of compensation'. Cattle got his way, but not before 22 December, when a coupling came undone and the side chains broke on a carriage attached to a goods train at Frankton; the carriage travelled nearly a mile towards Ellesmere before the guard managed to stop it. There had been three passengers in the carriage; the guard was rewarded with 5 shillings.

The Cemmaes Road incident had involved the train from Machynlleth derailing on the facing points, the loco, tender and seven wagons going off the rails. The station master had delegated to a porter the task of checking the points before the train's arrival. The engineer sent to repair the points said they were dirty and had not been properly cleaned or oiled. Cattle instructed the station master to attend the board, and reissued in more stringent terms the instruction about checking the facing points.

David Davies was involved with building the 6½-mile-long Van Railway from Caersws, hiring the locomotive *Meirion*, a Manning, Wardle 0-6-0ST, at £8 per week from November. The line was being built by a limited company registered on 9 June 1870 with the intention that it should be worked under the terms of the light railway clauses contained in the 1868 Regulation of Railways Act. Agreement with the relevant landowners avoided the need for compulsory purchase powers. Its purpose was to serve lead mines that had once been owned by Lefeaux. None of the directors or shareholders had any obvious connection with the Cambrian, although Davies did later have £500 in shares. Some sources give Powell and Swetenham as the contractors; the engineer was Evan Powell of Newtown.

Cattle imposed financial consequences on guards found to be bending the rules. In December 1870 T. Evans was reduced from being a goods guard at 20 shillings to shunter at 18 shillings because he had allowed staff to travel with him without either a ticket or a pass. In February 1871 guard Parry allowed a passenger with a 3rd class ticket to travel 2nd class without collecting the ticket or challenging it; he was demoted to the position of porter at 16 shillings per week, a reduction of 2 shillings. Staff changes consequential to the second case saved the company 9 shillings per week.

A letter to the *Daily Telegraph* published on 18 November took Rich back to the Cambrian to inspect the line at Friog with Owen on 30 December. He made several recommendations that the engineer agreed to undertake. In his report, Owen added that there was 9 feet of solid rock under the line at this point, which 'would not be known or … observed by inexperienced persons or by anyone casually inspecting the place'. The letter had its origins in a dispute between the railway and the adjacent Anna Maria mine. On 5 April 1871 Owen gave the mine's operator formal notice not to interfere with the company's property on threat of arrest and imprisonment.

The *Railway Times* had more to say about the Cambrian on 3 December 1870. The constituents had been forced into existence before their time, it said, without capital and without local repute. Land had been taken without payment and rolling stock obtained only to be sequestrated or pawned to pay financiers 5% on subscriptions that in any other way would not have earned legitimate interest. The several disreputable speculations that comprised the Cambrian had been kept in existence to provide a salary for their chairman.

Happily, the landowners were mollified, it continued, the undertaking had got rid of its parasites and a slender revenue had been secured. The paper considered that the history of the Cambrian, from the date of its first inception, should be forced, again and again, on the attention of Parliament, as well as rehearsed in the ears of credulous subscribers who were considered by speculating solicitors, engineers and contractors as their lawful prey.

Although the receivership caused by the suit of 'Robinson and others' had been ended in 1868 (see page 96), their suit was ended by consent on 12 January 1871, when a new Railway Companies Act scheme, the fourth attempt, dealing with the inland section, rendered it unnecessary. Filed in November 1870, the scheme was to be confirmed on 22 July. It enabled the inland capital debt to be converted into 5% debenture stock and the arrears of interest and guaranteed dividends up to July 1870 to be capitalised; it also authorised the payment of interest and guaranteed dividends in cash from July 1870 and the creation of a rolling stock renewal fund.

Without the scheme the company would be in no position to pay £107,680 interest arrears and to redeem £355,806 debentures and bonds. Shareholder objections forced the abandonment of the proposal to reduce the capital base. In future the annual interest would be £155,277.

The coast scheme was filed on 15 January 1871 and confirmed on 7 August. Under its terms the company could convert the debt and certificates of indebtedness into 4% debentures, capitalise the interest arrears, settle the advances made to the coast by the inland, and apply revenues in specified order of priority. The coast debenture interest was less than the inland interest, presumably because coast section costs were higher and it earned less.

A printed report dated March 1871 described the financial position in some detail and also made some comparisons with the Great North of Scotland Railway and Highland Railway, systems that were similar in size to the Cambrian. With a lower route mileage, the Cambrian might not attract the same benefits of scale as the others, but the maintenance cost was considerably higher, probably the consequence of lower construction standards being corrected. The details are shown in the accompanying table.

| | Half year to | Mileage | | % working expenses to traffic receipts | Railway expenses per train mile | Traffic receipts per train mile | Cost of maintenance | |
|---|---|---|---|---|---|---|---|---|
| | | Double | Single | | | | per railway mile | per train mile |
| **Cambrian** | 30 December 1870 | 9 | 169 | 61.68 | 2s 10d | 4s 7¼d | £121 | 13.78d |
| **GNSR** | 31 January 1871 | 7 | 271 | 53.51 | 2s 3¼d | 4s 3¼d | £35 | 5.68d |
| **Highland** | 31 January 1871 | 7 | 232 | 43.44 | 2s 0¾d | 4s 8¾d | £26 | 3.51d |

Some two years after Hutchinson had recommended doing away with mixed trains (see page 97) Cattle had been instructed to report on the implications. Writing on 19 January 1871, he had said that it would require an extra 240 miles per day and an extra passenger locomotive being kept in steam. Eventually the issue was to be scrutinised by the Board of Trade.

The PSNWR tried to extend its operations in 1871, in January applying for a rate to carry fluxing stone in its own wagons from Llanymynech Rocks to Llanymynech for onward transmission to Staffordshire, via its own line, for Savin. It also applied to work traffic over the Porthywaen branch with its own locomotives. On 18 February Owen inspected the locomotives at Llanymynech, identifying them as *Powis* and *Bradford*, Manning, Wardle 0-6-0STs with a 14ft 1in wheelbase bought by France to use on PSNWR construction in 1865. They were suitable for use on the main line or the Llanfyllin branch, he said, but not for the Porthywaen branch. .

The traffic committee decided that the PSNWR should be charged 8d per wagon, the same as charged to private owners. No comment was made about the locomotives and it seems likely that neither they nor the wagons saw service on the Cambrian beyond crossing between the PSNWR main line and the Nantmawr branch at Llanymynech.

Outstanding works to complete the coast-line station facilities would cost £23,095, Owen reported on 8 May. Expenditure on Pwllheli and Afon Wen stations and 'Minffordd siding' was estimated at £6,000, the Merionethshire Railway junction at £700, and the Croesor extension to Portmadoc harbour at £737. He also recommended doubling the track between Machynlleth and Dovey Junction, to 'materially facilitate the working of the traffic' and reduce the danger that existed because so many trains met at the junction, at a cost of £8,000.

The Merionethshire Railway was about to receive its Act for a standard-gauge branch from the Cambrian, 1,250 yards from the centre of the bridge over the Traeth Bach, to the Festiniog & Blaenau Railway at Ffestiniog, intended to take traffic from the Festiniog Railway. The new Pwllheli station had been completed by 21 September and at Minffordd only the permanent way for the shunting siding remained incomplete on 19 October. Fresh plans required from Spooner for the coal chute had prevented the works there being completed by 21 December.

Shunting goods traffic at Portmadoc, including the Beddgelert siding, had increased greatly during 1871, Cattle reported. He proposed allocating the locomotive used on the Van Railway at an estimated cost of £300 per annum. Train-engine shunting mileage would be reduced by two-thirds, saving £180 annually at 1 shilling per mile; in addition, £50 per year paid to the Portmadoc carter for horse-shunting wagons – 3d empty, 6d full – would be saved. The locomotive could also be used to work wagons between Portmadoc and Minffordd. Approval was given for a three-month trial.

Rich reported on the Van Railway on 31 August, finding its facilities wanting so far as passenger traffic was concerned; it is said to have been opened for goods traffic in August. On 7 September the Van company

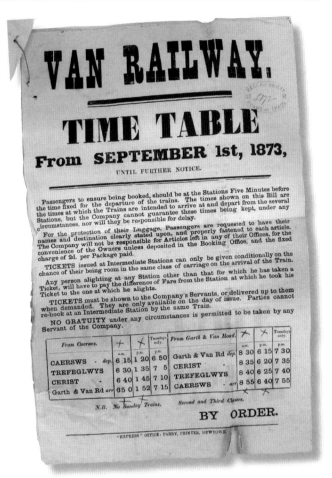

The Van Railway opened from an interchange with the Cambrian at Caersws for goods in 1871. Its passenger service only lasted until 1879 and its goods service until 1893. Leased by the Cambrian from 1895, it survived to be taken over by the GWR in 1922, that company paying £1,100 in cash for it. *National Archives*

was informed that in order for the railway to be worked as a light railway it required a licence from the Board of Trade and that such licence could not be issued unless the company had obtained either an Act of Parliament or a Railways Construction Facilities Act, 1864, certificate.

Acting on Rich's requirement, on 22 September the Cambrian asked the Van to install a headshunt between the two lines and to provide its own locomotive shed instead of using the Cambrian's goods shed; Davies reported on 20 October that these works had been completed. The MWR had dealt with the Van Mining Company's request to sell it a 2nd/3rd composite carriage on 5 July, but it was only prepared to hire; 3rd class carriages were the subject of an enquiry made in March 1876. It was to be 1873 before the Board of Trade certificate requirements were met and the Van opened for passengers.

An order for Sharp, Stewart to supply two goods engines had been approved on 22 September 1871. Priced at £2,270 each, they were to

be delivered on 1 March and 1 April 1872. On 20 October unspecified modifications proposed by the builder, costing £50 per locomotive, were approved.

Being built of timber and used by steam locomotives with inefficient ashpans, the Barmouth bridge was at risk of fire. Indeed, several fires had already been dealt with by the bridgeman, Edward Roberts, Owen reported on 20 February 1872, requesting approval to spend £54 on a small portable engine to be stationed there. In June he wanted to buy a boat to be used when maintaining the bridge. There were several at Portmadoc available for £4 or £5, and it cost that much to hire one.

Rich inspected the station and mineral branch at Minffordd on 22 March 1872, submitting his report three days later. The branch was made for the purpose of interchanging goods and minerals between the Cambrian, 4ft 8½in gauge, and the Festiniog Railway, 1ft 11¾in gauge. The interchange would take place using a large goods shed constructed to accommodate both railways. In fact, the branch was nothing more than a short siding that led from the Cambrian to the new goods yard constructed close alongside the Cambrian line, in the fork between the two railways. The junction was a single line with points locked with the station signals, and the sidings in the yard were controlled by catch points, which he said should be locked with the distant signals.

This Sharp, Stewart 0-6-0, seen at Oswestry, was one of two delivered in 1872. No 1 in the fleet, it was originally named *Victoria*.
*R. H. Bleasdale/John Alsop collection*

The station at Minffordd was intended mainly for the interchange of passengers between the railways, and there was no access to it except by crossing the Festiniog Railway on the level. Rich recommended that an approach should be constructed under the Festiniog Railway. Mineral and goods traffic could be taken into the yard, but the passenger station could not be used until the junction point was locked with the distant signals; the catch points were locked with the station signals and the approach had been made. Rich re-inspected the location and on 16 July reported from Borth that he had found everything to his satisfaction. The traffic committee gave instructions for the new facilities to be brought into use by 1 August.

In practice, the station was inconvenient to work because it was on a 1 in 50 gradient and heavy trains could not be restarted, Owen reported on 19 September 1872. However, a platform extension costing £41 9s 4d would allow the engine and tender and two carriages to stop on a gradient of 1 in 263.

Two years after the LNWR had taken over the Carnarvonshire Railway (page 113), Cambrian directors met Richard Moon, the larger company's chairman, to discuss items of mutual interest, including the effect of the takeover on the Cambrian's traffic. From the LNWR's perspective, the meeting might have been consequential on the Cambrian's objection to the its applications for powers to build the 2-foot-gauge Festiniog & Bettws Railway, included in Bills deposited in 1870 and 1871. The Cambrian would see any traffic abstracted from the Festiniog Railway affecting its own business at Minffordd and Portmadoc. There was also resistance to any proposals to amend long-standing rebate agreements, complete with a division in the board about whether to be conciliatory or combative in dealing with the LNWR.

Sharp Stewart 0-6-0 No 4 was built in 1872 and rebuilt in 1891. Originally it was named *Alexandria*. *R. H. Bleasdale/John Alsop collection*

Overend had not attended any MWR board meetings for nearly two years when he retired on 24 February 1871. William Bailey Hawkins, an MWR board member since September 1869, was to become a Cambrian director in 1884.

The MWR's use of the Brecon & Merthyr Railway's new station at Brecon had been discussed by the former on 26 April. Broughton reported meeting Henshaw, his BMR counterpart, and agreeing that the MWR should have the use of both goods and passenger stations, staff, fire and light, through sidings for traffic interchange, room for one engine at Talyllyn, a small engine shed at Brecon, water at Brecon and Talyllyn, together with signalling, switchmen and cleaning of carriages, for £800 per annum. The MWR had previously offered £750 against the BMR's call for £850, that sum being £120 less than previously paid.

The dispute between the Cambrian and the MWR over the cost of working Llanidloes station and the joint line had been going on since 1869 (page 98). However, its escalation escaped reference in the Cambrian records and was only mentioned obliquely in the MWR minutes. Some information was included in the MWR shareholders' reports. The Cambrian persisted with a long and expensive lawsuit over the costs, but reached a settlement in May 1871 when it agreed to let the MWR's carriages, but not its locomotives, run through to Moat Lane; in return the Cambrian's 'carriage' could run through to Brecon. The MWR's ambitions for further through running were restricted because the Cambrian worked the Moat Lane-Llanidloes section as a branch line.

Despite this settlement, the MWR claimed £624 17s 8d for materials used in constructing the joint line; they had been supplied to the MWR's contractor, the Cambrian replied.

The MWR's decision to cease maintaining the joint line from 1 February 1872 must have been behind the Cambrian's unrecorded decision to make use of the unused MMR line between Llanidloes and Penbontbren and work the parallel lines together. The necessary works were complete by 20 June, Owen reported. On the 24th Broughton informed the Board of Trade that 'the junction' had been put in by the Cambrian without the MWR's consent, was unnecessary, and was calculated to cause expense and accident. He refused to attend the inspection made by Hutchinson on 28 June.

The single line had been built by the Cambrian to connect its line at Llanidloes with the unfinished portion of the MMR originally intended to have been made between Strata Florida and Penbontbren. About 5 miles that had been partially constructed had been allowed to decay and there appeared to be no intention of repairing it. The MWR's single line that ran alongside had been inspected in 1864.

The new junction was put in with the objective of working the traffic between Penbontbren and Llanidloes as on an ordinary double line, which Yolland had recommended in 1864. Hutchinson, however, understood that the junction had been made to settle a dispute between the Cambrian and the MMR.

The single line presented for inspection was 1 mile 46 chains long and was constructed at the time of the parallel line used by the MWR, all details being similar, although the chairs weighed only 22lb each. The line was in good order and the signal arrangements at the new junction were complete and satisfactory. However, at the south end of Llanidloes station a crossover road with facing points would have to be removed and the points of another [crossover?] would have to be interlocked with the MWR's signals. Chairs weighing at least 30lb must be substituted for the lighter ones at each side of the joints and

The interchange with the Festiniog Railway at Minffordd was opened in 1872. The main line and station are off the right of the photograph.
*R. H. Bleasdale*

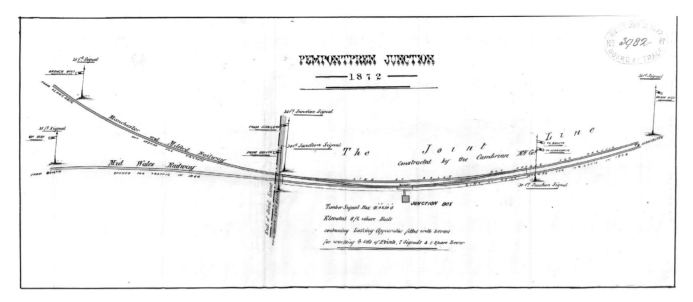

This signalling diagram shows the arrangements at Penbontbren after the Cambrian decided to work the joint line from Llanidloes as an ordinary double line in 1872. The Manchester & Milford Railway line to Llangurig was never used by ordinary traffic.

in the centre of each rail. Shelter was required on the down platform, 'which has not hitherto been used but will have to be with the completion of the new arrangements'.

Owing to the incompleteness of the works Hutchinson could not recommend approval being given for opening. He also questioned whether approval should be given even when his requirements had been met, given that the junction was not required for the traffic or by the company working over it. He concluded by noting that the joint chairs had not been upgraded on the MWR line despite the undertaking given in 1864.

Returning on 25 July, Hutchinson found everything to his liking, an interlocking error being corrected immediately, and he recommended approval. He made no reference to the 27lb chairs now used throughout; the state of the iron trade had made procuring 30lb chairs difficult, so Owen had upgraded the entire section with the 27lb variety from maintenance stock. The revised arrangement was brought into use on 1 August.

Power to extend the time available to acquire land and construct the MWR's western extensions had become effective on 27 June. Four years later the company was to be relieved of its obligation to build the extensions, having been unable to raise the money to do so.

The MWR's relationship with the Cambrian did not improve for some time. On 28 March 1873 the latter resolved to take action against the MWR to compel payment of its joint line and Llanidloes station maintenance contributions.

The financial situation of the smaller company was also not too good, for it was negotiating its second Railway Companies Act scheme, effective

from 6 June 1873. Its debenture debt was renewed for ten years at 4% or could be exchanged for 4½% perpetual debenture stock; £20,000 loan capital was also authorised. The company's position would be improved, shareholders were told, if there was a greater interchange of rolling stock with its neighbours.

That the North Wales Narrow Gauge Railways Act of 6 August 1872 had little impact on the Cambrian was mostly due to its parliamentary solicitor. The Bill is not mentioned in any of the Cambrian's surviving records, but NWNGR railway No 8 was a line from Abererch, near Pwllheli, to Porthdinlleyn, intended to be connected to the Croesor & Portmadoc Railway by making the Cambrian section that linked them mixed gauge. Despite admitting that its service was sparse, the Cambrian's objections prevailed.

Owen saw the worst possible motives for the Bala & Festiniog Railway Bill in December 1872. Noting that 2¾ miles of its route was substantially the same as that of the Merionethshire Railway, he thought that if the new company acquired the MR, or obtained running powers, it would have access to Portmadoc and the Lleyn and be capable of 'robbing the Cambrian' of the traffic from the Lleyn and Nevin districts that was not taken by the LNWR at Chwilog.

OPPOSITE TOP The Oswestry & Newtown Railway's Kilkewydd bridge crossed the Severn between Welshpool and Forden. Reconstruction of this bridge, completed in 1921, was the last major civil engineering project undertaken by the company before the Grouping. *Cambrian Railways*

OPPOSITE A lattice superstructure was used for the Newtown & Llanidloes Railway's Severn crossing at Scafell, between Newtown and Moat Lane. *Park*

# Old bridges

*View from Kilkewedd Bridge, Welshpool*

ABOVE The Newtown & Machynlleth Railway's timber bridge across the Severn at Caersws. The home signal and a siding buffer stop are on the left. *Park*

BELOW Holidaymakers enjoy the beach at Barmouth with Conybeare's lifting bridge and Cader Idris providing a backdrop. The spindly iron columns have been fully protected by fenders.

ABOVE This little bridge over the inlet at Barmouth is often overlooked. The station distant signal is this side of it and another post with two signals is just visible on the far side. *Renaud*

LEFT One of the lesser known timber bridges on the coast crossed the River Artro between Llanbedr and Pensarn. *Frith/John Alsop collection*

**TOP** The Briwet, or Traeth Bach, bridge at Penrhyndeudraeth crossed the Afon Dwyryd and also carried a toll road; the bridge is to be replaced with independent structures for railway and road.

**ABOVE** Running across the Traeth Mawr, the area reclaimed by Madocks as a result of the construction of the embankment at Portmadoc, the coast line gave its passengers the second-best view of the Snowdon range. This 1893 photograph shows the timber viaduct as it was before 21 spans on the right-hand side were replaced by an embankment in 1914. The watchman's hut is at the left-hand end of the bridge. *Valentine*

# Large station buildings

ABOVE The station building at Oswestry reflected its status as the company's headquarters. After some years of disuse Oswestry Borough Council restored it to community use in 2005.

BELOW Photographed circa 1905, Welshpool station, much larger and grander than its railway status ever required, was designed to impress the Earl of Powis. Horse-drawn vehicles wait for traffic. Now separated from the railway by the Welshpool bypass, it is used as a retail outlet. *Valentine*

ABOVE An early-20th-century parade gathers on the forecourt of Machynlleth station, an attractive building that remains in railway use today. *John Alsop collection*

BELOW Llanidloes was also much larger and grander than it ever needed to be; even if it had been the headquarters of the Newtown & Llanidloes Railway, which it was not, it did not need to have been this big. Now, traffic races past where trains used to call.

ABOVE Ellesmere, an intermediate station on the Oswestry, Ellesmere & Whitchurch Railway, served as the headquarters of the Wrexham & Ellesmere Railway. *John Alsop collection*

BELOW No large buildings here, for at Wrexham the Wrexham & Ellesmere Railway made use of the Wrexham, Mold & Connah's Quay Railway station, which occupied a large site close to the centre of the town.

# Branches

LEFT From the junction at
Llanymynech, the Oswestry
& Newtown Railway's Llanfyllin
branch was 8¾ miles long, its
terminus quite well appointed and
convenient for the community.
*John Alsop collection*

RIGHT Llansantffraid was the
largest intermediate station
on the Llanfyllin branch.
*Park/John Alsop collection*

BELOW This view of Llanfechan
the Llanfyllin branch's other
intermediate station, shows the
ground frame cabin, and wagons
loaded with timber in the goods
yard. *John Alsop collection*

OPPOSITE TOP The Llanfyllin
branch halt at Bryngwyn
attracted the postcard publisher's
attention because intending
passenger had to work the signal
to stop trains. *Park*

OPPOSITE The Cambrian soon
realised that the short branch
from Abermule to Kerry was
going to cost more than it earned,
but found that it could not be
closed. The branch train, hauled
by 0-4-0ST No 36 *Plasfynnon*, a
Sharp, Stewart locomotive built
for the Oswestry & Newtown
Railway in 1863, is seen at the
terminus.

BRYNGWYN RAILWAY STATION.

" You work the Signal to stop your Train."

OPPOSITE The Cambrian's platform just scrapes into this circa 1885 photograph of Dolgelley. The route to the coast was to the right.

OPPOSITE BELOW One of the crew of Sharp, Stewart 2-4-0T No 56 keeps an eye on platform activity at Penmaenpool. Built as a tender locomotive in 1865 and named *Whittington*, No 56 was one of the two locomotives rebuilt as tank engines for use on 'short trains' in 1907. *John Alsop collection*

ABOVE The junction between the Llanfyllin branch and the Shropshire Railways' Nantmawr branch; the latter runs to the right. *John Alsop collection*

RIGHT The Kerry branch's curvature and steep gradient, as much as 1 in 42, called for this special signal, which indicated whether the turn-out was set for the platform or the loop.

BELOW A feature of the Oswestry & Newtown Railway track when new was the use of tie bars to hold it to gauge, as seen in this photograph of the Kerry branch crossing a stream at Fron Fraith. *Park*

# 5

# Maturity
# 1873-1900

Concerns about operating costs caused the board to order savings in all departments on 21 February 1873, and by 20 April annual savings of £3,601 4s had been identified. The GWR's request for an improved service to Aberystwyth in May resulted in an examination of costs and reports demonstrating the 'heavy cost of working the coast section'. Cattle had already obtained approval for an increase in 3rd class coast fares to the 1½d per mile authorised in the coast Act on all trains except the first up and down, where the Government-mandated 1d per mile still applied. In the second half of the year one of the two ballast gangs had been laid off.

Owen had taken the need for economy to extremes, perhaps, with his proposal of 20 February for protecting shunting moves on the loop siding at Barmouth Junction. He thought that in fog or mist the overlaps were too short and suggested installing additional signals that would be worked by the shunter independently of the signal box;

*Marquis* was a Sharp, Stewart 0-6-0 built in 1873. It was photographed at Oswestry just before it went into the works for a heavy overhaul, completed in August 1889. Presumably it then lost its temporary cab.
*R. H. Bleasdale*

when the shunting had finished the arms could be lowered and the ordinary signals would protect the trains. The idea, which was approved, avoided the cost of rods and cranks that linking the signals to the signal box would require.

The prospect of the LNWR taking traffic at Blaenau Ffestiniog, despite being several years away, prompted Cattle to suggest a response. On 22 April he obtained approval to provide free storage space for the slate merchants at Minffordd and Portmadoc, the FR's Spooner having agreed with the idea. The railways would handle the slate for the merchants, charging 1 shilling per ton for the service. The LNWR provided such a facility at Mold and he expected that it would do the same at Bettws y Coed.

Savin's influence over the company's affairs and those of people associated with it continued for a long time, as illustrated by the case of Piercy v Fynney, reported in the *North Wales Chronicle* on 15 March. It also gives an indication of how much the debt was discounted. The case had been brought by Robert Piercy, the engineer's brother. Piercy had accepted £54,000 in Lloyds bonds for work carried out as Savin went bankrupt, assigning them to Fynney for £30,000 'in the panic of 1866'. Now Robert Piercy claimed one-third of the £30,000 from Fynney; he lost the case, the court ruling that Robert was owed the money by his brother. An active shareholder since at least 1864, Fynney was to be appointed to the board on 23 October 1874, but resigned on 23 July 1875.

'After several years' experience' traffic carried on the coast during the winter was found not to justify the service provided, leading to timetable reductions from 1873/74. Reductions were also applied to parts of the inland section. Income was unchanged while there was a 'great saving' in working expenses, although a rise in the price of coal had increased locomotive running expenses.

In November 1874 a group of London shareholders had been sufficiently dissatisfied with their lot to attempt to promote their own Bill in Parliament, to alter the arrangements between the inland and coastal sections and to increase the directors' remuneration. Giving notice of the Bill a month earlier than normal, they must have intended to bring the board to the table, in which strategy they succeeded because, with some amendments, including removal of the clause increasing the directors' pay, the Bill was adopted by the company and enacted on 30 June 1875.

On the MWR, Broughton's resignation to become the general manager of the Great Western of Canada Railway was accepted on 5 March 1875. In post since 1865, he was succeeded by Frank Grundy at a salary of £450 from 1 May.

Another resignation was that of S. E. Bolden from the Cambrian board, because of ill-health, accepted on 29 October 1875. He had been acting as managing director since 1870 (page 113).

One more legal case, Eaglesfield v the Marquis of Londonderry (Earl Vane), was heard at the High Court in December 1875. Ten years earlier the plaintiff had agreed with Savin to exchange £10,000 of Neath & Brecon Railway debentures for LNR No 1 preference stock. It turned out that the company issued him with the same amount of 'worthless' ordinary LNR stock. Savin's status as a bankrupt protected him from being joined in the case, which was not to be concluded until it reached the law lords on 11 April 1878; judgment was given in the Cambrian's favour.

A Bill to revive powers and to raise additional capital, deferred from 1874 because of the shareholders' intervention, was not proceeded with until September 1876. However, by the time the royal assent was given on 14 August 1877 the company had decided to set Porthdinlleyn aside. The Act authorised £50,000 capital to buy rolling stock and to pay arbitration costs; the acquisition of extra land at Criccieth and Talsarnau stations was also authorised. Shareholders had been warned that the mileage and demurrage account had been running in the red, indicating the need for more rolling stock.

Another 'great storm', on 20 January 1877, did damage that cost the Cambrian £3,317 to repair. Floodwaters from the Vyrnwy and Severn near Buttington and Pool Quay nearly reached the level of 'the great inundation of 1852', Owen reported. The sea walls on the Aberdovey deviation and at Friog were washed away and there were slips at Brow Bank on the OEWR. Cattle telegraphed 'to all parts of the country' to stop through bookings beyond Machynlleth. He provided road transport for passengers who arrived on the first day, but on the second day told them to make their own arrangements – the stoppage was an act of providence and the company was not liable. Claims of £13 4s should not be met, he thought, but the difference in the fare between the journey booked and that made should be refunded.

A few days later this event was followed by the highest tide known to the oldest inhabitants, combined with a hurricane. Owen's report required 14 handwritten pages. On the inland section the Moat Lane 1st class refreshment room chimney fell through the roof and signals were damaged at Oswestry and Montgomery. On the coast, the line was flooded at Glandovey Junction and washed out near Dolgelley and Ynys Las. The embankment between the junction and Ynys Las had been made of sand, another example of poor construction. Two years before, Owen had reported noticing that the tide was rising higher each year, attributing the effect on the deviation embankment stopping it from spreading as far as it did. Services were restored over the deviation in 24 hours and on the Dolgelley branch in 48 hours. The Aberystwyth line, however, was closed for 12 days.

Defence works at Glandovey, Ynys Las and on the deviation were completed in September. Some strengthening was still required on the Dolgelley branch and at a location three miles north of Barmouth. Advance notice of a cyclonic storm on 10 October was telegraphed to Owen from the USA, but it travelled with less velocity than anticipated and the only damage was two signals blown down at Borth.

The arbitrators appointed to apportion revenue between the coast and inland sections made their second award on 16 November, allocating 62% to the inland and 38% to the coast, compared with 65.43% and 34.57% awarded in 1869 (page 99).

Secretary George Lewis was appointed to the combined post of secretary and general manager on 28 September 1878; the purpose of the change, shareholders were told, was to consolidate the executive. Two out of ten directors had voted against the proposal, but they were all to approve the award of an extra £150 for the additional responsibilities on 28 February 1879. Cattle, the traffic manager, left on 30 November.

Lewis soon had to explain a significant decrease in traffic, reporting on 25 January 1879 that a reduction in the last two weeks in January had continued. Investigation had shown that passenger numbers had been affected by the weather, slate quarries had been closed for more than two weeks, mineral traffic from Savin & Company Ltd's quarries at Llanymynech and Porthywaen had nearly halved (2,072 tons compared with 3,898 tons), and there had been little lead ore from Van and Llanidloes.

On the bright side, he looked forward to a revival of the timber traffic and reported a significant, but unexplained, increase in parcels traffic originating at Newtown. On 29 March, however, he reported that slate and limestone trades were still in depression, although there had been some improvement on the inland section.

'Two new powerful passenger engines with bogie frames, for heavy summer traffic, four 3rd class carriages with brakes attached, and one goods brake van have been added to the rolling stock during the last

## 'Statistics of the gross revenue and expenditure of the company...'

| Year | Length of line | Miles run by trains | Gross Receipts Traffic Receipts | | | | | | Misc receipts | TOTAL |
| | | | Passengers | Parcels/ mails | Merchandise | Livestock | Minerals | TOTAL | | |
| --- | --- | --- | --- | --- | --- | --- | --- | --- | --- | --- |
| | Miles | Miles | £ | £ | £ | £ | £ | £ | £ | £ |
| 1869 | 178½ * | 711,591 | 66,488 | 8,917 | 35,180 | 7,390 | 25,135 | 143,110 | 2,883 | 145,993 |
| 1870 | 178½ | 729,789 | 71,029 | 9,720 | 40,358 | 7,331 | 29,214 | 157,652 | 5,855 | 163,507 |
| 1871 | 178½ | 775,056 | 72,847 | 10,005 | 43,257 | 8,397 | 29,911 | 164,417 | 8,395 | 172,812 |
| 1872 | 178½ | 817,495 | 72,879 | 10,062 | 47,959 | 7,998 | 32,990 | 171,888 | 8,078 | 179,966 |
| 1873 | 178½ | 778,154 | 74,416 | 10,444 | 50,672 | 7,993 | 33,107 | 176,632 | 8,835 | 185,467 |
| 1874 | 178½ | 758,436 | 78,675 | 11,100 | 52,479 | 7,843 | 33,863 | 183,960 | 7,080 | 191,040 |
| 1875 | 178½ | 774,782 | 80,138 | 12,372 | 52,389 | 9,706 | 36,117 | 190,722 | 7,374 | 198,096 |
| 1876 | 178½ | 811,407 | 88,590 | 12,563 | 56,736 | 9,013 | 35,147 | 202,049 | 7,765 | 209,814 |
| 1877 | 178½ | 821,799 | 85,465 | 12,956 | 54,253 | 9,438 | 37,633 | 199,745 | 7,005 | 206,750 |
| 1878 | 178½ | 802,311 | 84,054 | 13,834 | 53,917 | 8,980 | 36,796 | 197,581 | 7,658 | 205,239 |
| 1879 | 178½ | 805,398 | 75,958 | 14,397 | 48,835 | 7,791 | 35,679 | 182,660 | 6,739 | 189,399 |
| 1880 | 178½ | 826,236 | 77,632 | 14,148 | 49,035 | 7,908 | 35,664 | 184,387 | 6,766 | 191,153 |
| 1881 | 180¾ ** | 861,325 | 75,436 | 13,736 | 47,428 | 7,918 | 36,714 | 181,232 | | |
| 1882 | 180¾ ** | 855,374 | 77,061 | 14,250 | 49,525 | 8,847 | 31,567 | 181,250 | | |

\* The extension to Dolgelley (2 miles) was opened on 21 June 1869.      \*\* The company commenced to work to Llanyblodwel on 11 February 1881.

half-year,' shareholders were told on 19 February. The locomotives, 4-4-0s, had been ordered from Sharp, Stewart on 25 January 1878 for delivery by 1 June, the tender price of £1,995 each payable after they had run 1,000 miles satisfactorily. The wheel arrangement was unusual for the time, but became the standard for the Cambrian's passenger stock.

David Davies, the erstwhile contractor, caused a fluttering in the dovecotes with the publication of a letter discussing his perception of the company's situation, sent to the deputy chairman on 21 February. Apparently printed and distributed to shareholders before their meeting on 28 February, when he also retired as a director, he managed to upset the board, the shareholders and the officers. A copy of the document has not been seen, but the essence of it has been distilled from reports and letters transcribed into the minutes.

Starting from the point that the ONR's agreement with the AWCR, to work it for 45% of the gross receipts, was disastrous, as it cost 88% to run, Davies went on to show that the inland section had to service £325,329 of capital derived from the coast and the certificates of indebtedness, equal to the ONR's original capital. The company had £4,401,153 capital and had never paid interest on more than

Built by Sharp, Stewart in 1878, *Beaconsfield* was the first of the Cambrian's 4-4-0s. *John Alsop collection*

£1,600,000. In 15 years no dividend had ever been paid on the remainder – it was not worth the paper it was written on.

After 10 years as a director, he had been unable to find out how the inland section became liable for certificates of indebtedness to the value of £85,409. The railway cost more to maintain than similar lines, the locomotives were wrecked and £80,000 needed to be spent on the track.

When Londonderry replied to Davies's speech on the issues, saying that the 'worthless' capital had been issued to him and Savin to build the railways and that 'whilst he had been living in affluence there were numerous widows and orphans in Lancashire in very reduced circumstances whose husbands and fathers invested their moneys in that stock on the faith of its bona fides,' Davies walked out.

With remarkable speed, the company produced a 12-page pamphlet of its own, rebutting Davies's claims, distributing it to shareholders on 26 February. Compiled by John Conacher, the former accountant's clerk, it stated that expenditure on track maintenance had averaged 22.47% of gross receipts from 1869 to 1879. Comparisons made with other companies still showed that the Cambrian's costs were out of alignment. The proportion ranged from 6.5% (Lancashire & Yorkshire Railway), 10% (Midland Railway) and 11% (LNWR) to 15.31% (Highland Railway). Over the same period 100½ miles of track had been relaid, using 6,456 tons of iron rail and 4,717 tons of steel rail, the latter first used in 1875. Many of the timber bridges, whose locations were unrecorded, were renewed with iron during this period.

Conversely, the cost of rolling stock maintenance averaged 10.75%, only slightly less than the LNWR's 10.8% and noticeably less than the Midland's 12.52% and the Lancashire & Yorkshire's 15.30%. The Highland spent only 8.75% of its gross receipts on rolling stock maintenance. The LNWR would be expected to do well in such comparisons, having the economy of scale in its favour.

The rebuttal did not answer the question about the inland certificates of indebtedness, probably issued against claims for extras made by Savin's inspectors. Entitled 'statistics of the gross revenue and expenditure of the company, and of the expenditure on the permanent way and rolling stock', the rebuttal brochure was produced annually

| Year | Rate of receipts | | Working expenses | Rate of expenses | | Net revenue | |
| | Per mile of line | Per train mile | Amount | Per train mile | As proportion of gross receipts | Amount | Rate per train mile |
|---|---|---|---|---|---|---|---|
| | £ | d | £ | d | % | £ | d |
| 1869 | 819 | 49.24 | 96,246 | 32.46 | 65.93 | 49,747 | 16.78 |
| 1870 | 917 | 53.77 | 101,787 | 33.47 | 62.25 | 61,720 | 20.30 |
| 1871 | 969 | 53.51 | 105,205 | 32.58 | 60.87 | 67,607 | 20.93 |
| 1872 | 1,010 | 52.83 | 111,601 | 32.76 | 62.01 | 68,365 | 20.07 |
| 1873 | 1,041 | 57.20 | 106,328 | 32.79 | 57.33 | 79,139 | 24.41 |
| 1874 | 1,072 | 60.45 | 114,346 | 36.18 | 59.85 | 76,694 | 24.27 |
| 1875 | 1,111 | 61.36 | 113,033 | 35.01 | 57.06 | 85,063 | 26.35 |
| 1876 | 1,177 | 62.06 | 125,940 | 37.25 | 60.02 | 83,874 | 24.81 |
| 1877 | 1,160 | 60.38 | 130,932 | 38.24 | 63.32 | 75,818 | 22.14 |
| 1878 | 1,151 | 61.39 | 107,514 | 32.16 | 52.38 | 97,725 | 29.23 |
| 1879 | 1,063 | 56.44 | 102,332 | 30.49 | 54.03 | 87,067 | 25.95 |
| 1880 | 1,072 | 55.52 | 100,309 | 29.14 | 52.48 | 90,844 | 26.38 |
| 1881 | | 52.29 | 115,375 | 32.14 | 61.47 | 72,313 | 20.15 |
| 1882 | | 52.68 | 106,440 | 29.86 | 56.69 | 81,323 | 22.82 |

until 1882. The table above shows the basic data and demonstrates how the company had grown over the years since the settlement had been made with Savin's inspectors.

Capital works mentioned in the directors' reports during the 1870s were carried out at the locations listed in the table below.

### Capital works, 1870-79

| Location | | Half-year ending |
|---|---|---|
| Towyn | Permanent station | 31 December 1870 |
| Pwllheli | Permanent station | 30 June 1871 |
| Afon Wen | Permanent station | |
| Pensarn | Permanent station | 30 June 1872 |
| Portmadoc | Permanent station | |
| Glandovey Junction | Permanent station | |
| Criccieth | Permanent station | |
| Harlech | Permanent station | |
| Ynys Las | Permanent station | |
| Llwyngwril | Permanent station | |
| Talsarnau | Permanent station | |
| Minffordd | Permanent station | |
| Dyffryn | Permanent station | |
| Penrhyn | Permanent station | |
| Aberystwyth | Accommodation works | |
| Montgomery | Permanent station | 31 December 1872 |
| Fenn's Bank | Dwelling house | |
| Talerddig | Dwelling house | |
| Barmouth Junction | Permanent station | |
| Glandovey | Permanent station | |
| Portmadoc | Permanent station | |
| Barmouth | Permanent station | 30 June 1873 |
| Oswestry | Two dwelling houses | |
| Penmaenpool | Permanent station | |
| Criccieth | Important additions | 31 December 1879 |
| Pensarn | Important additions | |

Itemised capital expenditure from 1876 to the end of the decade included rebuilding timber bridges with iron and stone at Penstrowed and between Forden-Montgomery (two), costing £1,463 8s 8d, raising embankments on the Dovey and Mawddach estuaries and other sea defences (£3,614 13s 5d), building a sea wall on the Aberdovey deviation (£1,698 5s 9d) and a landing stage at Aberdovey (£885 15s 10d), adding more piles to the Traeth Mawr viaduct (£700), work on the footbridge at Oswestry, shared with the GWR (£675 14s 11d), and arching (lining) one of the Aberdovey deviation tunnels (£320 6s 9d). To save the time and cost of sending wagons from the coast to Oswestry, a repair shop was erected at Aberdovey at a cost of £527 6s 11d in 1880/81. Block telegraph installation and track renewals made regular appearances under this heading.

The Penmaenpool Bridge Company opened its private toll bridge across the Mawddach on 27 February 1879. The railway collected the tolls, charging 10% for the service. Lewis reported railway traffic increasing, recommending improvements to station facilities.

The importance of the LNWR rebate, 50% of the revenue on traffic (except minerals) handed over at the most convenient interchange, was demonstrated in a report compiled by W. M. Crouch, a Glasgow civil engineer, in January 1880. According to the National Archives' catalogue, it was commissioned by several Scottish banks and insurance companies, but there is nothing in it to substantiate that assertion. The rebate was worth £16,000 a year to the Cambrian and probably half of it was profit, making it worthwhile for the Cambrian to hand traffic to the LNWR at the expense of mileage over its own system.

The remainder of the report described the company's background and made observations on its prospects and scope for economies. Comparisons were made with the Great North of Scotland Railway. Maintenance could not be reduced while so many of the bridges were made of timber. Care should be taken not to reduce locomotive maintenance standards. Efficiency in carriage and wagon maintenance was good and Crouch recommended an increase in expenditure, worthwhile in the longer term.

Other working expenditure had been cut back, the only officers not

The toll bridge across the Mawddach at Penmaenpool was opened in 1879. The double-armed signal and single platform are just beyond the bridge in this photograph.

in subordinate positions being the general manager, who carried the roles of secretary, traffic manager and superintendent, and the engineer, who also served as locomotive superintendent. Whether this was real economy Crouch could not say, but he supposed that the directors were satisfied the officers concerned had the required experience and energy.

Crouch could not see any scope for an improvement in traffic receipts. There were no communities of 10,000 to generate passenger traffic, and no important factories or mineral fields. The slate traffic could only decline with the arrival of the LNWR and GWR at Blaenau Ffestiniog, while granite paving slabs and setts from Portmadoc [Moel y gest] could reach their market more easily by sea. The Cambrian had no prospects as a through route, the LNWR would see to that.

The company's only hope for improving its receipts was developing its local traffic, but it had cost much more than the traffic justified. There was little hope of all the stocks earning any dividend unless some scheme for consolidating the inland stocks and reducing its interest, as with the coast debenture stocks, was devised. The Cambrian would, Crouch concluded, have a value to the LNWR and the GWR, and possibly even to the Midland Railway, but without knowledge of those companies' policies it would be impossible to estimate what it would be.

On 10 May 1879, by agreement with the MWR, Penbontbren signal box was taken out of use, the windows and door boarded up, the lamps returned to the stores, and the MMR line abandoned. The MWR had been pressing for the signalman's position to be dispensed with since 1876.

Several people were injured when a part of the footbridge across the line near the castle level crossing at Criccieth collapsed on 30 June 1879. A fair was being held in fields on either side of the railway, and a crowd of some 200 had amused themselves by standing on the bridge and throwing sticks and stones at pedestrians and trains crossing beneath them.

On 21 February 1880 Owen reported that he had inspected the Barmouth bridge and found it requiring heavy repairs. He recommended increasing the number of bays, having them at 3-foot intervals instead of 5 feet.

During 1880 a directors' committee held several meetings with the MWR chairman to discuss terms for making a working agreement. A report submitted to the Cambrian board on 22 May was accepted; its contents or recommendations are not known, but there was to be no action on the proposal for several more years.

The possibility of operating part of another railway came with the

Space at Penmaenpool was short so the engine shed, visible here to the left of the boathouse, was remote from the station. Tied up at the landing stage is the steamboat that operated a service to Barmouth. *Pictorial Stationery Company*

closure of the Potteries, Shrewsbury & North Wales Railway on 19 June. France, now working the Nantmawr quarries and bankrupt, asked if the Cambrian would work his traffic over the PSNWR's Llanymynech-Llanyblodwel branch via Buttington. There was no response to this, but on 14 January 1881 the PSNWR accepted the Cambrian's offer to work the traffic for 3d per ton with a two-year contract. Services to Llanyblodwel were started on 11 February without comment; not even the shareholders were told, despite 2 miles 36 chains being added under the 'lines worked' heading in the reports from July 1881. The principal traffic was materials for the construction of Liverpool Corporation's Vyrnwy reservoir. With the quarry under different ownership, Nantmawr stone traffic was to be worked from 1885.

Henry Gartside, a director of four of the constituent companies and a Cambrian director since its founding, died in 1880. His erstwhile colleague, Whalley, had died on 7 October 1878, completely isolated from the railway network that he had played a key role in creating.

The retirement of Lefeaux from the MWR board on 23 February 1881 passed almost unnoticed. Another of the figureheads of the constituent companies, he had only attended one meeting since Whalley's resignation in 1866.

The carriage of slate from Blaenau Festiniog via the LNWR in 1881 was an ongoing topic. Breese, the Portmadoc solicitor, had persuaded the quarry proprietors to continue sending via Minffordd, 'notwithstanding the powerful influence and inducements held out to them'. In February 1882, however, the LNWR had not only set its rate to match the Cambrian's but also offered to pay the costs of connecting the principal quarries with its facilities. The Festiniog Railway was squeezed in the middle and had agreed to reduce its rate from 2s 1½d per ton to 2 shillings, the proprietors paying 10d and the Cambrian 1s 2d.

If he could get the FR to join the Railway Clearing House, Lewis reported on 26 April 1882, the Cambrian would get a share of the FR's mileage, reducing the 1s 2d by 4d or 5d per ton. The traffic was worth about £16,000 to the Cambrian. An agreement was made on 3 May for the Cambrian to charge the same rate as before, rebating the difference to the FR for remittance to the consignors.

George Lewis, the secretary who had joined the company from the ONR, had his appointment terminated at the board meeting on 30 March 1882. He accepted the position of traffic manager at £700 and agreed to work with John Conacher, who was appointed secretary and accountant with a salary of £500. Whether Lewis was underperforming or Conacher was shining with the production of his statistics is not clear. He resigned on 31 August and was replaced by one of 26 applicants for the post, Edwin Liller, on a salary of £600 from 1 November.

Other staff changes on 31 August 1882 saw Owen relieved of his responsibility for locomotive superintendence, with his salary reduced to £600, and the appointment of workshop foreman William Aston as locomotive superintendent, on trial at £250; his appointment was made substantive from 1 June 1884, at a salary of £300. Owen had taken responsibility for the locomotives after Walker had left the company on 31 March 1879.

A decision to renew 75 miles of track with steel rail by 1885 had been taken on 29 April 1882. The estimated £48,000 cost would be charged to revenue in equal instalments over five years. When completed, 141 miles of the railway's 187 route miles would be on steel rail. The remainder was lightly trafficked branch lines and parts of the main line renewed with iron 'in comparatively recent years'. The use of steel, the directors reported in February 1883, reduced track maintenance costs, making funds available for other purposes without increasing working expenses.

The remains of Sharp, Stewart 2-4-0 *Pegasus* after it had fallen 50 feet onto the beach at Friog on 1 January 1883. Only one carriage was badly derailed, as shown. *Cambrian Railways*

Heavy rain during the last few days of 1882 caused a few minor landslips on the NMR section, but none of them caused as much damage as the slip at Friog on 1 January 1883. Some 30 tons of peaty-loam overburden and 30 feet of stone wall 2ft 6in thick fell up to 68 feet and pushed ex-ONR Sharp, Stewart 2-4-0 *Pegasus*, hauling the 5.30pm from Dovey Junction, over the cliff. Both crew members were killed when it fell to the beach, a vertical distance of 50 feet. Three of the four vehicles in the train were derailed, one badly. The locomotive was destroyed.

Rich reported on the incident and found no fault with the company or its staff. The railway ran on a 6-foot shelf cut into the rock at the location of the accident, he wrote, and there had been no slip there in the previous two years. Altogether, 120 tons of material had fallen. The road should be better maintained and drained, he felt, and any remaining loam above the railway should be removed or the base should be repaired and supported with stone pitching.

On 15 January Conacher gave notice to the highway authority to keep the road in proper repair. The company contributed £10 to the fund started for the widow of William Davies, the fireman, who had a child to bring up. In May, a Sarah Lloyd of Barmouth made a claim for £1,500 compensation in respect of injuries alleged to have been caused by the accident; the board refused the claim, and it was heard at Chester Assizes in July 1884. The jury found in the company's favour, agreeing that it had not been negligent.

In January 1883 a writ had been issued against the Gorseddau Junction & Portmadoc Railway for £708 10s 10d – £379 18s 10d was owed for the signal box and interlocking installed in 1875, the remainder for working the crossing since 26 January 1875. Judgment had been obtained for the first amount on 29 June 1876 but no settlement had been made. Negotiations with the General Post Office on various matters were a feature of the 1880s. The issue of free passes to GPO personnel, approved on 23 January 1883, produced an objection because they excluded liability in case of accident, a standard railway company clause for them. The GPO also wanted reimbursement of fares paid before the passes were issued, obtaining judgment when the company refused. The solicitor observed that the GPO was only entitled to passes where its telegraph had been installed along the railway, for the purpose of construction, maintenance, repair or inspection, whereas the company had been in the habit of issuing annual passes for the entire system.

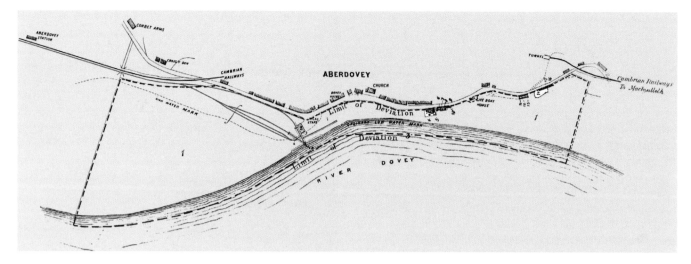

Track serving the wharf at Aberdovey, 1883. *Parliamentary Archives*

The GPO took the case to court in 1884, also obtaining judgment, the judge ruling that while the railway companies might understand that a free pass excluded liability, the GPO and other parties could not be expected to know. One rather suspects that the GPO chose to bring the case against what it perceived to be a weak company. On a less contentious note, on 23 May 1883 permission had been given for the installation of wall letter boxes at Barmouth and Newtown.

Also in the 1880s, the Festiniog Railway conducted a long-running dispute with the Cambrian over the payment of rebates due on the slate traffic. It had allowed the rebate to the quarry owners and wanted reimbursing by the Cambrian. For reasons that were never specified, the Cambrian resisted all requests to pay despite being in contravention of its agreement with the FR. Repelling pressure from Spooner, on 12 April 1883 it even went so far as to instruct Owen to survey an independent route from Penrhyndeudraeth to Duffws.

He reported on 22 May that he had taken trial levels and proposed a route 10½ miles long with a 600-yard-long tunnel, 'several rather heavy viaducts' and a ruling gradient of 1 in 40 for 2¼ miles. It would cost about £90,000. Having got to Duffws, he noted, connecting to the quarries could not be done without demolishing much housing, the land formerly available being occupied by the LNWR, the GWR and 'the Festiniog Railway proper'. It was not mentioned again, but the FR still fought for its rebate.

After 29 June 1883, armed with fresh Parliamentary powers, £4,777 15s 5d was spent on extending the pier at Aberdovey, £20,000 of pier stock being authorised for the purpose. Offering it to existing shareholders on 19 February 1884, the company said that it would only issue the stock in sufficient amounts to ensure that the profit from operating the pier was enough to pay 5% dividend.

Other powers permitted the issue of £30,000 No 5 coast debenture stock, £175,000 coast ordinary stock and £30,000 inland ordinary stock belonging to the inland section for 'such price or prices as they can get', to recoup the cost of the capital overspend, to establish and operate hotels at Moat Lane and Llanidloes and refreshment rooms at any station, and to establish a savings bank for the benefit of employees. Many stations already had refreshment rooms but the company was not empowered to operate them.

An unusual breach-of-duty claim was made against the railway in February 1884. A customer in Llanidloes had dispatched goods to London, then two days later asked for the delivery to be stopped, but the LNWR had already made it. The plaintiff paid the Cambrian's costs and the LNWR paid the amount of the claim. The logic of this is not understood.

On 15 April Conacher forecast that at the current level of business the company would run out of money on 30 June, when the debenture

interest was due and when an agreement with the National Provincial Bank to reduce the £40,000 overdraft to £20,000 came into effect. In due course, the bank started proceedings and on 12 July the directors were appointed managers and Conacher the receiver. A trade depression and the company's inability to issue fresh capital contributed to its difficulties.

Liller, the traffic manager, lost his job as a consequence of the downturn. On 18 August one of the directors gave notice of a motion, that 'seeing the continued decrease in the company's traffic, and the generally unsatisfactory explanations given by Mr Liller, he be called on for his resignation.' Three months notice was given on 30 September and Conacher was instructed to undertake the duties from 1 January 1885. On 21 January 1885 the board resolved that Liller could apply to the chairman for a reference and should be given £100 for his removal expenses.

The brutality of 19th-century justice is brought home by an entry in the solicitor's report of 27 September 1884. At Towyn, Mary and David Jones (aged 8 and 6 respectively) had placed seven stones on the line and the company decided to sue, as a warning to others. The magistrates, however, said that owing to the children's tender age all they could do was bind their father over to birch them and be responsible for their future behaviour.

The practice of naming locomotives came to an end with a minute of the traffic committee of 30 September 1884. No explanation was given and names remained on those locomotives that had them; they continued to be used in reports. In 1901 Herbert Jones, then locomotive superintendent, told *The Railway Magazine* that they were not used because of the difficulty in transmitting Welsh names accurately over the telephone. The magazine wondered why names could not be used on the locomotives and numbers on the telephone. Many of the names had their origins in the construction of the constituent companies, the nobility that supported them and the places served.

When Earl Vane, 5th Marquis of Londonderry since 1872, died on 6 November 1884, his executors asked the company to buy his saloon. Aston examined it, reporting that its woodwork was in fair condition considering the age of the vehicle, 14½ years, although the upholstery was considerably worn, not having been renewed since it was made. The wheels, axles, axle boxes and springs were in good order but the springs were over-weighted since the new brake gear had been fitted. The brakes were of no use to the company and the springs would need replacing. The carriage had cost £731 when new. The design was unsuitable for the company's use; it would be difficult to insert extra doors although it could be used as a family carriage. He estimated its value at £250. The saloon must have been new when Owen referred to it on 12 May 1870 (page 113). Provisions of the NMR's 1865 Act saw Vane replaced by Lord Henry Vane-Tempest.

The effects of the mid-1880s depression led to the MWR seeking economies, arranging for the Cambrian to take over its carting at Llanidloes from January 1885; the revenue was divided 60%-40% in favour of the Cambrian. In 1886 the MWR made the final instalment, £12,906, due on its rolling stock.

Most Cambrian capital expenditure during the 1880s went on the sea walls at Afon Wen (£534 15s 4), Llanaber (£387 14s 2d) and on the Aberdovey deviation (£6,999 2s 9d). Following the accident at Friog, £2,073 13s 1d was spent on the cliff and £293 8s 5d to install a check rail on the reverse curves. £1,874 16 11 was spent on extending the sea walls at Llanaber and Harlech. As the amounts got smaller towards the end of the decade the sites were amalgamated in the reports, to Aberdovey and Friog sea walls (£3,304 6s 5d) and Aberdovey, Friog and Afon Wen sea walls (£494).

Other works undertaken included a warehouse at the Aberdovey landing stage (£451 7s), renewing a third timber bridge between Forden and Montgomery with stone and iron (£300), arching (lining) Aberdovey tunnel No 4 (£1,680 18s 9d), and extending platforms (£2,127 12s 3d).

In 1885 another attempt was made to remove the stranglehold the company's debt had on its development. In a notice circulated on 19 February, the proprietors were told that it would be beneficial to consolidate and simplify the numerous classes of debentures and preference stocks, albeit at the expense of them making a 'small sacrifice'. If accepted, a new scheme that already had the support of holders of £1,459,477 capital would allow the receiver to be discharged and an application for listing on the stock exchange.

Made on 14 July, the scheme converted the capital into inland, coast and pier ordinary stock and four classes each of 4% preference and debenture stock – 11 types of stock instead of 14. Doing away with the 5% stock was helpful, of course, but did not change the underlying position, that with £2,684,757 ordinary stock and £2,220,000 loan stock the company was still over-capitalised. Indeed, it was to be nearly 10 years before all the interest was paid on all debenture classes.

The Abergynolwyn Slate Company had not settled its accounts with the Cambrian in full since the rate had been increased from 1 shilling to 1s 6d per ton on 1 May 1883, deducting 6d per ton from each invoice. The Cambrian's offer of 1s 4d per ton was put into effect, under protest, from 1 November 1885, leading to a hearing with the railway commissioners on 2 February 1886. Despite a finding in the slate company's favour, the matter rumbled on into 1887, matters at issue including the 2d per ton charge for horse shunting at Aberdovey, awarded to the Cambrian, and the threat to send the slate via Dolgelley despite it being no cheaper to do so.

From 21 February 1886 the MWR was allowed to work Sunday trains on the Llanidloes branch, using its own locomotives and guards, on payment of 12 shillings per day. Conacher could not see any advantage to the MWR working all branch services. Four locomotives were based at Llanidloes, three of them working onto the main line. Except for one return trip that a main-line locomotive could perform, the duties of the fourth could be taken over by the MWR, but that company would not alter the time of one of its goods trains to accommodate the change.

From 1 July 1886 through trains to Liverpool and Manchester from Aberystwyth were made up solely of Cambrian carriages and worked by Cambrian guards to and from Manchester. Conacher anticipated the service using six new composite carriages and at least four carriages and two vans built in 1885.

The adoption of the continuous vacuum brake in 1886 was responsible for £222 19s 7d being spent on locomotive steam brakes and £3,785 0s 8d on equipping both locomotives and carriages. Another safety measure was the installation of interlocking points and signals, which cost £1,740 10s 2d.

The Aberdovey wharf in use as a promenade in the early 20th century.
*Donald George/John Alsop collection*

The Porthdinlleyn Railway, engineer George Owen, had obtained its Act in 1884. On 26 January 1887 the Cambrian resolved to work the line for 50% of the gross receipts. Although an extension of time was obtained in 1888 the scheme was to be abandoned in 1892.

On 21 March 1887 Conacher submitted a report showing where savings could be made if the Cambrian leased the Festiniog Railway. Troubled by the depression and the loss of slate traffic since the LNWR had opened to Blaenau Ffestiniog in 1881 and the GWR in 1882, the FR had commissioned John Stevenson Macintyre, an engineer who had worked for the Eastern Counties Railway and Great Eastern Railway, to report on the prospects of reducing its working expenses. Completed in November 1886, the report was submitted to the FR's shareholders on 25 February 1887.

Conacher said that although he could not comment on Macintyre's conclusion that the FR was paying too much for its consumables compared with other railways without seeing the FR's books, there would be an immediate saving of £1,260 in management charges and expenses if the Cambrian ran it. However, he had been informed by a stockbroker that it would cost about £7,000 a year to lease, £269 short of 5% on the FR's ordinary stock and £539 in excess of 1886's profits and 'his' savings. On that basis the figures did not make sense. The Cambrian board accepted the report on 23 March without comment. Although the FR was put on the agenda in May and June, discussion was deferred each time and the issue was not raised again.

The long-held ambition for the Cambrian to be a part of a through route to Ireland came into effect on 19 April, when the Sligo Steam Navigation Company started a service between Aberdovey and Waterford, three return trips per week creating the shortest route between the south of Ireland and Lancashire, Yorkshire and the Midland counties and carrying passengers, goods and cattle. The exercise was not worthwhile. On 26 April Conacher reported that the amount of cargo carried from Waterford had been small because dry weather had lowered demand for Irish cattle and there was uncertainty about through rates. By 30 June a loss of £389 had been incurred.

On 4 May the vessel had been 3 hours overdue at Aberdovey, arriving too late to cross the bar. The Cambrian's agent went out in a small boat and discovered the captain drunk, a situation that was not unusual – he was sacked by the ship's owners. By 22 June the owners were complaining about the lack of profit being made, asking for a subsidy of £250 per month. The Cambrian blamed the ship, the SS

Sharp, Stewart No 21 was one of two 4-4-0s put into stock in 1886.

*Liverpool*, for being too slow. The owners blamed the firemen and the coal. Later, the four Waterford firemen were accused of deliberately keeping it short of steam. Their replacement by Liverpool firemen saw some improvement in timing but did nothing to make the service profitable. It appears that the Waterford Steamship Company applied pressure to some would-be shippers by threatening not to pay the annual bonus due on the number of beasts shipped.

Another incident occurred on 28 September, when the ship grounded on the Aberdovey bar after the captain had missed one of the buoys in the dark. It was floated off on the tide the next morning.

In a change of agent and ship, the Clyde Shipping Company's SS *Magnetic* took over on 24 October, but turned out to be just as unsatisfactory, despite a subsidy of £150 per month. On its second crossing stormy weather caused the death of 31 cattle and badly injured 25 more. The ship's agents, Conacher discovered, had failed to insure the cargo despite the shippers having paid for it; claims came to £719 2s 6d. By 16 December the ship had made only 13 out of 24 advertised crossings. (The White Star Line's SS *Magnetic* was launched in 1891.)

A working agreement between the Cambrian and the MWR was agreed during the last months of 1887, the contract being dated 29 February 1888. The Cambrian took over from 2 April. Conacher thought there was scope for improving services after he and William Aston, the locomotive superintendent, conducted a speed test during an inspection on 5 March 1888. The workshops at Builth should be retained for maintaining and repairing MWR carriages and wagons, he thought.

Owen made an inspection that started on 2 April, finding the bridges and tunnels in need of light repair that could be carried out at little cost over the summer. The track needed more work; steel rail had been laid on old chairs and sleepers, was of different lengths and had no provision for expansion. The keys were of elm and other softwood instead of seasoned oak and sleepers had not been pressure-treated with preservatives. Ballasting after relaying was in arrears; Conacher said that the worst section was between Builth and Penbontbren. Signals were in working order but interlocked only at Talyllyn, Three Cocks Junction and Glanyrafon siding. At Doldowlod level crossing and two private sidings there were no distant signals, just small point indicators. Only a home disc signal protected St Harmons and Aberedw stations from approaching trains. The loop on the MWR platform at Moat Lane was too short and should be extended by 70 yards to permit proper working.

Aston reported that MWR passenger locomotive No 2 was in good order, having been fitted with a new boiler. Nos 3 and 4 were in moderate condition, while No 1 had been put into the Builth workshop for general repairs that would take about six weeks. The locomotives were Kitson 0-4-2s, like the Cambrian's mixed-traffic 'Volunteer' class. Goods engines Nos 5 and 8 were in fair order, No 9 needed £100 of repairs, and No 7 was very poor and would cost £600 to overhaul, so No 6 was about to be fitted with No 7's boiler. No 10 had a cracked cylinder, which had been repaired. Nos 8 and 9 were working at 100lb boiler pressure and Nos 5 and 10 at 110lb. Nos 9 and 10, supplied in 1873, were Sharp, Stewarts identical to recent Cambrian purchases. The Cambrian board agreed to purchase MWR Nos 2, 9 and 10 for £3,000 on 21 March.

The MWR carriage stock was 'an old type' built by Ashbury and needed considerable work. Aston mentioned tyres, springs, underframes, solebars, tie rods, buffer springs, axle boxes and headstocks. Although the stock did not justify the cost of repairing to make it suitable for general use, it should be kept in fair repair for market and excursion traffic. There were 40 carriages, four brake vans, two horse boxes and a carriage truck; 10 vehicles were in works or stopped for repair, and 18 were running but not in good repair.

Wagons rebuilt in the last 10 years were in good condition, 21 cattle trucks were of a good size and a good type, and 19 covered vans were in poor condition. There were 439 goods vehicles in total; 56 had been broken up and 47 were stopped for breaking up.

In August Conacher reported that there was now a convenient and reliable connection between the Mid Wales section and the main line. The convenience of visitors travelling from South Wales to the 'watering places on the company's system' saw the operation of trains with through carriages from Cardiff, Merthyr and Newport.

Negotiations with the GPO over improvements to the mail service had started in 1887 and continued into 1888. When the GPO refused the Cambrian's offer to make the necessary changes for £9,000 a year, the company offered to maintain the status quo with a five-year contract for £5,500 plus an increase of £100 per year backdated to 1 July 1886. The amount must go to arbitration, the GPO countered, if the Cambrian did not accept £5,500, its final offer. The Cambrian gave in.

As a part of the contract, the Cambrian was required to supply a sorting carriage; the Metropolitan Railway Carriage & Wagon Company's tender of £568 for one vehicle was accepted on 9 August. Before producing the drawings, Aston travelled on the Travelling Post Office between Shrewsbury, Stafford and Crewe. The new vehicle was put into service during the first half of 1889.

During the year Aberystwyth town council pushed for mails to the town to be accelerated, but the GPO refused to pay the Cambrian's extra expenses for additional empty stock and light engine working.

The steamboat service was no more successful in 1888 than in 1887. On 30 January sailings had been reduced to two per week and the subsidy increased to £200. On 25 August the *Magnetic* broke its propeller when berthing at Aberdovey, and missed several sailings while a replacement was found and fitted. Ironically, the new propeller was more efficient, reducing the vessel's coal consumption by 20%. However, the ship was in liquidation and its use was terminated on 30 November, when services were said to be suspended.

Undeterred, the company obtained powers under the Cambrian Railways (Steamboats) Act, effective from 9 July 1889, permitting it to build, buy or hire and use, maintain or let steam vessels between Aberdovey, Aberystwyth, Portmadoc and Pwllheli and Wexford, Rosslare, Waterford, Wicklow and Arklow. The pier stock was

| Cambrian Railways mileage, February 1889 | | | | |
|---|---|---|---|---|
| | Miles | Chains | Miles | Chains |
| **Lines owned by the company** | | | | |
| Whitchurch junction to Pwllheli | 132 | 14 | | |
| Oswestry junction to junction with GWR | | 14 | | |
| Llynclys junction to Porthywaen | 1 | 65 | | |
| Llanymynech station to Llanfyllin | 9 | 13 | | |
| Abermule junction to Kerry | 3 | 55 | | |
| Moat Lane junction to Penbontbren junction | 9 | 21 | | |
| Glandovey junction to Aberystwyth | 16 | 59 | | |
| Aber dovey junction to Aberdovey harbour | | 38 | | |
| Barmouth junction curve between main and branch lines | | 21 | | |
| Barmouth junction to Dolgelley junction with GWR | 7 | 36 | | |
| | | | 181 | 16 |
| **Lines worked by the company** | | | | |
| Llanymynech junction to Nantmawr (PSNWR) | 3 | 75 | | |
| Penbontbren junction to Talyllyn junction (MWR) | 46 | 55 | | |
| Three Cocks station to junction with Midland Railway (MWR) | | 38 | | |
| | | | 51 | 8 |
| **Lines run over by the company** | | | | |
| Whitchurch junction to station (LNWR) | | 7 | | |
| Talyllyn junction (Brecon & Merthyr Railway) | 4 | 7 | | |
| Dolgelley junction to station (GWR) | | 30 | | |
| | | | 4 | 44 |
| **Total mileage** | | | **236** | **68** |

converted to A debenture stock and the pier stock surplus, £442 12s 7d, became the nucleus of the steamboat depreciation fund.

Compliance with the 1889 Regulation of Railways Act wrought enormous changes to the Cambrian, forcing it to modernise and to overcome, finally, the shortcomings of its impecunious origins. The Act's prime objective was to impose use of the block system of train operation, the interlocking of points with signals, and continuous brakes on passenger trains. Despite the company's best efforts the Board of Trade made an order on 20 November 1890, requiring the first within 12 months, the second within two years and the third within 2½ years. The Porthywaen branch and the Barmouth junction curve were treated as mineral lines.

To save all the companies from having to apply for fresh capital powers, the Act authorised them to issue debentures against a Board of Trade certificate verifying that the works were required. The Cambrian initially estimated the cost as £50,504: block working £543

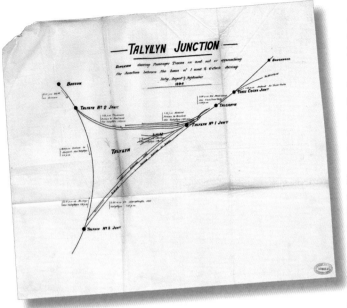

A diagram of Talyllyn Junction made in 1894 to show possible passenger train conflicts through the junction. *National Archives*

(only the Llanfyllin and Dolgelley branches required it); interlocking, including some alterations to layouts and additional platforms, £37,300; and continuous brakes, £12,661 (23 passenger and 10 goods locomotives, £5,115, 143 passenger carriages, £6,292, and 24 passenger brake vans at £1,254). When Conacher applied on 1 December 1890 he was told his estimate was excessive by £20,856.

The Board of Trade had not understood that the Cambrian's locomotives were too small or underpowered for the installation of vacuum brakes and needed either replacing or rebuilding with larger boilers. Fourteen brake vans, which probably had timber frames, were too weak to have automatic brakes fitted.

What really upset the Cambrian, though, were the restrictions placed on the operation of mixed trains, the conveyance of wagons behind passenger vehicles, the provision of one brake vehicle for every 10 wagons, the limit of 25 vehicles in a train, the restriction of speed to 25mph, and the requirement to stop at all stations or at intervals not exceeding 25 miles. The company had always run mixed trains and the loadings on them would not justify running more passenger trains. It would be unreasonable to expect it to run more unremunerative mileage, especially when it could not pay a dividend. In February 1893 28% of the company's passenger mileage ran mixed. The correspondence was to continue until 1912.

Compliance took nearly five years and was to cost £278,905. In all, 76 stations together with 52 junctions, sidings and crossings required interlocking, but it was not as straightforward as the Board of Trade thought it should be and there was some difficulty in persuading the civil servants that the knock-on effects of compliance should be included in the authorised expenditure. For example, a new carriage shed was needed at Oswestry because the interlocking required a new

down platform on the site of the existing shed. Also at Oswestry, the engine shed needed to be extended because the new locomotives were larger than their predecessors.

All passenger trains were worked using automatic vacuum-brake-equipped stock from 1 January 1894. Although the last vehicle in the train should be braked, to avoid delay in working 'occasionally' an unbraked cattle truck or van could be added to the end of the train. Provided it was equipped with vacuum pipe, sprung buffers and screw couplings, one of these vehicles could be included in a train, in front of the brake van.

On mixed trains the passenger carriages had to be next to the locomotive and the brake connected; the number of vehicles, excluding locomotive and tender, was not to exceed ten; a second brake van and guard should be used if the number of vehicles was more than ten; and 'under no circumstances' should the number of vehicles exceed 19. Three main-line trains, two on the coast section and one on the MWR, continued to operate under the old rules, with carriages following wagons, until 1 January 1896.

The Cambrian had justified the continued operation of mixed trains by citing the need to replace or rebuild locomotives. To accommodate the Board of Trade in the meantime, sidings were installed where carriages could be stabled while shunting took place, and mixed trains were run with two goods brakes instead of one, requiring 12 additional vehicles.

Exemptions from block working regulations were obtained at the larger stations, although that might be an oversimplification. By 1896 Pwllheli was the only station without interlocking, deferred while consideration was given to relocating it.

The Board of Trade had applied considerable, if not sometimes ill-considered, pressure to comply with its requirements. On 16 March 1893 Alfred Aslett, who had succeeded Conacher, dealt with its refusal to extend the time to finish the interlocking into the following year, setting a deadline of 20 May. Completing the outstanding 16 stations and junctions and 10 level crossings in two months was absolutely impracticable, he said. There were several big jobs, citing Llanymynech curve – needed to connect the Llanfyllin branch to the PSNWR's Llanyblodwel line and to avoid branch trains having to change direction at the north of the station – and Portmadoc, where the cattle pens, carriage dock, weighing machine and water tank and most of the track needed relocating to accommodate the second platform required by the interlocking, as well as others.

The expenditure was funded by offering A debentures to existing stockholders at 115%. After the rent charges, these debentures were the first charge on the company's net revenue, the highest grade of stock from an investment perspective. It said much about the company's financial position at this time that a premium was asked.

The Board of Trade, however, would not certify £28,480 spent on turntables, water columns, platforms and other structural improvements. This left the company in a quandary. The work had been paid for out of revenue; leaving it in the revenue account would be unfair on the D debenture holders, who would not be paid their interest. A Bill to obtain further powers was deposited in November 1895.

## Additions to stock 1891-5

|  | Tender engines | 1st Class | Composite carriages | 3rd Class | Passenger brake | Goods brake | Travelling gas holder |
|---|---|---|---|---|---|---|---|
| 1891 | 2 | 1 | 6 | 20 |  |  |  |
| 1892 |  | 1 |  |  |  |  |  |
| 1893 | 1 | 4 |  | 9 |  |  |  |
| 1894 | 5 |  | 7 | 10 | 6 | 3 | 5 |
| 1895 | 6 | 1 | 10 | 12 | 6 |  | 1 |
|  | 14 | 7 | 23 | 51 | 12 | 3 | 6 |

## Tenders accepted 1890-95

| Quantity | Item | Supplier | Unit cost |
|---|---|---|---|
| **20 November 1890** | | | |
| 40 | Timber trucks | Craven Brothers | £63 |
| 2 | Bogies passenger engines | Sharp, Stewart & Co | £2,120 |
| 20 | 3rd Class carriages | Metropolitan Railway Carriage & Wagon Ltd | £392 |
| **30 December 1890** | | | |
| 6 | Tri-composite lavatory saloons | Metropolitan Railway Carriage & Wagon Ltd | |
| **3 November 1892** | | | |
| 8 | Bogie engines and tenders | Sharp, Stewart & Co | £1,980 |
| 50 | Goods wagons with vacuum brakes | Metropolitan Railway Carriage & Wagon Ltd | £74 18s |
| 12 | Cattle trucks with vacuum brakes | Metropolitan Railway Carriage & Wagon Ltd | £141 1s |
| **14 December 1892** | | | |
| 14 | Passenger brake vans | Ashbury Railway Carriage & Iron Co | £299 |
| **28 March 1893** | | | |
| 30 | Timber trucks | Metropolitan Railway Carriage & Wagon Ltd | £74 4s |
| **27 April 1893** | | | |
| 3 | Passenger engine boilers | Sharp, Stewart & Co | £490 |
| 3 | Goods engine boilers | Sharp, Stewart & Co | £500 |
| **3 June 1893** | | | |
| 12 | 3rd Class carriages | Metropolitan Railway Carriage & Wagon Ltd | £393 |
| **8 November 1893** | | | |
| 9 | Composite corridor carriages with lavatory accommodation for 3rd Class | Metropolitan Railway Carriage & Wagon Ltd | £570 |
| 6 | 3rd Class corridor carriages | Metropolitan Railway Carriage & Wagon Ltd | £530 |
| 9 | 3rd Class corridor carriages | Ashbury Railway Carriage & Iron Co | £530 |
| **9 December 1893** | | | |
| 5 | Goods engines | Neilson & Co | £2,000 |
| **4 April 1894** | | | |
| 1 | Breakdown and travelling crane | Chapman & Co | £520 |
| **14 June 1894** | | | |
| 3 | Bogie Composite carriages with lavatory accommodation for 1st Class and luggage compartment | Metropolitan Railway Carriage & Wagon Ltd | £700 |
| **14 November 1894** | | | |
| 4 | Goods locomotive boilers | Nasmyth, Wilson & Co | £560 |
| 6 | 45-foot Composite bogie carriages with lavatory accommodation | Metropolitan Railway Carriage & Wagon Ltd | £780 |
| 12 | 35-foot 3rd Class carriages | Metropolitan Railway Carriage & Wagon Ltd | £474 |
| 6 | Passenger brake vans | Ashbury Railway Carriage & Iron Co | £360 |
| **13 December 1894** | | | |
| | | Metropolitan Railway Carriage & Wagon Ltd | |
| **16 January 1895** | | | |
| 4 | Bogie passenger engines (plus exhaust injectors at £50 each) | Sharp, Stewart & Co | £2,120 |
| 3 | Goods engines | Vulcan Foundry Co | £2,030 |
| 3 | Bogie tank engines | Nasmyth, Wilson & Co | £1,800 |

TOP A works photograph of 4-4-0 No 65, built by Sharp, Stewart in 1893. Nine engines built in 1893/94 had wrought-iron crank axles that did not last very long, only 39,476 miles in the case of No 65. Their replacements were made of steel. This locomotive was on the down mail involved in a collision at Tylwch on 16 September 1899.
*John Alsop collection*

LEFT Another works photograph. Neilson 0-6-0 No 74 was built in 1894, one of a batch of five. The Cambrian only placed one more order with this company.

RIGHT 0-4-4 No 83, seen at Brecon, was built by Sharp, Stewart in 1895, and was later used on the ill-fated Royal Train over the Mid Wales and the Cambrian on 21 July 1904. *John Alsop collection*

BELOW The construction of 4-4-0 No 84 in 1895 brought to an end the Cambrian's long-standing relationship with Sharp, Stewart. The locomotive was photographed in Aberystwyth.

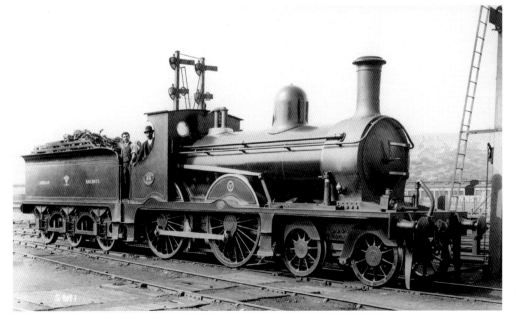

OPPOSITE The memorial to the contractor David Davies, who died in 1890, stands by the main road at Llandinam, next to the bridge that started his civil engineering career in 1846, and across the river from the first railway that he built. 'Broneirion', the house he built for himself, is on the right.
*Park*

With the Bill's enactment on 2 July 1896, the Cambrian had a wide range of fresh powers. It could:

- make access roads to the stations at Barmouth, Glandovey and Moat Lane Junction
- acquire additional land at Ellesmere, Oswestry, Pant, Four Crosses, between Towyn and Llwyngwril, Penrhyndeudraeth, Afon Wen and Pwllheli
- operate bus services between Llanidloes and Devil's Bridge, Aberystwyth and Devil's Bridge, Barmouth and Dolgelley and Harlech, and Portmadoc and Bettws y Coed, Snowdon, Pwllheli and Porthdinlleyn
- provide hotels or refreshment rooms at Aberystwyth, Borth, Aberdovey, Barmouth, Towyn and Portmadoc
- exercise running powers over the Van Railway and the Wrexham & Ellesmere Railway's loop line.

The Llanymynech curve was 'legalised' – it had been built without Parliamentary sanction.

The company could also raise £600,000 in D debentures, the money to be used to double parts of the existing line, to construct additional sidings, warehouses, engine and carriage sheds, and to obtain rolling stock. It could convert the existing 4% A, B, C and D debentures into 3% A, B, C and D debentures at the rate of 133%, the premium making them more attractive to investors while the interest accrued remained the same.

On 25 September 1890 the board had decided that working the Wrexham & Ellesmere Railway was conditional on having exclusive running powers and an Oswestry-facing curve at Ellesmere. The WER had obtained powers for a 13-mile-long line connecting the Manchester, Sheffield & Lincolnshire Railway, the Wrexham, Mold & Connah's Quay Railway and the Cambrian to enhance the through route between the English North West and South Wales in 1885. Piercy

had been the engineer to the Bill, but Owen had replaced him. Despite extensions of time obtained in 1888 and 1890, the WER had been unable to raise any capital.

The first sod was not cut until 11 June 1892, after £50,000 had been subscribed by the MSLR. Owen had gone over the route in July 1891 and had borings made to test the ground for the abutments of the Dee river bridge at Bangor; the 200-foot structure, 'possessed of merit from an artistic view', according to the *Wrexham Advertiser* on 11 July, was designed by Thomas Hughes, who had also designed bridges for the Cambrian. Mrs Kenyon, wife of the company chairman, G. T. Kenyon, cut the first sod in Wrexham's Caia Meadows, and Owen presented her with a miniature silver barrow and spade. Messrs Davies Brothers of Wrexham had contracted to build the line for £95,000.

David Davies had died on 20 July 1890, aged 72, the board acknowledging his role in building the railway and his services as a director on 7 August. There had been no such tribute when his one-time partner, Savin, had died on 23 July 1889, aged 63. Another key figure, Piercy, had died on 24 March 1888, aged 61; he had been a JP, living in some style at Marchwiel Hall, near Wrexham, and owned property in London and Sicily.

On 31 September 1891 Conacher left the Cambrian to be the North British Railway's general manager, the board paying tribute to his 26 years' service with the company on 27 October. Alfred Aslett, traffic manager and accountant of the Eastern & Midlands Railway, was appointed to replace him with a salary of £700.

One of Aslett's first tasks was to complete the arrangements that Conacher had started, for Cambrian officers and clerks aged under 45 to join the Railway Clearing System superannuation scheme, the company contributing 2½% of the salaries of those who joined. By 26 January 1892 86 applications had been received from 200 qualifying employees, incurring an annual cost of £121 3s to the company. Of course, no consideration was given to increasing the salaries of those who did not qualify for scheme membership by 2½%. This was the

Llandinam Bridge and Railway Station.

first time that any Cambrian employees could earn a pension and not be dependent on the directors' goodwill when they came to retire.

The combination of a disgruntled merchant, an outspoken employee and a Parliamentary select committee put the Cambrian's working practices under the spotlight in 1891/92 and saw three directors and Conacher summoned to the House of Commons to apologise for breaching Parliamentary privilege and to be admonished by the Speaker.

The sorry saga had started earlier in 1891, when the Board of Trade, having made the connection between the hours worked and the likelihood of accidents occurring, set about collecting information by requiring railway companies to make returns of men working for more than 10 and 12 hours at a time. On 3 February the House of Commons' railway servants (hours of labour) select committee was appointed to inquire whether the hours worked by railway servants should be restricted by legislation.

The committee heard not only from Board of Trade officers and company managers and directors but also from 33 railwaymen, the largest contingent, 10, employed by the Cambrian. The latter were supported by Frederick Bather, an Oswestry corn merchant and Cambrian customer with premises adjoining the station. During his dealings with the railway he had learned of its employees' concerns about the hours they worked. He became disgruntled with the company, however, when a subsidy was withdrawn as unjustified under the provisions of the Railway & Canal Traffic Act of 1888 and he failed to get a free pass in substitution. On 16 April he gave evidence to the committee, submitting a petition in support of shorter hours for railwaymen signed by some 500 Oswestry residents and several affidavits of affected Cambrian personnel.

Learning of Bather's appearance, Conacher not only offered to give evidence himself but circulated the company's employees, saying that they could apply for a free pass if they wished to give evidence, promising that anyone who did so would not be penalised.

Conacher was examined on 18 and 23 June. On the second occasion he was questioned about James Humphreys, a porter at Ellesmere, who had been held responsible for a derailment on facing points there on 6 November 1887. He had told Rich that he had been on duty for 19 hours at the time of the accident; in his affidavit he said that he had actually been on duty for 44 hours. Conacher said that Rich's report was correct. Humphreys had been dismissed and John Hood, the station master, had been suspended for two weeks and was later transferred to Montgomery, a demotion, for signing a petition in support of his reinstatement. Conacher added that the directors also blamed Hood for failing to instil discipline in his staff.

Hood was one of the last witnesses to appear before the committee on 16 July, anxious to defend his reputation. There had been no suggestion that he had been in any way responsible for the 1887 accident – he had been punished for signing the petition. He was certain that Humphreys had been on duty for 44 hours and thought that the cause of the accident was the poor state of the track, disputing Rich's report. Perversely, unlike previous sessions, which had been extensively reported, this day's evidence was not reported, yet Hood's brief appearance caused all the trouble.

Conacher thought that Hood had deliberately gone out of his way to contradict him. Without giving him a hearing, on 6 August the board agreed that he should be sacked with one month's salary in lieu of notice; at a meeting with the chairman (James William Buckley), two directors (John William Mclure, an MP, and William Bailey Hawkins), and Conacher on 30 September, he was censured for his evidence.

On 21 February 1892 the Amalgamated Society of Railway Servants alleged that some witnesses, including Hood, had been dismissed

On 7 April 1892 John Conacher, next to the serjeant-at-arms, and the Cambrian directors stand at the bar of the House of Commons to be admonished by the Speaker for their part in the dismissal of station master John Hood in breach of Parliamentary privilege.
*Illustrated London News*

because of their evidence, to deter others. From 25 February the committee took evidence again, hearing from Hood first. After he had given evidence in July he had felt that he was a 'marked man', with every trivial error examined in minute detail until he was dismissed without explanation. He had worked for the Cambrian for 22 years, transferring to Llanymynech from the North Eastern Railway as clerk in 1869. The day before he gave evidence he had been awarded £1 10s for keeping his station in good order, and had received an increase in salary nine months before that. The director who used his station would not say why he had been sacked. At the 30 September meeting Conacher had produced evidence relating to the 1887 derailment that appeared to be fabricated. Conacher had been reluctant to approve Hood's attendance at the 16 July hearing, leaving it until it was too late, he said, to issue the pass.

Humphreys, Conacher, John Stokes (the goods guard who was supposed to have been on duty at Ellesmere on the night of the derailment in 1887), Samuel Williamson (the shorthand writer on 30 September, later to be secretary and general manager) and Buckley, the chairman, were among those called or recalled to the committee. Conacher was examined over three days, Buckley over two.

On 24 March the committee decided that the allegations by three men that their dismissal was because of their appearance before it were unfounded and that Hood had been dismissed in consequence of giving evidence and to deter others.

The board tried to avoid censure on 31 March, minuting 'having learned that it is possible that Mr Hood's dismissal may be regarded

… as infringing the rules … and constituting a breach of the privileges … place on record that in discharging Mr Hood they were actuated solely by the consideration that he was entirely unfit to be retained in a position of trust. They certainly had no intention of deterring any of their servants from giving evidence …' But it was to no avail.

Under summons, Buckley, Hawkins, Mclure and Conacher attended the House of Commons to explain themselves on 7 April. For such an unusual event, the House and Strangers' Gallery were full. Mclure, the MP, stood in his place to read a prepared statement. The directors had

acted in the interests of the company and the public, he said, and they had no intention of discouraging railway servants from giving evidence or of infringing Parliamentary rules and privileges; if they had done so unintentionally they offered a full and unreserved apology. The debate on a motion for the Speaker to issue an admonishment took several

A map showing the Wrexham & Ellesmere Railway, opened in 1895, and its connections, illustrating how traffic could now be carried from the North West of England without using the LNWR. *National Archives*

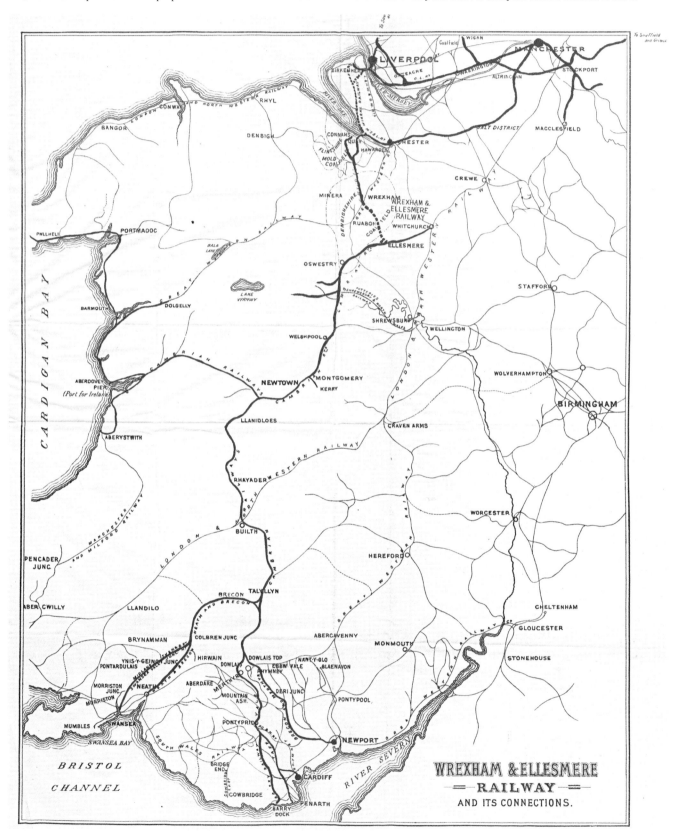

hours and four divisions before it was won, the Cambrian party being called in to hear it at 30 minutes past midnight.

Hood became something of a celebrity, appearing in support of Parliamentary candidates and writing letters to newspapers. Labour MPs contributed £213 3s 6d to a fund established in his name. Ironically, on 22 September, the day that Conacher's resignation had been accepted, another derailment had occurred on the facing point at Ellesmere, at the up end of the station instead of the down. Once again a porter was blamed for not checking the point. There had been a man called Humphreys on duty as well.

From 1 May 1893 2nd class was abolished and 1st class fares set at the 2nd class level, a change that saw the year's 1st class revenue increase by £1,302 and 3rd class by £2,053, as well as reducing the passenger duty by £181; 2nd class revenue the year before had been £3,143. Timetable changes from 1 July reduced the journey time from London to the coast by an hour, to 7 hours; the following year the time was to be reduced to 6¾ hours. A new contract made with the GPO was worth £6,900 per annum.

Construction of Birmingham Corporation's reservoirs near Rhayader brought with it the prospect of considerable traffic, and a draft agreement was accepted by the board on 27 April 1893. A signalled junction with the corporation's construction railway had been installed south of Rhayader Tunnel by 8 May 1894; Major H. Arthur Yorke inspected it on 13 July, and its cost, £3,976 11s 7d, was paid by 3 October.

Using the 0-4-0ST that had been working the Porthywaen and Nantmawr branches, the company started working the corporation's line as far as Caban (Nantgwillt) for £700 per annum from 13 August 1894; on 30 October the corporation complained that the arrangement was inconvenient and could not continue. It was not too convenient for the Cambrian, either, because the locomotive was restricted to 15mph on the main line. The Porthywaen/Nantmawr traffic was worked by a locomotive hired from the out-of-use Van Railway.

Aslett was certain that the junction was inadequate because the shunting neck, constrained by the adjacent tunnel, could only hold 10 wagons and there was no space for sidings on the company's land. There had been runaways on the 1 in 34 gradient on the corporation's line, including one incident involving 24 wagons with brakes pinned down. The corporation's proposed exchange sidings 500 yards from the junction were made unsuitable by 3-chain-radius curves on the access line and the site being on a 1 in 40 gradient.

More than five years after his death and nearly 30 years since his collapse, Savin's debts continued to haunt the Cambrian. Now under new management, Savin & Company Ltd still owed £1,627, and Aslett had been trying to obtain payment. He told the board on 15 January 1895 that his attempt to get £40 per month had been countered with an offer of £200 a year. Making no progress, the Cambrian took a lien on 158 wagons, and a liquidator was appointed on 17 December 1895. No payment had been made by May 1896, when the receiver made a counter-claim of £2,411 16s 3d. Notice to surrender the wagons on 27 July produced a cheque for £1,500 by return.

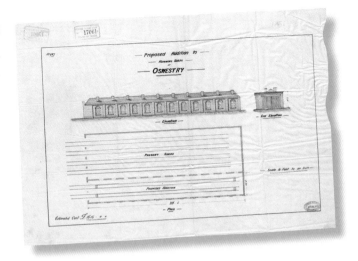

Elevations and plans of a two-road extension made to the locomotive running shed at Oswestry in July 1895. *National Archives*

With the completion of the Wrexham & Ellesmere Railway on the horizon, an extra-powers Bill deposited in December 1894 had given rise to a dispute between the Cambrian and the Manchester, Sheffield & Lincolnshire Railway. One of the clauses was intended to give the WER power to make agreements with the Cambrian, Wrexham, Mold & Connah's Quay Railway and MSLR, to use or work any part of it, in contradiction to the existing agreement giving the Cambrian exclusive rights.

Seeing the clause as the work of the MSLR, Aslett met its general manager, William Pollitt, who said that as his company had invested £50,000 in the WER it should have the right to work it and to exercise its running powers into Oswestry. Two companies could not work the line independently of each other, Aslett observed, offering the MSLR running powers into Oswestry in exchange for reciprocal access to Chester as an olive branch. The clause was withdrawn. The MSLR, later the Great Central Railway, and the Cambrian were each to underwrite one-third of the WER's losses.

A press trip over the WER was run on 10 October 1895, the contractor's 0-4-0, named *Bantam*, hauling a Cambrian saloon from Wrexham. Intermediate stations were located at Marchwiel, Bangor-on-Dee and Overton-on-Dee. The line was laid with 80lb steel rail on 47lb chairs, and the formation was 18 feet wide. There were eight underbridges and 12 overbridges, two of timber. King's Mill and Old Forge viaducts had five 50-foot spans. A steam navvy had been used in the excavation of 120,000 tons of earth from Pickhill cutting. The 190-foot Dee bridge comprised two bowstring steel latticed girders and abutments were made of Abenbury pink stone; only one end of the bridge was fixed, to allow for expansion. The bridge over Liverpool Corporation's Vyrnwy pipeline had abutments 22 feet apart, the span being 66 feet on the skew.

Yorke had required two visits before the line could be opened, the first on 24/25 September. It was, he reported, 12 miles 56 chains long,

## Traffic on the WER, 1895

|  | Passengers | | Parcels, milk, etc | | Goods | Coal |
|---|---|---|---|---|---|---|
|  | No | Receipts | Receipts | Local receipts | Foreign tonnage | Foreign tonnage |
| Ellesmere | 519 | £23 0s 5d | £1 16s 3d | £1 9s 4d |  | 36 tons |
| Overton-on-Dee | 479 | £17 10s 10d | 8s 6d | 10s 6d | 1 ton | 82 tons |
| Bangor-on-Dee | 519 | £15 6s 1d | 10s 6d | 8s 7d | 30 tons | 195 tons |
| Marchwiel | 266 | £4 3s 5d | 2s 3d |  | 21 tons |  |
| Wrexham | 1,217 | £42 6s 7d | 17s 10d | £10 | 5 |  |
| **Total** | **3,000** | **£102 7s 4d** | **£3 15s 6d** | **£12 8s 5d** | **36 tons** | **334 tons** |

4605

The shed after it had been extended, the extension showing differences in the size of the door openings and in the roof details.

single track with land taken and structures made for a second. Ballast was broken stone, gravel and colliery ash. The steepest gradient was 1 in 66 over 12 chains and the sharpest curve had a radius of 12 chains for 6 chains. There were passing loops with signal boxes at the three stations and signal boxes at Wrexham (South) and Ellesmere Junction. A turntable had been provided at Wrexham and another was being installed at Ellesmere.

The destruction by fire of the new WMCQR signal box, which was to control the junction between the two lines, a few days before, and the unfinished works at Wrexham station caused Yorke to postpone the opening. His second visit was made on 24 October, his report being submitted the next day.

The WER opened with little ceremony on 2 November 1895, the first train, hauled by a tank engine, setting off detonators as it left Wrexham at 8.10am. The *Wrexham Advertiser* thought that the 3rd class corridor carriages, with toilets and gas lighting, were of better quality than the 1st class stock on the same train. A saddler, Mr Knowles, had bought the first ticket. Dignitaries from the MSLR, WMCQR and Cambrian travelled over the line in an MSLR saloon later in the morning.

The initial service comprised three passenger trains, two mixed trains and a goods train. On 13 November Denniss, the new manager, reported traffic conveyed to date as shown in the table below. As goods traffic was higher than expected he had put on an extra train that would also benefit the South Wales coal business. A disagreement over the provision of Cambrian locomotive facilities at Wrexham was resolved by Denniss coming to an arrangement with the WMCQR.

Aslett had resigned to become the Furness Railway's general manager on 2 October. His replacement as general manager, Charles Sherwood Denniss, from the North Eastern Railway, at a salary of £800, was confirmed by the board on 17 October and Aslett was paid for services provided until 20 October. The assistant secretary, Richard Brayne, became secretary.

The start of construction of the 2ft 3in-gauge Plynlimon & Hafan Tramway on 11 January 1896 brought with it the possibility of another mixed-gauge crossing for the Cambrian to manage. On 16 January the promoter, Thomas Molyneaux of Earlestown, informed Denniss of his proposal to build a line from the quarries to Llanfihangel station and a branch crossing the Cambrian 300 yards from Ynys Las station to reach a wharf on the Dovey. Denniss recommended that approval be given, providing that the crossing met Board of Trade requirements. The Cambrian paid £83 14s of the £183 14s cost of the exchange siding. The tramway was to have a very short life and the branch to the river was never built.

Congestion on the main line during the summer brought complaints, 'unfortunately justified', reported Denniss on 25 February. He recommended doubling the line between Buttington and Pool Quay, 2 miles 6 chains, at an estimated cost of £9,795, to reduce the 7-mile 9-chain section between Buttington and Llanymynech. Doubling would soon be required between Pool Quay and Llanymynech and Moat Lane and Newtown; the last was the biggest bottleneck on the system, he said. A loop installed at Pool Quay before the summer improved the situation considerably, Denniss was to report in October, when he recommended doubling the section between Montgomery and Welshpool, 6 miles 17 chains, at a cost of £32,840 19s 3d.

Details of Arthur McDougall's proposals for the development of the Ynys Faig and Penrhyn estates at a location he called Fairbourne were submitted on 7 May. The board refused to contribute to the cost of a station so he declared that he would pay for it himself.

A visit by the Prince and Princess of Wales to Aberystwyth for the Prince's installation as chancellor of the University of Wales on 26 June was a three-day operation for the Cambrian. On the 25th it carried the couple from Buttington to Machynlleth, where they stayed at Plas Machynlleth, then took them to Aberystwyth and back on the day, and on to Talyllyn the day afterwards. Excursion trains were run from Leeds and London; 4,159 passengers used the Cambrian to see the royal visitors and the sale of extra tickets raised £326 4s 7½d.

The WER's Ellesmere loop, a north-to-west connection to the Cambrian's main line, was opened during September. Yorke inspected it on the 10th, reporting four days later that it was double track, 39 chains long and the interlocking at the north and south signal boxes was satisfactory. Some of the land required for the loop, and for the WER itself, was obtained from the trustees of Piercy's estate, requiring legal action to determine the price.

The 1896 Light Railways Act was to bring four light railways within the Cambrian's control by 1913. On 25 September Denniss suggested that its provisions could be used with advantage to the company. Proposals already seeking Cambrian support were the Llanfair & Meifod Light Railway and the Oswestry & Llangynog Light Railway. The lessee of the Nantmawr quarry had also asked for support in resuscitating the Shropshire Railways, formerly the Potteries, Shrewsbury & North Wales Railway, as a light railway.

A combination of gales and a high tide devastated the coast line on 8 October. The track was washed out, leaving sleepers suspended, between Glandovey and Ynys Las, and between Ynys Las and Borth. A mile on the northern bank of the estuary was damaged, and 2,000 yards of embankment from the level crossing north of Towyn to the Dysynni river bridge was completely washed away, demolishing one bridge and damaging two others. The Dolgelley branch was flooded up to 3 feet deep and closed for two days. One of the groins at Llanaber was washed away and the track washed out, while 700 yards of the Harlech sea wall was damaged. At Talsarnau the track was flooded and embankments damaged, and the embankments at either end of the bridge south of Afon Wen were washed away. All along the coast fencing was washed away and the house at Barmouth Junction was flooded to a depth of 4 feet. Subsequently Owen found that a 30-foot section of the formation at Friog, where it was 30ft high, had been dislodged.

Owen estimated repairs at £4,000-5,000. The rockmen and relaying gangs previously laid off would have to be re-employed, but the best of them had got jobs on the Rhayader reservoirs. Denniss paid tribute to the efforts of Owen and Gough, the traffic superintendent, in re-opening the line and keeping traffic moving. Two Cemmaes residents donated 3 guineas towards the cost of reconstruction.

The first reference to an extension at Pwllheli was recorded in January 1897. The town clerk, Evan R. Davies, had written to ask if the Cambrian would be prepared to work a narrow-gauge line from the west end of the town onto the Lleyn peninsula or, if the line was made in 'broad gauge', whether it would move its terminus to the town end of the harbour. Much of the existing traffic for the area was routed via Chwilog and it would be to the Cambrian's and the town's detriment if an independent line was built from that place to, say, Nevin. The Cambrian would not be involved in promoting a line, the board decided, but would support any scheme found to be practicable.

Another scheme that came to its attention was the Portmadoc, Beddgelert & Rhyd Ddu Light Railway. Denniss met its promoters in April and agreed to support it being a narrow-gauge line because of the gradients and 'necessarily sharp curves'.

Notwithstanding the powers of the 1889 Act, the Cambrian had ceased to operate ferry services from Aberdovey. In April 1897 the Manchester Ship Canal Company wanted to run a weekly Manchester-Waterford service that would not fully occupy the ship, so it suggested that the Cambrian be involved in a weekly Aberdovey-Waterford service. Denniss concluded that it could be made to pay, but that the English railway companies would not agree to through rates. It was not mentioned again.

John Bell had operated the Aberdovey-Ynys Las ferry service on payment of £1 per year since 1883. On 30 June 1897 he gave three months' notice of termination; his suggestion that the contract be replaced by a new one covering the summer months only for 10 shillings was accepted.

The LNWR obviously had a high opinion of the Cambrian's clerks, recruiting 12 of them in 1897. Denniss was annoyed, though, to be informed that on 19 May, while he was in London, two LNWR officers had established themselves in a waiting room at Oswestry to interview staff from Oswestry, Barmouth and Aberystwyth. It took some effort to stop the LNWR recruiting directly, Denniss informed the board. It was expected that personnel wishing to join another company would seek permission before making an application.

**Land required for expansion at Oswestry is indicated on this 1896 plan. Compare it with that on page 80.** *Parliamentary Archives*

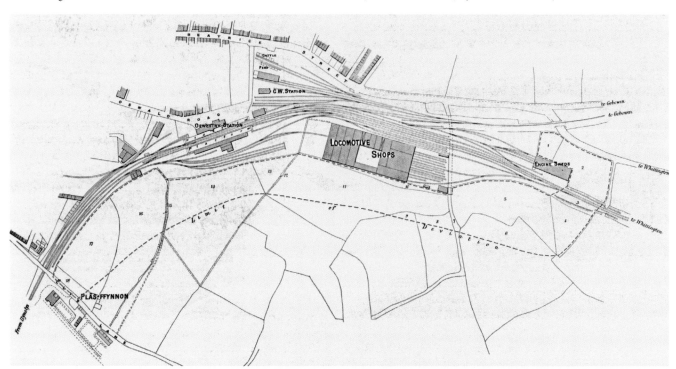

On 25 June 1896 No 68, suitably decorated, waits at Welshpool for the arrival of the Royal Train carrying the Prince and Princess of Wales, to convey them to their overnight accommodation at Plas Machynlleth; the next day the Cambrian carried them to Aberystwyth.
*Ted Talbot collection*

At the same time Denniss discovered that the company's Liverpool agent, W. H. Smith (not the newsagent), had been canvassing employees, on Cambrian notepaper, to take up appointments with the Western Australian Government Railways. Smith was acting, he found, on a request from his brother-in-law, the WAGR's general manager – and formerly the Aberdovey station master. Smith was sacked.

Summer congestion was further relieved by the introduction of a new passing place at Forden in June 1897. Denniss, however, objected to Yorke's requirement that a waiting shelter should be provided on the existing up platform – it was not a part of the inspection, the traffic did not warrant it, and there had been no complaint from the public about the lack of it. The Board of Trade replied, pointing out that provisional sanction for the use of the new works was subject to compliance with the inspecting officer's requirements. Yorke attached more importance to the up platform now that the station had become a passing place.

Refusing to recognise Yorke's right to make such a recommendation, Denniss proposed merely acknowledging the letter and resisting the 'interference'. Although the Board of Trade admitted that it was not competent to make its approval of the new works conditional on the waiting shelter, it resisted the Cambrian's objection until 19 March 1898, when it gave way.

Following a derailment at Welshampton on 11 June 1897, when 11 people died and 15 were badly injured, Yorke called upon the company to limit speeds and weights of trains until the entire line had been inspected. Only 31 miles had been upgraded for fast traffic and heavier engines. Dennis responded by having the timetable re-cast to impose a maximum speed of 35mph, regardless of the track conditions, from 1 October. Notifying the GPO that the mail would reach Aberystwyth 15 minutes later, he blamed Yorke.

Hardened GPO civil servants disagreed, pointing out that Yorke had made no specific recommendation and that speed was therefore entirely at the company's discretion. Denniss therefore rescheduled the train to arrive 10 minutes earlier from 1 April 1898, holding out the promise of improved timings from July. Informed of the 'improvement', the GPO decided that as the Cambrian had made little effort to comply with its contract it would withhold £250 from the

quarterly payment due on 31 March and £100 per month until the contract time was restored.

Denniss countered by saying that once the track works had been completed it should be possible for the train to arrive up to 30 minutes earlier than before. However, if the payment was not made in full the company would not feel obliged to improve the schedule. The GPO agreed to reconsider its position, but Denniss decided to give notice to cancel the contract. It took until June 1899 to agree to improved timings and until January 1900 to agree the £14,750 annual charge, an increase of £1,250.

In June 1900, however, it transpired that the GPO expected a new, larger, sorting carriage to be provided as well. Denniss explained that a new carriage had been offered when the company sought an annual payment of £17,500; having been beaten down so much, the company did not now expect to provide it. He offered to provide a carriage for an extra payment of £100 but the GPO refused. The carriage, No 293, was built at Oswestry at a cost of £726 2s 8d and entered service in December 1902.

Contrary to Gasquoine's account of the Welshampton accident, no children were killed or injured. £11,000 compensation was paid to victims at the expense of the preference share dividend.

Owen's resignation as engineer was accepted on 7 August 1897, probably a consequence of Welshampton, but he was also 70 years old and had been in post since 1864, when he had transferred from the OEWR. He was appointed consulting engineer on a salary of £400 and in April 1898 the board presented him with an illuminated address. His replacement, Alfred Jones Collin, formerly of the North Eastern Railway, took the position from 1 December, salary £500.

Collin's report on the track and structures was submitted on 28 January 1899. Twelve months previously he had found very little

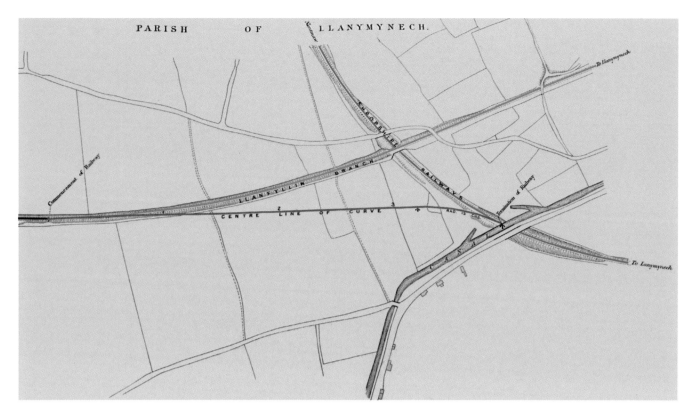

ballast under the sleepers, so he had formed two gangs to lift and ballast the track, starting at Whitchurch – 120 miles had so far been completed. The old 26lb and 28lb chairs had damaged the sleepers under the weight of traffic and were being replaced by 40lb chairs. The worst sleepers had been replaced but many more required renewing.

Much of the 72lb double-headed steel rail showed little sign of wear despite its age, but it was now too light; he recommended using 80lb steel rail unless rolling stock weights increased. Heavier fishplates were already being installed, the old ones being too light and worn.

The inland and Mid Wales sections used washed coarse sand from the Van lead mines; it was good, being heavy and easily handled, it packed well and did not set too hard. Gravel from company land at Afon Wen was used on the coast section due to the distance from Van, and was clean and suitable.

The stone and masonry bridges, and those with iron in them, were fine, but the timber bridges would always be a source of expense. Collin already had approval to replace the Doughty and Scafell bridges between Newtown and Moat Lane, and the Craig y don bridge at Aberdovey. Ironwork on the Barmouth bridge had been repaired, but parts of the timber section would soon require renewal. The iron road overbridge at Welshampton had been damaged by locomotives standing under it and would need replacing.

The tunnels were in good order but some were rather wet. Collin had arranged for deeper drains to be cut in some of them to remove water more quickly and to protect the track. Linings would need to be renewed in parts. The sea walls should be examined after every storm and slight damage repaired immediately. The Llanaber wall should be extended about 70 yards northwards to protect the railway from the approaching sea.

Although Denniss had failed to persuade the traffic committee to approve doubling the line between Welshpool and Montgomery, on 2 February 1898 approval was given to doubling between Forden and Moat Lane. The decision appears to have been aided by the need to replace the timber bridges.

William Aston was forced to resign with effect from 25 March 1899. The previous year Vincent Raven, the North Eastern Railway's

*An 1896 plan showing the curve connecting the Shropshire Railways' Nantmawr branch to the Cambrian's Llanfyllin branch. The section of the original Llanfyllin branch coloured pink was abandoned.*
*Parliamentary Archives*

locomotive engineer, had reported on the running of the locomotive department and Aston's position was decided when the board considered his response to it on 21 December. Herbert Edward Jones, from the Midland Railway, was appointed locomotive and carriage and wagon superintendent to replace him on 25 February, salary £600. Raven was paid £100 for his efforts.

The decision to appoint Raven was not recorded and his report has not survived, although the data given to him and some of his working papers are in the National Archives. Only the *Railway Engineer* (March 1899) commented on the matter, making the connection with Aston's certificate published in the shareholders' report, saying that the rolling stock had been maintained in good order, when it was 'common knowledge' that Raven's report was 'anything but complimentary to said rolling stock'. How could the directors reconcile the certificate with the report and not mention the latter to the shareholders? Opinions might differ but there was a consensus that for years Aston had been asked to make bricks without straw.

A crossing loop was brought into use at Four Crosses on 2 July 1899, less than five months after Denniss had obtained approval. Breaking up the 5-mile 3-chain section between Llanymynech and Pool Quay, it cost £1,250. In addition to the loop the works had included a cattle-loading dock, a down-side platform, a 290-foot siding and signalling.

One of the directors reported on outstanding accounts, mostly from railway companies, on 30 November. The Manchester & Milford Railway owed £43,373 19s 2d for maintenance of the joint line and use of Llanidloes station, accumulated since 1875. At Aberystwyth the Cambrian claimed £527 5s 9d, which the MMR thought was excessive, paying £400 on account. The Gorseddau Railway owed £1,185 14s up to 30 June 1894; the signal cabin was closed when the interlocking was completed and no further charges had been incurred since 1 July 1894.

The Cambrian effectively acted as banker to the MWR, making advances to cover interest payments, which were recouped from MWR traffic revenue. The Wrexham & Ellesmere Railway owed £1,281 6s 9d, which represented capital expenditure made on its behalf by the Cambrian.

During a period of low tide in August 1899 Collin had the Barmouth bridge inspected by divers and an engineer from the Cleveland Bridge Company, finding that all was not well. The bracing supporting the pier on which the drawbridge rested had rusted away, leaving it unsupported. Some of the columns were rusting, which was not expected with wrought iron permanently under water. The iron could be cut with a knife and chemical analysis showed that it had been of poor quality when made. He immediately imposed a 5mph speed restriction and later reduced it to 2mph.

Collin recommended renewing all the ironwork except the first two piers, which were in good order. New cylinders should be placed between the existing piers, the main girders fixed outside the existing structure and new cross girders placed between the original members. The channel would be spanned by a swing bridge turning on a roller path fixed on four cylinders built between piers Nos 3 and 4. The works could be carried out while the line remained open for traffic and would

The Cambrian's second GPO sorting carriage, No 293, entered service in time for the 1902 Christmas traffic. Built at Oswestry it cost £726 2s 8d. Only half of its length, to the right of the door, was required for sorting, the remainder being used for stowage. This carriage was the seventh built by the Cambrian with steel underframes, having been preceded by a batch of six bogie composite carriages.
*Cambrian Railways*

cost about £20,000. The new bridge would have a 20-ton axle load, and if the Dovey bridge was improved the locomotive exchange that was carried out at Machynlleth could be eliminated, reducing operating expenses. The work had been started by December, the contractors installing electric arc lights in order to be able to work at night.

Second class fares for through traffic had been reintroduced on an experimental basis in 1897, and this had been a success, reported Denniss on 16 January 1900, recommending that 2nd class be reintroduced on local journeys at 15% over 3rd class fares. Forty compartments could be provided at little expense: 'In previous cases

In 1898 4-4-0 No 85 was the first Cambrian locomotive built by Robert Stephenson & Company, costing £2,561. *John Alsop collection*

we have merely provided a mat on the floors and altered the lettering from "third" to "second" class.' The LNWR and GWR had adopted a similar policy, he said, and found it worthwhile. The *Railway Engineer* said that the move demonstrated the 'folly' of a small company surrounded by big ones taking the initiative in 'revolutionary changes'.

On 2 April Denniss made a case for extending at Pwllheli. The Board of Trade having apparently refused funding for a new harbour, he thought it unlikely that the council would be able to promote or carry out a scheme that would be of use to the Cambrian. The LNWR, on the other hand, was making much of its Chwilog station as the interchange for the peninsula's hinterland, renaming it 'Chwilog for Nevin' and reducing the fare to be less than the Pwllheli rate. Unless the Cambrian took action the LNWR would eventually build a light railway to Nevin and take all the traffic.

The embankment on which the extension was to be built was estimated to cost £57,000. The corporation had £15,000 and hoped that the Board of Trade would provide one-third, leaving £23,000 that it expected the Cambrian to contribute.

Renewal of the Doughty and Scafell river bridges was completed by May; they were made wide enough for a double track to facilitate doubling the line between Newtown and Moat Lane. Meanwhile, at Barmouth the Cleveland Bridge Company had difficulty in removing the old piles, one of them being 28 feet under the river bed. The first new cylinder was sunk 48ft 6in instead of the 20 feet anticipated by Collin. It passed through the 13 feet of stone put down by Conybeare, 1 feet of sand, 27 feet of soft blue clay, and 7ft 6in of soft blue clay full of oyster shells and shale before it reached a granite base.

The next three cylinders went in more easily once intruding ironwork from Conybeare's bridge had been removed; No 2 went down 53 feet, No 3 to 58 feet and No 4 to 65 feet. The four cylinders for the fixed span were treated differently. They were sunk 25 feet into the clay, then nine piles were driven that extended into the cylinders. All the cylinders were filled with concrete up to the water level. Collin

had a wind gauge installed so trains could be stopped from crossing the bridge if the wind pressure exceeded 20lb per square foot.

Talerddig station was put into use as a passing place on 24 August. On 20 June Denniss had reported that he had found it impossible to cast the timetable without crossing five trains there each day. The work had required signalling and a down platform to meet Board of Trade requirements, and a goods siding was also installed. Passenger trains had been passed unofficially and Denniss was aware that the company would be criticised if there had been an accident.

Without explanation, Brayne was demoted from secretary to be head of the rating and taxation department from 1 October, salary £200. Denniss combined the position of secretary with that of general manager, being paid an additional £250.

An application for fresh powers was approved on 6 November. Clauses covered the extension and new station at Pwllheli (estimate £34,500), conversion of the opening section of the Dovey bridge to a fixed bridge (it had not been opened for 10 years, estimate £250), excess payments to the MWR, use of steam vessels for excursions, erection or purchase of houses for personnel, and use of capital authorised by the 1896 Act for the purposes of the intended Act. With the Dovey bridge alteration dropped, the royal assent was given on 2 July 1901.

During 1899 the company had agreed to construct and work the Tanat Valley Light Railway and the Welshpool & Llanfair Light Railway, both of which would be constructed with the support of Treasury grants. Working privately, Collin was their engineer. Both companies had seriously underestimated the amount of capital required and needed fresh powers before tenders could be let. John Strachan of Cardiff was awarded both contracts during 1901.

**4-4-0 No 32 was built by Robert Stephenson & Company in 1897 and is seen on the turntable at Brecon.** *John Alsop collection*

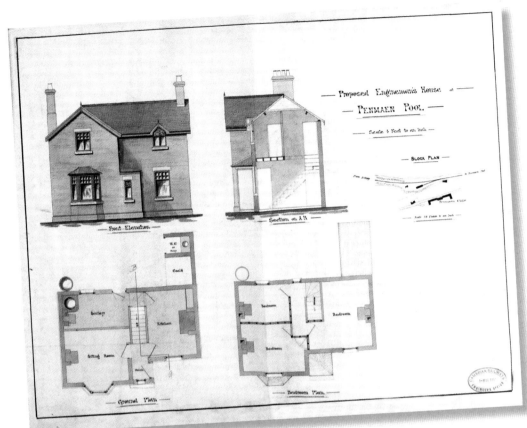

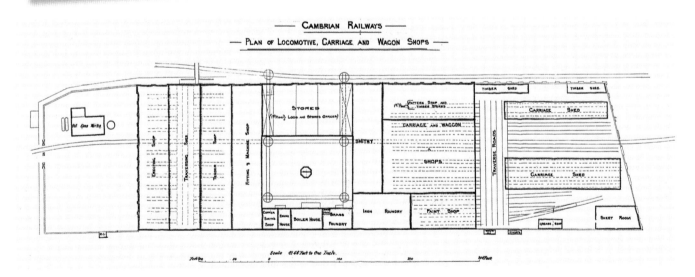

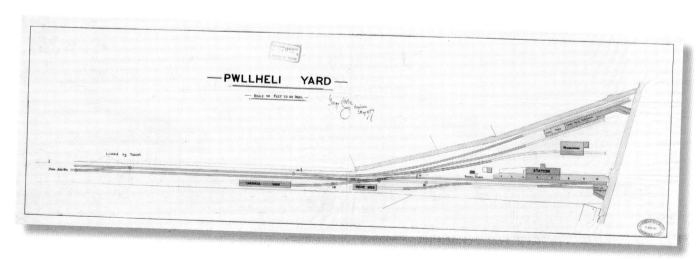

TOP Some of the plans for structures produced in the late 19th century were quite artistic. This one, dated 8 March 1897, is for a proposed engineman's house at Penmaenpool. *National Archives*

MIDDLE The layout of the works at Oswestry in 1898. *National Archives*

BOTTOM A plan of the original terminus at Pwllheli, dated 7 May 1897 and signed by George Owen, the engineer. Proposed alterations to track, cattle pens and the horse and carriage dock are coloured red. *National Archives*

# 6

# The 20th century: the world changes 1901-1914

During the 20th century the Cambrian was gradually to lose control of its own destiny. The change started with social legislation improving employees' conditions, increasing costs with no increases in fares or rates allowed to help balance the books. Then the Government took advantage of archaic legislation to control the railways during the 1st World War, with little apparent concern for the consequences, undermining the commercial basis on which railways had been established and leaving the smaller companies incapable of standing alone, when the only way forward was the 'Grouping' and, ultimately, nationalisation.

The Cambrian started the new century in reasonable condition. It went on to achieve a measure of expansion, built two steam locomotives and more rolling stock, and innovated with a steam railmotor, observation carriages and the tourist timetable. But it still had one more financial crisis to overcome before the final curtain fell.

In response to the Manchester & Milford Railway's proposal that the Cambrian should work its line for £6,000 per annum, Denniss was instructed to assess its condition and to see what savings could be made in January 1901. He recommended making a counter-offer of

These three six-wheeled carriages with a brake compartment and four 3rd class passenger compartments were completed in April 1901; the one nearest the camera is No 78. Using second-hand wheels and some second-hand brake equipment, they cost £427 net each. In 1890 the Metropolitan Carriage Company had supplied similar vehicles with three compartments that had cost £456 each. *Cambrian Railways*

Cambrian Railway Co's Engine

In the early years of the 20th century a postcard publisher thought that this view of 2-4-0 No 28, the erstwhile *Mazeppa*, a Sharp, Stewart engine of 1863, was sufficiently attractive to justify publication as a coloured postcard. *Knight/John Alsop collection*

£4,000 a year for the first three years, to pay for stations and locomotives to be brought up to scratch, but it was not pursued.

Another opportunity to expand the network followed the announcement on 17 April that the Mawddwy Railway was to close. This 6¾-mile independent branch from Cemmaes Road had become run down because its principal shareholder, Sir Edmund Buckley Bt, would not pay for repairs. It was offered to the Cambrian for £12,000. It had made a small operating profit but not enough to pay debenture interest or dividends.

It had potential for tourists, Denniss thought, but pointed out that the Cambrian had no capital to apply for such a purpose. There was nothing to stop the Mawddwy company from applying for an order to work the line as a light railway, however, and making an agreement with the Cambrian to reconstruct and work it, thus qualifying for a Treasury grant. Collin estimated that it would cost £8,950 to repair. Denniss therefore said that he could not recommend an offer being made. The traffic had been worth about £100 a month.

The impact of the Railway Employment (Prevention of Accidents) Act of 1900 was considered on 1 May 1901. The Board of Trade had given notice that it intended to make rules covering 12 aspects of railway operation: brake levers on both sides of wagons; labelling wagons; movement of wagons by tow rope; power brakes on engines; lighting where shunting was carried out after dark; protection of point rods and signal wires and location of ground frames; location of offices near working lines; marking of fouling points; protection of gauge glasses; working of trains without brake vans outside station limits; and protection of permanent way personnel.

The major expense for the Cambrian, Denniss reported, would be wagon brakes, engine brakes, protection of point rods and signal wires, and marking fouling points. There were six locomotives without power brakes, and it would cost £50 each to fit them.

Combined effort from the railway companies wrought concessions from the Board of Trade. Ten years were allowed for the wagon brakes

instead of two, and companies could refuse to accept wagons not labelled on both sides. Tow-roping was permitted where there were no other means of dealing with the traffic. Point rods and signal wires were to be covered within two years where they were in a position to be a danger to persons employed on the railway, and the requirement for permanent way lookouts applied to situations where danger was likely to arise. The requirement to mark fouling points had been withdrawn.

The Ellesmere loop line was also considered on 1 May. Through traffic between stations north of Wrexham and the Cambrian and South Wales not having developed as expected, the line was normally only used by goods trains except for three months in the summer, when there was a through passenger train each way between Seacombe and Manchester and Aberystwyth. This required two signal boxes to be manned at an annual cost of £205 8s. Denniss's recommendation that they be closed immediately was approved.

Reporting Owen's death on 5 June, Denniss said that he was 75 years old and had worked for the company for 37 years. He suggested that £100 of Owen's £400 salary should be paid to Collin, increasing his salary to £600.

No 19, the first locomotive to be built in Oswestry works, was completed by 7 August. A 4-4-0, Jones had been given permission to build it using one of two Nasmyth, Wilson boilers that had been in stock since 1898 (£827) and a set of wheels (£500) and cylinders (£50) already in stock, on 1 May 1900. Nasmyth, Wilson had quoted £1,680 to make a locomotive and tender using the parts, which Jones thought was ridiculous, estimating £550 to complete it without a tender; it turned out at £772 2s 11d. The last of the type, built by Robert Stephenson & Company in 1898, had cost £2,561 including tender. A

tender costing £478 was built for No 19 in 1903. The second boiler was used on another locomotive authorised in October 1903 and completed by 13 August 1904, No 11; its net cost was £1,995 1s 3d.

In addition to the locomotives, Oswestry works had a considerable output of new carriages and wagons around the turn of the century. Its foundry also met the railway's requirements for rail chairs.

At Barmouth the eight new bridge cylinders had been completed by October. By February 1902 the main girders for the fixed section had been installed and the flooring had been connected, taking the weight off three of the old spans. By 13 May the main girders and floor of the swing portion had been erected and the drawbridge removed. Although the swing section was not operational, the speed restriction was removed on 30 June.

On 7 July a steamboat towing a lighter downstream collided with the old structure. Had this happened before the bridge renewal started it would certainly have made the bridge unsafe for traffic and might have partially demolished it, Collin reported. The swing section was first tested in August, and by December only the cast-iron cap on the

*Using an unused boiler and other components from stock, No 19, a 4-4-0, was completed at Oswestry in August 1901. Cambrian Railways*

centre cylinders remained outstanding; the structure had been painted and the old one removed. Collin had provided photographs of the work in progress, but they were not retained with his reports.

Robert Stephenson & Company was awarded an order for five goods engines in February 1902. Because it was keen to get work for its new plant in Darlington, its tender had been resubmitted; originally £2,914, the engines were now £2,730 each, 'coincidentally' £5 less than the lowest tender. Its position was assisted by its willingness to take Cambrian debentures at 95% of market value in settlement, and to share any surplus with the railway if they were sold on the market at a profit. Jones noted that previous engines supplied by the Vulcan Foundry had been unsatisfactory.

Two locomotives should have been delivered in October 1902, the remainder by March 1903, but when Jones visited in November the first two were nowhere near complete. The builder explained that not only had there been problems with machinery but the workforce was taking advantage of the new works to try and obtain better terms of employment – there had been several strikes and a boycott. The first locomotive was delivered on 19 April 1903, three more by 9 June, and the last on 16 June. A £15-per-week late-delivery penalty was imposed.

Despite the delay with this order, the next, in January 1904, also went to Darlington, which prompted Stephenson to ask for the penalties to be reimbursed, saying that the strikes and other issues were beyond its control and were covered by the terms of the contract.

Denniss was offered the appointment of chief commissioner of railways for Victoria, Australia, in 1902, but decided not to take it. Telling the board on 30 September, he added that the salary was £3,500. The hint fell on deaf ears.

The moribund Shropshire Railways (formerly the Potteries, Shrewsbury & North Wales Railway) was offered to the Cambrian for £70,000 in January 1903. Denniss told the intermediary that the Cambrian would be prepared to consider working it if the present owner obtained running powers into Shrewsbury General station, and that it was not prepared to negotiate with the LNWR and GWR, the station's owners, on the issue. The Cambrian already had control of the only remunerative section of the railway, the Nantmawr branch, and Denniss knew that the GWR and LNWR would exclude other railways from using the station.

After many trials and tribulations, the Welshpool & Llanfair Light Railway was opened for goods traffic on 9 March 1903 and for passengers on 4 April, the Cambrian being responsible for its operation.

A survey of coast structures, a prerequisite to using heavier locomotives (page 151), was completed by 21 April, when Denniss reported that it would only require some cattle creeps to be strengthened and more packing to be provided under the Dovey drawbridge. The Dolgelley branch had also been cleared, releasing locomotives for use on the Tanat Valley Light Railway. Collin had been asked to survey the Mid Wales section for the same purpose.

In June Denniss tried to get the directors to plan ahead regarding the company's locomotive and rolling stock requirements. He said that 43 of the 85 locomotives were more than 20 years old, and 12 were 40 years old. Over the next five years 18 locomotives would require replacing and increased traffic would require one more locomotive each year, involving expenditure of at least £50,000 chargeable to renewals and £13,500 chargeable to capital.

Of the 216 carriages, 37 were four-wheeled, 35 were more than 20 years old, and 25 had been in service for nearly 40 years. The four-wheeled stock should be withdrawn and used for other purposes; it had

1,050 seats and could be replaced by 17 bogie vehicles at a cost of £13,600. Catering for growth would need one saloon, 12 composites, 12 3rd class (two with luggage and guards accommodation) and six passenger brake vans, at an estimated cost of £22,250. Overall, he calculated expenditure on renewals at £124,230 and on capital at £62,200.

In October Denniss returned to the subject of increasing track capacity. Despite extra loops installed at Pool Quay, Four Crosses, Forden, Whittington and Talerddig, the line had still run at maximum capacity during the summer. Double track between Welshpool and Moat Lane would increase revenue, he forecast, and was necessary to compete with motor traffic.

The most economical and practical way of improving the service, he said, would be to provide single cars similar to those at work on the Welshpool & Llanfair Light Railway; perhaps he meant tramway-like carriages. Worked by small engines, frequent services could be operated between Aberystwyth and Barmouth; Dolgelley, Barmouth and Pwllheli; Whitchurch, Welshpool and Llanidloes; Oswestry and Llangynog; and Oswestry and Llanfyllin.

The first two would attract tourists and require eight engines and vehicles. The carriages would cost about £520 each. The cheapest way of providing locomotives would be to convert the existing small locomotives already working on the coast section to tank engines, at £120 each.

Feeder omnibuses and coaches were unattractive and people would only use them when necessary, but more attractive vehicles would encourage traffic. Denniss proposed ten routes: Aberystwyth-Aberayron-New Quay; Llanfyllin-Vyrnwy; Pwllheli-Nevin; Portmadoc-Penrhyndeudraeth-Beddgelert; Cemmaes Road-Dinas Mawddwy-Dolgelley; Rhayader-Elan Valley waterworks; Newbridge-Llandrindod; Llanidloes-Devil's Bridge; Llanfair Caereinion; and Cann Office-Dinas Mawddwy-Cemmaes Road.

In June 1903 a recommendation from Jones, the locomotive superintendent, that the Builth Wells workshop should be closed, leaving a small presence to carry out running repairs on wagons 'as at Portmadoc', was accepted, saving £1,244 annually. Nineteen men and two apprentices were affected. He said he would give them jobs at Oswestry, but most of them were 'very old servants' who would not move. Builth (four locomotives) and Brecon (three) became outstations of Llanidloes (seven plus two at Caersws and two at Moat Lane). Watson, the Llanidloes foreman, was getting on in years but was trustworthy. Only four men transferred to Oswestry; 16 left the company.

A works photograph of 0-6-0 No 92, delivered by Robert Stephenson & Company in 1903. *John Alsop collection*

Another product of Robert Stephenson's Darlington works, 4-4-0 No 94 was delivered in 1904 and is seen at Aberystwyth. *John Alsop collection*

In January 1901 the Cambrian and Mid Wales companies decided that they should be amalgamated. No explanation was given by either party for the move or why it took until 1903 to deposit a Bill. In October 1903 Denniss suggested that if the amalgamation was to proceed the company should also obtain powers to acquire extra land at Pwllheli, to build or acquire hotels at Harlech, Criccieth and Pwllheli, to issue debentures in payment for road motor cars or other vehicles, and to authorise contributions to an employees' pension fund.

On 5 January 1904 the Dowager Lady Watkin Wynn ceremonially opened the Tanat Valley Light Railway by using a gold key, apparently engraved with the Cambrian's crest, to unlock a silver chain that blocked the passage of the inaugural train at Porthywaen level crossing. Around 300 passengers, mainly shareholders, travelled from Oswestry, some of them taking lunch with the TVLR board at Llangynog. Normal services started the next day, the first train taking 150 passengers to Oswestry market. Until a water tank was installed at Llangynog, services were subject to delay.

Like the Welshpool & Llanfair Light Railway, the TVLR was short of funds and in dispute with its contractor, the litigious John Strachan. The nature of the agreements, whereby the Cambrian was responsible for construction and operation, dragged it in, with creditors saying that they had only accepted contracts because the Cambrian was involved. Obtaining judgment for £4,000 spent on the TVLR's behalf, the Cambrian put the company into receivership on 30 April. The Treasury refused to make an extra grant because the TVLR had, it declared, spent too much on land purchases and legal expenses. Strachan's actions against both companies were eventually resolved at arbitration.

Some 35 years after construction, on 11 January services on the coast section were interrupted for five days by a rock fall from tunnel No 3 on the Aberdovey deviation. The fall occurred when the arch was being renewed and a cavity the full width of the tunnel was created. As the loose material was being removed, timber struts put in during construction were found, so the tunnel's builders were aware of the likely problem. Collin thought that heavy rain during the previous three months had aggravated the situation.

In January 1904 the LNWR's desire to give passengers on its expresses access to a dining car forced the Cambrian to order two corridor carriages for use on London-Aberystwyth services. The LNWR had requested the improvement the previous year, but Denniss had done nothing until the larger company set a deadline of 1 July 1904. If the LNWR ran the through carriages, he explained, the Cambrian would lose considerable mileage and the advertising value of its stock being seen as far away as London.

Existing carriages could be adapted for £40 each, Jones had told Denniss, but it would 'seriously cut up' the stock. It would be better to build new, at a cost of £1,100 for vehicles 54ft 6in long. The order was given on 20 January, the two carriages replacing two of six bogie carriages ordered on 19 February 1903.

The discussion concerning these carriages made the company realise that it had no idea about its loading gauge. Denniss had asked Owen and Aston to produce one in 1895 but it could not be found. Jones had therefore made a template and run it throughout the line, establishing that only minor alterations to platforms and the rebuilding of 12 yards of the roof of No 1 tunnel on the Aberdovey deviation would enable carriages 60 feet long and the height of the latest GWR stock to be operated without restriction.

On 13 February 1904 Collin submitted his resignation as engineer, citing ill health. He had also been acting as engineer of the light railways so may have been overworking. He aggravated the disputes with Strachan because, as the nominated arbitrator, he had agreed to act, then on 6 May announced his withdrawal because he was a creditor of the Welshpool company.

George C. McDonald, formerly the Midland Railway's resident engineer, new lines and works, was appointed to replace him on 7 April, at a salary of £450. When he complained about the mandatory membership of the Railway Clearing House superannuation scheme, which had not been mentioned at interview, he was awarded an additional

£36 to cover the subscription. He started with the Cambrian on 9 May.

A local landowner had raised concerns about the name of Glandovey station in March, pointing out that stations were normally named after the place they served, in this case Garreg, while the station carried the name of a local house. With its proximity to Glandovey Junction, it was misleading to passengers. He added that the name was actually half English and half Welsh, and should be Glandyfi; the Welsh form was adopted on 5 May. Another correspondent said that the Welsh form would be confusing to English passengers, and the confusion between the adjacent stations could be resolved by renaming the junction station. Denniss thought the last point had merit and the name Dovey Junction was adopted from 1 July.

The contract with Pwllheli Corporation for the extension was finally sealed in May. The key points were that the corporation would build the embankment and convey its freehold to the company, which would pay £20,000 in cash or D debentures and that provision would be made for a connection to any railway that might be built between Pwllheli and Nevin.

Jones inspected three former Lambourne Valley Light Railway 0-6-0Ts that had been placed on the market after that line had been taken over by the GWR. They had cost £1,300 when built in 1898 (Nos 1 and 2) and 1903 (No 3). Suitable for the Tanat Valley Light Railway or the other branches, they were being offered at £900 for No 3 and £650 each for Nos 1 and 2. He was instructed to offer up to £2,200 of D debentures at 95%. He subsequently bought them for £2,000 plus £7 10s for spares, but the agents refused to take stock. Numbered 24, 26 and 35 in the Cambrian list, two were delivered to Oswestry on 16 June and put into traffic by 7 July. The third was delivered on the 22nd.

Passage of the 1903 amalgamation Bill through Parliament had been hampered by LNWR game-playing. After saying that it would not object to the MWR amalgamation in return for running powers between Talyllyn and Llanidloes, it then produced a set of clauses intended to divert all the through traffic over the Central Wales line. Instead of the running powers between the MWR and Llandrindod

Wells, which the Cambrian sought, it offered to allow the passage of through carriages, which was already provided for but which it had refused to allow. Over six weeks the LNWR moderated its position and gave the Cambrian what it wanted, agreeing also to share the cost of making Builth Road junction suitable for passenger trains.

The royal assent was given on 24 June, the amalgamation taking effect from 1 July. In addition to Denniss's proposed powers and the LNWR clauses, there were also clauses for the GWR and the Midland, and one freeing the MMR from paying interest on the cost of building and maintaining the joint line and on maintaining Llanidloes station. It still had to pay interest on one-third of the cost of building the station, however, despite relinquishing its rights to both it and the joint line. £17,500 of B debentures could be issued to redeem the annual charge of £800 paid to the Brecon & Merthyr Tydfil Junction Railway for the use of Brecon and Talyllyn stations.

The Cambrian hosted another royal visit on 21 July 1904, when the King and Queen inaugurated the Rhayader waterworks. As the LNWR royal train was unsuitable for the corporation's railway, saloon No 9 was overhauled and used with saloon No 11, two other four-wheeled vehicles and a brake van to carry the royal party to the reservoirs.

Unfortunately, on 13 August Denniss had to explain to the board that, despite his best efforts, the day had not gone well. Approaching Rhayader from Builth, the royal train had stopped on the 1 in 60 gradient at Elan Junction to get the token. It could not then be restarted, even with the assistance of Birmingham Corporation's locomotive. Under Denniss's instruction, an excursion locomotive was then added to the train and it arrived 19 minutes late.

Restrictions on the Mid Wales bridges inhibited double-heading and Jones had not sanctioned the use of a banking engine because of the switchback nature of the line. Afterwards Jones admitted that he

**Completed in August 1904, 4-4-0 No 11 was the second locomotive built at Oswestry using a spare Nasmyth, Wilson boiler.** *J. B. Sherlock/John Alsop collection*

In October 1909 a London photographer was commissioned to take a set of 35 photographs of Oswestry works. In this view of the erecting shops nine locomotives are visible. *W. Brooks*

had known that a single locomotive would not restart the train if it stopped on any of the banks. W. H. Gough, the traffic superintendent, was criticised for failing to clear the line before the Royal Train's arrival; he also, in Denniss's view, failed to cope with the emergency when it arose. Unfortunately, he added, the 'type of men' in the traffic department, including the station masters, were unable to deal with extraordinary conditions. Gough was called before the traffic committee to be rebuked in person.

During his post-appointment inspection of the line, McDonald had found that want of ballast was causing parts of it to move during hot weather. Later, on 10 October, he said that track renewals should relate to rail life, about 24 years. Therefore, with 260 miles, 12 miles should be renewed each year, but over the last 13 years the average renewal had been 6¼ miles.

He also reported that the timber portion of the Barmouth bridge required complete replacement. It had not been maintained for five years, the piles were worn by the scouring action of the sand, and beams and planking were decayed. Suggesting that the work be carried out over three years, he estimated its cost at £16,000. Asked to report on the practicality of partly replacing it with an embankment and on the cost of replacing it with iron, on 1 November he said that steel would cost £285 per span, compared with £140 for timber. However, the steel would deteriorate rapidly in the exposed location, and creosoted timber would be more satisfactory. His remarks about creosote imply that preservative not had been used previously.

Pointing out that any change to the nature of the structure would require Admiralty approval, he thought that 60 spans could be filled in, leaving 53. Although more expensive at £17,620, the result would be more satisfactory. In December 1906 a contract was let for the

supply of 50,000 cubic feet of timber for delivery to Aberdovey over two years, valued at £5,404.

Denniss did not think much of the board's idea of moving the stock registry work to the Mid Wales London office, whose lease had two years to run. The work would require an experienced registrar, a clerk and an office boy. Williamson, his chief assistant, who had done the work, could not move to London on medical advice. In January/February and July/August five or six extra clerks were drafted in from other departments to prepare the dividend cheques. The expenditure would be £474 3s 4d, but the saving at Oswestry would be less than £150. It could be done if the expense was thought to be justified, he said. The proposal was deferred.

On 7 December 1904 Denniss paid tribute to the efforts of his clerical staff in handling the Mid Wales amalgamation, with overtime worked most days since October 1903. His recommendation that they be awarded £100 between them was accepted.

Reports in the *Liverpool Daily Post* and the *Liverpool Echo* on 24 August 1905, that negotiations for the LNWR to purchase the Cambrian were almost complete, generated some excitement, especially in Oswestry, where it was feared that the works would be closed in consequence. The *Daily Post* published a denial from the LNWR the next day. The Cambrian board merely noted the reports.

A serious decline in traffic receipts during the second half of 1905 called for savings in all departments. Oswestry works was put on short time from 21 August and one of the ballast trains was stopped.

By 13 September employees retiring or dismissed had produced annual savings of £692 8s 6d.

With some of the older locomotives costing more to maintain than they were worth, Jones was instructed to enquire about locomotives for sale. On 1 November he said that he had inspected locomotives belonging to the Metropolitan District, Metropolitan, and Lancashire, Derbyshire & East Coast railways. Locomotives being offered by the GWR and the Great Northern Railway were either unsuitable or obsolete. The Metropolitan locomotives were closest to being suitable and affordable but were still too heavy for the branches.

Nevertheless, on 2 November he bought five of them for £500 each and one for £550, which had a nearly new boiler, and spare parts for £70. They were delivered to Oswestry on 22 November and entered the Works to be made suitable for Cambrian purposes; work included removal of condensing apparatus and provision of cabs. Jones also bought two Metropolitan gas holders for £50 each; unexpectedly, they arrived fully charged with gas worth about £6, 'which of course I made use of'.

With the Pwllheli extension needing more time, Denniss suggested making an application for additional powers. The Bill sought permission to double the line between Three Cocks and Talyllyn, at Kilkewydd, and between Machynlleth and Dovey Junction (the second line at the last for obtaining ballast only), and for additional land to extend the Aberystwyth station yard and the Afon Wen ballast pit.

The Davies name was restored to the board with the election of David Davies, grandson of the contractor, on 3 January 1906. This followed the death of Arthur Charles Humphreys-Owen, the heir of Mrs Owen of Glansevern, who had been a director since 1876 and chairman from 1900 until 1905. Edward Davies, Davies's father, had been a director from 9 August 1892 until his early death on 1 January 1898.

The opening of a 30-bed hotel in Nevin, and LNWR proposals to serve it with a road service from Chwilog in 1906, prompted Denniss to suggest that the Cambrian should run a service from Pwllheli. Jones cautioned against using steam-powered vehicles – petrol gave much better results. Two Moss & Wood 'Orion' buses were therefore obtained at a cost of £770 each and a shed was built at Pwllheli to garage them. The vehicles carried 22 passengers, 12 in the main compartment, eight in the smoking compartment and two with the driver. Luggage was carried on the roof.

The service was launched on 16 June and started on the 18th. Three return trips were operated six days per week and parcels and bicycles were also carried. Based on first-month revenue of £121 11s, Denniss reckoned that earnings would be about £15 per week.

The Tanat Valley Light Railway's shortage of funds brought the Cambrian into dispute with the Earl of Bradford, who had provided land for it. At issue was railway No 2, as defined in the TVLR's 1899 Light Railway Order, the south-to-west curve at Llanyblodwel, intended to facilitate traffic from the TVLR to Llanymynech. Bradford had required its construction in return for withdrawing his objection and for making land available to the railway at £80 per acre. Because the light railway had run out of money it had not been built, but Bradford was determined that it should be and held the Cambrian responsible.

He had granted an exception in 1903 and three years later wanted compliance. Such was his persistence that railway No 2 became known as 'Lord Bradford's curve'. The Cambrian explained that the TVLR had insufficient funds and that it, the Cambrian, had already spent £16,000, and might have to pay more, despite having said at the outset

**The carriage workshops.** *W. Brooks*

that it would not contribute to TVLR capital. A 12-month extension was granted on the understanding that the curve would be put into use without further correspondence.

The Cambrian did consider installing the curve, but the estimate was £1,600, including £1,200 for the signalling associated with the two signal boxes needed to comply with Board of Trade requirements for passenger working. Despite the earl's efforts, it was never built.

In June a compromise was reached in the case that Liverpool Corporation had brought against the TVLR, the Cambrian and the subscribing local authorities for the non-payment of interest on the £3,000 it had subscribed to the TVLR to aid the delivery of materials for the Vyrnwy reservoir. It made the Cambrian responsible for paying the debenture interest and making a contribution to the expenses of the corporation and the other defendants. A Light Railway Order was obtained to confirm the arrangements.

The December 1905 Bill was enacted on 20 July, after its second reading had been ambushed by Labour members seeking free travel for MPs. Barry, Cardiff and Midland Railway Bills had been similarly attacked before the Speaker ruled the motions out of order. The track-doubling proposal and the extra land at Aberystwyth had fallen by the wayside, although powers were also obtained that improved the efficacy of existing powers for dealing with trespass.

The Bill approving the lease of the Manchester & Milford Railway by the GWR had been dealt with in the same session, and had been

*The lifting bridge at Barmouth was replaced by a swing bridge in 1902. Here a short train is making the crossing while those enjoying the seaside are dressed in accordance with the standards of the day.*

given the royal assent on 29 May. The GWR was to pay the Cambrian £11,000 in settlement of the MMR's debts and was to be allowed to use Aberystwyth station. The Cambrian also had a two-year option to require the GWR to convey the MMR's property from Penbontbren to Llangurig without charge; the existence of a £50 rent charge on the land seems to have deterred the Cambrian from exercising it.

On 29 July 1896 the Cambrian had taken a 14-year lease on the Van Railway that gave it unrestricted use of the line to collect mine waste for use as ballast. The Van had been in receivership since 12 March 1892 and closed since 30 June 1893. Under the lease the toll was £150 per annum, the Cambrian being responsible for maintenance. With the ballast becoming exhausted and the lead traffic worth only about £400 a year, less than the cost of maintenance and operation, the Cambrian decided to exercise its right to determine the lease when the dowager Marchioness of Londonderry died on 18 September 1906. Unfortunately, it had misread the lease and its term was absolute. Lord Herbert Vane-Tempest, the heir and a Cambrian director, reduced the toll to £100, and again in 1914 to £80, sufficient to cover rent charges of £61 2s.

The limitations of the Metropolitan locomotives soon became apparent, with reports of the Dolgelley branch track being damaged.

In September a trial was made with one of the 'Wrexham & Ellesmere class of tank engine' – Nasmyth, Wilson 0-4-4Ts built in 1896 and 1899 – in substitution. Although they were 1 ton heavier, their weight was better distributed and the trial locomotive caused no track damage. Limited coal and water capacity, 1½cwt and 900 gallons respectively, restricted the use of the 4-4-0Ts to shunting and banking.

On 28 September 1906, McDonald reported that the company employed 54 platelayers aged over 60, and 13 were aged over 70; 28 were incapable of doing the work and he would like to retire them, but there was no pension fund. Without assistance, their only refuge would be the workhouse. Could the board find a way of making an allowance of, say, 5 shillings per week? He had found that once a man got well over 60 he could not keep up with his work, and there was also the danger of accidents to consider. He got no useful response from the traffic committee. Jones also had infirm men retained on the books in Oswestry works.

After taking a month's special leave, Denniss returned to work 'intimating' that he wished to be relieved of the secretary's responsibilities. The board agreed on 4 October and appointed Samuel Williamson with a salary of £300. He had joined the company as a junior clerk in 1885 and trained under Conacher.

Over the years leading to the First World War, new legislation imposed more social obligations on the Cambrian. The 1906 Workmen's Compensation Act, effective from 1 July 1907, determined that the liability for compensation started from the date of the accident, not two weeks after, even if the accident was due to misconduct or did not occur on company premises. The 1880 Employer's Liability Act had put the onus of proof on the injured employee, a point addressed by the 1897 Workmen's Compensation Act but which the judiciary had interpreted restrictively. The company had created a compensation fund, paying £484 15s 10d out of £742 6s 6d over the 12 months to 16 January 1907.

The problem of small locomotives suitable for working the branches was resolved by converting two Sharp, Stewart 2-4-0s into tank engines in January and July 1907. Jones described them as 'engines for short trains', and the conversions cost £121 10s.

During 1907 E. R. Davies was keen to get the Cambrian to take possession of the new embankment at Pwllheli. The corporation was paying interest on a £17,500 overdraft it had taken to get the works completed and needed the Cambrian's £20,000 to settle it. McDonald, however, found that the embankment was still incomplete and the railway formation was crossed by the contractor's tracks and tramways in several places. The transaction was eventually completed on 25 May 1908. The extra land required to enable the line to be extended onto the new formation was secured for £205 instead of the vendor's £411 asking price.

The Cambrian's engine shed at Wrexham, capable of holding two locomotives, opened on 1 June 1907. McDonald estimated that it would save £45 in Great Central stabling charges and 778 light-engine miles per annum.

In July Denniss reported on the North Shropshire Light Railway Order application, a proposal to take over the derelict Potteries, Shrewsbury & North Wales Railway and operate it as a light railway. A formal notice had been submitted to him by Mr H. F. Stephens of Tonbridge. He recommended that the Cambrian should retain the powers already granted to it by the Shropshire Railways' 1888 and 1891 Acts.

Improved conditions of service and standardised rates of pay and grading came with the introduction of the railway conciliation scheme in November 1907. From the turn of the century, rising costs had brought home to railway companies that many of their employees were not sufficiently productive. Revised working practices led to improvements in train loadings, reduced train mileage and time at terminals. Men could now do more work in 8 hours than they had previously done in 10. At the same time the cost of living, which had fallen for many years, had started to rise, leading to trades union demands for higher wages, payment for overtime and Sunday working, and shorter hours.

The companies refused to meet the Amalgamated Society of Railway Servants on the issues, and in the autumn of 1907 its members voted to

An uncommon view of the bridge in the open position. *Shaw*

ABOVE No 97 was one of three 4-4-0s supplied by Robert Stephenson in 1904, the order concluding a seven-year relationship with the Darlington company.

BELOW The first of four light railways to come under Cambrian control during the 20th century was the Welshpool & Llanfair Light Railway, opened to goods on 9 March 1903 and to passengers on 4 April. This photograph, taken shortly after the opening, shows one of the 2ft 6in-gauge railway's Beyer, Peacock 0-6-0Ts with a train of passenger stock and vans at Castle Caereinion. The short-lived overbridge is visible just behind the train.

to make any payment to other personnel involved so 'some expression of thanks … may be a more convenient acknowledgement'.

A general transport strike that started in Liverpool on 14 June spread to railwaymen on 5 August, reaching the Cambrian on the 18th, when four men at Welshpool and two at Wrexham withdrew their labour. The entire workforce at Aberystwyth followed suit the next day, and services were terminated at Bow Street. The Government negotiated a settlement on 19 August that ensured strikers would be reinstated, and the railwaymen returned to work on the 21st – 221 out of 1,250 Cambrian employees had joined in. All non-striking personnel received double pay and 32 received extra cash awards for meritorious service.

In return for the railway companies agreeing terms to end the railwaymen's strike, the Government agreed to support, by legislation if necessary, increases in rates because improved conditions had increased labour costs. A royal commission was appointed to report on the 1907 conciliation scheme's performance and to make recommendations.

John Conacher died on 18 October 1911, aged 66. Ironically, within three months the company was to pay off the last of its short-term debt for the first time in 20 years. On 1 November David Davies was elected chairman and Williamson was appointed to be general manager as well as secretary (salary £900).

Second class accommodation was abolished again from 1 January 1912 (page 151). The LNWR had notified the Cambrian of its intention to make this move on 31 July 1911. The GWR, the Midland and GCR had already done so, traffic manager Conacher reported. It represented only 5% of the Cambrian's traffic revenue, he said, and train weight could be reduced if it was abolished – 100 carriages had 160 2nd class compartments. This time the 2nd class passengers transferred their allegiance to the 3rd class.

The arrangements for through-carriage working were explained to the board by Williamson in January 1912. The mileage fee payable on the incoming stock would ideally be offset by fees paid for Cambrian stock going to London or other destinations. However, in the summer the Cambrian received more 'foreign' stock than it had of its own to send out, so it owed money – for July-September 1910, for example, the amount was £364 9s 8d to the LNWR and a smaller amount to the GWR. During the winter months, when some of its better stock would otherwise be idle, the Cambrian allowed the larger companies to use it, offsetting the summer's debt.

The Shropshire & Montgomeryshire Light Railway had asked about terms for obtaining running powers between Oswestry and Ellesmere, as permitted by the SMLR's Light Railway Order. Williamson said that the only reason for granting such powers was an expectation of increased traffic. That being unlikely, on 10 January he recommended declining the application. In the appeal court on 27 October 1913 the Cambrian's contention that running powers could be granted by agreement was denied. However, the light railway company was wrong-footed by the ill-founded impression that the Cambrian intended to appeal to the House of Lords and did nothing to give effect to its success.

Traffic on the Nantmawr branch, worth £1,800 a year to the Cambrian, was also of interest to the SMLR, the branch being originally part of the Potteries, Shrewsbury & North Wales Railway. Correspondence had started in 1910, and on 8 January 1912 the Cambrian's solicitor summarised the exchanges in a special report.

The Shropshire Railways, which owned the branch, had authority to operate its own trains but had no locomotives or rolling stock, so had suggested licensing the SMLR to work them. It was doubtful that it could do this, but the Cambrian could stop it using a small section of its line at Llanymynech that was not covered by any of the previous

agreements. It could also divert the stone traffic onto the Tanat Valley Light Railway and the Porthywaen branch, reducing the tolls payable to the Shropshire Railways and, because of the reduced mileage, the customer's costs, although that was not stated. Over the following years the Cambrian, LNWR and GWR worked together to keep the SMLR away from the Nantmawr traffic.

Although the Pwllheli-Nevin bus service was unprofitable – in 1907-10 the average income was £1,080 against expenditure of £1,199 – it was useful to the Cambrian in deterring any competition based on the LNWR's Chwilog station. In January 1912, therefore, two 30hp Daimler chassis were obtained from the London General Omnibus Company for £175 each exclusive of tyres and spares, delivered to Oswestry. Fitted with suitable bodies, they could run up to 20mph, more than double the maximum speed of the original vehicles.

The Dovey bridge had not been opened for 26 years when McDonald discussed it on 8 January 1912. Although local opposition had stopped the repeal of article No 9 of the AWCR's 1865 Act in 1901, no one had noticed that strengthening works had stopped it from being opened at all. He recommended making another attempt to have the article repealed, forecasting that there would be very little opposition. New girders on the existing piers would cost about £600, while providing a new opening bridge would cost up to £5,000.

On 4 July McDonald reported on another structure that needed attention. The Traeth Mawr viaduct, crossing the Glaslyn between Minffordd and Porthmadog, had 36 spans, was 'getting shakey' and needed extensive repairs. Less than half of its length crossed the waterway, so he suggested filling in 21 spans and making that section an embankment. The adjoining quarry could supply the material needed and he did not anticipate any local objections. He also did not expect any objections from the Admiralty, as there was no navigation and the outfall to the sea was through sluices smaller than the spans he proposed to leave. The cost was estimated at £2,500.

The national coalminers' strike in 1912 had threatened the company's ability to maintain its operations. On 27 February Williamson issued precautionary 14 days' notices to guards, porters, station clerks, gangers and Oswestry works personnel, giving him the flexibility to dismiss them with one day's notice after the 14 days expired. The train service was reduced from 4 March, and by 3 April

| Mixed trains run on the Cambrian Railways, May 1911 | |
|---|---|
| Whitchurch-Oswestry | 2.25am |
| Welshpool-Newtown | 7.05pm |
| Welshpool-Oswestry | 1.40pm (Monday only) |
| Welshpool-Oswestry | 7.10pm |
| Barmouth Junction-Dolgelley | 6.05pm |
| Barmouth-Machynlleth | 7.20pm |
| Llanymynech-Llanfyllin | 8.40am and 8.00pm |
| Llanfyllin-Llanymynech | 7.25am (Wednesday only); 7.35am (except Wednesday); 6.25pm |
| Abermule-Kerry | 10.20am; 12.05pm; 4.45pm |
| Kerry-Abermule | 9.00am; 11.30am; 3.45pm |
| Wrexham-Ellesmere | 3.50pm (Monday only) |
| Tanat Valley Light Railway | All trains, three in each direction daily; 6.40am |
| Llangynog-Oswestry | (Wednesday only) |
| Welshpool & Llanfair Light Railway | All trains |
| Mawddwy Light Railway (from July 1912) | All trains |

receipts had been reduced by £4,450, despite carrying all traffic offered. Working expenses had been reduced by £1,553 and some trains were being run mixed; Board of Trade approval for the latter had been received by telegram on 28 February. At 1 April the company had 5,349 tons of coal in stock, about eight weeks' supply. The strike ended on 6 April, after 37 days, and the dismissal notices were withdrawn.

Items requiring fresh or amended powers were approved on 11 June. They included acquisition of the Vale of Rheidol and Tanat Valley light railways, running powers on Welshpool corporation's Smithfield siding, conversion of the Dovey bridge to a fixed span (estimate now £930), the embanking of 132 yards of the eastern end of the Traeth Mawr viaduct (estimate £1,237), and the purchase of additional land for sidings at Moat Lane. The VRLR had been controlled by Cambrian nominees since August 1910.

The work to double the Newtown-Moat Lane section proceeded with very little comment. On 12 June McDonald reported that the bridges had been completed and forecast that the work would be finished in July.

Lord Michelham started the directors' benevolent fund on 3 August 1912, donating his half-year director's fees (£14 14s 4d) for the purpose. The gesture might have been driven by guilt, because he had not attended a board meeting since February 1910. Another director contributed £20, but none of their colleagues followed suit. Disbursements totalling £7 were made to former employees or their families during the fund's first year. Michelham continued the practice until he died on 7 January 1919.

The final pre-war legislation to affect the railway companies came into effect in 1913. The Railway Companies' (Accounts and Returns) Act of 1911 required them to prepare accounts and returns annually and relieved them of the obligation to report to shareholders more than annually.

A local publisher adapted his postcard of Forden to commemorate the collision. *Park/John Alsop collection*

A head-on collision that occurred at Forden on 26 November 1904 was the fault of the station master and the driver of a down passenger train. The station master had an up goods shunted into the down platform because it would be easier to unload horses there, persisting when reminded that the passenger was due and when told that it had left Welshpool. The passenger train was being driven with disregard for the conditions and the driver had not abated his speed in fog; when he saw the home signal was against him he braked but was too late to avoid the collision. Six passengers and a fireman sustained light injuries. The front ends of both locomotives were badly damaged and other stock was damaged. The driver, normally restricted to goods trains, had a history of reckless behaviour that in itself was not serious, but Jones, the locomotive superintendent, had not linked the incidents. The driver was sacked. Denniss was left to deal with the station master, who was probably demoted; he had long service and a good reputation. *Cambrian Railways*

The prospect of signing 2,500 dividend warrants over a short space of time prompted Williamson to find an alternative in February 1913. He had heard that the Midland Railway issued its warrants with a facsimile of the secretary's signature included in the design and countersigned by the assistant secretary. The board agreed to follow this precedent. What Sydney George Vowles, the Cambrian's assistant secretary, thought of it was not recorded.

The residents of Scafell, a scattered community between Newtown and Moat Lane, petitioned for their station to be re-opened in March. A halt there had been closed in 1891, because the company did not want to incur the cost of meeting the Board of Trade's signalling requirements, although goods were still handled. Now, the £300 cost of building a down platform, required because of the track doubling, was an unwanted complication. The existing platform was re-opened for four eastbound trains a day from 9 June.

A 4-hour gap in the morning of the coast line's winter timetable was inconvenient for the early-season holidaymakers, so from 12 May Williamson transferred the railmotor from the WER, running a service to Aberystwyth that left Portmadoc at 9.00am and returned in the evening. With costs of £10 per week, its revenue was £353 over the nine weeks it ran before the start of the summer timetable.

The Nevin motorbus service came to an end with the sealing of a contract with the Nevin & District Motor Omnibus Company on 2 June. On 27 February Williamson had reported that it had been performing poorly, with 26 breakdowns in two months. The Nevin company had agreed not to start a competitive Chwilog service if the Cambrian ceased operating, and was prepared to maintain an 'efficient' service from Pwllheli for five years.

The 1912 Bill was enacted on 4 July, giving the company the powers that it sought. Responding to concerns that had been expressed over the intention to replace the opening section of the Dovey bridge with a fixed span, the Act included a clause requiring the company to replace it with an opening span if after five years the Board of Trade decided that such was necessary. Obtaining Welshpool corporation's assent to the use of its Smithfield siding had required the Cambrian to agree to the removal of the Welshpool & Llanfair Light Railway's terminal track from the road, to fence it off and to illuminate the adjacent level crossing.

Denniss had been one of the objectors to the Vale of Rheidol Light Railway acquisition, complaining that the issue of A debentures in exchange for the light railway capital would reduce their value. On 9 July Williamson was instructed to take instructions from director Alfred Herbert if he had any questions arising from the VRLR purchase.

On the same day Williamson informed the board of the Shropshire & Montgomeryshire Light Railway's first full year of trading, having been lent a copy of the railway's report. It reported receipts of £3,848, £3,062 expenditure, £784 Shropshire Railways' guaranteed debenture interest, and £2 2s carried forward. He noted, however, that 4½% on the SR's £20,654 debentures was actually £929, not £784, and that more than one-third of this amount was accounted for by a £140 reduction in the managing director's salary and the transfer of £150 into a locomotive repair suspense account.

Fatal accidents at Hawes (Midland Railway) on 21 December 1910 and Ditton (LNWR) on 12 November 1912, which were aggravated by the ignition of leaking train-lighting gas, prompted the Board of Trade to push for the universal adoption of electric train lighting. On 18 August 1913 Williamson replied that the Cambrian's main line could hardly be compared with the trunk lines and that the company had no funds to carry out the conversion.

Despite the additional loops and the double track, the Cambrian still struggled with timekeeping. On 4 November Williamson told the board that it was time to make a serious effort to improve passenger train running. During the week ended 18 October, only 21 of the 75 main-line down passenger trains had arrived on time, 28 having been between 15 and 53 minutes late. Of the 87 up trains, only 22 arrived on time, the worst of the late arrivals being 31 minutes. The Mid Wales service was no better – only seven down arrivals out of 54 were on time, and three trains were less than 10 minutes late just twice during the week. Of the 42 trains run in the up direction, only 15 arrived on time. Even the self-contained and short WER could not keep time; 24 of the 37 up trains

were late, as were 30 of the 36 down trains. Williamson highlighted one train that was between 20 and 36 minutes late every day.

On weekdays the up mail arrived at Welshpool on time only once during the whole of October; it only kept time on Sundays. On the coast, however, trains 'ran with commendable punctuality'. Few goods trains ran on time, six being between 197 and 280 minutes late; such late running invariably meant increased operating costs because of overtime and locomotives being kept in steam for longer than anticipated.

He identified three causes for unpunctual running: the late arrival of other companies' trains at junctions, tablet failure, and difficulties at crossing places. There were other factors that he thought were capable of adjustment by observation and foresight. If it was impossible to improve the operating, the company's best interests would be served by adjusting the timetables. Congestion in the summer might make punctual running impossible, but there was no reason to be unpunctual during the remainder of the year. Something should be done in case the railway ever had to face road competition in the future.

One of the traffic inspectors was promoted to chief inspector with responsibility for timekeeping. He also oversaw the carriage cleaning – many required re-upholstering, but would be improved if the cleaning was better. Williamson had also sometimes found carriage lavatories 'in a somewhat objectionable condition'. On 7 January 1914 approval was given to the installation of a passing loop at Clatter, between Caersws and Carno, as a seasonal measure to reduce congestion; it cost £1,430 and commenced operation on 26 June.

Charles Conacher retired on 28 February 1914. Traffic officer W. Herbert Williams was promoted traffic superintendent with a salary of £350, and W. H. Gough became goods manager on his existing £400 salary. On 26 September 1913 Williams had applied for a salary increase, from £250, saying that he had 36 years' service, worked hard

Despite understanding that they were not ideal for the Cambrian's purposes (pages 161/2), five 4-4-0Ts were bought from the Metropolitan Railway in 1905. With their condensing apparatus removed, the addition of a cab and a fresh coat of paint, they no doubt looked the part but it was soon found that their small tanks and heavy axle loads restricted their usefulness. No 2 had been the Metropolitan Railway's No 10.
*Cambrian Railways*

and had not been given an increase since 1910; the application was deferred three times but had obviously not counted against him.

Two struggling or failing companies looked to the Cambrian to help them out during 1914. On 13 February Williamson submitted a 10-page report about the Festiniog Railway. Since 1900 it had suffered from the effects of a depression in the slate trade caused by slackness in the building trade and extensive use of alternative roofing materials and foreign competition, its dividends falling from 4% to nothing. Greaves, the FR's chairman, had enquired if the Cambrian was interested in taking another narrow-gauge railway into its portfolio.

To do so, the Cambrian would have to pay the interest on the debentures and preference and ordinary shares – £5,776 in 1912 – but, Williamson noted, the net revenue had only been £3,878. Some savings could be made on administration, but the working expenses had already been cut to the minimum. He thought, however, that the Cambrian should consider the proposition; the risk to the slate trade could be considered reasonable and passenger traffic might be developed.

Portmadoc harbour was at risk of silting up, and if it did the traffic would probably not be routed via the FR, and the Minffordd traffic might also be lost. Therefore the Cambrian would have to be satisfied that the harbour would remain open if it took on the FR. He had met Frederick Vaughan, the FR's managing director, and suggested that a committee of the board meet the FR directors to see if a deal could be done. He concluded his report by pointing out that the FR's rolling stock could be used on the Vale of Rheidol branch. Discussions continued for some time before eventually petering out.

Board concern about locomotive operating costs led to the locomotive and traffic departments producing a joint report on 18 February 1914. They were satisfied that traffic requirements could not be met with fewer engines in steam. With train services limited to 14-15 hours per day, the engines were required at the same time and there was no scope for greater utilisation. The time taken by some goods trains, long turn-round times and the restriction of certain classes to branch lines also reduced the average mileage worked. When timetable changes were considered, the departments co-operated to avoid steaming locomotives unnecessarily.

This travelling gas holder was purchased from the Metropolitan Railway for £50 in November 1905. The company had previously paid £335 for similar. *Cambrian Railways*

No 9, the saloon used when King Edward had visited the Elan Valley waterworks, had another royal outing on 25 March. Lever Brothers had asked to borrow it to convey King George V when he visited the company's soap factory and model village. The equerry and minister-in-attendance were participants in both visits.

Following a petition from the men concerned, the short-time working introduced at Oswestry works in 1905 (page 160) was ended with the resumption of Saturday working on 1 July. The downside was that the number of men employed was to be reduced, either by dismissal or retirement, to maintain the wages bill at the same level.

The Railway Fires Act 1905, effective from 1 January 1908, prevented railway companies from using their statutory status to repudiate liability for damage caused by fires started by steam locomotives. Williamson referred to it in relation to a fire that had damaged 5,000 larches near Cemmaes Road on 17 April. McDonald said that the damage was probably not as bad as it looked, but it would take 12 months to establish the true position. When the owner offered to settle for £20 plus his solicitor's costs, £2 2s, Williamson pointed out that the incident had not been reported in accordance with the Act's requirements – notice of claim to be submitted within seven days and particulars of damage within 14 days. It was settled for £5 plus costs in July 1915.

The Bishop's Castle Railway's receiver got very short shrift in July 1914. He suggested that the Cambrian acquire the line, in receivership since 1893, and extend it to Montgomery. Instructed to investigate, Williamson made a brief report and rejected the proposal.

The amount of safety legislation affecting the railways was clearly having an impact on their management. On 8 July Williamson reported the purchase of 1,000 copies of a booklet entitled *The Safety Movement* from the GWR for £8. Distributed to staff, they were overprinted 'presented by the Cambrian Railways Company to their employees'.

On the other hand, the cost of complying with Colonel J. W. Pringle's recommendation following the accident at Ais Gill on 2 September

1913 – that brake vans be equipped with tools that could be used in the event of an accident – was felt to be too much. The 'fast trains' included LNWR vans that were already equipped and there had never been any need for tools on the remainder. Tools and cupboards for the 61 vehicles affected would cost about £4 4s each. In September approval was given to spend £68 on fire extinguishers for 40 passenger brake vans.

A revised timetable and advertising combined to attract 26,566 more 3rd class and 378 more 1st class passenger bookings at coast-section stations over the three months from May 1914. Just before the outbreak of war with Germany on 28 July the company carried substantial military traffic; 2,000 men of the 16th Brigade had been at Llanidloes, 500 artillerymen had been at Rhayader, and the Welsh Territorial Division had 5,000 men at Aberystwyth and 4,000 at Portmadoc.

The relocation of the Llanidloes camp to the North East, ordered at 9.00pm on 29 July, required every item of rolling stock the company possessed, six trains leaving at 90-minute intervals from 7.00am the next day. The Rhayader camp was sent to Plymouth on 31 July. From 3 August 26 trains were required to return the Aberystwyth and Portmadoc camps to their home bases.

BELOW During 1906 the Cambrian experienced considerable problems with its water supplies due to a drought. Shortage at Wrexham meant that engines working the branch had to run to Oswestry to take water after each journey. The photograph shows the shed, turntable and water tank at Aberystwyth before the latter's capacity was increased from 15,956 to 28,721 gallons by the addition of another tier of plates that cost £57. *Cambrian Railways*

BOTTOM Bogie corridor Composite carriage No 325 was one of two built at Oswestry that entered service in July 1908. Designed for through trains to London over the GWR, they had heating and cost £1,159 each. Two similar vehicles completed in 1906 for internal use had cost £950 each. *Cambrian Railways*

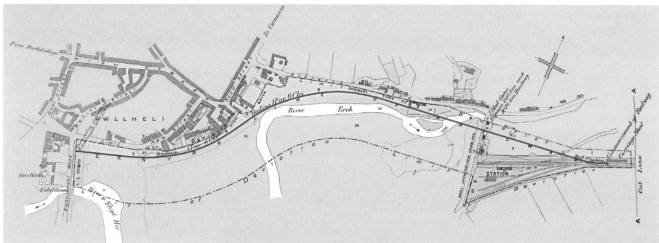

TOP This is one of two poultry vans built on second-hand underframes and put into service at the end of 1907, having cost £225 1s each. The end doors allowed them to be used for other purposes, such as carrying stage scenery. *Cambrian Railways*

ABOVE Powers to extend the coast line at Pwllheli in connection with the corporation's harbour development scheme were obtained in 1901 although the extension was not opened until 1908. The plan shows the extension but not the embankment on which it was constructed. *Parliamentary Archives*

RIGHT The 1909 station at Pwllheli is seen shortly after opening. The two 'Orion' motor buses and two horse-drawn vehicles wait for passengers. *John Alsop collection*

LEFT Aberdovey station was reconstructed with the ironwork from the original Pwllheli station. Loading gauges erected over each line protect the tunnels from overloaded trains and make allowances for eastbound trains leaving from either platform. The canopy ironwork is today incorporated in the canopy of the Bala Lake Railway's Llanuwchllyn terminus. *John Alsop collection*

BELOW Railmotor No 211 and 2-4-0 No 56 pose for the camera at Oswestry in 1911. Intended for use on the Wrexham & Ellesmere Railway, the ensemble proved to be very popular when used on the coast. *Cambrian Railways*

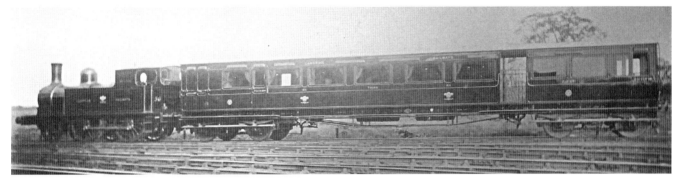

BELOW On 2 August 1911 a Pwllheli-Machynlleth goods train became derailed while passing the motor train at Pensarn. C. L. Conacher, the traffic manager, told the board that everything had been done correctly, except that the loco crew lost control of the engine. He complained, though, that the arrangement for passing trains here was irregular and the station was not equipped or signalled for it. The same applied at Penrhyndeudraeth, Penmaenpool and Bettisfield. Safety would be improved if changes approved at Harlech and Fenn's Bank in April and May were extended to the four stations mentioned. It seems that at these places the loops were intended for shunting, not for passing trains. *Cambrian Railways*

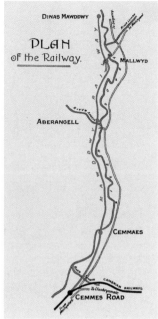

TOP LEFT Mawddwy Railway's terminus and locomotive shed at Dinas Mawddwy. Following the making of a Light Railway Order on 2 March 1910 the railway was reconstructed by the Cambrian and re-opened.

TOP RIGHT A plan of the Mawddwy railway published in 1911.

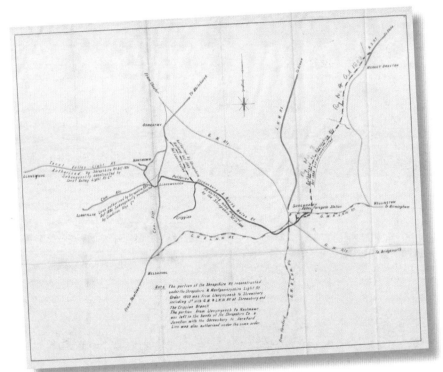

LEFT A plan of the railways around Shrewsbury and Llanymynech produced in support of the Cambrian's case against the Shropshire & Montgomeryshire Light Railway's claim for running powers to Oswestry and for the use of the Nantmawr branch. *National Archives*

RIGHT Despite not owning the Welshpool & Llanfair Light Railway, in 1913 the Cambrian obtained powers to make a small diversion of that line at Welshpool, moving the terminal track out of the road. This plan shows the diversion in red, the other narrow-gauge tracks in green and the corporation's Smithfield siding in blue; this was partially mixed gauge with the light railway. *Parliamentary Archives*

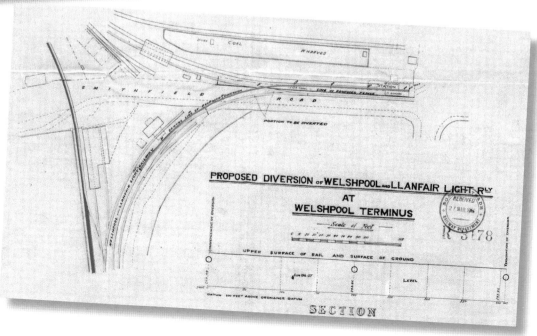

OUR LOCAL EXPRESS.
Ellesmere to Oswestry
Good old Cambrian !

CAMP OF THE WELSH REG'T. PORTMADOC. 1914.

ABOVE This Vale of Rheidol Light Railway 2-6-2T has enlarged bunkers, a modification made after the Cambrian took control of the 2-foot-gauge railway in 1913. With a coastal terminus at Aberystwyth, this 12-mile railway was authorised by Act of Parliament in 1897 and opened in 1903. Cambrian nominees took control in 1910, running the line until Parliamentary sanction for the Cambrian to do so had been obtained.

MIDDLE Of all the railways picked on by Cynicus for their supposed bucolic and rumbustious charm, the Ellesmere-Oswestry section of the Cambrian might be the most unfitting.
*Cynicus Publishing Company*

LEFT The Cambrian carried thousands of troops and their equipment to and from various camps along the line from 1910; this photograph shows the Welsh Regiment's encampment at Portmadoc in 1914. The Traeth Mawr level crossing and crossing-keeper's house is lower left. The buildings at Gelert's Farm, above the crossing-keeper's house, are between the Croesor Tramway, then officially the Portmadoc, Beddgelert & South Snowdon Railway, and the Beddgelert siding. *C. H. Teed*

# 7

# War and its aftermath
# 1914-1922

An order under the Regulation of the Forces Act 1871 was made on 4-5 August 1914, placing most British railways under Government control, directed by the Railway Executive Committee. In compensation the Government would make up net receipts to their 1913 levels. All military traffic, personnel and munitions, had to be carried without charge. Off-duty officers had to be carried 1st class at quarter-fare.

Williamson informed the board of the new regime immediately, formally recording the situation in his report on 18 September. The Van and Mawddwy railways had been excluded from the order. The omission of the Van was of little consequence, and if the demand for timber increased both the Mawddwy and Cambrian would benefit from the former's exclusion. From a day-to-day perspective the railway carried on as before, although Williamson and his staff had to prepare a statement to determine the company's position for compensation. They also had to prepare weekly statements of cash taken and expenditure, including wages, and a monthly estimate of earnings and outgoings.

The Railway Service badge issued to railwaymen to wear to explain why they had not enlisted during the war.

The Railway Clearing House system of dividing revenue according to mileage was suspended, with each company keeping its revenue. The Cambrian was a loser from this as its outward traffic was much less. Initially, the REC had ordered all important bridges and tunnels to be placed under 24-hour guard but had soon reduced this requirement to the Bangor-on-Dee and Barmouth bridges and the Wrexham viaducts.

Already 135 men had been called up or enlisted; in future they could only enlist with the company's permission. The company had agreed to reinstate them when they returned to civilian life and to meet their superannuation contributions. It had also agreed to make allowances to their wives, families and dependents.

Despite the war, on 4 November Williamson obtained approval to convert two six-wheeled carriages into observation vehicles for use on the coast line. He had got the idea from travelling with the directors in the inspection saloon on their annual tour. He thought the carriages would be profitable and enable the railway to compete more effectively with motor cars. Costing £165 each, they were completed by October 1915, delayed by a shortage of materials. The compartments were removed, tramcar-type seats installed and large windows placed in the sides and ends; they seated 48 instead of 36.

A report on the prospects of what became the Welsh Highland Railway was dealt with on the same date. Would the Cambrian be prepared to find £36,000 to acquire the North Wales Narrow Gauge Railways and the Portmadoc, Beddgelert & South Snowdon Railway, complete the construction of the Portmadoc-Carnarvon route, and take on its operation? Describing various scenarios, Williamson said that the company had 'not been fortunate in [its] experience of light railways', and if it had £36,000 it could use it more profitably. A suggestion that it operate the line if the promoters found the capital, except for rolling stock, was refused on 4 January 1915.

When the Park Hall estate, between Oswestry and Whittington, was taken over for military purposes, the REC authorised construction of a siding, which was available for traffic from 23 November. Williamson anticipated 5,000 tons of materials being shipped to the site. A second siding was put into use on 28 June 1915.

Conversion of the Dovey bridge was completed by 30 November 1914. To secure local agreement, the Cambrian had agreed to re-open the junction station to passengers and to make a footpath over the bridge. Coming under pressure to fulfil these obligations, Williamson agreed to provide a halt at Gogarth in substitution. It would supply a public need and the capital cost would be the same but there would be no need to pay a lad to act as a booking clerk, which would be required at the junction. The repairs and modification to the Traeth Mawr viaduct were also completed by November.

In connection with the requirement for more locomotives and boilers, Jones produced a breakdown of the locomotive fleet on 6 January 1915, as shown in the table below. He and Williamson recommended the purchase of five goods locomotives by 1918 and the trial conversion of one of the Metropolitan tanks into a tender engine. Assuming that re-boilering of the present stock continued, the new locomotives would meet the company's renewal requirements. They also thought that as the older locomotives were replaced by 'superior engines' there would be some redundancy in the fleet. The order for five Belpaire goods locomotives and four large bogie passenger locomotive boilers was placed with Beyer, Peacock on 1 February. The same company agreed to convert the Metropolitan tanks for £305; the first, No 34, was sent to Gorton on 22 March.

## Locomotive stock, 1915

| Class | Number | Year purchased | Year re-boilered | Total in class |
|---|---|---|---|---|
| Bogie Belpaire passenger | 94-98 | 1904 | | 5 |
| Large passenger bogie | 11 | 1904 | | |
| | 19 | 1901 | | |
| | 32, 47 | 1897 | | |
| | 61-68 | 1893 | 1914 (No 62) | |
| | 69-72 | 1894 | 1912 (No 69), 1914 (No 71) | |
| | 81-84 | 1895 | 1914 (No 84) | |
| | 85, 86 | 1898 | | 22 |
| Small bogie passenger | 16, 17 | 1878 | 1913 (No 16), 1911 (No 17) | |
| | 20, 21 | 1886 | 1914 (No 20), 1910 (No 21) | |
| | 50, 60 | 1891 | 1914 (No 60) | 6 |
| Belpaire goods | 89-93 | 1903 | | |
| | 38, 99-102 | 1908 | | 10 |
| Neilson goods | 73-77 | 1894 | | |
| | 78-80 | 1895 | | |
| | 87, 88 | 1899 | | 10 |
| Rebuilt goods | 1, 4 | 1872 | 1893 (No 1), 1891 (No 4) | |
| | 6, 10 | 1873 | 1895 (No 6), 1894 (No 10) | |
| | 14 | 1878 | 1897 | |
| | 18 | 1879 | 1890 | |
| | 27, 39, 40 | 1863 | 1896 (No 27), 1895 (Nos 39, 40) | |
| | 45, 46 | 1864 | 1896 (No 45), 1895 (No 46) | |
| | 48, 49 | 1873 | 1889 (No 48), 1897 (No 49) | |
| | 51, 52 | 1865 | 1894 | 15 |
| Bogie side tanks | 3, 5, 7 | 1895 | | |
| | 8, 9, 23 | 1899 | | 6 |
| Metropolitan tanks | 2, 12, 33, 34, 36, 37 | 1905 | 1900, 1899, 1897, 1903, 1892, 1899 (age of boilers) | 6 |
| Small passengers | 28 | 1863 | 1893 | |
| | 41, 43 | 1864 | 1893 (No 41), 1892 (No 43) | |
| | 53, 55 | 1865 | 1892 (No 53), 1894 (No 55) | 5 |
| Small side tank | 44 | 1864 | 1894 | |
| | 56 | 1865 | 1890 | 2 |
| Small side tank | 57 | 1860 | 1893 | |
| | 58, 59 | 1866 | 1894 | 3 |
| Side tank shunting | 13 | 1875 | | 1 |
| Small side tank | 26, 35 | 1904 | 1898 (age of boiler) | 2 |
| Small side tank | 24 | 1904 | 1903 (age of boiler) | 1 |
| Small saddle tank | 30 | 1864 | 1893 | 1 |
| Small saddle tank | 22 | 1901 | | 1 |
| Small saddle tank | 25 | 1877 | | 1 |
| Side tank Rheidol | 1, 2 | 1913 | 1902 (age of boilers) | 2 |
| Side tank Rheidol | 3 | 1913 | 1896 (age of boiler) | 1 |
| Side tank Welshpool & Llanfair | 1, 2 | 1902 | | 2 |
| | | | **Total** | **102** |

War bonus was awarded from February, initially 3 shillings per week to men earning less than £1 10s, and 2 shillings to those earning more, the railway companies paying 25% of it from their own funds. By May 1918 the bonus reached £1 5s, of which the companies paid 2½%.

The public status of men of military age who remained in railway employment, who might be accused of shirking their call-up, was resolved by the REC commissioning a badge. On 3 February it said that numbered badges would cost 5d each and the die for the company's name would be 18 shillings. A supply was obtained for Cambrian employees.

A benefit of being under Government control was manifest in March. An investigation into the detention of wagons throughout the railway network drew Williamson's attention to delays at Whitchurch. He was able to arrange for certain goods trains to be worked through to Crewe by Cambrian locomotives and thought that it set a useful precedent for the future.

Wartime inflation struck when a new boiler was wanted for one of the Nielson locomotives. Beyer, Peacock quoted £995 in March, compared with £830 for those ordered in February. The maker cited increases in the cost of materials and wages, reducing the price to £795 when steel tubes were specified instead of copper.

Oswestry works was unsuited for the manufacture of munitions, Williamson reported on 13 May. The REC had suggested that railway companies should defer, as far as possible, all capital or renewals work in favour of munitions manufacture. If that was done, said Williamson, it would be necessary to reach an understanding with the Government over the arrears. Thus was the independent future of the railway companies further undermined. An order for the manufacture of 50 No 4 adapters weekly was issued on 9 June; this subject was not mentioned again and is not known if the order was repeated.

Men in reserved occupations were now being allowed to volunteer for military service, and 22 enlisted, although applications from two accounts clerks were refused. The employment of female typists at Oswestry to replace absent men was started and suitable women were recruited for training as booking clerks and ticket examiners. In June Williamson objected when he learned that workshop men were being

The four Beyer, Peacock 0-6-0s delivered in 1908 as Nos 15, 31, 42 and 54 were renumbered 99-102 respectively after the war. The last was photographed heading for the coast. *H. W. Burman*

encouraged to register for service elsewhere in the munitions industry. Twenty men had applied by the end of the month, probably expecting the wages to be better. Anticipating that more clerks would be called up, on 15 October Williamson made arrangements for more girls to be appointed as clerk-apprentices.

The two Daimler bus chassis that had been bought in 1912 had never been used (page 169). They and the spares were sold for £80 on 16 June, a loss of £240 on the purchase price. The company still owned an 'Orion' chassis purchased in 1906 that it wished to sell.

On 7 July approval was given to the removal of the South signal box at Barmouth Junction. Although it would cost £220 to remove and make the necessary alterations to the signalling, its closure would save £60 in wages annually.

To pay for the war individuals and companies were encouraged to subscribe to 4½% war loan stock. The company made arrangements for its staff to subscribe on a pay-as-you-earn basis and agreed to subscribe £1,000 on its own account on 11 August. The employees had subscribed £436 7s 11d by 15 September. The company also adopted the policy of investing its spare cash in 90-day 5% Treasury bills.

The war did not stop passengers and their friends from larking about on the railway. In August Ivor Evans, a clergyman in training, was seeing off friends from Dyffryn and, as a joke, took the guard's green flag from the van and waved it, starting the train. Fortunately the guard was able to apply the brake. Evans was prosecuted and fined £2, the maximum. One might ask why the driver had not noticed, despite the crowded platform, that carriage doors were still open.

On 13 October Williamson seemed quite pleased that, by dint of co-operation between the traffic and locomotive departments, the 1915/16 winter timetable had been arranged to operate with two fewer locomotives in steam per day and a reduction of 145 light-engine miles per week, while providing the same service that had operated 12 months previously. In an attempt to maintain the timetable, he had also restricted the attaching and detaching of vehicles from certain trains at intermediate stations. He expected complaints to start with.

Former Metropolitan Railway 4-4-0T No 34 was returned from Beyer, Peacock as a 4-4-0 in October. Coupled to an old tender and painted at Oswestry, it entered service on the Mid Wales section on 8 November. In its modified form its tractive effort was calculated to be 'somewhat less' than that of the large bogie passenger locomotives that normally worked the service. Over four days from 9 November it was tried with two types of coal in comparison with No 84, one of the aforementioned locomotives, and consumption was found to be almost the same.

On 5 January 1916 approval was given to convert No 36 at Oswestry. It was dispatched from the works on 5 October, tested on the Llanfyllin branch the next day and, like No 34, transferred to the Mid Wales section. As modified, the locomotives had a capacity of 3½ tons of coal and 1,700 gallons of water. Their (modified) tenders had been built for 0-6-0s in 1872 and 1873 respectively. No more conversions were made.

Five employees who had lost their lives in battle were recorded at the shareholders' meeting on 25 February. M. R. Williams (goods clerk) and T. Mills (booking clerk) fell at Gallipoli, W. E. Lewis (apprentice carriage joiner) in France, and Stanley Mason (platelayer) and E. G. Harries (engineering pupil) of wounds inflicted at Gallipoli. Thirteen men had been wounded. Traffic reliefman W. E. L. Jones had been mentioned in despatches in the Dardanelles.

Locomotive No 22, an 0-4-0ST formerly used on the Van branch, had been at Caersws for some time, nominally as spare but effectively out of use. Jones had been resisting Williamson's attempts to dispose of it for more than a year when it was sold to Armytage & Jones Ltd, Sheffield, for £700 on 22 May and sent to the camp at Prees Heath, near Whitchurch.

Before the war the LNWR had asked for the river bridge at Afon Wen to be strengthened to accommodate its 'heaviest class of engines'. It was a double-track structure, each company using one track. Claiming that the Cambrian side was strong enough for its traffic, McDonald offered to deal with the LNWR side if that company paid. The work was done in June.

The question of Lord Bradford's curve was postponed for another five years by means of a legal agreement made in July. A settlement

| Engines in steam, 1-7 September 1913-16 | | | | | |
|---|---|---|---|---|---|
| Date | Day | 1913 | 1914 | 1915 | 1916 |
| 1 | Friday | 85 | 76 | 72 | 66 |
| 2 | Saturday | 86 | 74 | 72 | 70 |
| 3 | Sunday | 8 | 6 | 6 | 7 |
| 4 | Monday | 79 | 72 | 72 | 66 |
| 5 | Tuesday | 83 | 74 | 70 | 61 |
| 6 | Wednesday | 80 | 77 | 68 | 62 |
| 7 | Thursday | 83 | 74 | 69 | 65 |

had been reached between the company and the Shropshire Railways and the Shropshire & Montgomeryshire Light Railway.

To discourage optional travel, the REC abolished tourist tickets during 1916, and on 7 September extended the ban until the war ended. In the short term the Cambrian benefited from this as it sold the ticket for the return journey; the revenue would be retained by the issuing company when a return ticket was sold. In the longer term, however, it encouraged would-be tourists to seek alternative means of transport.

As former railwaymen who had enlisted were returned home wounded or otherwise unfit to resume their railway careers, on 18 October the REC issued a notice instructing railway companies to issue them, and their dependents, with privilege rate tickets for local journeys for 12 months from the date each started to receive his military pension, each case being reviewed at 12 months. One imagines that other industries were not required to provide subsidised transport for their former employees.

On 2 November Williamson gave the traffic committee details of a reduction in the number of locomotives steamed over a four-year comparative period, and an extract is shown in the table above. On 6 December he produced details of daily locomotive running costs. The large passenger bogie locomotives cost £3 17s 7d, compared with £2 14s for the Llanfyllin branch loco. The biggest component of the expense was coal.

The LNWR confined Cambrian locomotives to their own system, but during the war the Railway Executive Committee saw their range extended to Crewe, a practice that continued afterwards. 0-6-0 No 93 was the last of the six locomotives built by Robert Stephenson at Darlington in 1903.

Seen at Llanidloes with 4-4-0 No 71, 4-4-0 No 34 was the first of two ex-Metropolitan Railway 4-4-0Ts converted to tender engines in 1915-16. No 71 stands in front of the new shed, completed in 1902.
*John Alsop collection*

Approved on 13 October 1915, the timber flood-relief bridges at Buttington were renewed with concrete piers and steel girders during 1916 at a cost of £1,142. One of the timber piles had collapsed and there was much rotten timber in it, McDonald had reported. Ten 13-foot spans were replaced by five of 26-foot.

The REC instructed that all open wagons should be pooled from 1 January 1917, an arrangement the Cambrian found to be satisfactory, shareholders were informed in February. The company had all the wagons it needed and there had been a considerable reduction in the haulage of empty stock. The board hoped that the arrangement would be made permanent after the war ended.

The use of ticket barriers at Welshpool from 1 January 1917 brought to light a case of fraudulent travel by Montgomeryshire's chief constable, Major Holland, on 19 January. His public position had enabled him to purchase a season ticket at a reduced rate for 15-16 years. Because the Welshpool station master had not given him the accountant's renewal notice after the last one expired on 16 September 1914, he had continued travelling on the old ticket, avoiding inspection by replying 'season' to any request for tickets. The board decided that he should pay for the 'free' travel at the old rate and pay the full price in future; he paid the arrears on 17 February.

A locomotive shortage on the LNWR, because it had allowed so much of its own stock to be sent to the continent, saw Cambrian locomotives working through to Crewe and Shrewsbury at weekends from February. In April two passenger engines and one goods were loaned as well. A special traffic during 1917 was the operation of 10 trains conveying 500 crippled LNWR wagons between Whitchurch and Talyllyn for repair at Cardiff.

Seven more men had died by the time the shareholders met on 28 February. They were W. H. Lewis (passed fireman), H. Tudor (labourer), W. W. Boak (fireman), Arthur Roberts (boilermaker), C. H. Loose (sheetmaker), H. E. Stokes (relayer) and F. Phillips (goods clerk). The last was also awarded the Military Medal. Fourteen more of his colleagues had been wounded. At the date of the meeting, 372 Cambrian employees were engaged on military service.

On 22 March eight men from the permanent way department left for three months' work in France. Many more volunteered to go, but McDonald could not justify releasing them. Even in wartime it would have been a big adventure, for it was unlikely that any of them had been overseas before.

In April the solicitor obtained counsel's opinion on the TVLR's debt to the Cambrian, to confirm that it could not be eliminated by any statute of limitations. The debt was £47,276 13s 1d plus 4% compound interest, making £69,097 15s 1d, mostly incurred before 1906. The Cambrian had retained the TVLR's share of the traffic receipts, £22,086 12s 7d plus 4%, totalling £29,523 17s 6d. The receiver had been appointed in 1904 but had never filed any accounts. Neither the TVLR's directors nor shareholders had met since 1907. When the Cambrian issued a writ for £40,676 16s 8d on 30 June, the TVLR board, with only the chairman present from the 1907 meeting, met on 20 November, discussed the issue and resolved to take no action.

The TVLR was underequipped with loading and other station facilities and was unable to provide them; the Cambrian could not spend capital on another undertaking. The only solution would be for the Cambrian to take over the TVLR. This opinion was expressed by Williamson and the solicitor to a representative from Liverpool Corporation on 4 January 1918. Uncertainty surrounded the £6,000 Treasury loan that had been made to the TVLR – the takeover would not happen if the Treasury insisted on repayment.

The use of oxy-acetylene for repairs would save time and labour, Jones reported on 4 July. Using equipment borrowed from the LNWR, he had been able to effect repairs that could not otherwise have been done except by replacing frames or cylinders. The British Oxygen Company had demonstrated the equipment and offered to supply a set for £100. It would be useful in the works and could be used on bridges as well; the main cost would be the bottled oxygen, and men would have to be trained to use it.

Newtown became a closed station from 1 August 1917, generating extra revenue of £30 3s 7d from platform tickets over the first two months; a ticket machine was installed on 15 August. The Montgomery Education Authority requested a special permit because it was often necessary for its staff to visit the station to meet committee members or public officials, and the new arrangement would 'entail considerable annual expenditure', between 10 and 15 shillings a year. The Newtown Traders' Association also asked for a special rate. Both were refused. Two ticket machines had already been installed at Aberystwyth (31 December 1914) and two at Barmouth (24 July 1916).

In January 1918 the solicitor negotiated the purchase of a house in Queen's Park, Oswestry, for occupation by Williamson. The asking price of £1,500 had been reduced to £1,450 plus the vendor's costs. What prompted this move is not known. As the company had no statutory power to buy houses, the solicitor advised legitimising the purchase the next time the company obtained Parliamentary powers.

At the REC's request, two brake vans were sent on loan to the Highland Railway to assist that company in handling anticipated 'important Admiralty traffic'.

A head-on collision between two goods trains occurred at Park Hall on 18 January. One fireman was killed and the other three enginemen were severely injured. The locomotives and six wagons were badly damaged, seven wagons were destroyed and seven slightly damaged. While it was quickly ascertained that both trains carried tablets for the Oswestry-Ellesmere section and there was a discrepancy between the signalmen's versions of events, there was no evidence of any misconduct to account for it. In his report, Pringle concluded that one or both signalmen had something to hide and the traffic was not being worked in accordance with regulations.

A committee of signal engineers had also been unable to determine if there was any fault with the equipment, recommending that insulated cables should be used on token circuits wherever there might be any risk of contact. As a precautionary measure, four sets of McKenzie & Holland instruments, implicated in the accident, were taken out of use and replaced by Tyer's instruments from stock.

It had been the practice for Cambrian permanent way employees to provide their own shovels. The near doubling of their price during the war, from 2s 6d to 4s 8d, had prompted them to ask for company provision. McDonald's proposal to pay an allowance of the difference

between the two prices for the current year and making them company issue from 1919 was accepted on 8 February. To prevent misuse or theft, an old shovel, or its remnants, would have to be produced before a new one was issued.

Thirteen more employees had lost their lives on military service when the shareholders met on 28 February. They were T. E. Owen (passed cleaner), H. H. Owen (blacksmith), R. Evans (carriage joiner), E. J. Caine (goods porter), H. P. Evans (station master), F. Jones (warehouseman), J. Lloyd (platelayer), D. R. Jones (cleaner), W. Jones (porter), E. S. Ellis (labourer), S. Vaughan (labourer), E. Evans (relayer) and J. H. Dyas (passed cleaner). Nineteen more had been injured. J. H. Davies, an Oswestry works labourer, and J. H. Howells, a platelayer, had both been awarded the Military Medal. The number of men on military service had increased to 414.

The Aberystwyth Travelling Post Office had been suspended at the start of the war, and the Cambrian's two vehicles were stored. No 293 was loaned to the LNWR for work on the Crewe-Manchester service at the GPO's request from June.

The declaration of peace in November 1918 did not mean the end of Government control, it was to be three years before this occurred. The effect of the war on traffic is shown in the tables below, produced by Williamson in July. No allowance was made for traffic carried without charge, which included 111 loaded coal trains covering 9,990 miles. The effect of the 50% mandatory fare increase, imposed from 1 January 1917 to discourage discretionary travel and to make equipment available for use on the continent, is clear, although the numbers travelling increased again in 1918.

The first of five locomotives ordered from Beyer, Peacock on 1 February 1915 was delivered on 20 October 1918, followed by the second on 12 November. The remainder were dispatched on 30 May, 6 June and 26 June 1919, the last two in undercoat as McDonald wanted to get them into service. Thanks to the war the £15,900 contract price had increased to £28,485. The board resisted the manufacturer's claim for the increased costs until June 1920, paying on production of an auditor's certificate and an undertaking that half of the excess would be refunded if the REC objected to it.

Williamson produced figures concerning locomotive use during the winter of 1918/19. In 1890 57 locomotives had earned the company £4,081 each; in 1913, 102 locomotives earned £3,510 each. In November 1913 the company had steamed an average of 65 locomotives per day; during the same month in 1918 52 locomotives

## Passenger receipts

| Month | Number of passengers | | | Receipts | | |
|---|---|---|---|---|---|---|
| | 1916 | 1917 | 1918 | 1916 | 1917 | 1918 |
| January | 132,647 | 103,693 | 118,559 | £7,644 | £9,079 | £10,695 |
| February | 125,091 | 88,790 | 109,483 | £6,643 | £7,337 | £9,339 |
| March | 129,571 | 103,183 | 126,886 | £7,476 | £8,255 | £10,626 |
| April | 154,155 | 110,595 | 140,517 | £9,419 | £10,422 | £13,315 |
| May | 176,669 | 135,429 | 169,797 | £11,041 | £12,150 | £15,892 |
| June | 184,688 | 140,914 | 161,471 | £13,875 | £13,849 | £15,814 |
| | **902,821** | **682,604** | **826,713** | **£56,098** | **£61,092** | **£75,681** |
| | | | | | | |
| **Train miles** | | | | | | |
| Coaching | 500,585 | 417,344 | 398,524 | | | |
| Goods | 277,717 | 259,594 | 299,882 | | | |
| Shunting | 156,415 | 144,239 | 150,138 | | | |
| Other | 74,333 | 49,354 | 55,510 | | | |
| | **1,009,050** | **870,531** | **904,064** | | | |

| Platform ticket sales, 1918 | | |
| --- | --- | --- |
| | Expenditure | Receipts |
| Newtown | £174 15s 1d | £201 6s 9d |
| Aberystwyth | £700 18s 1d | £1,092 3s 7d |
| Barmouth | £236 10s 9d | £290 6s 1d |
| Rhayader | - | £22 18s 3d |

had been steamed. The first comparison implies that the company had more locomotives than it needed, while the second suggests that more efficient use was being made of the fleet.

Another step towards the absorption of the Tanat Valley Light Railway occurred on 8 January 1919, when two agreements were sealed, as to services and accommodation to be provided for Liverpool Corporation, and between the TVLR, the company and the investing authorities regarding the proposed amalgamation.

Under the heading 'closed stations', on 12 February 1919 Williamson reported on platform ticket sales and expenses up to 31 December 1918, as shown in the table above. Platform tickets had been issued at Pwllheli during August and September, earning £23 7s 9d against expenses of £19 1s 10d. They were issued at Oswestry, Welshpool, Caersws and Borth on Sundays and at Machynlleth after 4.00pm on Sundays, earning £15 2s 3d, £22 3s 8d, £1 13s 11d, £2 13s 5d and £36 2s 8d respectively. It is not clear if 15s 5d spent on tickets applied to those five stations or just to Machynlleth.

Following attempts to improve wagon loadings, Williamson produced figures for November 1918. About 1,000 goods wagons had been in use, loading to slightly less than half of their capacity. Around 500 mineral wagons were more efficient, loading nearly full. During 1918 the company's 119 coal wagons made 2¼ trips to the colliery per month. Utilisation was poor, he explained, because the Government's coal controller insisted on the Cambrian using coal from South Wales.

Since the Government had taken control, the company had submitted monthly reports of expenditure to the REC, claiming any revenue shortfall compared with 1913. Over the four years of war, maintaining the locomotives and rolling stock had cost a total of £6,716 more than the 1913 benchmark; this was not reimbursed, despite the increase being attributable to wartime inflation.

The directors also lost out on the strict interpretation of the rules. In 1917 they had reinstated their fees to their pre-1909 level, when they had been reduced to help pay for Conacher's salary. On 23 December 1918 the REC disallowed the claim against the company's expenses because the higher rate had not been paid in 1913.

Herbert Jones, the locomotive superintendent, retired at the age of 64 on 31 December 1918. Twenty years earlier, he had been released from the obligation to join the superannuation scheme, the premium being too high, on the understanding that he did not ask for support when he left the company. He asked for the situation to be reconsidered and was awarded £1,000 tax free and allowed to retain his gold travel pass. McDonald, the engineer, replaced him.

With the cessation of hostilities, local authorities established reconstruction committees, those served by the Cambrian asking for various sections of the line to be doubled to reduce or eliminate congestion. Aberystwyth town council wanted the line doubled from Shrewsbury, Criccieth UDC thought that it should be doubled from Portmadoc to Pwllheli and extended to Porthdinllleyn, and Brecon County Council thought that Talyllyn Junction-Brecon should receive attention. Montgomeryshire County Council had grander ambitions in wanting the entire Cambrian network to be doubled, calling on all the authorities affected to apply pressure on the company and to get

their MPs to put their case to the Board of Trade and the minister of reconstruction. The cost of doubling, excluding branches, was estimated at £3,064,514.

The consequences of the 447 men who had joined the forces were summarised at the shareholders' meeting held on 28 February 1919. Forty-one had died and five were missing, while J. C. Morris and W. Davies had joined those awarded the Military Medal. It was to be established that 51 men had died. Allan Gairdner Wyon received the £250 commission for a memorial to be erected at Oswestry station.

Camps established near Oswestry and Bettisfield had generated considerable traffic, involving more than half a million men, the company estimated, and more than 40,000 wagons at Oswestry. The 400,000 tons of timber carried from 1915 contrasted with 21,000 tons carried in 1914. No attempt was made to estimate the volume of coal bound for Scotland carried from Talyllyn to Oswestry.

The war bonus had increased the wages bill from £122,000 in 1913 to £243,000, despite the employment of fewer personnel. Without consulting the companies, the Government had given railwaymen an 8-hour day, adding another £30,000 to the wages bill. Government traffic originating on the Cambrian was estimated to total £15,008. In every direction costs were being increased but the railways' charges were strictly regulated.

W. Herbert Williams, traffic superintendent, died on 28 February 1919 after a short illness. He had joined the company in 1877. He had not, Williamson reported, earned more than £160 until 1910, so his widow was not well provided for. The board awarded her a year's salary, £450, and agreed that the company should pay Williams's outstanding income tax, about £50.

A directorial complaint about the company's failure to connect with the LNWR's 1.10pm departure from Afon Wen caused Williamson to explain some of the issues that had to be dealt with when planning its timetables. The 1.15pm from Pwllheli was timed to

The cover of one of the last timetable booklets produced by the Cambrian reflected the austerity of the era.

connect with the 2.45pm GWR departure from Barmouth and the 6.35pm LNWR departure from Welshpool. As a result time was wasted on the journey – there was a 32-minute wait at Barmouth – and the average speed to Machynlleth was 16½mph. If the 1.15pm was retimed to 12.50pm it would be necessary to lose another 20 minutes between Barmouth and Welshpool to avoid a long wait at Shrewsbury. A train was run from Pwllheli at 12.25pm but the (very few) passengers then had to wait 35 minutes at Afon Wen.

In the eastbound direction, the 8.20am from Oswestry did not reach Afon Wen until 1.27pm. Williamson had, therefore, arranged for the LNWR to run its train from Afon Wen to Portmadoc and back before going on to Carnarvon at 1.10pm.

He concluded that he was ashamed of the service operated. In Whitchurch-Pwllheli (133 miles) and Whitchurch-Brecon (112 miles) the Cambrian had a splendid trunk system, destroyed by a policy of connecting with other companies at 13 junctions, ruining its homogeneity. A passenger on the 1.15pm from Pwllheli bound for Oswestry, for example, would arrive at 6.09pm if he changed to the GWR at Barmouth, but not until 7.21pm if he remained on the Cambrian.

On 9 May Williamson reported that Easter traffic had been comparable with earlier years. Instead of duplicating the ordinary trains, express relief trains had been run in each direction. This policy had allowed passengers returning on the morning train to leave 90 minutes later and still make the same connections at Shrewsbury and Crewe. The midday express was also worked through to Birmingham and Manchester, presumably being divided at Welshpool.

Precautions had been taken to ensure that the holiday service was reliable, and it generally worked well. However, there were three incidences of delays caused by two signalmen and an inspector blocking the road with a light engine, a goods train, and branch-line stock left in a platform. They illustrated 'the difficulties we have to contend with, although the staff are … receiving far higher wages than they have ever before received and are working less hours.' Unusually, he identified neither the locations nor the individuals concerned.

The REC had recently made further concessions on service conditions, including payment of overtime at time-and-a-quarter, night duty (10.00pm-4.00am) at time-and-a-quarter, and overtime between those hours at time-and-a-half, Sunday working at time-and-a-half and a week's holiday to be given after 12 months' service. Williamson estimated the annual cost at £11,000.

The Cambrian's objection to the Shropshire & Montgomeryshire Light Railway's proposed Market Drayton extension explained the resumption of 'Mr Stephens's "pin-pricking"' over the issue of running powers, Williamson reported on 7 May 1919. On 26 April Stephens had written that he wished to discuss the question of the SMLR exercising its running powers between Llanymynech or, alternatively, provision of a through carriage from Oswestry to Shrewsbury.

Williamson had asked Stephens to explain his proposals, the number and times of trains to be run and the tolls and rents offered, or the trains to which the through carriage would be attached. He told the board that 304 passengers had booked to the SMLR, mostly to Kinnerley, from Cambrian stations during 1918, an average of one per working day. He doubted that any more booked in the reverse direction. Replying on 9 May, Stephens suggested that SMLR trains should be routed via the Nantmawr branch and Porthywaen to avoid shunting at Llanymynech. Williamson waited a week before saying that that would not be possible.

Track relaying having got into arrears during the war, McDonald was anxious to get the relaying gangs up to strength. This work was carried out in addition to the routine maintenance undertaken by the permanent way gangers. By 9 May 1919 he had recruited an extra 23 men to bring the strength up to 48. There had been 200 applicants and he had given priority to those without jobs.

The war bonus had not kept pace with inflation, and demands for better wages and conditions was behind widespread unrest and disruption, the coalition Government being slow to realise that pre-war standards could not be reinstated. The unionisation of labour also had an effect. An attempt to reduce railway industry wages resulted in a national strike from 27 September, in which 1,573 Cambrian personnel participated, 76% of the payroll; 757 strikers were from the operating departments, representing 95% of operating staff. A national settlement was reached on 5 October but the transport of mail by air between London and what *The Times* called 'the great provincial cities' from 30 September was surely an indication that the railways did not hold the key to the nation's transport needs. The settlement maintained wages at a weekly minimum of £2 11s for at least 12 months. In December Williamson reported that bonuses – double pay – paid to those who had stayed at their posts amounted to £397 8s 3d. The men who went on strike lost £6,041 5s 5d, while £92 11s 5d was paid to volunteers.

The Government also had a problem deciding on an acceptable mechanism for handing the railways back to their owners without putting most of the smaller companies into liquidation. Without consulting the companies nationalisation was considered, and the Ministry of Ways & Communications Bill, the Ministry of Transport Act from 15 August 1919, included a clause that ignored the 1844 Regulation of Railways Act. This had given the Government power to purchase railways any time after 21 years of obtaining their Acts of incorporation, the price being set at a sum equivalent to 25 years' dividends based on the average of the three years preceding the purchase and an allowance for future prospects. Supported by the banks and the Stock Exchange, the companies' objections forced the Government to back down. As it was, the 1919 Act extended the period of control by two years to give the Government some breathing space.

Davies, the chairman, had been absent from his company duties during the war, serving in the Army, and Thomas Craven had taken charge as acting chairman. On 7 May 1919 Craven was presented with a silver inscribed cigar case as a record of his colleagues' appreciation.

When cylinders were required for the Class 61 passenger engines in September 1919 McDonald was unable to obtain quotes so decided to try and cast them in the company's own foundry. The North British Locomotive Company agreed to lend a set of patterns for £15. Nothing so complicated had been attempted at Oswestry before, but he was confident that the moulders would rise to the occasion.

Twenty-four machine tools in the works had an average age of 50 years, and as a result locomotive servicing was taking longer than it should. McDonald's attempt to improve the situation was delayed by an ironfounders' strike deferring the manufacture of a replacement lathe and a drill. The order was completed in April 1920.

From an operating perspective, 1919 was a good year for the Cambrian: 2,458,262 passengers had been carried, up from the 1,661,849 in 1917, when the fares had been increased. Also 887,758 tons of freight had been carried, an increase of 110,386 tons over 1913. Punctuality had also improved: 8,219 of 13,341 passenger trains operated had arrived at their destinations on time and 2,576 had been less than 5 minutes late.

Statistics such as these were regularly produced and published to operating staff in the weekly notice, a practice highlighted by the *Railway Gazette* as an example that should be followed by other companies, to 'encourage the staff'.

CAMBRIAN BUYS SMASH 'TALERDDIG' JAN. 18, 1921

0-6-0T No 54 was one of the two locomotives hauling the 10.25am from Aberystwyth that derailed after colliding with a rock fall at Talerddig on 18 January 1921. It took two days to clear the line. The locomotive had been built by Beyer, Peacock in 1919 and was re-numbered 102, the highest number carried by a locomotive in the Cambrian fleet.
*John Alsop Collection*

Installation of electricity on railway premises was not the subject of advance planning. When a Llanfyllin builder erected a power station in the town he suggested installing lighting in the station when he sought permission to erect poles and wires on railway property. The installation would cost £12 and each lamp 2s 7½d per annum, half the usual price. On 3 December 1919 approval was given for the installation of eight lamps at £1 1s annually; gas lighting had cost £4.

On 3 May 1920 the Ministry of Transport informed the TVLR that if it was vested in the Cambrian the claim for repayment of the £6,000 loan would be waived in exchange for £6,000 fully-paid Cambrian No 1 stock. An application for a Light Railway Order to give effect to the transfer was immediately deposited; it was made on 12 March 1921.

Since the war many of the contracts for the supply of equipment or materials were accepted with a caveat that the supplier reserved the right to increase prices in line with increased costs, and at least one tried to take advantage of this. On 5 May an order was placed with Bolchow, Vaughan of Middlesbrough for 1,000 tons of steel rail and 60 tons of fishplates. The order was completed by 2 June, when it was inspected, and 698 tons was delivered on 18 June, a shortage of wagons delaying delivery of the remainder until 21 August and 15 September. When Williamson queried a £2 per ton price increase on the August delivery he learned that prices had been increased in July. Bolchow, Vaughan claimed that the increase was permitted by the contract but decided not to press its claim.

In June the Government published its white paper on 'the future organisation of transport undertakings … and their relation to the state'. Excluding light railways, it proposed that railways should be formed into regional groups. With some changes, the proposals became effective with the Railways Act on 19 August 1921. Under the Act's terms the Cambrian, together with the GWR and five other Welsh railway companies, became a constituent of the western group. The Mawddwy, Van, Welshpool & Llanfair and Wrexham & Ellesmere railways were among the designated subsidiary companies.

Building on the success of the seasonal express trains in 1919, several innovations came with the start of the 1920 summer timetable on 12 July. Notably, for the first time it was possible to travel from Paddington to Pwllheli, via Welshpool, without changing trains. A luncheon and tea car was worked between London and Aberystwyth and lunch was served on the Cambrian on the return journey. On Fridays and Saturdays a new train ran from Whitchurch to Aberystwyth, calling only at Machynlleth and Borth. The South Wales service was also augmented. The enhanced service was operated at the expense of 350 extra miles per day.

A recommendation by the rates advisory committee that train fares should be increased by 25% was accepted by the Government and put in place from 6 August. Nationally, the railways were said to be running at a deficit of £54,500,000 and the increase was intended to help bring them back into balance before the companies resumed control. Goods traffic rates had been increased by an average of 50% in January. One of the effects of the fare increase was to produce fares that included quarters of a penny (farthings); newspapers noted that booking offices rounded up such fares to the next halfpenny.

In an effort to improve operating, Williamson had adapted the gentlemen's waiting room at Moat Lane to serve as a control office. Installing telephones to connect it with Oswestry, Builth Wells, Aberystwyth, Barmouth and intermediate stations had cost about £20. The arrangement would be crude, he said, but the company would gain valuable experience.

On 30 September the traffic superintendent reported that the system had worked well, forcing station staff and signalmen to take a closer interest in the operating. The controller was also chasing up delay incidents immediately, obtaining information while it was still fresh in the minds of the staff concerned. From the start of the winter service on 4 October the superintendent was going to have the control manned from 12.00pm until 8.00pm to pay special attention to the working of goods trains.

On 9 October 1920 Williamson produced the data shown in the table below to demonstrate the impact of the war on the wages bill, and the increase in the number of employees following the reduction in working hours. On 4 October he had written to the officers, reminding them that the 'pre-war necessity for economy still exists', that no one should be employed unnecessarily, that overtime should be kept to a minimum, purchasing should be controlled, and stores used with care. The company could not afford, he concluded, to maintain the same standard of efficiency achieved by main-line companies.

| The impact of the war on the Cambrian's wages bill | | | | |
|---|---|---|---|---|
| | **1913** | | **1920** | |
| *Department* | *Wages* | *Employees* | *Wages* | *Employees* |
| Locomotive | £39,726 | 672 | £161,653 | 812 |
| Permanent way | £25,961 | 488 | £113,111 | 636 |
| Traffic | £39,658 | 735 | £166,515 | 909 |
| | **£105,345** | **1,895** | **£441,279** | **2,357** |

Another miners' strike saw the Cambrian reducing its services from 25 October. It had 5,821 tons of coal in stock and used 787 tons per week on the reduced service.

At some unspecified date goods trains had been run early in the morning and in the evening, and timekeeping had benefited as a consequence. As a result, goods trains had become more heavily laden, reducing mileage and the number of engines in steam. Over the four weeks ended 13 November, 824 goods trains had run; 593 (72%) had arrived on time and 37 (4%) had been less than 15 minutes late. However, 104 (13%) had arrived more than 45 minutes late.

As the post-war boom proved to be short-lived, heavy-engineering companies looked to the smaller railway companies for work. Receiving offers from Beyer, Peacock and Vickers, the Cambrian decided to send three locomotives to the former on 17 November. Williamson

explained that with the growth of the locomotive fleet from 48 in 1880 to 102 there had been no corresponding increase in works capacity and the company had more locomotives than it needed as a result. The offer was to do the work for the cost of materials and wages, an overhead charge of 110% on the wages and 10% profit, accurate records of the work done to be made available to the company. Nos 67, 69 and 85 were sent to Gorton, but when Beyer, Peacock issued a provisional invoice for £2,500 for No 67 on 10 May 1921 it was decided to send no more. McDonald said that the work could have been done for less than £1,000 at Oswestry; the total bill amounted to £3,025 13s.

In July 1913 a 4% increase had been allowed on goods traffic. In 1920 the Government realised that some companies had been transferring the extra revenue to reserves, a practice that affected the compensation paid. Although Williamson had explained that the Cambrian had treated the money as revenue and kept it for the company's general purposes, on 30 December the compensation due for November was paid with £11,238 deducted to account for the 4% increase. Williamson gave notice that the company did not accept the deduction and reserved its right to appeal against it.

In January 1921, McDonald reported that an old Sharp, Stewart 0-6-0T, No 13, had been set up in the Oswestry works copper shop to drive the line shafting, at a cost of £2,240. It was the most convenient place to access the shafting but made it difficult for the coppersmiths to work, so a lean-to outside the erecting shop was built for them at a cost of £400.

Traffic was stopped for two days at Talerddig after the locomotives hauling the 10.25am express from Aberystwyth derailed on 18 January 1921. Following a period of heavy rain rock had fallen into the cutting. Little damage was done to rolling stock and track and there were no injuries. Buses carried passengers around the site while recovery and repairs were carried out; one passenger wrote that despite this interruption he had still completed his journey on time.

Rarely can the destruction of a locomotive have been so graphically illustrated as in this photograph of the wreckage after the collision at Abermule on 26 January 1921. *John Alsop Collection*

At Abermule, the presence of the parallel main road nearby must have helped the rescue effort, and made it easier for those who wanted to watch. Only the man using a saw to cut a hole in the carriage roof appears to be doing anything. It took three days to clear the line and re-open it.

With 14 passengers and three train crew killed, the collision between two trains on the single line 1 mile west of Abermule on 26 January is notorious among British railway accidents. Even the Ministry of Transport inspector called it deplorable. Just as at Carno in 1869, the single-line tablet was mishandled; in this case a westbound goods train took back the Montgomery-Abermule token it had handed in a few minutes before. No one checked either the tablet or the instruments, and some of those who had handled the tablet were not authorised to do so.

The *Railway Gazette* noted that the incident marred British railways' accident record of the previous five years, of 13 passengers killed in 10 incidents. In terms of fatalities it was the worst incident since the collisions and fire at St Bede's Junction, Jarrow, on 17 December 1915, which had resulted in 18 passengers and one fireman losing their lives. The journal noted that there had been no fire, despite the use of gas lighting on both trains, and also commented that the brake vans and compartments had contained first aid materials, fire extinguishers and 'wrecking' tools; this was not because the company had had second thoughts about complying with Pringle's 1913 request (page 176), but because the vehicles concerned were LNWR stock.

Among the dead was Lord Sir Herbert Vane-Tempest, a director since 1905. His uncle, the Cambrian's first chairman, had been on the train at Carno in 1869 (page 100). A donation of 200 guineas was made to the Montgomery County Infirmary at Newtown and gratuities totalling £210 were made to the doctors and nursing staff. The line was re-opened on 29 January, the *Railway Gazette* commenting on the scale of this achievement, considering that it had been deemed to be unsafe to work at night. It also mentioned the use of oxy-acetylene equipment, the use of portable telephones connected to the overhead wires and the small amount of damage sustained by the track, amounting to some broken chairs and bent rails.

The four men held responsible were sacked on 16 February. The enginemen on the up train were awarded bonuses of £5 and full pay until they returned to work. Approval was given to the erection of a memorial stone at the site on 23 February.

Having received Pringle's report on the collision, on 14 June the traffic committee resolved that, except on the light railways, tablet instruments at all stations should be interlocked with the starting or advanced starting signals, and where feasible the instruments should be moved to the signal boxes and that ground frames working main-line facing points should be removed. Of the 29 main-line stations with

tablets housed in the station buildings, 18 would require new signal boxes costing £4,500 in total. After trials at Bettisfield and Whittington, McDonald obtained a quotation of £3,995 5s to install interlocking at 27 stations. Parry, the Abermule station master who had been on holiday when the accident occurred but who had allowed a culture of slack practice to develop, was demoted to the position of clerk.

Two locomotives, Nos 82 and 95, and a carriage were destroyed in the accident. No 82's boiler was repaired with a new tubeplate and smokebox and transferred to the Oswestry works boiler house. No 95's boiler was repaired for locomotive use, and its tender was also repaired. Two carriages with bodies destroyed were repaired using components salvaged from the wreck.

During its existence, 32 incidents on the Cambrian were subject to a Board of Trade investigation; many more were recorded internally. Where there had been a fatality, the sigh of relief in reporting an inquest verdict of 'accidental death' was almost palpable. Managing any compensation claims was the next priority. When the company's doctor, Dr R. de la Poer Berresford, had been awarded 100 guineas and a gold pass for his part in dealing with the derailment at Welshampton (page 149), the board was not just rewarding his clinical contribution but his part in reducing claims of £13,059 1s to £9,058 4s 2d.

Shareholders attending their meeting on 23 February had learned of the effects of Government control on their railway. The wages bill, £120,000 in 1913, had been nearly £500,000 in 1920; the 8-hour day cost £70,000 per annum; a signal box that had cost £1 1s per week to run in 1914 now cost £1 14s 6d; a station that had cost £3 13s now cost £15 11s 6d. A boy porter paid £1 15s received £3 3s on his 18th birthday. A station clerk who worked 50 minutes in two shifts on a Sunday was now paid for 8 hours, costing £1 12s. In 1913 the gross revenue had been £365,000 and the net revenue £148,000; to earn that now would require £875,000 gross revenue.

The Cambrian Railways (Tanat Valley Light Railway Transfer) Order was made on 12 March, signifying the last expansion of the Cambrian's network. On 7 July Williamson asked the TVLR shareholders to send in the certificates for exchange for the equivalent nominal value of Cambrian ordinary No 1 inland stock.

Another miners' strike caused the Government to declare a state of emergency on 1 April, accompanied by an instruction that passenger train mileage should be reduced by 25% to conserve coal from 6 April. (The transfer of the collieries back to their owners on 31 March had been accompanied by mandatory wage reductions.) By 10 May Cambrian passenger services had been reduced by 50%. Although coal stocks were low because deliveries had been interrupted for some weeks before the strike started, some coal and patent fuel had been obtained from South Wales through Government sources. One of the directors had obtained 800 tons of coke that was being mixed with coal for locomotive use. The Ministry of Transport's request to supply coal to the Festiniog and Corris railways, because they had run out, was accepted.

Further cuts were made to the passenger service from 23 May, reducing mileage to 52% less than that operated in March. Goods train mileage was about 30% less. More coke and patent fuel and 2,500 tons of French 'reparation' coal were obtained to help keep the reduced services going.

Two venerable GWR 2-4-0s bought for £850 each from the Bute Works Supply Company in May could not be put to work immediately because of the strike. Built as 2-2-2s for the West Midland Railway in 1861 and rebuilt as 2-4-0s at the GWR's Wolverhampton Works in 1883, they had been sold for automatic train operation trials on the West Somerset Mineral Railway in 1911. Nos 212 and 213 on the GWR, they were Nos 1 and 10 on the Cambrian. They would be useful for branch lines and lighter trains on the coast, McDonald explained.

| Effect of the 1921 miners' strike | | | | |
| --- | --- | --- | --- | --- |
| | Passengers | | Revenue | |
| *Month* | *1920* | *1921* | *1920* | *1921* |
| March | 155,944 | 168,873 | £13,579 | £16,813 |
| April | 184,030 | 133,294 | £19,912 | £15,233 |
| May | 229,849 | 144,007 | £22,323 | £16,703 |
| June | 222,512 | 142,134 | £24,488 | £18,205 |
| July | 303,764 | 216,672 | £44,649 | £31,595 |

The coal strike ended on 4 July. On the same date *The Times* said that the cheeriest optimist could find only two points in its favour: the surprising clearness of the smokeless atmosphere and the stimulus given to road transport. The public had learned the delights of the motor coach and the convenience of door-to-door transport. When, in more recent times, railwaymen acted to support miners in disputes, the damage done to their industry in the past had obviously been forgotten. The effect on the Cambrian's passenger traffic was considerable, as shown in the table above.

On 21 May a special board meeting was held to discuss the company's participation in the 'Grouping', when the directors resolved to obtain amendments to the Bill covering the value of the absorbed companies, to be calculated as not less than the 1913 net revenue, and a requirement that proprietors should receive not less than the capital value of the subsidiary. A letter proposing terms of absorption was drafted for sending to the GWR.

The 1921 summer timetable started on 11 July. The lunch/tea express that had run between Paddington and Aberystwyth in 1920 was extended to Pwllheli, and the return Saturday workings loaded so well that they ran non-stop between Welshpool and Paddington.

Traffic crossed the new Kilkewydd bridge for the first time on 14 August. Its renewal had been started in 1920. McDonald had been unable to place a contract to build the abutments so the railway took on the job itself, using labour supplied by a Welshpool contractor and supplying the plant and materials. The old structure was removed by October and McDonald thought that some of the ironwork could be re-used in the renewal of timber overbridges.

When the Cambrian took back control from the Government on 16 August, £21,000 required to meet personal injury claims arising from the Abermule accident was disallowed from the net revenue claim because a similar expense had not been incurred in 1913. The £51,258 outstanding comprised £11,258 in respect of the 4% rates increase and £40,000 deemed to have been overspent on the locomotives and rolling stock accounts.

The majority of the £33,000 claims made in respect of the Abermule collision were thought to be excessive and the insurance company, responsible for £10,000, was 'not exercising any undue haste in settling'; only £2,000 had been paid. The solicitor had advised that, as the Government was in control of the railway at the time, it was liable for the claims, a position the Government appeared to accept, saying that it would consider further claims as they were disbursed.

The GWR's general manager, Felix Pole, opened a dialogue with Williamson, asking that he be invited to 'do a deal'; if the Cambrian required any locomotives, boilers or vehicles, the GWR could offer better prices than elsewhere, 'to our mutual advantage'. Any answer Williamson received to his query about the GWR doing locomotive repair work was not recorded. Two second-hand locomotives were bought for £7,735; formerly Nos 3521 and 3546, the 4-4-0s were given the numbers of those destroyed at Abermule, 82 and 95, and put to work on the coast.

Despite having the lowest number, 2-4-0 No 1 only joined the Cambrian fleet in 1921, having had a very varied history since it was built as a 2-2-0 by Beyer, Peacock for the West Midland Railway in 1861. Cambrian passengers must have wondered about the appearance of such a vintage machine on their trains. It was photographed with a Barmouth train at Machynlleth.

A requirement for heavier brake vans followed the more efficient loading of goods trains, so six 20-ton vehicles were hired from the Government. They were purchased at valuation, £400 each, when offered for sale later in 1921.

The return of No 85, the last of the three locomotives sent to Beyer, Peacock for repair, was followed by a letter of complaint from McDonald about the quality of the work, sent on 3 September. His request for £218 10s 9d as the cost of putting them right was countered by an offer of half that amount. The repairs to No 69 had cost £3,196 10s.

On 14 October Williamson gave the board a forecast of the company's financial position until 31 December 1921. The details were not recorded but the outcome seems to have been a decision that the amalgamation should be completed as soon as possible. Shareholders were subsequently told that the company was struggling to pay its way, a loss of £3,000 was forecast for the period from the end of Government control until the end of 1921 and that uncertainty about the amount due from the Government in compensation made it impossible to borrow to pay the debenture interest.

To ease matters a little, in November and December Williamson made agreements with the National Union of Railwaymen and the Associated Society of Locomotive Engineers & Firemen for their members to refund 10% of the wages to the company from the end of January 1922. He told the unions that the alternative would be a reduction in the workforce and that the company's officers, including the directors, had already agreed to this – an agreement of which, if the minutes are anything to go by, they had no knowledge.

The company was notified that it had been allocated £73,093 as its share of the first tranche of the £60 million compensation fund created for the controlled railways on 13 December. The fund was still insufficient to compensate them adequately for the service they had given and to restore them to pre-war health. Collectively, they were most unhappy about the way they had been treated, being the only industry not allowed to profit from the war and having their viability undermined

| Operating receipts, 1913-1921 | | |
|---|---|---|
| | **Gross receipts** | **Net receipts** |
| 1913 | £357,817 | £141,191 |
| 1914 | £367,108 | £149,185 |
| 1915 | £371,564 | £138,634 |
| 1916 | £389,443 | £138,885 |
| 1917 | £421,224 | £139,087 |
| 1918 | £513,222 | £134,566 |
| 1919 | £661,175 | £133,761 |
| 1920 | £897,785 | £133,930 |
| 1921 | £880,722 | £113,966 |

in the process. Had the Government been strong enough it should have nationalised them then – the Grouping just deferred the day.

The Cambrian's results for railway operating from 1913 are shown in the table above. The D debenture holders only received 2½% interest in 1921.

During the war the company had invested £33,994 13s 1d in Government stocks with a nominal value of £37,500. When sold on 9 January 1922 they incurred a loss of £944 17s 10.

'Keen negotiations' were required on 25 January 1922 to reach an agreement with the GWR over the amalgamation; the company employed Price, Waterhouse & Company, the accountants, to act for it. The settlement reflected the market value of the different stocks, some of which had never earned a dividend, on 30 December 1921. Over the 10 years from 1904 dividend payments had averaged £112,914, the settlement therefore giving slightly more than a 5% increase at the expense of some reduction in capital value. The status of the No 1 preference stock had been a sticking point in the negotiations, because it had only received interest in 1918 (2%) and 1919 (4%).

The details are shown in the table below; in round figures, the system was valued at slightly less than half of what it had cost, truly a

| Cambrian Railways stocks at 30 December 1921 | | | | |
|---|---|---|---|---|
| **Cambrian stock** | **Market value at 30 December 1921** | **GWR stock to be given in exchange** | **Interest on GWR stock** | **Interest on Cambrian stock** |
| A 4% debenture stock £1,421,211 | £916,681 | 4% debenture stock £1,421,211 | £56,848 | £56,848 |
| B 4% debenture stock £855,848 | £483,554 | 4% debentures to produce 3⅛% = £748,875 (87⅛%) | £29,955 | £34,234 |
| C 4% debenture stock £400,000 | £206,000 | 5% preference stock to produce 3½% = £280,000 (70%) | £14,000 | £16,000 |
| D 4% debenture stock £507,565 | £241,093 | 5% preference stock to produce 3% = £304,540 (60%) | £15,227 | £12,689 |
| No 1 preference stock £163,829 | £53,244 | Ordinary stock (7%) to produce 2% = £46,814 (28.57%) | £3,277 | |
| **£3,348,453** | **£1,900,572** | **£2,801,440** | **£119,307** | **£119,771** |
| | | | | |
| No 2 preference stock £484,000 | £72,600 | (21.454%)* | | |
| No 3 preference stock £415,729 | £27,022 | (9.297%)* | | |
| No 4 preference stock £856,120 | £47,086 | (7.866%)* | | |
| Ordinary stock (inland) £738,464 | £14,769 | (2.86%)* | | |
| Ordinary stock (coast) £682,982 | £13,660 | (2.86%)* | | |
| £3,177,295 | £175,137 | * £250,500 deferred consolidated ordinary stock to bear dividend from 1 January 1929 | £17,535 (if 7% dividend maintained) | |

ABOVE 2-4-0 No 10 had a similar history to No 1 and must have evoked similar responses from Cambrian passengers seeing it for the first time in 1921. *H. W. Burman*

reflection of the havoc that Savin, Piercy and Whalley had wreaked on the fruit of their ambitions.

The agreement was backdated to 1 January 1922, the Cambrian management meeting all revenue liabilities up to 31 December 1921 and paying the 1921 debenture interest at the 1913 rate. The balance of the revenue and all the assets and the liabilities, including the reserves and the share of the Government's £60 million, less £7,000 for the directors' loss-of-office compensation, would be passed to the GWR.

A special proprietors' meeting to approve the agreement, incorporated in the 'Great Western Railway (Western Group) Preliminary Amalgamation Scheme, 1922', was held on 14 February. The Cardiff Railway, Rhymney Railway, Taff Vale Railway and Alexandra (Newport & South Wales) Docks & Railway companies were included in the same scheme. The final ordinary meeting, the 107th, was held four days later, when several directors paid tribute to the efforts of Williamson and his staff in the pursuit of efficiency and economy during the previous 10 years. James Fraser, the auditor since 1901, was also recognised; his father had been elected auditor in 1879.

The directors met for the last time on 15 March 1922, nominating David Davies to be a director of the GWR and voting allowances for special services to the company, £2,750 to Williamson and £200 each to the accountant and the assistant secretary. The amalgamation was sealed on 25 March.

LEFT The last major engineering project undertaken by the Cambrian was the renewal of the Kilkewydd bridge, used for the first time on 14 August 1921. Provision was made for the line to be doubled at a later date if required.

ABOVE In May 1922 the Cambrian's last directors and officers made a farewell visit to Aberystwyth, commissioning a local photographer to record the occasion. From left to right they are: W. K. Minshall (solicitor), Sir Joseph Davies MP (director), Alfred Herbert (director); Lord Kenyon (director), N. W. Apperley (director), G. C. McDonald (engineer and locomotive superintendent), S. G. Vowles (assistant secretary), C. B. O. Clarke (traffic superintendent), H. Warwick (superintendent of the line), Thomas Craven (deputy chairman), David Davies MP (chairman), T. C. Sellars (general manager's assistant), S. Williamson (general manager and secretary). The Earl of Powis was absent. *H. H. Davies*

BELOW Seen shortly after the Grouping, 4-4-0 No 96 carries its GWR number, 1029, while its tender still betrays its origins. Some of the Cambrian locomotives had quite a good innings with the GWR. *John Alsop collection*

ABOVE The GWR could obviously see no use for six-wheeled brakes Nos 121 and 135 and they were soon sent to Swindon for breaking up.

LEFT In contrast, four-wheeled carriage No 74 lasted long enough to have its new number, 4044, applied before it, too, was sent to Swindon.

# Afterword

The determination of George Whalley, Benjamin Piercy and Thomas Savin to complete the Newtown & Llanidloes Railway and to develop a Welsh railway network centred on Montgomeryshire created the Cambrian Railways, albeit they were ejected as soon as their dream became reality. Their determination to proceed at any cost left their creation saddled with enormous debt, however, that hampered the Cambrian throughout its existence. Failure would have discouraged investment in Montgomeryshire railways for many years. The reader might like to speculate on the likely outcomes. The Welsh railway map would have been very different. Under Great Western Railway control, the Cambrian was cared for and prospered, gaining additional halts and only losing passenger services on the Kerry branch and the narrow-gauge light railways in 1931.

In the British Railways era, chipping away at the edges started with the closure of the Tanat Valley Light Railway during a coal shortage in 1951 and ended with the privatisation of the Vale of Rheidol Light Railway in 1989. That so much of it survives in the 21st century says a great deal about its value to the places and communities that it serves.

## Appendix 1 Constituents

| | Miles | Incorporation |
|---|---|---|
| Llanidloes & Newtown | 12¼ | 4 August 1853 |
| Oswestry & Newtown | 30 | 26 June 1855 |
| Newtown & Machynlleth | 23 | 27 July 1857 |
| Mid Wales (*worked in perpetuity from 2 April 1888, amalgamated July 1904*) | 46½ | 1 August 1859 |
| Oswestry, Ellesmere & Whitchurch | 18 | 1 August 1861 |
| Aberystwyth & Welsh Coast | 86 | 22 July 1861 |
| Vale of Rheidol Light (*amalgamated July 1913*) | 12 | 6 August 1897 |
| Tanat Valley Light (*amalgamated March 1921*) | 15 | 4 January 1899 |

## Appendix 2 Opening dates

| | |
|---|---|
| Llanidloes-Newtown | 11 August 1859 |
| Oswestry-Pool Quay | 1 May 1860 |
| Pool Quay-Welshpool | 14 August 1860 |
| Welshpool-Newtown | 10 June 1861 |
| Newtown-Machynlleth | 25 February 1863 |
| Machynlleth-Borth | 1 July 1863 |
| Aberdovey-Llwyngwril | 24 October 1863 |
| Ellesmere-Whitchurch | 1 May 1863 |
| Oswestry-Ellesmere | 25 (or 27) July 1864 |
| Llwyngwril-Penmaenpool | 5 July 1865 |
| Borth-Aberystwyth | 1 August 1864 |
| Llanidloes-Talyllyn Junction | 1 September 1864 |
| Llwyngwril-Barmouth Junction | 3 July 1865 |
| Barmouth Junction-Barmouth (goods, horse-drawn) | June 1866 |
| Barmouth Junction-Barmouth (passengers, horse-drawn) | After 18 April 1867 |
| Glandovey-Aberdovey | 14 August 1867 |
| Pwllheli-Penrhyndeudraeth (by Carnarvonshire Railway) | 20 September 1867 |
| Barmouth-Pwllheli | 10 October 1867 |
| Penmaenpool-Dolgelley | 21 June 1869 |
| Ellesmere-Wrexham | 2 November 1895 |
| Vale of Rheidol Light | 22 December 1902 |
| Tanat Valley Light | 5 January 1904 |
| Pwllheli extension | 19 July 1908 |

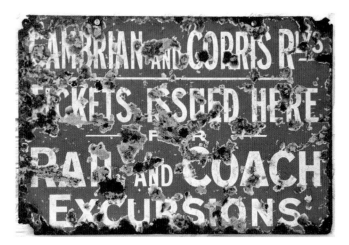

This enamel sign advertising rail and coach excursions is displayed in the Corris Railway's museum in Corris.

## Appendix 3 Running powers, etc

*Brecon & Merthyr*

| | |
|---|---|
| Talyllyn Junction-Brecon | all traffic |
| Talyllyn Junction-Deri Junction | not exercised |
| Talyllyn Junction-Morlais Junction | not exercised |
| Brecon & Merthyr & LNWR Joint | |
| Morlais Junction-Merthyr, GWR and Taff Valley Junctions | not exercised |

*GWR*

| | |
|---|---|
| Dolgelley Junction-Dolgelley station | all traffic |
| Dolgelley station-Llangollen | not exercised |
| Merthyr, Rhydycar Junction, to Merthyr, High Street Junction | not exercised |

*LNWR*

| | |
|---|---|
| Builth Road Junction-Llandrindod Wells | not exercised |
| Whitchurch Junction-Whitchurch station | all traffic |

*Midland*

| | |
|---|---|
| Three Cocks Junction-Hereford | not exercised |

*Neath & Brecon*

| | |
|---|---|
| Brecon, BMR Junction-Brecon, Mount Street | not exercised |

*Shropshire*

| | |
|---|---|
| Blodwell Junction-Nantmawr | merchandise |
| Llanymynech-Blodwell Junction | all traffic |

**Other companies' running powers over the Cambrian Railways**

*Midland*

| | |
|---|---|
| Three Cocks Junction-Talyllyn Junction | all traffic |

*LNWR*

*Powers obtained over whole line – portions exercised:*

| | |
|---|---|
| Afon Wen Junction-Afon Wen station | all traffic |
| Buttington Junction-Welshpool | all traffic |

*GWR*

| | |
|---|---|
| Buttington Junction-Welshpool | all traffic |
| Dolgelley Junction-Aberystwyth | not exercised |
| Dolgelley Junction-Barmouth | not exercised |

*Brecon & Merthyr*

| | |
|---|---|
| Talyllyn Junction-Llanidloes | not exercised |

*Wrexham & Ellesmere*

| | |
|---|---|
| Ellesmere Junction-Ellesmere station | not exercised |

**Lines leased or worked**

| | |
|---|---|
| Van Railway | from 1896 |
| Wrexham & Ellesmere | in perpetuity |
| Welshpool & Llanfair Light | opened 4 April 1903 |
| Mawddwy Light | re-opened 31 July 1911 |
| Shropshire (Nantmawr branch) | not included in 1921 Railways Act |

**Junctions with other railway companies**

*LNWR*: Whitchurch, Welshpool, Builth Road, Afon Wen

*GWR*: Oswestry, Buttington, Aberystwyth, Dolgelley, and over Wrexham & Ellesmere line

*Midland* : Three Cocks

# **Appendix 4** Rolling stock (December 1920)

**Locomotives**

| Type | Number in class | Numbers | Maker | Works number | Date built, and re-built | Tractive effort |
|---|---|---|---|---|---|---|
| 0-4-4T | 6 | 3, 5, 7 | Nasmyth, Wilson | 460-462 | 1895 | 14,037 |
| | | 8, 9, 23 | | 558-560 | 1899 | 14,037 |
| 0-6-0ST | 1 | 25 | Manning, Wardle | 374 | 1872 | 7,344 |
| 0-6-0T | 2 | 26, 35 | Chapman, Furneaux | 1161-2 | 1898[1] | 8,540 |
| | 1 | 24 | Hunslet | 811 | 1903[1] | 9,020 |
| 2-4-0T | 3 | 57 | Sharp, Stewart | 1681 | 1866, 1893 | 9,255 |
| | | 58, 59 | | 1682-3 | 1866, 1894 | 9,255 |
| 2-4-0T | 2 | 44 | Sharp, Stewart | 1488 | 1864, 1894[2] | 9,891 |
| | | 56 | | 1656 | 1865, 1890[2] | 9,891 |
| 4-4-0T | 4 | 2, 12, 33, 37 | Beyer Peacock | - | 1864, 1905[3] | 13,008 |
| 0-6-0 | 15 | 27 | Sharp, Stewart | 1344 | 1863, 1896 | 14,506 |
| | | 39, 40 | Sharp, Stewart | 1445-6 | 1863, 1895 | 14,506 |
| | | 45 | Sharp, Stewart | 1530 | 1864, 1896 | 14,506 |
| | | 46 | Sharp, Stewart | 1531 | 1864, 1896 | 14,506 |
| | | 51, 52 | Sharp, Stewart | 1590, 1597 | 1865, 1894 | 14,506 |
| | | 1, 4 | Sharp, Stewart | 2231-2 | 1872, 1891 | 14,506 |
| | | 6 | Sharp, Stewart | 2306 | 1873, 1895 | 14,506 |
| | | 10 | Sharp, Stewart | 2307 | 1873, 1894 | 14,506 |
| | | 14 | Sharp, Stewart | 2511 | 1875, 1897 | 14,506 |
| | | 18 | Sharp, Stewart | 2510 | 1875, 1890[4] | 14,506 |
| | | 48, 49 | Sharp, Stewart | 2339, 2347 | 1864[5] (reboiled 1897) | 14,506 |
| 0-6-0 | 10 | 73-77 | Neilson | 4691-5 | 1894 | 18,629 |
| | | 78-80 | Vulcan Foundry | 1445-7 | 1895 | 18,629 |
| | | 87-88 | Neilson | 5401-2 | 1898 | 18,629 |
| 0-6-0 | 15 | 89-93 | R. Stephenson | 3089-93 | 1903 | 18,629 |
| | | 99-102 | Beyer, Peacock | 5029-30, 5032-3 | 1908 | 18,629 |
| | | 38 | Beyer, Peacock | 5031 | 1908 | 18,629 |
| | | 15, 29 | Beyer, Peacock | | 1918 | 18,629 |
| | | 31, 42, 54 | Beyer, Peacock | | 1919 | 18,629 |
| 2-4-0 | 5 | 28 | Sharp, Stewart | 1400 | 1863, 1893 | 9,891 |
| | | 41 | Sharp, Stewart | 1485 | 1864, 1893 | 9,891 |
| | | 43 | Sharp, Stewart | 1487 | 1864, 1892 | 9,891 |
| | | 53 | Sharp, Stewart | 1633 | 1865, 1892 | 9,891 |
| | | 55 | Sharp, Stewart | 1655 | 1865, 1894 | 9,891 |
| 4-4-0 | 6 | 16, 17 | Sharp, Stewart | 2789-90 | 1878 | 12,412 |
| | | 20, 21 | Sharp, Stewart | 3356-7 | 1886 | 12,412 |
| | | 50, 60 | Sharp, Stewart | 3696-7 | 1891 | 12,412 |
| 4-4-0 | 22 | 61-68 | Sharp, Stewart | 3901-8 | 1893 | 14,688 |
| | | 69-72 | Sharp, Stewart | 3976-9 | 1894 | 14,688 |
| | | 81-84 | Sharp, Stewart | 4070-3 | 1895 | 14,688 |
| | | 32, 47, 85-6, 11 | Stephenson | 2871-5 | 1897 | 14,688 |
| | | 19 | Oswestry | | 1901 | 14,688 |
| 4-4-0 | 2 | 34 | Beyer, Peacock | | 1864, 1905[6] | 13,008 |
| | | 36 | Beyer, Peacock | | 1864, 1905[6] | 13,008 |
| 4-4-0 | 5 | 94-98 | R. Stephenson | 3031-5 | 1904 | 17,859 |

[1] Ex-Lambourne Valley Railway, 1905

[2] Built as 2-4-0, converted 1908 and 1909 respectively

[3] Ex-Metropolitan Railway, 1905

[4] Ex-LNWR, 1879

[5] Ex- Mid Wales Railway, 1888

[6] Ex-Metropolitan Railway, 1905, converted to tender engines 1915 and 1916 respectively

Plus 73 tenders and Vale of Rheidol locomotives

**Livery:** black, lined grey and red, tenders lettered 'Cambrian'

## Appendix 4 Continued

**Passenger train vehicles**

Coaching vehicles
  221 (137 uniform class; 84 composite)

Other coaching vehicles
  118 (2 observation carriages; 2 Post Office vans; 48 luggage, parcel and brake vans; 8 carriage trucks; 47 horse boxes; 11 miscellaneous)

**Livery:** bronze green, lined yellow

**Merchandise and mineral vehicles**

2065 open wagons (under 8 tons 82; 8-12 tons 1,264)
  110 covered wagons
  6 exceptional loads
  191 cattle trucks
  372 rail and timber trucks
  38 brake vans
  2 miscellaneous

**Service vehicles**

213 (10 gasholder trucks; 109 locomotive coal wagons; 62 ballast wagons; 15 mess and tool vans; 2 breakdown cranes; 12 travelling cranes; 3 miscellaneous)

## Appendix 5 Permanent way etc

*Permanent way*
Rail      80lb per yard (British Standard section)
Sleepers   9ft x 10in x 5in, spaced 11 to every 30 feet of track
Chairs    42lb each

*Steepest gradients*
Main line                            1 in 52
Mid Wales section                    1 in 80
Vale of Rheidol Light                1 in 50
Welshpool & Llanfair Light           1 in 30 for 1,738 yards
Kerry branch, falling towards Abermule   1 in 43 for 1,467 yards

*Summit level*
941 feet above sea level between Pantydwr and St Harmons

*Turntables*
Aberystwyth      50 feet diameter
Dolgelley        42 feet diameter (joint, maintained by GWR)

(Two 45-foot turntables were sold to Cambrian Railways by GWR on 6 August 1920)

## Appendix 6 Employees (March 1921)

| | Adults | Juniors under 18 years of age |
|---|---|---|
| Locomotive department | | |
| Engine driver and motormen (male) | 131 | |
| Firemen (male) | 130 | |
| Engine cleaners (male) | 27 | 29 |
| Carriage & wagon department | | |
| Carriage cleaners | | |
| Carriage and wagon examiners (male) | 20 | |
| Carriage and wagon oilers and greasers (male) | 1 | 6 |
| Locomotive, carriage & wagon department | | |
| Labourers (male) | 107 | 4 |
| Mechanics and artisans (male) | 297 | 39 |
| All departments | | |
| Clerks (male) | 227 | 39 |
| Clerks (female) | 19 | 1 |
| Cranesman (male) | 1 | |
| Inspectors (male) | 19 | |
| Messengers (male) | 1 | |
| Miscellaneous (male) | 94 | 2 |
| Miscellaneous (female) | 4 | |

## Appendix 7 Route mileage

| | Miles | Chains | Miles | Chains |
|---|---|---|---|---|
| Main and principal lines | | | | |
| Whitchurch-Aberystwyth | 96 | 32 | | |
| Moat Lane-Talyllyn | 56 | 34 | | |
| Dovey Junction-Pwllheli | 54 | 50 | 207 | 36 |
| Minor and branch lines | | | | |
| Porthywaen branch | 1 | 65 | | |
| Llanfyllin branch | 9 | 13 | | |
| Kerry branch | 3 | 55 | | |
| Dolgelley branch | 7 | 36 | | |
| Vale of Rheidol Light | 11 | 60 | | |
| Tanat Valley Light | 15 | 00 | 48 | 69 |
| Total mileage owned by the company | | | | |
| | 256 | 25 | | |
| Lines leased and worked | | | | |
| Wrexham & Ellesmere | 12 | 57 | | |
| Nantmawr branch | 3 | 75 | | |
| (Shropshire Railways) | | | | |
| Welshpool & Llanfair Light | 9 | 6 | | |
| Van | 6 | 40 | | |
| Mawddwy | 6 | 61 | 38 | 79 |
| Grand total | | | 295 | 24 |

Appendix data extracted from National Archives file RAIL92/135

# Bibliography

Ahrons, E. L.; Locomotive and train working in the latter part of the 19th century: the Cambrian Railways; *The Railway Magazine*, April/May 1922

Allchin, M. C. V.; *Locomotives of the Cambrian, Barry & Rhymney Railways*; Author, revised edition 1943

Anon; Illustrated Interview: Herbert Edward Jones; *The Railway Magazine*, April 1901

Anon; *Picturesque Wales*; Cambrian Railways official issue, Photochrom, 1910

Booth, T.; On the Cambrian Railways from Moat Lane to Brecon; *The Railway Magazine*, 1899

Briwnant-Jones, G.; *Railway Through Talerddig*; Gomer Press, 1990

Christiansen, Rex & Miller, R. W.; *The Cambrian Railways Volume 1 1852-1888*; David & Charles, 1967, 1971

Christiansen, Rex & Miller, R. W.; *The Cambrian Railways Volume 2 1889-1968*; David & Charles, 1968

Coe, Reginald H.; The Whitchurch-Aberystwyth main line section of the Cambrian Railways; *The Railway Magazine*, April 1916

Conybeare, Henry; *Description of the viaducts across the estuaries on the line of the Cambrian Railway*; Proceedings of the Institution of Civil Engineers, 1871

Cox, David & Krupa, Christopher; *The Kerry Tramway and other timber light railways*; Plateway Press, 1992

Cozens, Lewis, Kidner, R. W., & Poole, Brian; *The Mawddwy, Van & Kerry Branches*; Oakwood Press, 2nd edition, 2004

D., J.; The Cambrian Railways' modern rolling stock; *The Railway Magazine*, 1903

Dalton, T. P.; *Cambrian Companionship*; Oxford Publishing Company, 1985

Gasquoine, C. P.; *The Story of the Cambrian – a biography of a railway*; Woodall, Minshall, Thomas & Co, 1922

Green, C. C.; *Cambrian Railways Album*; Ian Allan Publishing, 1977

Green, C. C.; *Cambrian Railways Album 2*; Ian Allan Publishing, 1981

Green, C. C.; *The Coast Lines of the Cambrian Railways Volume 1 – Machynlleth to Aberystwyth*; Wild Swan Publications, 1993

Green, C. C.; *The Coast Lines of the Cambrian Railways Volume 2 – Dovey Junction to Dolgelley*; Wild Swan Publications, 1996

de Havilland, John; *Industrial Locomotives of Dyfed & Powys*; Industrial Railway Society, 1994

Jenkins, Stanley C. & Strange, John M.; *The Wrexham & Ellesmere Railway*; Oakwood Press, 2004

Jones, Elwyn V.; *Mishaps on the Cambrian Railways and the Great Western Railway (Cambrian Section)*; Author, 2003

Judge, Colin; *The Elan Valley Railway*; Oakwood Press, 1987

Johnson, Peter; *An Illustrated History of the Festiniog Railway*; Oxford Publishing Co, 2007

Johnson, Peter; *An Illustrated History of the Great Western Narrow Gauge* Oxford Publishing Co, 2011

Johnson, Peter; *An Illustrated History of the Shropshire & Montgomeryshire Light Railway*; Oxford Publishing Co, 2008

Johnson, Peter; *An Illustrated History of the Welsh Highland Railway*; Oxford Publishing Co, 2nd edition, 2010

Johnson, Peter; *Rails in Wales: The Cambrian Lines*; Ian Allan Publishing, 1984

Kidner, R. W.; *The Mid Wales Railway*; Oakwood Press, 1990

Kidner, R. W.; *The Cambrian Railways*; Oakwood Press, 2nd enlarged edition, 1992

Lerry, George G.; *Henry Robertson – pioneer of railways into Wales*; Woodall (Printers & Stationers), 1949

Mitchell, Vic & Smith, Keith; *Shrewsbury to Newtown*; Middleton Press, 2008

Mitchell, Vic & Smith, Keith; *Newtown to Aberystwyth*; Middleton Press, 2008

Mitchell, Vic & Smith, Keith; *Machynlleth to Barmouth*; Middleton Press, 2009

Mitchell, Vic & Smith, Keith; *Barmouth to Pwllheli*; Middleton Press, 2009;

Mitchell, Vic & Smith, Keith; *Branch Lines around Oswestry*; Middleton Press, 2009

Mitchell, Vic & Smith, Keith; *Bangor to Portmadoc*; ; Middleton Press, 2010;

Perkins, T. R.; The Welsh "Kerry Express"; *The Railway Magazine*, January 1901

Pole, Felix J. C.; The administrative reorganisation of the railways following the war; *Modern Railway Administration*; Gresham Publishing Co, 1927

Rear, W. G. & Williams, M. F.; *The Cambrian Coast Railway*; Foxline Publishing, 1988

Sekon, G. A.; Illustrated Interview: Charles Sherwood Denniss; *The Railway Magazine*, October 1898

Shackleton, Frank; A Terrible Accident [Welshampton, 1897]; *Journal of the Railway & Canal Historical Society*, No 210, March 2011

Stephenson, W. Tetley; The Railway Conciliation Scheme 1907; *The Economic Journal*, Vol 21, No 84

Thomas, Ivor; *Top Sawyer – a biography of David Davies*; Longman, Green, 1938

Wade, E. A.; *The Plynlimon & Hafan Tramway*; Twelveheads Press, 1997

Williams, Herbert; *Davies the Ocean – railway king and coal tycoon*; University of Wales Press, 1991

Wren, Wilfrid J.; *The Tanat Valley – its railways and industrial archaeology*; David & Charles, 1968

# Index

| Hampshire County Library | | |
|---|---|---|
| C015621188 | | |
| A & H | Jul-2013 | |
| 385.094245 | £30.00 | |
| | | 9780860936442 |

3976447

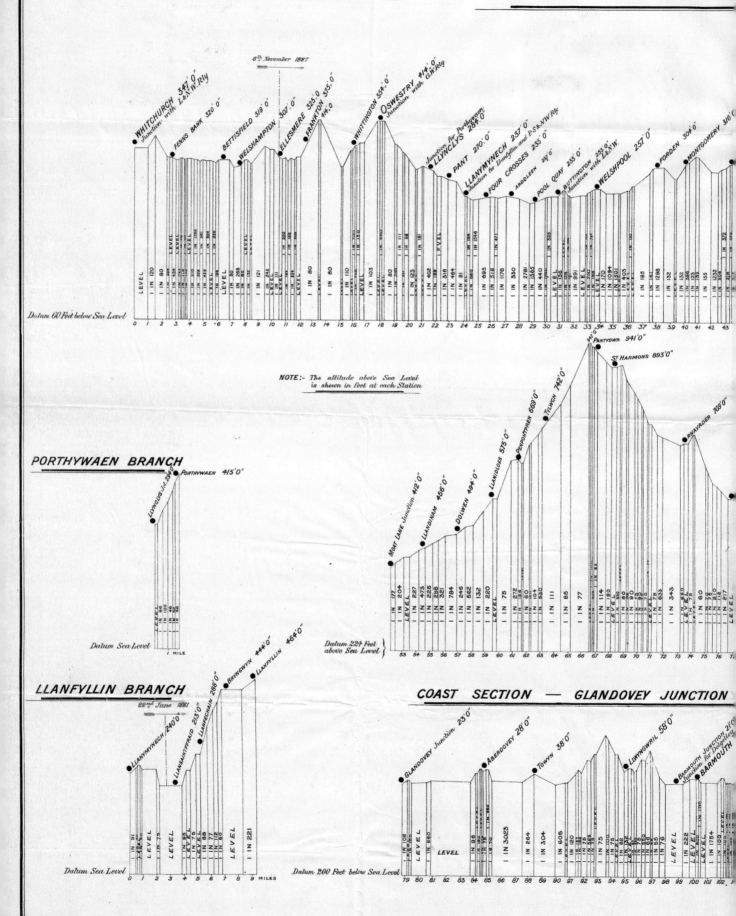

MAIN LINE — WHITCHURCH TO

Datum 60 Feet below Sea Level

NOTE:- The altitude above Sea Level
is shewn in feet at each Station

PORTHYWAEN BRANCH

Datum Sea Level

LLANFYLLIN BRANCH

Datum Sea Level

Datum 224 Feet
above Sea Level

COAST SECTION — GLANDOVEY JUNCTION

Datum 200 Feet below Sea Level

PRINTERS, SIR J